THE CURIOUS
VIEWER

CONTENTS

INTRODUCTION JENNIFER M. WOOD

For more than twenty years, Mental Floss has been the home for "all things curious." No matter what the topic, there's nothing our entire team of writers and editors likes more than to take a straightforward story and uncover the little-known details you have never even thought to ask about. There are few places where this inclination for inquisitiveness is more evident than in our television coverage.

How else could we explain our willingness to ask a physicist whether Scrooge McDuck could indeed take a dive into a swimming pool full of gold coins on *DuckTales*? (He couldn't—at least not without breaking several bones, and that's a best-case scenario.) Or why we'd take the trouble to bother an ornithologist and paleontologist to discuss whether Daenerys Targaryen's dragons on *Game of Thrones* could really fly?

To some, our interest in entertainment *could* be considered fanatical. But great television has a tendency to do that. Especially since the medium has progressed so far beyond its days as the "boob tube"—so much, in fact, that you don't even need an actual television at all to enjoy its many diversions. That's just one of the ways Mental Floss has watched the TV landscape change over the past two decades. Sure, the physical appliance itself has become sleeker and cheaper while the imagery has become more lifelike. But the major shift has been in the type of content we consume.

Though there's some disagreement about when and which show kicked it off, there's no arguing that we're currently in a Golden Age of Television. While some experts point all the way back to *Friends* and *Buffy the Vampire Slayer* as the opening salvo, others credit HBO's earliest cable lineup of "it's-not-TV" series including *Oz* and *The Sopranos*. Meanwhile, the ubiquity of streaming services such as Netflix, Hulu, and Amazon Prime has created more avenues for today's most inimitable creative minds to share their stories with the world, as well as a way for classic shows to find their way back into modern-day conversation. We still have a long way

to go to achieve parity for women, people of color, and LGBTQ individuals both in front of and behind the cameras, but we're undoubtedly moving in the right direction. Which is why there's never been a better time to be a fan of great television, and that's what *The Curious Viewer* is all about.

In the pages that follow, you'll find a trove of behind-the-scenes secrets and little-known stories about the making of your favorite shows of the last twenty years. You'll learn which mega-hit series first introduced Mental Floss to viewers (hint: someone was reading it while sipping coffee at Central Perk) and which lovable curmudgeon saved a man from death row. You'll read about how *Law & Order*'s iconic "dun-dun" sound effect came to be—and who gets a royalty check every time you hear it.

And while I promise I didn't play favorites, I definitely made room to mention some of my own favorite TV series. So *The Wire*, *Breaking Bad*, and *The Crown* are all in here; as are *The Office* (both the British and American versions are included, though my heart will always belong to Ricky Gervais and Stephen Merchant's original), *It's Always Sunny in Philadelphia*, *Curb Your Enthusiasm*, and the painfully short-lived *Freaks and Geeks*. At the same time, I'd be hard-pressed to name a better few hours of television than *Fleabag*'s second season, so that's in here, too.

We hope that you'll enjoy reading *The Curious Viewer* as much as we loved researching and writing it. And that you'll discover many fascinating facts about your favorite shows, as well as be intrigued enough to start watching a few series you've never seen before.

(2001–2010)

CREATED BY: Joel Surnow and Robert Cochran

SEASONS: 9

EPISODES: 192

OTHER SHOWS BY JOEL SURNOW AND ROBERT COCHRAN:
La Femme Nikita (1997–2001)

With its American tough-guy hero and conveyor belt of terrorist attacks to foil, *24* accidentally became the zeitgeist marker for 2000s television. The series, which started filming before 9/11 but premiered just two months after the terrorist attacks, stars Kiefer Sutherland as Counter Terrorist Unit (CTU) officer Jack Bauer and tells an epic story of imminent threats and last-minute saves to the soundtrack of a beeping clock. It was an innovative show that presented events as close to real time as anything with commercials can get, filling an hour slot with an hour of in-universe action. For an espionage thriller, the structure was perfect for making the audience feel the temporal constraints of having to work faster than your enemies.

Presidential assassination attempts, nuclear weapon detonations, cyberattacks, and beyond—Bauer hustled to prevent them all from happening, regardless of the required methods. The end (almost) always justified the means in Bauer's mind, which is why the show took on both the good and the evil elements of the post-9/11 culture in America.

24 was an undeniable phenomenon, resurrecting Sutherland's career, and earning massive audiences and prestigious awards.

....

THE ORIGINAL CONCEPT FOR *24* WAS ABOUT A WEDDING.

Joel Surnow's initial concept was solely about the real-time format. When he called co-creator Bob Cochran to pitch the idea, it was about the day leading up to a wedding, but that was quickly discarded in favor of a thriller in which someone's daughter was kidnapped. Eventually, that morphed into the anti-terrorist drama that became *24*.

24'S CREATORS ALMOST SCRAPPED THE REAL-TIME FORMAT.

Even after the massive success of *24*'s first season, the producers tossed around the idea of doing away with the show's unique format. Fortunately, several of the actors—Sutherland included—lobbied the creators to keep the ticking clock and real-time format. Co-writer Virgil Williams told *The Guardian* that losing it "would be like killing Tony Soprano."

THE SHOW'S FORMAT PLAGUED ITS WRITERS.

Despite saying that the real-time format was freeing in certain aspects, writer Michael Loceff told *Slate* that it also boxed *24*'s writers in for one simple reason: They couldn't magically transport people to where they needed them to be. "You want the character of Curtis to be at CTU, but he's at the airport, so we can't have him at CTU right then," Loceff explained. Fortunately, they made it work.

THE COUNTDOWN CLOCK WENT SILENT WHENEVER TRAGEDY STRUCK.

24 reminded viewers of its real-time gimmick with every commercial break and credit sequence by ending scenes and episodes with its iconic digital clock beeping down the seconds. To mark something like the death of a major character or a moment of intense sadness, the clock would appear silently as a tribute.

MARY LYNN RAJSKUB LANDED THE ROLE OF CHLOE BECAUSE OF *PUNCH-DRUNK LOVE*.

Mary Lynn Rajskub's Chloe O'Brian became one of *24*'s most important characters after joining the show in its third season, but the fit wasn't always obvious. The actor had a background in stand-up, and she cut her teeth on the absurdity of the HBO sketch comedy series *Mr. Show with Bob and David*. But she was called in to audition for *24* to play Jack's most trusted sidekick because one of the show's producers loved her as Adam Sandler's overbearing sister in *Punch-Drunk Love* and wanted to write a part for her.

FREEZE FRAME

"DAY 3: 7:00 P.M.– 8:00 P.M." // SEASON 3, EPISODE 7 Jack Bauer has a tattoo of the Virgin of Guadalupe from his time in deep cover. But rather than spend hours in the makeup chair every time it would appear on screen (as it does in the last few minutes of this episode), Sutherland just got the tattoo for real. Presumably it was also a big time-saver.

Rajskub, however, rarely did dramatic auditions. And having just come off a bad one, she was reluctant to read for *24*. Her agent was eager to see her do it, but Rajskub had another major cheerleader in her corner: her mom, who raved about the series. So Rajskub binge-watched the first two seasons and liked it, which made her feel better about trying out.

DAVID PALMER WAS THE ONLY PRESIDENT TO SERVE HIS FULL TERM ON *24*.

Presidents didn't make out so well on *24*. The show went through a series of presidents in eighteen years (of in-universe time, as each season was generally set at least eighteen months after the previous chapter), getting rid of its POTUSes using everything from assassinations to potential Alzheimer's. Of those, President David Palmer (Dennis Haysbert) was the only one elected to office who actually finished a full term.

THERE'S A NOD TO *STAND BY ME*.

Milo Pressman is a character in *Stand by Me* who owns a junkyard. Milo Pressman is also a character in *24*. Either that's a major coincidence, or it's a subtle tip of the cap to the movie that helped launch Kiefer Sutherland's career.

KIM BAUER WAS ABDUCTED FOUR TIMES.

Nicknamed "Spawn" by hateful "fans," Jack's profoundly unlucky daughter, Kim (Elisha Cuthbert), was kidnapped three times in the first season alone, and then once more in season 2 at the hands of a prepper who lied to her about an atomic bomb going off in Los Angeles. That doesn't count the handful of times she was detained by police or held up in a convenience store robbery. Just about the only thing producers didn't do was tie her to train tracks.

CUTHBERT GOT INTO A TANGLE WITH *24*'S INFAMOUS COUGAR.

Happy Days featured Henry Winkler's Fonzie jumping a shark on water skis, and *24* had Kim Bauer randomly encounter a cougar while lost in the woods. The second-season episode "Day 2: 6:00 p.m.–7:00 p.m." is infamous for its over-the-top treatment of Kim— a character who was already known for her absurd story lines—but filming was no joke for Cuthbert, who had to be hospitalized when the cougar bit her hand during introductions. "Because of the show, I had all these [fake] cuts and fake blood on me," Cuthbert told

Vulture. "They thought I was, like, totally mauled. I was like, 'No, it's just my hand! I just got bit on the hand!'"

THERE WAS ALMOST A *24*/*DIE HARD* CROSSOVER.
We don't have a lot of details about how any of this went down, but in 2010 it was revealed that a deal was in the works for Sutherland to return as Jack Bauer alongside Bruce Willis's John McClane for a crossover movie event. Sadly, it fell apart.

THERE ARE INDIAN AND JAPANESE VERSIONS OF *24*.
After appearing as President Omar Hassan of the fictional Kamistan, actor Anil Kapoor bought the rights to adapt *24* for a Hindi-speaking audience, spawning two seasons in which Kapoor starred as the Bauer-esque Jai Singh Rathod. Similarly, Toshiaki Karasawa stars in a Japanese version of the show in which his CTU Japan Agent Genba Shidō must safeguard Urara Asakura (Yukie Nakama) as she prepares to become Japan's first female prime minister.

FREEZE FRAME

**"DAY 5: 1:00 P.M.–2:00 P.M." //
SEASON 5, EPISODE 7**
Is there really anything that screams Bush-era anti-terrorism drama more than having a cameo from Senator John McCain? Yet instead of playing a politician or some other Important Person in a Suit, McCain (who is uncredited) can be seen for about one second as a CTU staffer handing off a folder at the 1:32:22 split screen. McCain landed the gig simply by being an enthusiastic fan of the show. While speaking with Jon Stewart on *The Daily Show* in 2007, the late politician admitted that he watched *24* "all the time. I'm sort of a Jack Bauer kind of guy."

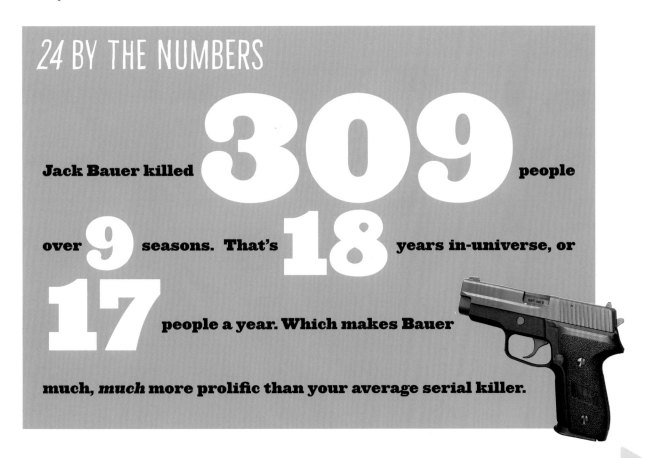

24 BY THE NUMBERS

Jack Bauer killed **309** people over **9** seasons. That's **18** years in-universe, or **17** people a year. Which makes Bauer much, *much* more prolific than your average serial killer.

30 ROCK

(2006–2013)

CREATED BY: Tina Fey

SEASONS: 7

EPISODES: 138

OTHER SHOWS BY TINA FEY:
Unbreakable Kimmy Schmidt (2015–2020)

30 *Rock* is a rewarding watch for fans of *Saturday Night Live*. Inspired by Tina Fey's tenure as head writer for *SNL*, this show about the production of a fictional sketch series is set at NBC's real-life headquarters at 30 Rockefeller Plaza in New York City. In addition to Fey's award-winning portrayal of Liz Lemon, *30 Rock* stars *SNL* alum Tracy Morgan as comedian Tracy Jordan and frequent *SNL* host Alec Baldwin as network executive Jack Donaghy.

For viewers who have never seen an episode of *Saturday Night Live*, *30 Rock* still has a lot to offer. The show helped make Fey's surreal brand of comedy instantly recognizable. Though characters like Jane Krakowski's attention-seeking Jenna Maroney and Jack McBrayer's optimistic (and possibly immortal) Kenneth Parcell are larger than life, they're also easy for audiences to love. Critics had plenty of love for *30 Rock* as well: The series earned twenty-two Emmy nominations in 2009 alone, a record for a comedy in a single year. Based on *30 Rock*'s enduring legacy, we'd say that praise was well deserved.

30 ROCK WAS SUPPOSED TO BE A SHOW ABOUT THE NEWS, NOT SKETCH COMEDY.

Fey originally pitched a show like HBO's *The Newsroom* about a news program with a Bill O'Reilly–like host in which she'd play the producer and (in an ideal world) Alec Baldwin would play the pundit. But an NBC exec suggested she use her time at *SNL* as inspiration. Initially, she wasn't into the idea—until she thought about casting Tracy Morgan. (It didn't hurt that they had the blessing of *SNL* creator Lorne Michaels, who was an executive producer on *30 Rock*.)

NO ONE EXPECTED ALEC BALDWIN TO SAY YES TO A STARRING ROLE.

Fey created the character of Jack Donaghy for Alec Baldwin, but she never thought he'd actually do the show; she didn't even reach out to him before holding auditions. But Baldwin was hosting *SNL* around that time, so Michaels mentioned the part to him. For Baldwin, who was flying between New York and Los Angeles every other week to see his daughter, the timing could not have been better. "The idea of flying around and making my visitation with my daughter dependent on the whims of a film producer was always excruciating," Baldwin told Salon in 2012. "*30 Rock* was primarily about Lorne saying, 'I will protect your schedule and you will not lose any time with your daughter. Come do this show.' And I really needed a harbor at that time."

BALDWIN BASED HIS PORTRAYAL OF JACK DONAGHY ON LORNE MICHAELS.

Baldwin told NPR, "As I always say, 'Lorne is someone who has a tuxedo in the glove compartment of his car.' And Lorne is a friend, and I adore Lorne. But we do stick it to Lorne a lot."

FREEZE FRAME

"THE AFTERMATH" // SEASON 1, EPISODE 2
In the second-ever episode, Liz Lemon is surprised to learn that Tracy Jordan owns a yacht (he didn't). Tracy responds, "I got a yacht. I got a solid gold jet ski, two Batmobiles, the AIDS monkey's bones..." That part was scripted but, according to Fey, Morgan's line ended there, and they needed him to keep talking as his character rounded a corner. So he improvised a few additional items, like "the first moped," "a pair of Rock Hudson's socks," and "a pair of Bill Bixby's glasses from when he used to be your best friend."

DONALD GLOVER WAS A WRITER ON *30 ROCK*.

Before he starred on *Community*, made it big as rapper Childish Gambino, or created *Atlanta* (his own award-winning series), Donald Glover was a writer on *30 Rock*. "Donald started right out of college as a writer at *30 Rock*," Fey told *Entertainment Weekly*. "He was actually still ... living in an NYU dorm. He was an RA, and he would work and go home to a dorm." Glover made appearances in a few episodes, then returned to play young Tracy Jordan in a live episode. He also wrote some of the lyrics to *30 Rock*'s iconic "Werewolf Bar Mitzvah" and whipped out his spot-on Tracy Morgan impression to record some of the song's lyrics when Morgan wasn't available.

TRACY MORGAN WAS KNOWN FOR HIS IMPROVISING.

According to the other cast members, Morgan improvised quite frequently. Kevin Brown, who played Dot Com, joked that it was because Morgan "never looked at the script." But Morgan explained, "If I didn't read the script, I wouldn't have been able to do my lines. I read the script all the time. Every day. It's just that [Brown] never saw me reading the script. I like to have fun. . . . I come from a standup background and the first three letters in the word *funny* are fun. So I always had fun with it and I guess I made it look easy."

FEY THOUGHT THE SHOW WOULD GET CANCELED DURING SEASON 1.

In 2006, *30 Rock* was often mentioned in the same sentence as Aaron Sorkin's *Studio 60 on the Sunset Strip*. They both premiered on NBC at around the same time, and both were peeks behind the scenes of a sketch comedy show. Many people wondered which one would last. Meanwhile, Fey was busy thinking about whether *30 Rock* was just too out there. Krakowski later recalled, "Today I was remembering Paul Reubens being on the show in season 1. . . . I remember Tina was calling the episode 'Goodbye America' because she thought we wouldn't stay on the air after that one. That was the first time that we knew the show was not going to be normal."

FEY USED THE REAL JACK McBRAYER AS INSPIRATION FOR HIS CHARACTER, KENNETH THE PAGE.

McBrayer loves to eat chickpeas out of a can, and he told Conan O'Brien that Fey made his character a fan of that snack as well. She used his quirks as inspiration for other characters, too: Like McBrayer, Nancy Donovan (Julianne Moore) wrapped a can of Sprite in tinfoil to keep it cold.

CHRISTOPHER CROSS WAS A FAN OF THE SHOW.

In the season 4 episode "Floyd," Liz cries and sings a made-up Christopher Cross song when she learns her ex-boyfriend is getting married. After watching the episode, Cross actually finished the song, which he titled "Lemon's Theme," then sent it to Fey. Likely not-that-coincidentally, the writers named Liz's boyfriend Criss Chros.

SPOILERS! THE WRITERS DIDN'T WANT TO END THE SHOW WITH A LIZ LEMON WEDDING.

This is why she got married halfway through the final season. Fey wanted Liz to "find happiness," she told *Entertainment Weekly*, but didn't want marriage to "be the accumulation of her time."

THE WRITERS TOOK INSPIRATION FROM MANY SITCOM FINALES FOR THE *30 ROCK* FINALE.

The *30 Rock* writers watched a handful of other television show finales, including *The Mary Tyler Moore Show*, *Frasier*, *Cheers*—and *iCarly*. "I was moved to tears by the *iCarly* finale," Fey told *Entertainment Weekly*. "It didn't hold up in the room because they didn't know the characters like I did. But that was another one where they really let people say goodbye!"

30 ROCK BY THE NUMBERS

The show averaged more than **7** **jokes per minute.**

30 Rock was known for its fast-paced writing. In 2014, one reporter calculated that there was an average of 7.44 jokes per minute.

THE STORY OF *STUDIO 60* ON THE SUNSET STRIP

The stars seemed aligned for success when *Studio 60 on the Sunset Strip* debuted in September 2006. Creator Aaron Sorkin had won six Emmy awards for his previous foray into televised dramedy, *The West Wing*. Star Matthew Perry was sitcom royalty after ten seasons on *Friends*. And the cast was rounded out by actors who had already found success on TV, like Bradley Whitford and Steven Weber, along with relatively unknown talents who would later find major success on the small screen, including Simon Helberg and Sarah Paulson. The well-received pilot made *Studio 60* the landslide winner for Best Overall New Program in a critics' poll conducted by *Broadcasting & Cable*. Less than a year later, the show was off the air.

Today, *Studio 60* is remembered as a rare blemish on Sorkin's résumé and an odd historical footnote for *30 Rock*, the series that debuted the same year, also on NBC, also covering the behind-the-scenes antics of a *Saturday Night Live*–like sketch show. *Studio 60*'s viewership declined from a high of more than 13 million viewers for its premiere to fewer than 5 million for its finale.

Theories abound to explain the show's untimely demise. Weber suggested that critics were partly looking to take the notoriously opinionated Sorkin down a peg. According to Sorkin, the show had the top "time-shifted" audience in an era before DVR views were accounted for in television ratings. While its ratings were generally better than *30 Rock*'s, *Studio 60*'s reported $3-million-per-episode cost certainly didn't help its cause.

While *Studio 60* has its defenders, even more than a decade after its cancellation, perhaps its ultimate undoing was the dissonance between Sorkin's soaring dialogue and the show's prosaic setting. While the verbose writer's impassioned monologues fit right into *The West Wing*'s high-stakes milieu, the relatively insignificant goings-on of a TV sketch show seemed to call more for the mordant satire of Tina Fey. Sorkin, for his part, was uncharacteristically concise in his own postmortem. He told *The New York Times*, "I think that everything that was wrong with *Studio 60* was my execution."

THE AMERICANS

(2013–2018)

CREATED BY: Joe Weisberg

SEASONS: 6

EPISODES: 75

The Cold War comes to a sleepy Washington, DC, suburb when undercover KGB spies Philip and Elizabeth Jennings (Matthew Rhys and Keri Russell) are greeted by their new neighbor, Stan Beeman (Noah Emmerich), who just happens to be an FBI agent.

For six seasons, *The Americans* follows the Jenningses as they work to infiltrate the United States' intelligence system, all while protecting their true identities from Stan and raising two children who have no idea why their seemingly square parents work such odd hours and get suspicious phone calls every night. But it's only a matter of time before Philip and Elizabeth's suburban façade begins to show cracks. The only question is: Who will suffer as a consequence?

The brainchild of Joseph Weisberg, a former CIA case officer, *The Americans* offers up a grounded family drama with the type of political intrigue that's usually only found in the works of genre masters like John le Carré and Robert Ludlum. Weisberg, who shocked his family by joining the CIA three years after graduating from Yale, wove his real-life experience in spycraft into *The Americans*—so much so that its authenticity impressed many former spooks.

THE PILOT OF *THE AMERICANS* WAS INSPIRED BY A REAL ESPIONAGE CASE.

In 2010, the Department of Justice announced that it had cracked a Russian spy operation that had been active in the United States for years. Federal agents arrested ten suspects, eight of whom had posed as regular Americans to obtain intelligence for the Russian government. They even went by innocuous-sounding American names like Anna Chapman and Richard Murphy. All ten were charged with conspiracy to act as foreign agents, but were eventually sent back to Russia in a prisoner exchange. This was the seed for the story of Philip and Elizabeth Jennings.

THE CIA REVIEWED EVERY SCRIPT.

As a former agent, Weisberg was required to submit scripts he wrote to the CIA's Publications Review Board. The agency would make sure that no classified information was divulged in the episodes—but the government works at a much slower pace than the TV business, so Weisberg had to request an expedited review each time.

THE AMERICANS TAKES PLACE IN THE WASHINGTON, DC, AREA, BUT IT WASN'T FILMED THERE.

Ostensibly normal American couple Philip and Elizabeth Jennings own a travel agency and are raising their daughter, Paige, and son, Henry, in the leafy Washington suburb of Falls Church, Virginia. But, as we soon learn, the Jenningses are actually undercover Soviet spies—and the show's filming locations are nowhere near DC.

The Jennings home is located in White Plains, New York, and most of the show was filmed in and around New York City. Production designer Diane Lederman told DNAInfo that they filmed in front of Grant's Tomb, a "very DC-looking monument," and used the

Javits Center as an airport. But sometimes the sets were a little too convincing. "We had a scene [where] Keri Russell walks out of a bar, except it wasn't a bar, it was an empty storefront, and we just dressed the front of it. And all day long, people kept coming up and wanting to know when the new bar was opening," Lederman said.

THE WARDROBE CAME FROM VINTAGE STORES.

Costume designer Katie Irish told *The New York Times* that she sourced most of the show's authentic 1980s clothes from New York City resale shop Rue St. Denis. She was able to find plenty of eighties suits for FBI agent Stan Beeman, plus the multitude of disguises that Elizabeth and Philip wear. "Honestly, I don't know how we would have done the show without them," Irish said when the store closed in 2018.

THE SHOW'S FINAL SEASON WAS BASED ON A HISTORIC SUMMIT THAT LED TO THE END OF THE COLD WAR.

The sixth and final season of *The Americans* revolved around Elizabeth Jennings's part in disrupting a high-stakes meeting in Washington between Ronald Reagan and Mikhail Gorbachev. A handler tells Elizabeth that if the two leaders were to agree on ratcheting down the arms race, the KGB—concerned that such a treaty would leave the Soviet Union vulnerable to attack—would overthrow Gorbachev's government. And if that wasn't scary enough, the operative reveals that the USSR has a doomsday device dubbed Dead Hand. This computerized system will unleash the Soviet nuclear arsenal if the US attacks the USSR and wipes out its military.

The actual Washington Summit did take place in December 1987, where the leaders negotiated nuclear arms control to prevent mutually assured destruction. They signed the Intermediate Nuclear Forces (INF) Treaty, reducing the US and Soviet nuclear weapons stockpiles. The summit also set the stage for both nations to sign the Strategic Arms-Reduction Treaty (START) in 1991, which is the title and backdrop of the gripping series finale.

SPOILERS! U2 ALMOST DIDN'T LET *THE AMERICANS* USE ITS SONG IN THE SERIES FINALE.

In the final episode, Elizabeth, Philip, and Paige are unmasked as Russian agents, and they flee Washington by train for Canada. U2's 1987 smash "With or Without You" plays as the jaw-dropping events unfold—a perfect match between action and soundtrack that almost didn't happen. As co–music supervisor Amanda Krieg Thomas told Vulture, the band rarely licenses the song for TV. "The last possible day it could be cleared, it cleared," she said.

SPOILERS! THE GARAGE SCENE WAS THE MOST DIFFICULT TO WRITE—AND PERFORM.

In six seasons stuffed with suspense and surprises, the writers kept the series tightly focused on its complicated characters. But the writers and the actors described the garage scene in "START"—in which Stan Beeman realizes he has been betrayed, and must choose between loyalty to his country and loyalty to his friends—as the most difficult of the whole series.

Weisberg and co-showrunner Joel Fields wrote and rewrote the scene over several seasons. Then, when it came time to film it, they shot ten-minute takes from every angle. "Rarely have you worked that hard to earn a scene," Noah Emmerich, who played Beeman, told Vulture. "It's a painful moment for Stan, certainly, and it was my last scene with Matthew and Keri, in terms of production schedules, so it was a doubly resonant moment. It was the end of our story line and the end of our work together."

Everyone's efforts paid off, though. Weisberg and Fields's script won an Emmy for Outstanding Writing, and Matthew Rhys's performance as Philip won the Emmy for Outstanding Lead Actor in a Drama Series.

FREEZE FRAME

"MARTIAL EAGLE" // SEASON 2, EPISODE 9
In the second season of *The Americans,* Elizabeth and Philip attempt to infiltrate a Contra (right-wing rebel groups that were active throughout the 1980s) training base by disguising themselves as employees of a septic company so that they can surveil the scene. In order to paint as accurate a portrait of what the Contra camps were like, the show's producers decided to tap someone with real-world knowledge to help get the details right. They ended up recruiting Oliver North, a former National Security Council aide who was at the center of the Iran–Contra affair, a major political scandal in the mid-1980s. North gave them so much information that they gave him a story credit.

ARRESTED DEVELOPMENT

(2003–2019)

CREATED BY: Mitchell Hurwitz

SEASONS: 5

EPISODES: 84

OTHER SHOWS BY MITCHELL HURWITZ:
The Ellen Show (2001–2002)

This smart, snarky series follows the riches-to-rags story of the Bluths, a dysfunctional Orange County family that loses their real estate fortune after the SEC begins investigating the family business for fraud. When the family patriarch, George Bluth Sr. (Jeffrey Tambor), goes to prison, his son Michael (Jason Bateman) is left to grudgingly hold the family together.

Arrested Development's intricately crafted plotlines, recurring gags, and relentlessly clever wordplay earned the adoration of a cult following, but it didn't drive ratings high enough to keep Fox from canceling the show after its third season. Still, the show's producers—along with the series' die-hard fans—wouldn't let *Arrested Development* go down without a fight. In 2013, seven years after being axed by Fox, the Bluth family was revived on Netflix for a fourth season, followed by a fifth in 2018, proving yet again that there's always money in the banana stand.

RON HOWARD WASN'T SUPPOSED TO BE THE PERMANENT NARRATOR.

From the start, the producers behind *Arrested Development* wanted the show to be as different from a traditional sitcom as possible, and one idea was to have a narrator enhance the plots and break the fourth wall throughout each episode. But before hiring someone to provide the voice, series creator Mitchell Hurwitz decided to have producer Ron Howard narrate the pilot as a temp track solely for test audiences. Howard's narration turned out to be one of the highest-testing aspects of the episode, so Hurwitz persuaded Howard to take the gig full-time.

THE SHOW DREW THE IRE OF THE OTHER ARRESTED DEVELOPMENT.

While critics praised *Arrested Development*'s arrival in fall 2003, the Atlanta-based hip-hop group of the same name, known for their songs including "Tennessee" and "Mr. Wendal," was none too pleased. Right as the series premiered, the musicians sued Fox for trademark infringement; they eventually settled for an undisclosed sum of money.

DAVID CROSS'S MUSTACHE BROKE FOX'S COMEDY RULES.

According to David Cross, during the mid-2000s, Fox's president of entertainment Gail Berman had three rules for comedies: no characters in baseball hats, no puffy sleeves, and, most importantly, no facial hair. So when Cross sported a mustache for the role of Tobias Fünke on his first day of filming, he immediately found himself in a heated debate with the network to save the character's trademark lip fuzz. Eventually, Cross won out, but he had to promise that the 'stache would never get too bushy.

NEVER NUDES ARE REAL.

Tobias's phobia of being nude, even when alone, tops his ever-impressive list of eccentricities. But while his "never nude" lifestyle might seem like something created just for a gag, there is a similar condition in the real world called gymnophobia; people who suffer from the condition share similar anxieties about being (or seeing others) in the buff.

THE BLUTH BANANA STAND WAS PARTLY BASED ON MITCHELL HURWITZ'S CHILDHOOD COOKIE BUSINESS.

Much like George Michael's (Michael Cera) foray into the frozen banana business, a twelve-year-old Mitchell Hurwitz learned the value of a dollar by slinging cookies near Newport Beach, California, in 1976. It began with a small stand outside the family home, but his father soon encouraged him to satisfy his entrepreneurial spirit by renting out an abandoned taco restaurant nearby. The business expanded so much that Hurwitz made enough to pay his way through college, all without the money laundering and arson that befell the Bluth banana stand years later.

BUSTER BLUTH'S LOST LIMB BEGAN AS A THROWAWAY EMAIL JOKE.

If you think Buster Bluth (Tony Hale) losing a hand to a loose seal was some long-term payoff to make a joke about his overbearing mother Lucille (Jessica Walter)—*loose seal*, *Lu-cille*—you might be giving the writers too much credit. Turns out the plot point simply started as a throwaway suggestion from Hurwitz in a brainstorm email for season 2. During a speech at the 2013 New York Television Festival, Hurwitz said the joke made the writers "look more ingenious than they were."

THE BLUTH COMPANY STAIR CAR BECAME PART OF THE MARVEL CINEMATIC UNIVERSE.

Before helming four Marvel blockbusters, including *Avengers: Infinity War* and *Avengers: Endgame*, Joe and Anthony Russo collectively directed more than a dozen episodes of *Arrested Development*, including a joint effort for the pilot. The brothers didn't forget their roots on the series once they were in the land of superheroes; in 2016's *Captain America: Civil War*, the duo put the Bluth company stair car in the background during the famed airport fight scene.

THE NETWORK WANTED MITCHELL HURWITZ TO "DUMB" THE SHOW DOWN.

Arrested Development was adored by critics for its intricate running jokes and dense humor, but executives at Fox weren't always laughing, especially when ratings began to slip. Their fear was that the show was too complicated for viewers, so after season 2, Hurwitz received a note from the network to "dumb it down" by 25 percent—yes, they gave him an exact number. Hurwitz later revealed that when he told executives he would only make the show his way, he was told, "You can make it, but we'll basically just make your life miserable."

5 TV SHOWS SAVED BY STREAMING

Unlike networks, streaming services don't have to worry about ratings or selling commercials. If a show has a following, fans might be devoted enough to pay a subscription fee to keep watching. At least that was the thinking when Netflix greenlit *Arrested Development* for two additional seasons. Here are five other series that got a second life on streaming.

BREAKING BAD
(2008–2013)

One of the most popular series of all time nearly didn't make it to a third season. Creator Vince Gilligan said that he didn't believe AMC would have stuck with the show if it hadn't become a watercooler hit on Netflix.

DESIGNATED SURVIVOR
(2016–2019)

The political drama starring Kiefer Sutherland as a man thrust into the role of president spent two seasons on ABC. When the network declined to renew it, Netflix ordered ten more episodes—but no more. Sutherland said complicated contracts with actors who had moved on to other projects were to blame.

LUCIFER
(2016–2021)

The Fox series about the literal devil who moves into the nightclub business ran for three seasons before Netflix ordered two more seasons. In a rare move, Netflix then un-canceled *Lucifer* a second time, deciding to order a sixth season to make sure the devil (and his fans) got their due.

THE EXPANSE
(2015–PRESENT)

The trippy sci-fi series spent three seasons on Syfy before being canceled. *A Game of Thrones* author George R. R. Martin was one of many fans who petitioned Amazon head Jeff Bezos to save it, which he did.

THE KILLING
(2011–2014)

AMC's moody drama lasted three seasons. When Netflix saw its popularity among its own viewers, it ordered six episodes for a fourth and final season.

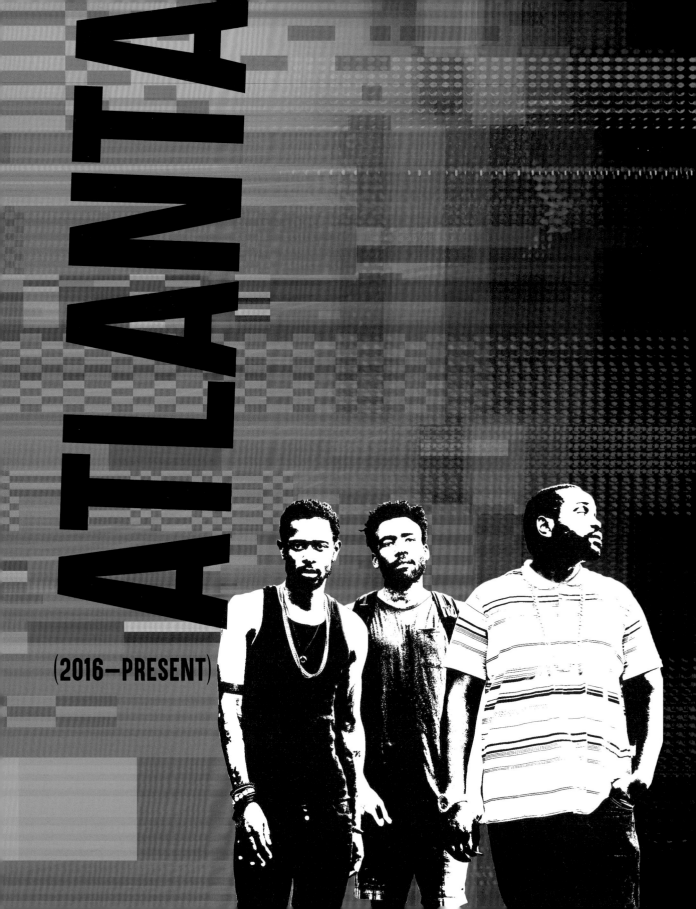

ATLANTA

(2016–PRESENT)

CREATED BY: Donald Glover

SEASONS: 2

EPISODES: 21

In just two seasons, Donald Glover's *Atlanta*—a show about fame and friendship—has burned down screens by subverting expectations for what a TV series can be. The show sets up a classic narrative: Rapper Paper Boi (Brian Tyree Henry) is making a name for himself as he rises from underground to commercial success in the rap world, with his cousin/manager Earnest, aka Earn (Glover) at his side. Then the show pushes that deep into the background in favor of heavy atmosphere and fraught character relationships.

The principal cast, including Glover, Henry, LaKeith Stanfield, and Zazie Beetz, anchors the show with some of the most charismatic and human performances on television. *Atlanta*, which is equal parts funny, frightening, entrancing, and enlightening, revels in a freedom few shows ever attain. And it does so in nearly every episode. Trippy and grounded, silly and brutal, *Atlanta* defies a singular label and demands a seat at the VIP table.

DONALD GLOVER TRICKED FX INTO ORDERING THE SHOW.

The concept of Trojan Horsing your way onto TV is something a few creators (including Jenji Kohan of *Orange is the New Black*) have talked about. You sell the studio one familiar thing then introduce them to the real, innovative story hiding inside it. According to Glover, *Atlanta* followed in that grand tradition by telling FX the series would be more of a traditional hang-out show than it is. "I just kinda Trojan Horsed it," Glover told reporters after winning two Golden Globes. "I told FX [the show] was something it wasn't until we got there and then hoped it would be enjoyable."

DONALD GLOVER THINKS OF *ATLANTA* AS "*CURB YOUR ENTHUSIASM* FOR RAPPERS."

Along with surrealism, *Atlanta* trades in the kind of wry humor that would make Larry David proud, which explains why Glover describes the show as a rapper version of *Curb Your Enthusiasm*. "Being a rapper is super awkward," Glover told Stephen Colbert in 2018. "You're in a video and you got, like, champagne and butts close to your face . . . and then you have to go to Whole Foods and the person is like, 'Hey, you're that dude!' and you're like, 'Please, I really want to buy this ice cream.'" Cue the theme music and deadpan stare.

GLOVER IS A RAPPER IN REAL LIFE, SO HE DIDN'T WANT TO PLAY ONE ON TV.

There are plenty of TV stars who echo their real careers in the fictional world—think Jerry Seinfeld playing an increasingly successful comedian on *Seinfeld* and Lena

Dunham playing an increasingly successful writer on *Girls*. But Glover didn't want to go that route. "That would have been whack to me," Glover said. "I don't think anybody wants to see a show about making it."

MARIJUANA INSPIRES THE SHOW'S CHAOTIC STRUCTURE.

Given that *Atlanta*'s structure is marked by disorientation and disconnection, it makes sense that marijuana is a muse for the show. "We do everything high," Glover told *The New Yorker*. "The effortless chaos of *Atlanta*—the moments of enlightenment followed by an abrupt return to reality—is definitely shaped by weed. When shit is actually going on, no one knows what the fuck is happening."

ZAZIE BEETZ IS CAREFUL ABOUT HOW HER CHARACTER IS VIEWED.

Beetz plays Van, Earn's sometime-girlfriend and the (mostly single) mother to their child. She's intelligent and caring and represents a version of Black womanhood not usually seen on TV. "What I like about *Atlanta* is that it offers audiences a space to see roundness within characters and more fullness to them," Beetz told *Elle*. Van is representative, but also a fully fleshed-out individual. It was important to Beetz and *Atlanta*'s creators that she not be written or portrayed as a minor character or some one-dimensional trope.

FREEZE FRAME

"JUNETEENTH" // SEASON 1, EPISODE 9
As a rapper, Glover goes by Childish Gambino. When his third studio album, *Awaken, My Love!*, dropped on December 2, 2016, sharp-eyed internet denizens realized he'd already hidden its album art in an October 25, 2016, episode of *Atlanta*, where Glover's Earn and Beetz's Van go to a Juneteenth party. That's next-level Easter egging.

"A big thing from the beginning was that they wanted her to be more than an angry Black woman. That resonated a lot with me," Beetz said. "*Atlanta* provides insight into parts of Black culture that some people may not understand, because they're not exposed to it."

THEY NEEDED A "WHITE TRANSLATOR" TO USE THE N-WORD ON THE SHOW.

FX initially told Glover not to use the N-word in the pilot, which would have been a dilution of natural speech. "I'm Black, making a very Black show, and they're telling me I can't use the N-word," Glover told *The New Yorker*. "Only in a world run by white people would that happen." To solve the problem, the creative team brought in Paul Simms—an executive producer known as the "white translator" to several Black showrunners—to make the case for why FX should allow the show to use the word. If you watch *Atlanta*, you know who won that argument.

ATLANTA MADE A CHICKEN WING ORDER SO POPULAR, A RESTAURANT CHAIN ADDED IT TO ITS MENU.

If you don't know Atlanta (the city), this can get a little confusing: J. R. Crickets is a real restaurant depicted in the show, but the lemon pepper wet chicken wing order that Paper Boi and Darius (LaKeith Stanfield) get wasn't on its menu in real life. Glover based the dish on an item on American Deli's menu; he found it funny that someone would treat Paper Boi to something at J. R. Crickets that wasn't actually on the menu. The show's depiction of the item, however, led to a run on people attempting to order it, so J. R. Crickets decided to add it to the menu. (Which kind of kills the joke.)

BATTLESTAR GALACTICA

(2003–2009)

DEVELOPED BY: Ronald D. Moore (based on Glen A. Larson's original series)

SEASONS: 4

EPISODES: 76

OTHER SHOWS BY RONALD D. MOORE:
Outlander (2014–PRESENT)

In the early 2000s, a producer named David Eick and a writer named Ronald D. Moore began working together on a reboot of *Battlestar Galactica*, the 1978 sci-fi TV series that much of the world didn't even seem to remember anymore. The series follows the adventures of a human battleship in deep space attempting to avoid the Cylons, a race of AI beings intent on destroying the fifty thousand humans left in the world. By tapping into some of their own past storytelling frustrations, as well as the fears and concerns of post-9/11 America, Eick and Moore began constructing what would become one of the most acclaimed television series of the twenty-first century, as well as one of the great science fiction stories of all time.

The road to *Battlestar Galactica* becoming a giant of 2000s television was not an easy one, though. Its creators fought through uncertain early plans, a fandom who hated the very idea of a reboot, and a supposed "plan" that didn't really exist to establish a new vision of sci-fi television with an all-star cast that included Oscar nominees Edward James Olmos and Mary McDonnell—and Katee Sackhoff in the role of Starbuck, which caused some unexpected controversy.

RONALD D. MOORE KICKED OFF HIS REBOOT WITH A MANIFESTO.

With a new sci-fi property to work with, and years of experience on multiple *Star Trek* series to pull from for inspiration, Moore wanted to make his intentions for *Battlestar Galactica*—which began as a miniseries for Syfy before the cable channel ultimately greenlit it as an ongoing series—clear from the beginning. To do this, he included a three-page manifesto at the beginning of the miniseries script, a document that has now become legendary to fans. Titled "Naturalistic Science Fiction, or Taking the Opera out of Space Opera," Moore began the document with a simple but grand mission statement: "Our goal is nothing less than the reinvention of the science fiction television series."

The document remained attached to the script as it went out to actors, and the philosophy drew some of the show's most important stars, including Edward James Olmos, to the series.

CHANGING STARBUCK'S GENDER WAS ESSENTIAL—ALBEIT CONTROVERSIAL.

When he first began developing his new approach to the series, Moore began looking at ways to reinvent the series' original characters. He quickly turned to the problem of what to do about Apollo and Starbuck, the two pilots who were the stars of Glen A. Larson's original series. Moore saw the friendship between a straitlaced pilot and a rule-breaking pilot as a cliché of genre television, and wanted to change that. Then a simple idea occurred to him: What if Starbuck were a woman?

"I just realized that would change everything," Moore later recalled in Edward Gross and Mark A. Altman's *So Say We All: The Complete, Uncensored, Unauthorized Oral History of Battlestar Galactica.* "It would change the whole dynamic…That was an early idea that then came to be a big influence in the show."

RESPONSES TO EARLY SCREENINGS OF THE SERIES WERE HORRIBLE.

When news broke that *Battlestar Galactica* was getting a reboot, fans of the original series rebelled against the idea—as did Larson, who'd been trying to revive his franchise for years. The objections of its creator aside, the *Battlestar Galactica* reboot moved ahead with production of the initial miniseries (though Moore and Eick always intended to continue the story if the miniseries did well). The next obstacle was showing footage from the reboot to fans, and to test audiences, neither of which yielded positive results.

"I mean, they, like, really fucking hated it," Moore recalled. "The cover sheet said something like, 'This is one of the worst testings we've ever had. We see no reason why you would want to pick this show up as a series.' And analytics were even worse." Die-hard *Battlestar Galactica* fans also weren't happy, as Moore found out firsthand when he attended the 2003 Galacticon to screen a few clips from the miniseries and take questions…but was instead met with boos and hisses.

THE CYLONS HAD A PLAN, BUT THE WRITERS DID NOT.

One of the hallmarks of the *Battlestar Galactica* revival was the decision to make the Cylons not just the metallic Centurions but also human-looking sleeper agents who would be revealed as the series went on. Initially, Moore and company planned the idea of Cylon sleeper agents to be an even more subtle element of the plot than it eventually became. Moore compared the Cylons to "a shark," something we wouldn't see much in the series, in part because the show's writers were still figuring out exactly who the Cylons were and what they wanted.

The initial approach to the Cylons was also vague enough that the famed opening text of the series, in which it declares that the Cylons "have a plan," was actually just pure marketing copy, inserted at Eick's suggestion. "So for the next fourteen years of my life, people have asked me 'What was the plan?'" Moore said at the 2017 ATX Television Festival. "There was no fucking plan!"

THE WORD *FRAK* GAVE THE SHOW A LICENSE TO CURSE AS MUCH AS THEY WANTED.

One of *Battlestar Galactica*'s major contributions to the pop culture lexicon was the use of the word *frak* as an alternate curse word that could be dropped in at will because, in the eyes of censors, it didn't really mean anything. The word was used in the original series, but not nearly as much as the reboot's writers employed it into scripts. When asked why he chose to make such liberal use of the word, Moore called it "a brilliant opportunity to say 'fuck' over and over again."

SPOILERS! VIEWERS WEREN'T ENTIRELY SURE WHAT HAPPENED TO STARBUCK, AND NEITHER WERE THE WRITERS.

One of the great mysteries of *Battlestar Galactica* is what exactly happened to Kara "Starbuck" Thrace, who seemed to die toward the end of the show's third season, only to mysteriously reappear after a two-month absence. She's the character who plugs in the coordinates for the blind jump that leads the fleet to our Earth, only to vanish into thin air in the series finale. A number of fan theories have since sprung up about what happened to Starbuck, what she really was after returning to the series, and what her role in the story was. But if you're looking for definite answers, it turns out not even the show's writers have them—in part because they weren't looking for them.

"I can tell you that in the writing room, there were multiple theories as to who Kara Thrace really was, how did she come back, why did she disappear in the end," writer-producer David Weddle said in *So Say We All*. "We never answered those concretely, nor do I think we ever should. The opinions of the writers in the room are just like the opinions of the viewers. It's open to interpretation, and there are multiple ways to interpret it."

WHEN GEORGE LUCAS SUED *BATTLESTAR GALACTICA*

The box office success of 1977's *Star Wars* made sci-fi the hottest commodity in entertainment, with plenty of film and television projects—like 1979's long-promised *Star Trek* feature—making the lightspeed jump to screens. But *Star Wars* creator George Lucas thought that Universal's attempt to capitalize on the trend hit a little too close to home.

When *Battlestar Galactica* premiered on the network in September 1978, Lucas found its aesthetic derivative of his own space saga. He had a point: *Star Wars* concept artist Ralph McQuarrie and special effects expert John Dykstra both worked on *Battlestar Galactica*. There were space dogfights; a cocky, Han Solo–esque pilot in Starbuck; and the stormtrooper-inspired Cylons. Lucas and *Star Wars* studio 20th Century Fox filed a copyright infringement lawsuit against Universal that named thirty-four similarities between the productions. A judge admitted the presence of a "friendly robot" and space vehicles "made to look used . . . and old" was indeed suspicious.

After years of legal entanglement that far outpaced the show's original run of just twenty-four episodes, Fox and Universal settled out of court.

When *Battlestar Galactica* was ultimately rebooted to great critical acclaim more than twenty years later, there wasn't a peep from Lucas. In fact, when Lucas was setting his sights on crafting a *Star Wars* television series in the 2000s, he enlisted none other than Ronald D. Moore—who had brought *Battlestar Galactica* back to life—to help. Unfortunately, that series never materialized.

BETTER
CALL SAUL

(2015—PRESENT)

CREATED BY: Vince Gilligan and Peter Gould

SEASONS: 6

EPISODES: 63

OTHER SHOWS BY VINCE GILLIGAN:
Breaking Bad (2008–2013)

FREEZE FRAME

"MARCO" // SEASON 1, EPISODE 10

In a moment of comedic relief, we learn that Jimmy has seduced a (presumably inebriated) woman by telling her that he is Kevin Costner. When she wakes up in the morning, she clearly sees that it's not the *Dances with Wolves* star she went home with. But if something feels familiar about the scenario, it's probably that Jimmy (as Saul) told Walter White about this ruse back in 2010 in "Abiquiu," a season 3 episode of *Breaking Bad.* "If you're committed enough, you can make any story work," he tells Walt. "I once told a woman I was Kevin Costner, and it worked because I believed it."

If making *Breaking Bad* was a high-wire act of maintaining perfection, Vince Gilligan stepped onto an even thinner wire when he decided to create a prequel to the beloved series. But *Better Call Saul* is the rare show that manages to enrich its predecessor's backstory while standing alone as its own stellar creation.

Before he was Saul Goodman, lawyer to everyone's favorite chemistry-teacher-turned-meth-kingpin Walter White, Bob Odenkirk was Jimmy McGill, the ne'er-do-well brother to highly respected Albuquerque attorney Chuck McGill (Michael McKean). Though deep down Jimmy clearly cares about people—well, *some* people, including fellow lawyer and perfectly ponytailed Kim Wexler (Rhea Seehorn)— he cares about winning more, despite his better instincts. Played with exhausting enthusiasm by Odenkirk, Jimmy's journey to strip mall success is as harrowing and taut as watching Walter White navigate the meth business, but it's (thankfully) a whole other animal.

THE *BREAKING BAD* WRITERS USED TO JOKE ABOUT MAKING A SAUL GOODMAN SPINOFF.

While whittling down a huge pile of ideas into what would become *Breaking Bad*'s scripts, Gilligan and the other writers had a lot of lines for Saul that got scrapped. "We love writing for the character," Gilligan told Uproxx in 2015. "We love putting words in his mouth. And we had so much fun, indeed, doing that, that it started as a lark; we'd come up with some great term or phrase, and we'd laugh about it in the writers' room, and then we'd say, 'You know, when we're doing the Saul Goodman show we'll be able to blah, blah, blah.'" Be careful what you joke about.

THERE ARE HIDDEN MEANINGS IN THE EPISODE TITLES.

You can take nothing for granted in the *Better Call Saul* universe, including the episode titles. In the first season, every episode (from "Uno" to "Marco") ended in the letter O, except "Alpine Shepherd Boy," which was supposed to be called "Jell-O," but they weren't able to clear it. Season 2 went even deeper: The first letters of all the episodes (S-C-A-G-R-B-I-F-N-K) unscramble to spell "Fring's Back"—a clear message for *Breaking Bad* fans.

YOU CAN TELL A LOT ABOUT WHAT KIM WEXLER IS FEELING BY THE STATE OF HER PONYTAIL.

Kim Wexler, attorney at law and Jimmy's love interest, is as memorable for her tenacity as she is for her perfectly positioned ponytail. In an interview with Vulture, Rhea Seehorn explained the significance of Kim's ponytail: "Whenever women with long hair need to get shit done, you just get your hair out of your face." Though decided on for practical purposes, it meant that when Kim is feeling vulnerable, she lets her hair down—literally.

BETTER CALL SAUL (SORT OF) USES THE *BREAKING BAD* THEME SONG.

Dave Porter's title theme for *Breaking Bad* used a dobro guitar stretching the sound over a moody, percussive vibe. For *Better Call Saul*'s outro titles, Porter remixed that sound into something that's a bit more surf rock. Listen closely and you'll hear the *Breaking Bad* theme in the mix.

CHUCK MCGILL WASN'T INTENDED TO BE A BAD GUY.

Everyone who watches the show hates Chuck McGill, Jimmy's brother. But it wasn't until writing the seventh episode that Gilligan and the writers realized Chuck was a villain. "Believe it or not, the idea of Chuck being the 'bad guy' was a late addition to season one," Gilligan explained during a 2015 Reddit Ask Me Anything (AMA) chat with fans. "This points out one of the things I love most about writing for TV. There are enough episodes and enough lead time (if you're lucky) for writers to change the direction of a story midstream."

SAUL ENDS UP LIVING HIS "BEST-CASE SCENARIO."

In the penultimate episode of *Breaking Bad*, Saul erases his identity, prepares to move away from Albuquerque, and claims his best-case scenario is managing a Cinnabon in Omaha, Nebraska. That's exactly what he's doing as "Gene" in the very opening of *Better Call Saul*. Congrats, Saul. You're living the dream.

FREEZE FRAME ▶

"SWITCH" // SEASON 2, EPISODE 1

Better Call Saul regularly pays homage to its predecessor—especially with its preferred brand of tequila. On *Breaking Bad*, Gus Fring poisons an entire drug cartel with Zafiro Añejo tequila, the same fictional brand that Jimmy and Kim down while trying to bilk an investor in the season 2 premiere. The brand makes another appearance in season 3 ("Fall"), and the same bottle is pulled out again during the season 4 premiere ("Smoke").

BINGE-WORTHY TV SPIN-OFFS

The TV spin-off is a time-honored tradition, going back decades to a time when characters would be introduced in sketches on a variety show and then given their own full-fledged series just months later. As *Better Call Saul* has shown, the right character or concept can launch a spin-off into the pop culture stratosphere, where it can both blaze its own trail with new stories and possibly even become a bigger hit than its predecessor. In that spirit, here are some of the best TV spin-offs of all time.

THE JEFFERSONS
(1975-1985)

With *All in the Family*, TV legend Norman Lear and company gave the world one of the most influential, incisive, and celebrated sitcoms ever made. Then, just four years later, they did it again. *The Jeffersons*—about the title family's move from their home next door to the Bunker family in Queens to a "deluxe apartment" in Manhattan—took *All in the Family*'s fearless approach in addressing the social issues of its era and added its own spin, giving us one of television's most revered Black families, as well as the first major TV depiction of an interracial married couple.

LAVERNE & SHIRLEY
(1976-1983)

Happy Days (which itself was a spin-off of *Love, American Style*) was such a television powerhouse that it spawned no fewer than seven spin-off series, two of them animated—and that's not even counting the pilots that *didn't* get picked up. While *Mork & Mindy* is still well known for its introduction of Robin Williams to a national audience, the biggest success story to come out of the wider *Happy Days* family is without question *Laverne & Shirley* (which co-starred *Better Call Saul*'s Michael McKean).

FRASIER
(1993-2004)

Cheers ran for eleven seasons and was one of the defining sitcoms of the 1980s. *Frasier*, starring Kelsey Grammer as the eponymous psychiatrist-turned-radio-host who traded Boston for Seattle, somehow managed to at least equal, if not surpass, its parent series in terms of sheer pop culture influence. *Frasier* won five consecutive Emmys for Outstanding Comedy Series, tied *Cheers*'s run of eleven seasons, and remains a syndication staple thanks to the unforgettable performances from its ensemble cast. In early 2021, it was announced that *Frasier* is getting a reboot on Paramount+.

XENA: WARRIOR PRINCESS
(1995-2001)

In 1995, the syndicated fantasy series *Hercules: The Legendary Journeys* introduced a warrior princess named Xena, played by a then-unknown actress named Lucy Lawless. Later that same year, the character got her own fantasy series set in a fictionalized version of Ancient Greece, and rapidly outpaced her parent series. Today, *Xena: Warrior Princess* is remembered as a cultural phenomenon that catapulted Lawless to stardom and inspired dreams of a particular kind of badass woman in the hearts of nineties kids everywhere.

DARIA
(1997-2002)

A recurring character from *Beavis and Butt-Head* landed her own sitcom in which she analyzes high school life and her suburban surroundings through bespectacled eyes and a trademark monotone, and an unofficial mascot for Generation X was born. *Daria* remains one of the most specific and brilliantly constructed animated series to emerge from the adult-leaning animation wave of the 1990s. More than 20 years after *Daria*'s original premiere, it's about to get its own spin-off. MTV recently announced *Jodie*, a new animated series that will follow the post-college life of Jodie Landon (a minor character on *Daria*) as she enters the tech world. *Black-ish* star Tracee Ellis Ross will both executive produce the series and voice the role of Jodie.

ANGEL
(2016-2019)

A *Buffy the Vampire Slayer* spin-off seemed like a no-brainer in 1999, when the series was one of the hottest things on TV, but *Angel* was not necessarily the safest choice. Centering a show on the brooding vampire with a soul (David Boreanaz) as he moved to Los Angeles and began helping people while atoning for his own past sins required a darker touch, while still maintaining the wit and pacing of *Buffy*—and somehow the creators managed to pull it off.

THE BIG BANG BANG THEORY

(2007–2019)

CREATED BY: Chuck Lorre and Bill Prady

SEASONS: 12

EPISODES: 279

OTHER SHOWS BY CHUCK LORRE:
Dharma & Greg (1997–2002)
Young Sheldon (2017–PRESENT)

OTHER SHOWS BY BILL PRADY:
The Muppets (2015–2016)

Sitcom veterans Chuck Lorre and Bill Prady created *The Big Bang Theory*, which premiered on CBS on September 24, 2007. The comedy followed nerdy Caltech physicist roommates Sheldon Cooper (Jim Parsons) and Leonard Hofstadter (Johnny Galecki), who befriend their non-scientist neighbor Penny (Kaley Cuoco). For twelve seasons, the gang—which also included regulars Simon Helberg as Howard Wolowitz, Kunal Nayyar as Rajesh Koothrappali, Melissa Rauch as Bernadette Rostenkowski-Wolowitz, and Mayim Bialik as Amy Farrah Fowler—bonded over science and pop culture.

A decade after *The Big Bang Theory* debuted, CBS aired the first episode of *Young Sheldon*, a *Big Bang* prequel created by Lorre and Steven Molaro. In 2019, Parsons, citing personal reasons, opted to not renew his contract; thus, the producers decided to end the show's epic run. After 279 episodes and four Emmy awards for Parsons, the extremely popular sitcom concluded on May 16, 2019, when millions watched Sheldon and his friends experience a happy ending—and finally see their building's elevator get fixed.

THE SHOW WASN'T PITCHED IN A TRADITIONAL WAY.

Instead of writing up a premise—which includes outlines of the characters and the long-term vision for the show—and pitching it to CBS, Lorre and Prady wrote a complete script, hired actors, and, as Lorre explained, "put on a show" for CBS president Les Moonves. Lorre found the experience to be "crazy," but it obviously worked.

IT TOOK TWO PILOTS FOR THE SHOW TO GET PICKED UP TO SERIES.

The show filmed two different pilots, because CBS didn't like the first one but felt the show had potential. The first pilot began with a different theme song and featured Sheldon, Leonard, and two female characters, including a different actress playing what would become the Penny

role. Lorre thought the initial pilot "sucked" but is open to having the unaired pilot included as part of a DVD extra.

ED ROBERTSON OF THE BARENAKED LADIES HESITATED TO WRITE THE THEME SONG.

As the story goes, Lorre and Prady went to a Barenaked Ladies concert and were impressed that lead singer Ed Robertson sang a song about cosmological theory, so they tapped him to write the series' theme song, called "The History of Everything." In 2013, Robertson told CBS News that he'd previously written some songs for TV and film, only to have his work rejected, so he was initially reluctant to take on the project.

"I was like, 'Look, how many other people have you asked to write this? I'm at my cottage, I got a couple of weeks off right now and if you've asked Counting Crows and Jack Johnson and all these other people to write it, then I kinda don't want to waste my time on it,'" Robertson told them. Lorre and Prady told Robertson he was their only choice, so Robertson agreed to come on board. The first version was thirty-two seconds long, but Robertson had to trim it down to fifteen seconds. The original version was also acoustic, which Lorre loved, but Robertson insisted that his bandmates be on the track, and Lorre loved that one even more.

IT'S AMERICA'S LONGEST-RUNNING MULTI-CAMERA COMEDY EVER.

With 279 episodes, *Big Bang* is America's longest running multi-camera sitcom—beating out *Cheers* by four episodes. (*Cheers* ran for eleven seasons, from 1982 to 1993, and ended with 275 episodes.) It's apt that *Big Bang* topped *Cheers*, because both shows share the same DNA. "One of the things that was really inherent to the success of *Cheers* was that these people weren't related to one another but they clung to each other like a family," Lorre told *The Hollywood Reporter*. "That happened on *The Big Bang Theory*. The characters aren't related but they behave and operate like a family even to the point of making each other miserable."

KUNAL NAYYAR SPOKE IN HIS REAL ACCENT.

In recent years, white actors and South Asian actors speaking in an exaggerated Indian accent have come under fire. Raj spoke in a heavy accent, which was totally authentic. "I've lost count of the number of times I've had to tell people that my pure Delhi, St. Columba's School accent is the real deal, not something I consciously practice to sound more 'Indian' or to make fun of Indian accents like, say, the Apu character in *The Simpsons*," Nayyar told *The Times of India* in 2015. The actor was born in London, grew up in India, and moved to America in 1999 to attend college. "I'm proud of my culture; I wear it on my sleeve. The only thing is in fifteen years in the US, I haven't 'lost' my Indian accent."

AMY FARRAH FOWLER WAS MADE A NEUROSCIENTIST ON PURPOSE.

Mayim Bialik, who in real life has a PhD in neuroscience, told *Variety* how Fowler's profession came to be. "They didn't have a profession for my character when I came on in the finale of season three," she says. "In season four, Bill Prady said they'd make her what I am so I could fix things (in the script) if they were wrong. It's

neat to know what things mean. But most of the time, I don't have to use it."

BIALIK JOINED THE SHOW SO SHE COULD SECURE HEALTH INSURANCE.

In 2010, Bialik's grad school health insurance was expiring. She had a toddler and a newborn and needed insurance through a job. "I did not expect to be a regular on a television show," she told the Canadian talk show *The Social*. "I had been teaching neuroscience. I've tutored Hebrew. I've tutored piano. I wear a lot of hats, you know. I eventually auditioned for this show, called *The Big Bang Theory*, which I had never seen, and it changed my life and I got insurance [through the Screen Actors Guild]."

ASTROPARTICLE PHYSICIST AND SCIENCE CONSULTANT DAVID SALTZBERG ONCE GOT A JOKE ON THE AIR.

The Big Bang Theory had David Saltzberg on retainer from the beginning of the series. He attended the tapings every week, offering up corrections and ensuring the whiteboards used in the scenes were accurate. During episode nine of the first season, Saltzberg wrote a joke for Sheldon, who has a fight with another scientist. Penny asks Sheldon about the misunderstanding, and Sheldon replies, "A little misunderstanding? Galileo and the pope had a little misunderstanding!"

Even though Saltzberg teaches at UCLA and publishes papers, he thinks his work on *The Big Bang Theory* was more impactful. "This has a lot more impact than anything I will ever do," he told NPR. "It's hard to fathom, when you think about 20 million viewers on the first showing—and that doesn't include other countries and reruns. I'm happy if a paper I write gets read by a dozen people."

WIL WHEATON GOT THE "EVIL WIL WHEATON" GIG THROUGH TWITTER.

Wheaton told Larry King, "I was talking on Twitter about how much I loved the show and how I thought it was really funny." Executive producer Steven Molaro saw the tweet and told Wheaton to let him know if he wanted to come to a taping. A few days later Wheaton received an email from Bill Prady's assistant about appearing on the show. "I just thought the email was a joke from one of my friends, so I just ignored it," Wheaton said.

When Wheaton realized that the email was legit, he called Prady, who explained they wanted a nemesis for Sheldon. "It's always more fun to be the villain,"

Wheaton said. Even though the character has evolved into Sheldon's ally, Wheaton said, "I still call him Evil Wil Wheaton."

PARSONS ATTRIBUTES THE SHOW'S SUCCESS TO ITS LACK OF CHARACTER ARCS.
In a 2014 interview with *New York* magazine, Parsons gave his theory (if you will) on why *The Big Bang Theory* attracted more than 20 million viewers per week—a number unheard of since the *Friends*-era sitcom reign. "There's not anything to keep up with," he said. "You don't go, 'I didn't see the first three seasons, and now they're off with prostitutes, and they no longer work in the Mafia, and I don't understand what happened.' People have so many choices on TV now, so no one's asking for you to marry us. You can enjoy our show without a weekly appointment."

SPOILERS! THE PILOT AND THE SERIES FINALE BROUGHT THE SHOW FULL CIRCLE.
The series ends with a callback to the show's beginning, with Sheldon saying during his Nobel Prize speech that expectant parents Leonard and Penny's babies will be "smart and beautiful," — the same words Leonard said in the pilot. "Now that they're expecting, I have no doubt that will be the case," Sheldon said. In the pilot, after Leonard said those words, Sheldon jabbed Leonard with "Not to mention imaginary." Thankfully, he got that wrong.

SPOILERS! PENNY DOESN'T HAVE A LAST NAME.
Penny is the only character who doesn't seem to have a last name—that is, until she married Leonard and took his last name. "There really is no answer. She's Cher," Cuoco joked on *The Late Show with Stephen Colbert*. "One name. It became a little superstitious for me." Fan theories speculated her maiden name might be Wyatt, but Cuoco and the producers wouldn't confirm. In 2021, the mystery got a little deeper as a Redditor saw you could just barely make out a name on the label of a package Penny received in the episode "The Work Song Nanocluster." The poster said it was Teller, while others argued it was so blurry you couldn't really make out a name.

BINGEABLE COMIC BOOK–BASED TV SHOWS

Comics have been inspiring television since *The Adventures of Superman* in the early 1950s. Naturally, depictions of caped heroes have gotten a little bit more sophisticated since then.

1 ***Black Lightning* // (2018–2021)**
Cress Williams stars as Jefferson Pierce, a teacher-turned-high-school-principal with electrical powers who has to suit up once more when his family is targeted by a criminal gang.

2 ***The Boys* // (2019–PRESENT)**
Superheroes take a hard and R-rated turn in this Prime Video adaptation of the Garth Ennis and Darick Robertson series about the Seven, a super-team with corporate sponsors and dreams of ruling the world—if only rogue Billy Butcher (Karl Urban) would let them. Barack Obama is a fan.

3 ***The Flash* // (2014–PRESENT)**
Grant Gustin helps anchor the CW's DC Universe with his portrayal of Barry Allen, the Fastest Man Alive, who finds himself in a world where no comic book idea is too out-there, from time travel to a talking man-shark.

4 ***The Umbrella Academy* // (2019–PRESENT)**
Netflix scored one of their biggest original hits with this adaptation of the Gerard Way and Gabriel Bá series from Dark Horse Comics about a group of adopted siblings, now grown, who reunite for their father's funeral and remain a (dysfunctional) unit to stop a looming threat.

5 ***WandaVision* // (2021)**
Marvel Studios ushered in a new era of media domination with this delightfully demented miniseries about the Scarlet Witch, aka Wanda Maximoff (Elizabeth Olsen), and her android lover, Vision (Paul Bettany), who appear to be trapped in a sterile world of classic sitcoms. Unwrapping the mystery is part of the fun of this offbeat series, which launched a post–*Avengers: Endgame* Marvel Cinematic Universe.

BLACK-ISH

(2014–PRESENT)

CREATED BY: Kenya Barris

SEASONS: 7

EPISODES: 162

OTHER SHOWS CREATED BY KENYA BARRIS:
Grown-ish (2018–PRESENT)
Mixed-ish (2019–PRESENT)
BlackAF (2020–PRESENT)

B*lack-ish* could have easily been yet another toothless, trope-filled network sitcom about an upper-middle-class family. Instead, it has become a work of important social significance—and one that isn't afraid to tackle the issues facing Black families in America today. Anthony Anderson and Tracee Ellis Ross have received a ton of accolades for their roles as Dre and Rainbow Johnson, a couple who are worried that their kids are losing touch with their Black culture.

Though the series has been critically acclaimed since its premiere, its second season took the show's message even further and tackled everything from racial slurs to police brutality. Now several seasons in, *Black-ish*'s social conscience is regularly compared to *Good Times, A Different World,* and other pioneering series before it. And now it has launched its very own mini-franchise with spinoffs *Grown-ish*, *Mixed-ish*, and *Old-ish*, with each series speaking to a distinct audience.

THE SHOW'S TITLE REFERS TO RACIAL IDENTITIES . . . AND JUSTIN BIEBER.

When *Black-ish* debuted in 2014, there was a big discussion about its title and what it meant. Show creator Kenya Barris told NPR that it's a reflection of his anxieties about raising his children in a more privileged world than he knew as a kid. "I wanted to be honest with what it's like sort of raising your kids in a different environment than you were accustomed to being raised in," he explained. "My kids are nothing like I remember Black kids being when I was a kid."

When *Black-ish* star and executive producer Laurence Fishburne was asked about the show's title on *The View*, his explanation was more blunt: "For some people, it means when Black folks kind of act white. For some people, it means when white folks kind of act Black. . . . I think of it this way. Two words: Justin Bieber. Justin Bieber acts blackish but he doesn't get shot by the police; he gets a police escort home."

FREEZE FRAME

"PILOT" // SEASON 1, EPISODE 1

As the star and an executive producer on *Black-ish*, Anthony Anderson has contributed some of his own real-life experiences to the show. One of them? The "bro mitzvah" that Dre throws for his eldest son in the pilot. Anderson hosted a similar bash for his own son. If you remember the episode, you might recall a moment in the middle of all that revelry when Dre attempts a backflip on the dance floor . . . and lands flat on his back. According to Marcus Scribner, who plays Andre Jr., that move was not scripted—Anderson actually wiped out. "I think that everybody in the entire room thought Anthony died," Scribner said in an interview with *J-14*. "We all rushed over to Anthony like, 'Are you OK? Are you OK?' He just kept it moving and it made it . . . into the show."

KENYA BARRIS GOT HIS BREAK ON *AMERICA'S NEXT TOP MODEL*.

After graduating from Clark Atlanta University with a film degree, Barris picked up a few writing credits on the Showtime series *Soul Food* and WB sitcom *Like Family*. But he was hungry to develop his own show, so he worked with his childhood friend Tyra Banks on a reality competition pitch. That series was *America's Next Top Model*, and Barris got a handsome cut of the profits as a co-developer of the series.

NORMAN LEAR WAS A MAJOR INFLUENCE ON THE SERIES.

Barris has repeatedly cited Norman Lear as a primary influence on *Black-ish*. Lear developed and created such groundbreaking sitcoms as *All in the Family*, *The Jeffersons*, *Maude*, and *Good Times*. Barris is such a fan of *Good Times* in particular that he turned the *Black-ish* season 2 finale into a homage. "He's beyond an influence for me," Barris told *Variety*. "I feel like I am so derivative of Norman Lear and what he was doing and what he was about. It's hard to even think about being a writer without him having been there."

Lear clearly admires Barris's work, too. In 2016, the television legend stopped by the *Black-ish* writers room to pitch a few ideas, one of which inspired the season 2 episode "The Johnson Show."

MUCH OF *BLACK-ISH* IS SEMI-AUTOBIOGRAPHICAL.

Barris has always described the show as semi-autobiographical, but some of the parallels between the Johnsons and Barris's own family are much more direct. For instance, the *Black-ish* matriarch, Rainbow Johnson, is an anesthesiologist with a Black mother and a white father. Barris's real-life wife is also a biracial anesthesiologist named Rainbow.

Many episodes are based on real conversations with Barris's kids, too. The series received wide critical praise for the season 2 episode "Hope," which discussed police brutality. It opens with one of the youngest Johnsons, Jack, staring at news footage and asking his parents, "Why are all these people so mad?" That specific query came from Barris's then-seven-year-old son, who asked him the exact same question when his family watched the Ferguson grand jury decline to indict a police officer for shooting Michael Brown Jr., an eighteen-year-old Black teenager, in 2014.

LARRY WILMORE WAS ORIGINALLY A CO-SHOWRUNNER.

The star of *The Nightly Show* was originally set to run *Black-ish* with Barris. ABC had proposed Larry Wilmore as a co-showrunner on *Black-ish* in 2014. Given Wilmore's work on *In Living Color* and *The Bernie Mac Show*, Barris was eager to partner with him. But then Comedy Central offered Wilmore his own talk show, *The Nightly Show*, and he had to exit. He still stayed on for the first twelve episodes of *Black-ish*, but Barris called in TV veteran Jonathan Groff (the producer, not the *Glee* and *Hamilton* actor) as backup. Groff has been an executive producer ever since.

MARCUS SCRIBNER BEAT OUT ANTHONY ANDERSON'S SON FOR THE ROLE OF ANTHONY ANDERSON'S SON.

Marcus Scribner—who plays Andre Johnson Jr. (aka Junior), to Anthony Anderson's Andre Johnson Sr.—had what some might consider unfair competition when auditioning for the role of Anderson's son…because Anderson's actual son read for the part. "It was kinda funny 'cause, when we first went in for the audition, Anthony made sure to come out and let everybody know that his son was auditioning," Scribner told *Nylon*. "And he was like, 'None of y'all have a good chance 'cause my son is auditioning for this role!' And we were all super nervous…But I ended up getting the role, and I talked to Nathan [Anderson] afterward, he's a really cool guy…there are no hard feelings at all."

Anthony Anderson agrees that his son is a really cool guy, which is why they couldn't cast him. "You know, he just has a little too much swag, and I don't know where he gets it from," Anderson told Rachael Ray. "I sometimes question if he's mine or not. His swag factor is just off the charts! And we needed him not to be goofy, but just be a nerdy kid, and he couldn't shake that. And so I couldn't cast him!"

TRACEE ELLIS ROSS HAS A MEGA-FAMOUS (AND SUPER SUPPORTIVE) MOM.

Tracee Ellis Ross is the second oldest child of Diana Ross, which means she grew up in a household where Michael Jackson called frequently, and Andy Warhol painted her portrait. And Diana is clearly incredibly proud of her comedienne daughter: When Tracee was nominated for an Emmy in 2016, Diana took out a full-page ad in *The Hollywood Reporter* congratulating her daughter on the success.

But Ross isn't the only *Black-ish* cast member with celebrity kin. Yara Shahidi, who plays Zoey, boasts rapper Nas as a relation. She was even the flower girl at his wedding.

"PLEASE, BABY, PLEASE": THE LOST *BLACK-ISH* EPISODE DEEMED TOO DIVISIVE FOR TV

On February 27, 2018, *Black-ish* was scheduled to air "Please, Baby, Please," the fourteenth episode of the series' fourth season. Instead, viewers who tuned into ABC that night saw a repeat of a previously aired episode. Less than a week before the episode was set to air, the network decided to remove it from their schedule over concerns it would upset audiences. It was arguably more upsetting for fans who believed *Black-ish*'s creative team was being silenced.

"Please, Baby, Please" centers on Dre (Anderson) putting his newborn baby Devante to sleep during a thunderstorm by telling him a bedtime story—one that encapsulated the tumultuous state of America at that very moment. As Dre explains the nation's tense political animosity to his infant son, the show plays footage of white supremacist rhetoric, the NFL kneeling protests, climate change, and then-president Donald Trump. Dre's other children chime in with their own impressions and worldviews. Oscar-winning filmmaker Spike Lee, who partially inspired series creator Kenya Barris to write the episode with *Black-ish*'s executive producer Peter Saji, helps narrate.

"Daddy's scared, too, but not about the thunder," Dre tells his son, referring to the divisiveness engulfing America.

Although ABC had usually embraced Barris's social commentary, network executives believed this particular episode would be too polarizing. Officially, the shelving of "Please, Baby, Please" was attributed to "creative differences." But it was also widely speculated that this creative clash was a key factor in Barris's decision to part ways with the network and sign a $100 million deal with Netflix later that very same year. While ABC fielded criticism that their decision to pull the episode was a case of censorship, fans were left to wonder just how provocative the 22-minute episode could really be.

The answer was: not very. At the urging of Barris, the Walt Disney Company (which owns ABC) agreed to stream "Please, Baby, Please" on Hulu (also owned by Disney) beginning in August 2020—more than two years after its originally scheduled release date. What viewers saw was an honest depiction of a concerned father examining the world around him and wondering how it will treat his son. While the content has a political slant that some viewers may find uncomfortable, Dre's real story—a parent wanting to protect his kids—proved relatable to everyone. Dre's final words, in which he expresses hope that people can be there for one another, is a message of unity. He tells Devante the storm will let up soon.

CREATED BY: *Vince Gilligan*

SEASONS: 5

EPISODES: 62

OTHER SHOWS BY VINCE GILLIGAN:
Better Call Saul (2015–PRESENT)

FREEZE FRAME

"GRILLED" // SEASON 2, EPISODE 2

The fight scene between Jesse (Aaron Paul) and Tuco (Raymond Cruz) turned serious when Cruz ended up accidentally knocking Paul unconscious. "Tuco takes Jesse and he throws him through the screen door outside, and if you watch it back you'll notice that my head gets caught inside the wooden screen door and it flips me around and lands me on my stomach and the door splinters into a million pieces," Paul said in a Reddit AMA. "Raymond just thought I was acting, so he continued and kicked me in the side and picked me up over his shoulder and threw me against the house, but in reality I was pretty much unconscious."

As *Breaking Bad* was coming to a close in 2013, Bryan Cranston received an email from a fan congratulating him for his work on the series. "Your performance as Walter White was the best acting I have seen—ever," it read, with compliments extended to the entire cast. The letter was sent by Sir Anthony Hopkins.

During its five seasons, *Breaking Bad* elicited that kind of enthusiasm from millions of viewers—for its actors, for its sweeping portrayal of a sweltering New Mexico drug scene, and for its anxiety-provoking story about a high school chemistry teacher (Cranston) diagnosed with lung cancer who decides it would be better to use what time he has left to cook methamphetamine than to leave his family financially compromised. As Walter White descends further into the abyss, shaping his morality to fit the circumstances, the audience is tugged along with him, torn between the inherent ugliness of his criminality and his relatable devotion to his family. Creator Vince Gilligan described it as affable teacher Mr. Chips becoming Scarface. For the audience, it was another kind of transformation: A television show had taken on the urgency of a page-turning thriller that left them exhilarated and exhausted. Years after its finale, getting into a casual chat about favorite shows on TV will inevitably lead to someone asking: "You've watched *Breaking Bad*, right?" The answer is usually yes. A better question might be how many times.

PRACTICALLY EVERY NETWORK PASSED ON MAKING *BREAKING BAD*, INCLUDING HBO.

They're probably kicking themselves now, but most of the major networks—including HBO, Showtime, and TNT—passed on *Breaking Bad*. In fact, Gilligan described his meeting with HBO as "the worst meeting I've ever had…The woman we [were] pitching to could not have been less interested—not even in my story, but about whether I actually lived or died."

NETWORK EXECUTIVES *REALLY* WANTED MATTHEW BRODERICK TO PLAY WALTER WHITE.

It's impossible to imagine *Breaking Bad* with anyone other than Cranston in the lead role, but he wasn't as well known when the series kicked off, and AMC wanted a star. They were particularly interested in casting Matthew Broderick in the lead. "We all still had the image of Bryan shaving his body in *Malcolm in the Middle*," a former AMC executive told the *The Hollywood Reporter* about their reluctance to cast Cranston. "We were like, 'Really? Isn't there anybody else?'" But Gilligan had worked with Cranston before, on an episode of *The X-Files*, and knew he had the chops to navigate the quirks of the part. The network brass watched the episode and agreed.

JESSE PINKMAN WASN'T SUPPOSED TO LIVE PAST THE FIRST SEASON.

While *Breaking Bad* ultimately ended up being largely about the tumultuous partnership between Walter White and Jesse Pinkman, Jesse wasn't originally intended to be a major character. It's often stated that he was supposed to be killed off in episode nine, and that it was the 2007–08 Writers Guild of America strike that saved him, but Gilligan set the record straight in 2010, saying it became clear much earlier that Jesse's character—and his relationship to Walter—was integral to moving the show forward.

"I knew by episode two—we all did," Gilligan said. "Everybody knew just how good [Aaron Paul is], and a pleasure to work with, and it became pretty clear early on that that would be a huge, colossal mistake to kill off Jesse."

THE DEA TAUGHT BRYAN CRANSTON AND AARON PAUL HOW TO COOK CRYSTAL METH.

Because of the subject matter, the show's creators thought it prudent to inform the Drug Enforcement Administration (DEA) what *Breaking Bad* was about—then welcome their help. "We were taught how to make meth [by] DEA chemists who were our consultants on the show," Cranston told Howard Stern in 2012. "We didn't cook it, but we were told exactly the process at that high level." Presumably, knowing the right way to cook meth allowed the actor to look like they knew what they were doing without actually showing the full process onscreen.

WALTER'S BOSS AT THE CAR WASH IS A SCIENTIST IN REAL LIFE.

Breaking Bad marked the acting debut of Marius Stan (and his eyebrows), who played Bogdan, Walter's boss at the car wash. In real life, Stan has a PhD in chemistry and, according to a Reddit AMA, is a "Senior Computational Energy Scientist at Argonne National Lab—which is one of the national laboratories under the US Dept. of Energy—and a Senior Fellow at the University of Chicago, the Computation Institute." He landed the role accidentally: While Stan was working at the Los Alamos National Laboratory, *Breaking Bad* was looking for extras, and his kids wanted to try out. He and his wife took them to audition, and they were all hired. Stan was as surprised as anyone when he was given some lines then became a recurring character. One year after his *Breaking Bad* debut, he appeared in the TV series *Crash*. It's his only other acting credit (so far).

THE SCIENCE IN THE SHOW ISN'T PERFECT, AND THAT WAS ON PURPOSE.

Dr. Donna Nelson, a chemistry professor at the University of Oklahoma, worked as the show's science advisor and was tasked with making sure the show got its science right—or at least as "right" as is safe.

"I don't think there's any popular show that gets it a hundred percent right, but that's not the goal," Nelson told *Mental Floss* in 2013. "The goal is not to be a science education show; the goal is to be a popular show. And so there's always going to be some creative license taken, because they want to make the show interesting." One prime example of the show's imperfect science is Walt and Jesse's signature blue meth. "In reality, it wouldn't be blue; it would be colorless," Nelson said. "But this isn't a science education show. It's a fantasy. And Vince Gilligan did a fantastic job of getting most of the science right."

THE ICONIC BLUE METH IS ROCK CANDY.

Walter and Jesse's signature blue meth is blue rock

candy. More specifically: blue rock candy originally from The Candy Lady, a candy store in Albuquerque. (They have a whole line of *Breaking Bad*–inspired treats.)

⟍⟍⟍⟍⟍ SPOILERS! ⟋⟋⟋⟋⟋ THE WALKING DEAD CREW HELPED FILM GUS FRING'S FINAL MOMENTS.

Fring's final sendoff is one of the most memorable visual images from the entire series—and Gilligan was able to enlist the help of some true gore experts. "Indeed we did have great help from the prosthetic effects folks at *The Walking Dead*," Gilligan told *The New York Times*.

AARON PAUL DOESN'T SAY "BITCH" AS MUCH AS YOU THINK.

While any Jesse Pinkman impression ends with "bitch," by one calculation Paul uses the word a total of fifty-four times throughout the series. Considering there are sixty-two episodes, that seems a little on the low side.

Even if that number seems underwhelming, Pinkman's favorite add-on became so synonymous with the actor that, in 2014, Paul released an app called "Yo, Bitch."

WALTER WHITE'S ALTER EGO IS A NOD TO A REAL PERSON.

Walter White's drug kingpin alter ego, Heisenberg, is a reference to Werner Heisenberg, a Nobel Prize–winning physicist who developed the quantum mechanical uncertainty principle.

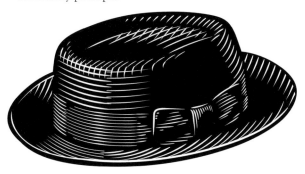

HEISENBERG'S TRADEMARK HAT WAS A MATTER OF PRACTICALITY.

Heisenberg's porkpie hat came to identify Walter White's dark side, but it originated from a very practical place.

FREEZE FRAME ▶

"PHOENIX" // SEASON 2, EPISODE 12

Filming Jane's (Krysten Ritter) death scene was the hardest thing Aaron Paul had to do in *Breaking Bad*. "Looking at Jane through Jesse's eyes that day was very hard and emotional for all of us," Paul said. Cranston reportedly spent fifteen minutes crying after filming was complete.

"Bryan kept asking me, after he shaved his head, 'Can I have a hat?' because his head was cold," Kathleen Detoro, the show's costume designer, explained.

VINCE GILLIGAN HAS ONE REGRET: JESSE'S TEETH.

When asked about whether he had any regrets about the show or any of its story lines, Vince Gilligan admitted, "One thing that sort of troubled me, looking back over the entirety of the show: Jesse's teeth were a little too perfect. There were all the beatings he took, and, of course, he was using meth, which is brutal on your teeth—all that living he did, he'd probably have terrible teeth in real life."

THERE ARE SIXTY-TWO EPISODES IN TOTAL, WHICH HAS A SPECIAL MEANING.

Over the course of five seasons, *Breaking Bad* produced a total of sixty-two episodes—which is probably no accident. The sixty-second element on the periodic table is samarium, which is used to treat a range of cancers, including lung cancer.

⟍⟍⟍⟍⟍ SPOILERS! ⟋⟋⟋⟋⟋ THE FINAL DEATH TOLL IS PRETTY HEFTY.

Just as you may have underestimated the number of times Jesse uttered "bitch," you might be surprised by how many people were killed throughout the show's entire run: 270 (though 167 of those deaths occurred when two planes collided because of Jane's father).

IN 2012, A METH COOK NAMED WALTER WHITE WAS WANTED BY THE AUTHORITIES.

That year, fifty-five-year-old Walter White rose to the top of Tuscaloosa, Alabama's, most wanted list for manufacturing and selling meth. Though White wasn't a teacher, there have been other real-life stories that mirrored Walter White's descent into the criminal underworld: In 2012, a chemistry teacher named William Duncan was arrested for selling meth, and in 2011, Irina Kristy, a seventy-four-year-old math professor, was arrested for running a meth lab. In the case of Kristy, the charges were dropped.

5 ACTORS WHO ASKED FOR THEIR CHARACTERS TO BE KILLED OFF

SPOILERS!

Sometimes an actor's relationship with a character just runs its course. Case in point: Dean Norris, aka *Breaking Bad*'s Hank Schrader. With the series coming to an end, Norris asked if there was a way to kill off Hank during the first half of the final season so that he could pursue other projects. Unfortunately, they needed him. As a result, Norris had to turn down the opportunity to star in a pilot in order to finish filming *Breaking Bad*'s fifth season. Here are five other actors who asked for their characters to be killed off—though not all of them got their wish.

1 SOPHIE TURNER // Sansa Stark on *Game of Thrones*

Sophie Turner wanted Sansa Stark to be killed off before *Game of Thrones* ended—because she wanted her character to die in a memorable and shocking way. "I don't want to survive," Turner told *The Wall Street Journal* in 2016. "If you're on *Game of Thrones* and you don't have a cool death scene, then what's the point?"

2 ADEWALE AKINNUOYE-AGBAJE // Mr. Eko on *Lost*

Adewale Akinnuoye-Agbaje grew more and more unhappy living in Hawaii and working on *Lost*, and after the death of both of his parents, the English actor wanted to return home to London as soon as possible. Executive producers Damon Lindelof and Carlton Cuse weren't happy to see him leave, but they respected Akinnuoye-Agbaje's wishes. "Our Mr. Eko plans very quickly derailed," Lindelof explained. "Originally he was going to be someone who challenged Locke for the spiritual leadership of the castaways." Eventually, they changed the character of Desmond to fill part of Eko's planned arc.

3 DAN STEVENS // Matthew Crawley on *Downton Abbey*

For three years, Dan Stevens played Matthew Crawley on *Downton Abbey*. But at the end of season 3, Stevens wanted to broaden his career—so Matthew was killed off in a car accident. "We were always optioned for three years," Stevens explained to *The Telegraph*. "And when that came up it was a very difficult decision. But it felt like a good time to take stock, to take a moment. From a personal point of view, I wanted a chance to do other things. It is a very monopolizing job. So there is a strange sense of liberation at the same time as great sadness because I am very, very fond of the show and always will be."

4 T. R. KNIGHT // Dr. George O'Malley on *Grey's Anatomy*

Although Dr. George O'Malley was a fan favorite character, T. R. Knight, the actor who played him, found it increasingly difficult to work with *Grey's Anatomy* creator Shonda Rhimes. He said that there was a gradual "breakdown in communication" over the years and that he became frustrated with seeing his screen time dwindle at the beginning of season 5. As a result, Knight asked to be written off the show, and Dr. O'Malley was subsequently hit by a bus.

5 JOSH CHARLES // Will Gardner on *The Good Wife*

In the middle of *The Good Wife*'s fifth season, Josh Charles's character, Will Gardner, was fatally shot in the courtroom by his client. While the decision to kill off Gardner had been made a year earlier, fans were shocked—and upset. In truth, it was Charles's decision; he simply decided not to return for season 6 after his contract was up. "It was just a creative decision for me wanting to go and explore new stuff—in my life, in my career," Charles told Deadline. Still, fans were not happy, and *The Good Wife*'s creators had to issue an open letter to fans to justify his death.

CREATED BY: Ilana Glazer and Abbi Jacobson

SEASONS: 5

EPISODES: 50

What began as a YouTube web series morphed into a small-screen phenomenon. Under the guidance of comedy veteran Amy Poehler, who served as executive producer, Abbi Jacobson and Ilana Glazer's *Broad City* made the jump from online to TV, premiering on Comedy Central in 2014. It's no wonder it regularly raked in positive reviews for its delightful portrayal of female friendship. For five seasons, fans followed the lives of dynamic duo Abbi Abrams (Jacobson) and Ilana Wexler (Glazer)—fictionalized versions of the show's creators—as they navigated their twenties in New York City. You won't find any sanitized, glamorous accounts of millennial life in the big city, and much of what you see is semi-autobiographical. From dodging professional responsibilities to navigating roommate squabbles to bumbling through the city's dating scene, the two best friends get up to a regular medley of hilarious—and for them, at times humiliating—hijinks.

ABBI JACOBSON THOUGHT ILANA GLAZER WAS ALIA SHAWKAT FROM *ARRESTED DEVELOPMENT*.

Jacobson and Glazer met while working together on an improv team. Jacobson told *The New York Times* that before they met, Jacobson thought Glazer was Alia Shawkat, the actress who played Maeby Fünke on *Arrested Development*.

"After the first night of practice, we go to a bar and we're talking about where we're from, and it turns out she knew two of my best friends from college," Jacobson recalled. "And in that moment, I was just like…this is not Maeby anymore. I would know if my friends were friends with Maeby. We really hit it off immediately; I was just like trying to become friends with Maeby, and then I thought, I'll just stay friends with this girl."

JACOBSON AND GLAZER UPSET WHOLE FOODS.

In the series' third season, Lincoln (Hannibal Buress) extracts Abbi's wisdom teeth. Ilana gets her hopped up on a weed s'mores milkshake called a firecracker. High as a kite, Abbi wanders off to a Whole Foods in Brooklyn, where she hallucinates that her stuffed animal friend, Bingo Bronson, is life-size and is egging her on to buy expensive items, like manuka honey. During an interview with Jimmy Kimmel, the women said they pestered Whole Foods on Twitter until they let them film there: "It had to be Whole Foods," Jacobson said. After some negotiations about what they could or could not do while filming there, Whole Foods granted their wish—then seemed to have regretted saying yes. The high-end grocery store chain wasn't offended by the hallucination. "They cared about us truly naming the price of their manuka honey," Glazer said. Abbi ended up spending a whopping $1,487.56 at the store—part of that on that pricey honey.

JACOBSON AND GLAZER DON'T MIND NUDITY— BUT PREFER TO BLUR IT OUT.

Occasionally, the women appear nude on the show. But unlike Lena Dunham on *Girls*, Jacobson and Glazer use blur bars to cover up their nether regions. "Lena Dunham is awesome," Glazer told *New York* magazine. "I love seeing her body on TV. Lena is like a vessel for the message that normal bodies are so beautiful and sexy and powerful. But I don't think we would be that brave to be that vessel, even though you still, like, get that and people are like, 'Wow, they're not . . . bony!'

Even though you get that same message, it's not as strong as Lena's. Lena's isn't for a joke, you know? Ours is always for a joke. We're very grateful for those blurs. So grateful."

HILLARY CLINTON MADE AN APPEARANCE ON THE SHOW.

In a March 2016 interview with *Entertainment Weekly*, Jacobson said that Hillary Clinton's cameo on the show, in which she played herself, wasn't supposed to be a political statement—but then she backtracked.

"Of course it's a political statement!" Jacobson told *The New York Times* in October 2016. "For us, it felt like we were justifying our show in a different way—it felt historic."

SOULSTICE IS BASED ON A REAL GYM.

One of Jacobson's odd jobs was handing out flyers for an Equinox gym near Grand Central Terminal. "I didn't even get paid, it was just a membership," Jacobson told *Time*. "But at the time I was like 'this is amazing!'" At least Jacobson didn't have to clean up gym vomit like her fictional character did.

GLAZER DIDN'T WANT HER BROTHER WRITING FOR THE SHOW.

Glazer's brother, Eliot, wanted to write for the show, but his sister thought "it would be too close for comfort," he told *The New Yorker*. "It was a source of tension for a while." Eliot eventually appeared in several episodes of *Broad City* as Ilana's brother and went on to write for *New Girl* and *Younger*.

GLAZER AND JACOBSON DON'T SMOKE WHILE THEY'RE WORKING.

On the show, Glazer and Jacobson can frequently be found indulging in marijuana, but fans shouldn't expect the stars to smoke with them. "Giving us a joint is one thing—I'm like, 'Thank you *soooo* much,'" Glazer told *New York* magazine. But Jacobson insisted they can't work while stoned. "Everyone thinks we smoke in the writers' room," she said. "It's like, we would never be able to do anything high!"

CLASSIC COMEDY CENTRAL SHOWS

Comedy Central made it to the airwaves in 1989 as the Comedy Channel, later merging with rival comedy network Ha! to create a basic cable humor empire. While they scored groundbreaking hits in the 2000s with *Chappelle's Show*, *The Daily Show*, and *Key & Peele*, the network's tradition of original programming began much earlier on.

MYSTERY SCIENCE THEATER 3000
(1989–1996)

Comedy Central's first cult hit was picked up from a small Minneapolis-St. Paul UHF station and featured stand-up comedian Joel Hodgson riffing on movies with his robot pals Crow T. Robot and Tom Servo. "The 3000 was a joke on all the people that were attaching the year 2000 to various programs," Hodgson said. "In the late '80s it was everywhere: 'America 2000' was something that George Bush, Sr. was talking about a lot so I thought, 'Wouldn't it be cool if I name it 3000 just to confound people?'"

VIVA VARIETY
(1997–1999)

Thomas Lennon of *Reno 911!* fame headlined this spoof of variety shows. Emerging from an unnamed foreign country, each episode showcased acts of questionable talent and the marital discord of Lennon's Mr. Laupin and Kerri Kenny's Mrs. Laupin, whose divorce proceedings included equal hosting rights to the show.

STRANGERS WITH CANDY
(1999–2000)

Amy Sedaris—sister of writer David and an equally adept comic powerhouse—starred in this bizarre riff on high school life. Playing Geraldine Blank, Sedaris navigated social cliques as a forty-six-year-old woman determined to complete her education after kicking a drug habit. The *Orange County Register* dubbed it a "grotesque pantomime of an ABC After School Special."

WIN BEN STEIN'S MONEY
(1997–2003)

Droll character actor Ben Stein (*Ferris Bueller's Day Off*, *The Mask*) was pitted head-to-head with contestants looking to win money that purportedly really belonged to him, all of them egged on (initially) by host Jimmy Kimmel. But don't worry: Win or lose, Stein got a salary for appearing.

UPRIGHT CITIZENS BRIGADE
(1998–2000)

Amy Poehler, Matt Besser, Ian Roberts, and Matt Walsh took their improv skills to cable with this inventive (scripted) sketch comedy series that helped usher in a new era of absurdist humor.

BUFFY
THE
(1997–2003)
VAMPIRE
SLAYER

CREATED BY: Joss Whedon (based on the movie written by Joss Whedon)

SEASONS: 7

EPISODES: 144

OTHER SHOWS BY JOSS WHEDON:
Angel (1999-2004)
Firefly (2002)
Dr. Horrible's Sing-Along Blog (2008)
Dollhouse (2009-2010)
The Nevers (2021-PRESENT)

A lot of people can say that high school was hell, but for Buffy Summers (Sarah Michelle Gellar) and her peers, the horrors of young adulthood were truly demonic. Whether dealing with the undead consequences of sleeping with your first love or being literally silenced in an episode about the difficulty of communicating one's true self, *Buffy*'s simple stroke of genius was using monster movie genre conventions in service of deeply human stories.

Series creator Joss Whedon's behavior on set has (retroactively) called his own ethics into question, but the worldview his seminal series espoused will no doubt go on to influence new generations of fans. *Buffy*—which was loosely based on Fran Rubel Kuzui's 1992 movie featuring Kristy Swanson in the title role—celebrated the power and pain of relying on other people. The show made it clear that, even for a superhero protagonist living atop a portal to infernal dimensions, "the hardest thing in this world is to live in it."

BUFFY MIGHT HAVE STARRED KATIE HOLMES AND RYAN REYNOLDS.

Can you imagine Katie Holmes as Buffy or Ryan Reynolds as Xander? Katie Holmes told Jimmy Fallon that before she was *Dawson's Creek*'s Joey Potter, she was up for the role of Buffy, but the scheduling didn't work out. Reynolds refused a role because, as he told the *Toronto Star* in 2008, "I didn't want to play a guy in high school. I had just come out of high school and it was fucking awful." It's often stated that the role in question was Xander, but Reynolds said in 2004, "Everyone says [I auditioned for Xander], but I'm never going to say that on record."

SARAH MICHELLE GELLAR AUDITIONED TO PLAY CORDELIA CHASE.

Sarah Michelle Gellar originally auditioned for the role of Sunnydale High queen bee, Cordelia Chase, before being cast as Buffy. "At the time, we were all trying to find our way to make the show something, its own thing apart from the film," original casting director Marcia Shulman said in *The Watchers Guide*. "We didn't think of Sarah as Buffy because we thought she was too smart and too grounded and not enough of a misfit in a sense." Ultimately, it was the network that suggested Gellar for the lead role, which is when the series really fell into place.

"I think that the way it turned out is the way it was meant to have turned out," Charisma Carpenter, who auditioned for the part of Buffy before being cast as Cordelia, told the BBC. "I don't know that I would have been ready for that kind of fame if I'd gotten Buffy."

FREEZE FRAME

SPOILERS! **"THE BODY"** // **SEASON 5, EPISODE 16** The shot that follows the coroner after he examines Joyce's body out to where Buffy waits with her friends was done in a single take, and it was inspired by Paul Thomas Anderson. "I had been watching *Magnolia* obsessively before I shot this," Whedon said. "So these endless tracking shots probably owe something to that. What can I say, I'm a hack."

DAVID BOREANAZ WAS DISCOVERED BY THE CASTING DIRECTOR'S FRIEND.

A number of actors read for Buffy's eventual boyfriend (and vampire!) Angel before David Boreanaz auditioned. "The breakdown said 'the most gorgeous, mysterious, fantastic, the most incredible man on the face of the Earth,'" Marcia Shulman said. She was sure she had auditioned every actor in Los Angeles when a friend of hers called to tell her about a neighbor of his whom he regularly saw walking his dog. The friend didn't know what the man did for a living, but he embodied everything Shulman had been talking about. "And the minute he walked in the room, I wrote down in my notes: 'This is the guy,'" Shulman said. (Fun fact:

Philadelphia-area fans of *Buffy* might remember Boreanaz's dad, Dave Roberts, who was the main weatherman on WPVI-TV from 1983 until his retirement in 2009.)

THERE WAS A GOOD REASON FOR THE VAMPIRES' CREEPY TRANSFORMATIONS.

In the *Buffy* movie, the vampires looked like regular people, only with sharper teeth and paler skin. But for the TV show, Joss Whedon wanted to increase the sense of paranoia by making the vampires resemble normal people until it was time to feed—at which point, they transformed into monsters. It was both a stylistic choice and a logical one. "I didn't think I really wanted to put a show on the air about a high school girl who was stabbing normal-looking people in the heart," Whedon said. "I thought somehow that might send the wrong message, but when they are clearly monsters, it takes it to a level of fantasy that is safer."

Getting into vamp mode—which required a prosthetic that fit from the forehead down to the bottom of the nose—took about an hour and twenty minutes. "It can be tedious," David Boreanaz said in 1998, "and taking it off is the worst part, because you have to sit there and you just want to rip the damn thing off—but you can't, because you'll take a piece of your skin with you. It has to be removed very delicately. But the end result is definitely worth it."

GELLAR HAD SOME PROBLEMS WITH THE DIALOGUE.

The show was famous for its "Buffyspeak," which was partially inspired by California Valley girl–isms. For Gellar, however, that dialogue could be an issue. "I grew up in New York. We didn't have Valley girls," Gellar said in 1998. "There's a very funny story about [my audition] where the first line is 'What's the sitch?' And there I go walking in, and my first [question was,] 'What does this mean?' No idea it meant situation. Talk about blowing a job instantly."

DARLA WASN'T SUPPOSED TO BE A RECURRING CHARACTER.

Darla (Julie Benz) was originally cast as Vampire Girl #1 and was going to be killed in the pilot. But Whedon decided to give her a name and kill her in the next episode. When they filmed her death scene, Benz later recalled, "Joss came up to me and said, 'We decided not to kill you. You're gonna be back next episode. And then we're gonna kill you.' This went on for a few episodes." So she continued to pop up in other episodes—and in the spin-off show, *Angel.*

GELLAR AND BOREANAZ PRANKED EACH OTHER BEFORE ROMANTIC SCENES.

In a 2002 interview with *The Independent*, Gellar described her intimate scenes with Boreanaz as "the unsexiest thing in the world." It didn't help that she and Boreanaz would purposely try to make the scenes as unpleasant as possible for the other person. "We would do horrible things to each other. Like eat tuna fish and pickles before we kissed," Gellar said. "If he had to unbutton my shirt or my trousers I would pin them or sew them together to make it as hard as I could."

THE SHOW BUILT ITS OWN GRAVEYARD, WHICH CAME IN HANDY.

In the first season, *Buffy* shot in a graveyard in Hollywood. "It meant going out all night, until sunrise, a lot of times," Whedon said. So in season 2, the production built their own graveyard in the warehouse's parking lot. "We . . . backfilled it with dirt and planted grass and lots of trees and stuff and that's our graveyard set," production designer Carey Meyer told the BBC. "At night, with a couple of headstones in the background with all the trees and such, you can really cheat to make it look quite large."

FREEZE FRAME

"HELP" // SEASON 7, EPISODE 4

According to Charles Arthur's book *Digital Wars*, the first use of the word "Google" as a verb on American television was in this 2002 episode, when Willow asks Buffy, "Have you Googled her yet?"

AT LEAST TWO ACTORS PLAYED MORE THAN ONE VILLAIN.

Brian Thompson, who played vampire Luke in the first two episodes, returned in the second season to play the Judge. "Quite frankly, we were in a hurry," Whedon said. "We already had his face cast and we knew he could put makeup on and give us a good performance." Camden Toy, meanwhile, played a number of villains, including one of the Gentlemen in season 4's "Hush," a skin-eating demon called Gnarl in season 7's "Same Time, Same Place," and übervamp Turok-Han throughout the seventh season.

SPOILERS! GELLAR KNEW WHAT WOULD HAPPEN IN SEASON 5 WELL IN ADVANCE.

Several moments in the final episode of season 3 foreshadowed two major events in season 5: Namely, that Buffy would get a sister, Dawn (Michelle Trachtenberg), and that the slayer would die at the end of season 5. Gellar told the BBC that she was given this information ahead of time. She also knew that *Buffy* would be coming to an end before her many castmates learned this devastating piece of news.

In the March 7, 2003, *Entertainment Weekly* cover story, Gellar announced that *Buffy* was coming to an end after seven seasons. "I love this job, I love the fans," she said. "I love telling the stories we tell. This isn't about leaving for a career in movies, or in theater—it's more of a personal decision. I need a rest." The rest of the cast found out the day the story hit stands. "I was devastated," Alyson Hannigan, who played Buffy's BFF, Willow, said in 2013. "I was just very shocked."

***BUFFY* BECAME A POPULAR TOPIC FOR COLLEGE COURSES.**

A number of colleges and universities have offered courses on fears and fantasies explored in the show; they're called "*Buffy* Studies." People have written books and held conferences dedicated to discussing the multidimensional themes of the show and presenting papers on it. According to the *Los Angeles Times*, attendees at a 2004 *Buffy* conference "were presenting 190 papers on topics ranging from 'slayer slang' to 'postmodern reflections on the culture of consumption' to '*Buffy* and the new American Buddhism.' There was even a self-conscious talk by David Lavery, an English professor at Middle Tennessee State University, on *Buffy* Studies 'as an academic cult.'"

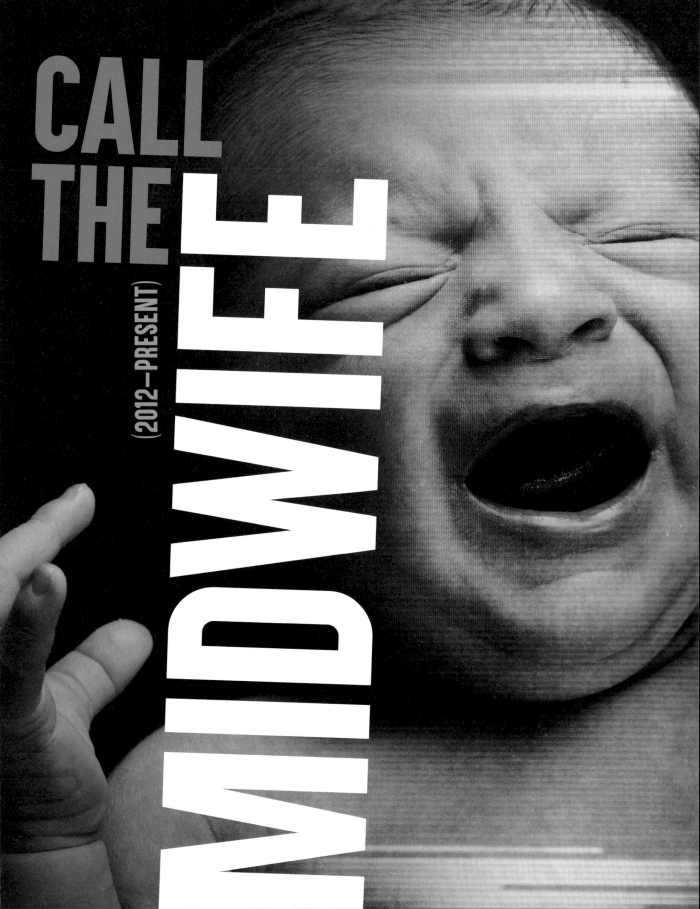

CALL THE
WIFE
(2012–PRESENT)
MIDWIFE

CREATED BY: Heidi Thomas

SEASONS: 10

EPISODES: 79

OTHER SHOWS BY HEIDI THOMAS:
Lilies (2007)
Upstairs Downstairs (2010–2012)

S ince it premiered in 2012, *Call the Midwife* has charmed audiences in England and beyond, regularly ranking as one of BBC One's most watched programs. Inspired by real stories, the show dives into the gritty details of daily life in London's Poplar neighborhood during the 1950s and 1960s. Midwives, working with the nuns of Nonnatus House, zip around the city's postwar East End, delivering babies and treating all sorts of medical ailments with a dash of their own intimate dramas added to the mix. Early seasons follow nurse Jennifer Lee (Jessica Raine), the character series creator Heidi Thomas based on a real-life London midwife. Later, as *Call the Midwife* transitions from the fifties to the sixties, the show focuses on the personal and professional lives of mainstays like Nurse "Trixie" Franklin (Helen George), Nursing Sister Shelagh Turner (Laura Main), Sister Julienne (Jenny Agutter), and Sister Monica Joan (Judy Parfitt).

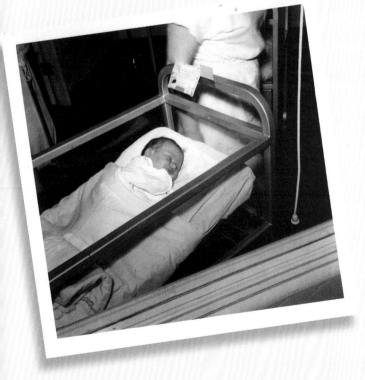

CALL THE MIDWIFE WAS INSPIRED BY A TRILOGY OF MEMOIRS.

Call the Midwife was adapted from Jennifer Worth's memoirs about her time working as a nurse and midwife in London's East End. Seasons 1 through 3 focus on Nurse Jennifer Lee (Lee was Worth's maiden name). Other characters in the series, like Sister Julienne, handyman Fred Buckle (Cliff Parisi), and Nurse Cynthia (Bryony Hannah), are fictionalized versions of Worth's real-life colleagues and friends as well.

JENNIFER WORTH NEVER GOT TO SEE HER STORIES ON THE SCREEN.

Worth died from esophageal cancer on May 31, 2011, shortly before *Call the Midwife* began filming its first season. "Mother was fading fast in the summer, just as the series was starting to be brought to life, and that was a very unusual, but quite magical and positive dovetail of events," Worth's daughter, Juliette Walton, told the *Radio Times*.

AN ACTUAL MIDWIFE HELPS WITH THE BIRTHING SCENES.

In order to ensure a certain level of realism, *Call the Midwife* has a trained midwife to coach actors through the scenes. "I have taught the actors how to take blood pressure or listen to a baby's heartbeat through a pregnant abdomen using a Pinard (stethoscope, which allows one to listen to a baby's heartbeat) correctly using the (vintage) equipment," Terri Coates, the show's midwife advisor, told the BBC.

But Coates's connection to the material goes even deeper: It was an article Coates had written for the journal *The Royal College of Midwives* that originally inspired Worth to adapt her own stories. "Jennifer said that she had always planned to write in her retirement and that my article provided the catalyst for her memoirs," Coates told the BBC. "I knew and worked with Jennifer for 13 years on the trilogy of her memoirs—I was her advisor and clinical editor."

CALL THE MIDWIFE FEATURES REAL NEWBORNS.

The actors rehearse with "jelly babies"—silicone dummies—before the real stars arrive on the scene to shoot. "When the time comes to shoot, we use a real baby," series producer Ann Tricklebank told the *Radio Times*. "We pass it under the actor's thigh and she brings it up, holding the baby and its umbilical cord, which is made of silicone." Parents often reach out to offer their freshly arrived bundles of joy for filming. But because the show's filming schedule demands the babies be available at specific times, the producers source their tot-sized talent from a specialist agency.

THE BIKE SCENES CAN BE TOUGH FOR THE ACTORS TO FILM.

Though they may look like they're biking around London's East End with ease, nailing the cycling scenes isn't as easy as, well, riding a bike. From navigating deeply grooved cobblestones to lugging around their nursing gear while dodging cameras, the actors really have to put their cycling skills to the test.

THERE'S A BOOK BASED ON *CALL THE MIDWIFE*.

When he isn't delivering babies and tending to Poplar's ill as Dr. Turner, actor Stephen McGann (who is married to showrunner Heidi Thomas) is bringing science to the public in different ways. McGann, who is a science communicator in addition to being an actor, contributed to a book, *Doctor Turner's Casebook*, that functions as a fictionalized diary about the events in the show.

THE SHOW DOESN'T SHY AWAY FROM DIFFICULT TOPICS.

"It lulls people into a warm, cuddly trance, but the subject matter is thought-provoking," Helen George, who plays Nurse Trixie Franklin, told *The Guardian*. In addition to birth and death, *Call the Midwife* has tackled difficult topics like abortion, racism, and domestic violence. It also regularly shines a spotlight on diseases and ailments that plagued London in the mid-twentieth century. The show has grappled with issues like diphtheria outbreaks, Huntington's disease, and leprosy.

THE CHI

(2018—PRESENT)

DEVELOPED BY: Lena Waithe

SEASONS: 3

EPISODES: 30

OTHER SHOWS BY LENA WAITHE:
Boomerang (2019–PRESENT)
Twenties (2020–PRESENT)

Lena Waithe's timely series showcases the intertwined lives of a dozen characters all living on Chicago's South Side. It begins with the murder of a teenage boy named Jason Roxboro (Lucien Cambric), but the allure of the show isn't as simple as solving one big mystery. *The Chi* flips the standard TV drama tropes upside down, taking characters who would have been bit players in an episode of *Law & Order* and making them the protagonists to provide a fuller, more human picture of this particular Black experience. The material is a perfect match for Waithe, who in 2017 became the first Black woman to win an Emmy for comedy writing for the "Thanksgiving" episode of *Master of None*.

Compare it to *The Wire* if you must, but it's reductive to call *The Chi* a crime drama. Although a violent crime is one of its catalysts and criminal activity flows through its veins, *The Chi* blossoms far beyond the typical elements of the genre to give viewers an intimate look at the totality of its characters through their connections, joys, and grief. Crime is the humming background noise, not the theme song.

Of those living with Jason's murder ringing in their ears, there are Jason's father figure, Ronnie (Ntare Guma Mbaho Mwine), a middle-aged screwup who takes out his need for revenge on the wrong person; Brandon (Jason Mitchell), the chef dreaming of opening his own restaurant; Jerrika (Tiffany Boone), an upscale real estate agent who is dating Brandon and trying to build a better life for them; Emmett (Jacob Latimore), a teen sneakerhead who learns he has a child; and Kevin (Alex Hibbert), a middle school kid who witnesses a murder yet still has to deal with the drama of rehearsing for the school play. That's just the tip of the iceberg for a large ensemble of characters who dip in and out of one another's lives in both familiar and unexpected ways.

SHOWTIME BOUGHT THE SERIES IN 2015.
Following her groundbreaking Emmy win in 2017, Waithe's profile skyrocketed. But she had already set the stage for the next step in her career when Showtime ordered a pilot for *The Chi* two years earlier. Just as she was earning the highest praise of her career so far, she was already a few months into shooting *The Chi*.

THE CITY OF CHICAGO IS ITS OWN CHARACTER IN *THE CHI*.

Waithe grew up in the same neighborhood depicted in the show, and was raised by her mom in the very same house her mom grew up in. She says growing up in Chicago gave her a different perspective than New Yorkers like Dick Wolf and Spike Lee. "My mom still lives here and my family still lives here, so I'm always connected to it," Waithe told *Chicago* magazine. "Chicago has such a huge impact on who I am."

WAITHE HAS KNOWN SHE WANTED TO BE A TV WRITER SINCE SHE WAS SEVEN YEARS OLD.

"I watched a ton of TV because I was raised by a single mom and spent a lot of time with my grandmother," Waithe told *Vogue*. "Like most grandparents do, she would spend hours and hours in front of the TV box. I also loved spending time reading and writing, so when it came time to really figure out what I wanted to do, I put those two loves together and my family was very supportive."

TV EXECUTIVES WERE CONFUSED ABOUT BRANDON'S CHARACTER.

Waithe started shopping the pilot script before a sea change in the industry led to more inclusiveness and an appetite for Black stories told by Black creators. TV executives who read it kept asking what the hook was—as in, were the characters going to deal drugs or go pro in basketball? Waithe told The Cut that Brandon, a talented chef with aspirations and dedication to his family, was particularly puzzling to potential buyers of the show. She responded, "It's about being Black and human in a city that's very complex. That's it. I write Black people in rooms talking."

JASON MITCHELL RELATED TO GROWING UP SURROUNDED BY VIOLENCE.

The show focuses a lot on the experiences of young people having to mature quickly on the periphery of violence. Mitchell related to that aspect of *The Chi*, saying, "I'm from New Orleans, Louisiana, and I went to the top four worst schools in the nation…It was imperative to be able to be tough and still have to be happy. It's hard to be a kid when you're in this really grown-up environment, you know, when you are pressed to bring some sort of money home…you never really know these people's story."

THE SHOW GETS SOUTH SIDE FOOD RIGHT.

Chicago magazine's Charles Preston noted that food is one of the elements of South Side life at *The Chi* nails—from the corner store to Brandon's food truck, and the potential commentary on the area as a food desert. The show got into trouble with its neighbors when it first started filming because they threw out food and home goods used as set dressing for the show's 77th Mart corner store. As a result, they subsequently promised to donate all safe, unexpired food and goods as well as make contributions to enrich the neighborhood.

ALLEGATIONS OF MISCONDUCT LED TO A MAJOR BEHIND-THE-SCENES SHAKEUP.

As Brandon and Jerrika, Mitchell and Boone led one of *The Chi's* major storylines. But in 2018, Boone opted to leave the show. One year later, it was announced that Mitchell would not be returning for season 3 of *The Chi* following complaints of inappropriate behavior on the set. Though the details were kept rather vague and accounts varied on what happened, season 2 showrunner Ayanna Floyd Davis told *The Hollywood Reporter* that she had been informed of issues between Mitchell and Boone by Waithe directly when she took over the show. "As showrunner, I did everything I could to deal with his behavior, by speaking with the studio's HR department multiple times and instructing one actress to call HR herself," Davis said, adding that she then "became a target of [Mitchell's] rage and inappropriateness, and had to report him to HR, as well." Davis, too, left after season 2.

For his part, Mitchell said that he was never able to give his side of the story. "When you're dealing with HR, it doesn't work like that at all," he said. "They'll never pop out and tell you, 'Oh, this is what was said by that person. This is what was said by that person.' You never get the luxury of finding out exactly how somebody felt about something."

THERE'S AN EDITED TV-14–RATED VERSION.

One of the smartest things a show featuring preteens and teens learning about life through tragedy could do is to make it as accessible as possible to that audience. So they created a version suitable for younger teens looking for a solid prestige drama.

7 OF SHOWTIME'S MOST BINGE-WORTHY SERIES

The Chi is one of the most recent additions to Showtime's impressive library of prestige dramas (and comedies and dramedies), whose eccentric antiheroes and ensemble casts can make it hard to turn off the TV. Here are more must-watch modern classics from the network.

1 **The Affair // (2014–2019)**
A family man (Dominic West) and a married Montauk waitress (Ruth Wilson) embark on an especially ill-advised affair in this slow-burning emotional drama with a twist. The same events unfold twice—once from each character's perspective—which highlights the fallibility of human memory and also leaves it up to the viewer to decide whom to believe. Bonus: *Mental Floss* magazine makes a brief appearance during a pivotal moment in the show's third season.

2 **Billions // (2016–PRESENT)**
Billions is a titillating game of cat and mouse between hedge fund billionaire Bobby Axelrod (Damian Lewis) and the US attorney (Paul Giamatti) trying to nail him for white-collar crimes. The characters' questionable morals will make you wonder what really goes on in the deepest circles of finance, and not just because the show was inspired by an actual investigation of hedge fund manager Steven Cohen by Preet Bharara, former US attorney for the Southern District of New York.

3 **Episodes // (2011–2017)**
There are British comedies, American comedies, and American remakes of British comedies. And then there's *Episodes*, a British-American comedy in which two married Brits (Tamsin Greig and Stephen Mangan) migrate to Los Angeles to write an American remake of their British comedy. The star of the show-within-the-show is Matt LeBlanc, spoofing his *Friends* celebrity as an egocentric actor.

4 **Homeland // (2011–2020)**
Claire Danes guides viewers on an enthralling—and nerve-racking—journey through the cryptic world of US counterterrorism as Carrie Mathison, a shrewd CIA agent with bipolar disorder. Not only is *Homeland* the most thrilling of political thrillers, it also demonstrates the difficulty of trying to do the right thing when it's not clear what the right thing actually is.

5 **Nurse Jackie // (2009–2015)**
Edie Falco successfully extricated herself from what could've been a lifetime of being called "Tony Soprano's wife" with her Emmy-winning turn as Jackie Peyton, a New York City ER nurse with a prescription drug addiction. Falco's performance was so masterful, in fact, that the New York State Nurses Association criticized the series for painting such an ethically corrupt portrait of nurses.

6 **Queer as Folk // (2000–2005)**
Based on the British series of the same name, *Queer as Folk* depicted a group of LGBTQ friends in Pittsburgh with a level of candor and comprehensiveness that had yet to be seen on American television. Not only does the series cover topical issues like HIV and gay marriage, but its cast—led by Gale Harold and Hal Sparks—offers a moving, magnetic portrayal of universal themes like love and loss. In 2021, NBC's Peacock ordered up a New Orleans-set reimagining of the show.

7 **Shameless // (2011–2021)**
Shameless is both a comedy and a tragedy of Shakespearean proportions that revolves around the Gallagher family on Chicago's South Side. The fact that the children and their deadbeat dad (William H. Macy) screw up so often and so epically somehow just makes them all the more endearing—perhaps because they also try so hard to redeem themselves.

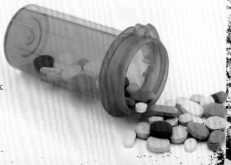

THE

CROWN

(2016—PRESENT)

DEVELOPED BY: Peter Morgan

SEASONS: 4

EPISODES: 40

OTHER SHOWS BY PETER MORGAN:
Metropolis (2000)
The Jury (2002)

When Netflix first announced its plans to produce *The Crown* in 2014, all viewers really knew was that they were getting a ten-episode series based on Peter Morgan's play *The Audience*, which revolved around Queen Elizabeth II's weekly meetings with the prime minister. Several seasons later, *The Crown* has become one of the most ambitious, most lauded projects in the history of streaming—and daring in its decision from the get-go to regularly replace its main actors as the characters grow older. So while the series kicked off with Claire Foy and Matt Smith playing the roles of the queen and Prince Philip, they were replaced by Olivia Colman and Tobias Menzies in season 3, who will be replaced by Imelda Staunton and Jonathan Pryce when season 5 arrives.

Morgan's sweeping epic, which is set against a truly opulent backdrop (Netflix has spared no expense when it comes to re-creating historic places like Buckingham Palace), has as much to offer history lovers as it does royal enthusiasts—all of it brought to life by the best and brightest actors Britain has to offer. But *The Crown*'s real genius lies in the way it makes every small moment a massively memorable one; the single tear shed by the queen (Olivia Colman) after visiting the Aberfan mining disaster zone, for example, or Margaret Thatcher's (Gillian Anderson) fish-out-of-water facial expression as she tries to hold her own during a goofy parlor game at Balmoral Castle. The cumulative result is a surprisingly human portrait of the Windsors and all their affiliates that exists somewhere between history textbook and tabloid headline.

PETER MORGAN DIDN'T HAVE MUCH INTEREST IN THE ROYAL FAMILY.
Considering that Morgan also wrote the 2006 film *The Queen*, it would be easy to think that he has had a deep and lifelong interest in the royal family—but you'd be wrong. "It was a horrible mistake," Morgan told *Entertainment Weekly* in 2019. "I don't know how we've ended up here."

The road to *The Crown* started with *The Deal*, a 2003 TV movie starring Michael Sheen about former prime minister Tony Blair's rise to power. *The Queen* continued that story, with its focus on a newly elected Blair (played again by Sheen) working to push the queen to take action in the wake of Princess Diana's death. That led to *The Audience*, a play that opened in London in 2013 and eventually made its way to Broadway. In 2016, when asked by *Variety* why he was interested in telling the story of the queen's rise to power, Morgan's response was honest: "I didn't really. I'm sick of writing the world of Elizabeth. But when we did the play *The Audience*, the scene between Churchill and the young queen struck me as having lots of potential."

CLAIRE FOY FLEW UNDER THE RADAR DURING AUDITIONS.

Though it's hard to imagine the first two seasons of *The Crown* with anyone but Claire Foy in the role of Elizabeth, Morgan admits that she did not stand out to him at first. "I tried to cast almost everyone in Britain before Claire Foy," Morgan told *Variety*. "Every time I went to a read-through where we were doing auditions for *The Queen*, I was interested in actress A or B. I would skip the bit where Claire was in there. And then after about the fourth time, I went, 'This one is sensational, who's this?'" And it was Claire.

MORGAN DIDN'T THINK THERE WOULD BE A SHOW WITHOUT MATT SMITH.

As much a challenge as it was casting the role of Elizabeth, the role of Prince Philip was equally difficult—albeit for different reasons. "When those two read together, there was complete electricity. They worked so perfectly," Morgan told *Variety*. "I just said to the casting director, 'He's the only one. I don't care if this plays to his agent's advantage. It's him or nobody. Don't posture. We won't have a show.' I'm afraid I gave them no negotiating position. I'm sure Matt's being hideously overpaid as a result. He was the only one."

THERE *WAS* A PAY DISCREPANCY.

Though Foy was the undoubted star of *The Crown*'s first two seasons, Morgan wasn't kidding when he said that Smith may have been overpaid for his role. In March 2018, during a Q&A, one of the producers revealed that Smith was paid more than Foy for *The Crown*. This ignited a global debate regarding the gender pay gap, with lots of people involved in the production making their voices heard. Jared Harris, who played King George VI (Elizabeth's father), called the situation an "embarrassment" for the production team and made it

clear that Foy should be compensated. "I understand they made an apology but, you know, an apology and a check would be more welcome," Harris told Digital Spy. "She worked longer hours. Her performance is a huge reason why this thing is going to have a season three, four, five, and six…send her a paycheck and, in retrospect, bring her pay up to parity."

TO CHANNEL HIS INNER WINSTON CHURCHILL, JOHN LITHGOW STUFFED COTTON UP HIS NOSE.

Though Winston Churchill has been portrayed by dozens of actors over the years, Lithgow's interpretation of the former prime minister was one of the series' acting highlights. But there was some skepticism when casting director Nina Gold suggested him for the role, partly because he's American (even though Churchill's mother was American). It all worked out, though. In 2017, Lithgow won an Emmy for Outstanding Supporting Actor in a Drama Series for his work on *The Crown*. In an interview with *USA Today* he explained that getting Churchill's somewhat nasal sound just right wasn't easy, or pretty—and that it included shoving bits of cotton up his nose. "It was rather repulsive watching me pluck cotton out of my nose after every scene, but they just had to put up with it," Lithgow said.

OLIVIA COLMAN WAS THE ONLY CHOICE TO PLAY THE QUEEN IN SEASONS 3 AND 4.

In 2019, Colman took over the role of Queen Elizabeth II from Foy, and according to Morgan, it was Colman or no one. "Olivia Colman was a list of one," Morgan told *Entertainment Weekly*.

HELENA BONHAM CARTER MET PRINCESS MARGARET . . . AND SHE WAS SCARY.

In season 3, Carter took over the role of the wild—and wildly intimidating—Princess Margaret, and had a little personal history from which she could pull. "My uncle was actually very close to her," Bonham Carter told *Entertainment Weekly*. "She was pretty scary. At one point, she met me at Windsor Castle and she said, 'You are getting better, aren't you?'" Bonham Carter presumed the princess was referring to her acting.

RE-CREATING ROYAL WEDDING DRESSES IS NO EASY TASK.

Having to re-create a royal wedding dress can be a nerve-racking experience for a costume designer. During *The Crown*'s first season, costume designer Michele Clapton told *Harper's Bazaar* that making Queen Elizabeth II's wedding dress was the most challenging costume she and her team worked on. "I thought it was so important that it was as close as we could possibly make it," Clapton said. "That whole procession with the bridesmaids and the train and everything was something which I thought, 'If we don't get that right, then we don't actually have the right to make anything else up.'"

In season 4, costume designer Amy Roberts faced a similar challenge, only this time it was Princess Diana's wedding dress—an iconic item of clothing that 750 million people around the world had tuned in to see live on her wedding day. But Roberts's approach was to not be intimidated. It helped that David Emanuel, who had a hand in designing Diana's actual dress, "was very light about the whole thing," Roberts told Bustle. "He said, 'Just do it. Just do it and enjoy it.' So that kind of released us from the fear." Though Roberts and her team took some creative liberties with the dress, it still took three people four weeks and 600 hours to make it.

THE CROWN'S CORGIS EAT A LOT OF CHEESE.

In *The Crown*, the queen is never too far away from her beloved corgis. Foy revealed that one of the ways the trainers on the set get them to behave is with cheese. "[Y]ou sort of worry that they're going to have a heart attack when you're giving it to them," Foy told *Vanity Fair*. "These corgis are cheesed up to the max—they're eating like a whole block of cheddar every day. It's scary."

THE SHOW HAS SOME ROYAL FANS.

Before Meghan Markle became the Duchess of Sussex, the *New York Post* reported that she had already moved into Kensington Palace with her now-husband Prince Harry, and that their nights often consisted of home-cooked meals and watching Netflix shows…including *The Crown*. In 2021, while being interviewed by James Corden, Prince Harry confirmed that he had indeed watched the show. "I'm way more comfortable with *The Crown* than I am seeing the stories written about my family or my wife or myself," he said. "Because… [*The Crown*] is obviously fiction." As for who Harry thinks should play him on the show if and when the time comes? *Homeland* and *Billions* star Damian Lewis is his pick.

THE QUEEN IS RUMORED TO HAVE WATCHED *THE CROWN*—AND LIKED IT.

In 2017, an unnamed source told the *Daily Express* that Prince Edward and his wife regularly drive to Windsor Castle on the weekend to have dinner with the Queen and watch some TV. "They have a Netflix account and urged her to watch [*The Crown*] with them. Happily, she really liked it, although obviously there were some depictions of events that she found too heavily dramatized."

Philip, on the other hand, must have been in another room. When a friend of Matt Smith's met the late prince at an event, he asked him if he had watched any of the series. Prince Philip's response, according to Smith? "Don't. Be. Ridiculous."

10 MOST EXPENSIVE TV SERIES

Some of the most beloved series in TV history have had massive budgets (and, perhaps surprisingly, so have some of the worst). Here are ten of the priciest programs ever put on television.

1 Game of Thrones
$15 million per episode
You knew HBO's smash fantasy epic was going to take the top spot—especially considering that virtually everything was shot in an exotic location. Plus: They needed to make those dragons look as realistic as possible.

2 The Crown
$13 million per episode
Netflix's dedication to getting royal history just right doesn't come cheap. Producers spent $35,000 just to re-create Queen Elizabeth II's wedding dress in the very first episode.

3 ER
$13 million per episode
In the late 1990s, *ER*—the NBC medical drama that turned George Clooney into a household name—was a huge cultural force. (Quentin Tarantino even directed an episode.) It also maintained a huge cast of up-and-coming stars whose salaries rose with their popularity, all of which added up to a big price tag.

4 Band of Brothers
$12.5 million per episode
With its massive cast, on-location shooting, period costumes and set dressings, and impressive action sequences, it's probably not surprising that this 2001 miniseries about "Easy Company" of the 101st Airborne Division during World War II, cost a fortune.

5 The Get Down
$11 million per episode
Netflix's whole business model is based on its appeal to niche audiences, which can be remarkably successful or an unmitigated disaster. Unfortunately, Baz Luhrmann's *The Get Down* turned out to be the latter. After spending a reported $120 million on the first season alone—much of that for music clearances and the show's hectic production—Netflix canceled *The Get Down* after one season.

6 Friends
$10 million per episode
By the end of its run, *Friends* had become a generation-defining show—and its stars knew it. How else could NBC have justified paying each of the six main actors more than $1 million per episode in the final seasons?

7 The Big Bang Theory
$9 million per episode
The stars of *The Big Bang Theory* took a cue from the cast of *Friends* by negotiating massive paydays for the show's final seasons. Add in shooting costs, numerous celebrity cameos, and the royalty fee they pay to the Barenaked Ladies for the theme song, and producers spent about $9 million for twenty-two minutes of airtime.

8 Marco Polo
$9 million per episode
Netflix had high hopes for *Marco Polo*, an epic historical drama that traced the early years of the explorer's life. The show debuted in December 2014 with a $90 million budget for its first ten episodes. Shortly thereafter, Netflix renewed the series for a second season with the same basic budget, which ultimately ended up being its last.

9 Rome
$9 million per episode
It's fine if you want to blame HBO's *Rome*—John Milius, William J. MacDonald, and Bruno Heller's historical drama about two Roman soldiers who regularly become entangled in real-life historical events—for the major financial hit Netflix took on *Marco Polo*. But its initial success is also regularly cited as the reason we have shows like *Game of Thrones*, so…*Rome* FTW!

10 Sense8
$9 million per episode
It might be the most successful thing the Wachowskis have made since *The Matrix*, but Netflix still had to cancel this sci-fi sleeper hit because it was costing them a pretty penny. The Wachowskis reportedly insisted on filming everything on location, which meant that Netflix had to pay for long-term filming permits in nine different metropolitan areas around the world.

CURB YOUR ENTHUSIASM

(2000–PRESENT)

CREATED BY: Larry David

SEASONS: 10

EPISODES: 100

OTHER SHOWS CREATED BY LARRY DAVID:
Seinfeld (1989–1998)

Only Ann Landers has gotten more mileage out of social etiquette than Larry David. After co-creating and spending several seasons on *Seinfeld*, the writer—who had taken only sporadic onscreen roles in his career, most of them without lines—brandished himself as the ultimate disruptor of acceptable behavior with *Curb Your Enthusiasm*.

As "Larry David," David shares his onscreen alter ego's success, wealth, and tony Los Angeles zip code. But where David and David differ is that TV Larry is a "social assassin" at large, who is willing to offend and insult without a moment's hesitation. He moves to New York City to avoid appearing at a charity event; he confronts people who strike up a chat to cut in line; he yells at children; a wobbly table ignites an entire season's story line. (Larry opens a coffee shop. Naturally, it ends in a fire.) Supporting cast members J. B. Smoove, Susie Essman, Cheryl Hines, and Jeff Garlin are either co-conspirators or victims. Mostly improvised, the show is clearly an outlet for the real David to give voice to the thoughts that would see him shunned if spoken out loud in the real world. There is no situation David cannot make worse, and television is better off for it.

CURB YOUR ENTHUSIASM'S VERSION OF LARRY DAVID IS AN "IDEALIZED" VERSION OF THE REAL LARRY DAVID.

Sure, there are some obvious similarities between TV Larry and real-life Larry, but David told *Rolling Stone* that it wouldn't be smart for him to be TV Larry all the time. "The character really is me, but I just couldn't possibly behave like that," he said. "If I had my druthers, that would be me all the time, but you can't do that. We're always doing things we don't want to do, we never say what we really feel, and so this is an idealized version of how I want to be."

EACH EPISODE OF *CURB YOUR ENTHUSIASM* IS BASED ON AN OUTLINE, AND VIRTUALLY NO DIALOGUE IS EVER WRITTEN.

Curb Your Enthusiasm became a milestone show because of its mostly improvised format. David writes rough outlines for each episode and lets the actors fill in the rest. "I write the scenes where we know everything that's going to happen," David told NPR. "There's an outline of about seven or eight pages, and then we improvise it."

CHERYL HINES WASN'T WORRIED ABOUT HER AUDITION, AS SHE HAD ALREADY CONVINCED HERSELF SHE WASN'T RIGHT FOR THE PART.

Hines's background was with The Groundlings improv troupe, but she didn't have much TV work to speak of when she auditioned for the role of Cheryl David (minus bit parts like an episode of *Swamp Thing* and a two-episode arc on *Unsolved Mysteries*). Because of that, she didn't think she was experienced enough to get the part of Cheryl David and neither she nor her agent thought she "was right for the part." At the time of her audition, Hines was working as a personal assistant to Rob Reiner's family. Four hours after reading for the part she got a call that she'd won the role. "I know now that they were looking for an unknown, so it worked in my favor that I had absolutely nothing on my résumé," she said.

WHEN LARRY DAVID SAVED A MAN FROM THE DEATH PENALTY

On August 12, 2003, twenty-four-year-old Juan Catalan had arrived to work at his family's machine shop in California when he was arrested for the murder of Martha Puebla, a sixteen-year-old girl who had testified in court as a witness to yet another murder, in which Juan's brother—Mario Catalan—was being charged. Juan attempted to plead his innocence in the matter and swore that he could not have been at the purported crime scene because he had been with his daughter at a Los Angeles Dodgers baseball game at the time of the murder. Though he produced their ticket stubs, the cops weren't buying it.

Remarkably, Larry David and the *Curb Your Enthusiasm* crew just happened to be filming an episode—season 4's "The Carpool Lane"—at the stadium during the very same game Catalan swore he was attending with his daughter. Given that there were tens of thousands of people in attendance, it was a long shot. But Catalan requested the raw footage to see if it could be of any help to his defense.

It took just twenty minutes of watching the raw footage for defense attorney Todd Melnik to spot Catalan and his six-year-old daughter in the stands. Juan Catalan was exactly where he said he was; that footage, coupled with cell phone ping data, proved there was no way he could have committed the murder. After five months behind bars awaiting trial for a murder he did not commit, Catalan was a free man.

In 2007, Catalan was awarded $320,000 after filing a lawsuit against the city of Los Angeles and its police department. In 2017, Netflix released a short documentary, *Long Shot*, about the incident. As for Larry David? "I tell people that I've now done one decent thing in my life, albeit inadvertently," he has joked.

AS A TITLE, *CURB YOUR ENTHUSIASM* HAS TWO MEANINGS.

David titled the series *Curb Your Enthusiasm* as an ode to *Seinfeld* fervor, meaning that people shouldn't expect this to be another *Seinfeld*. "Also, people should keep enthusiasm curbed in their lives," David told *Time*. "Always keep it. To not is unattractive. It's unseemly."

FREEZE FRAME ▶

"MARY, JOSEPH AND LARRY" // SEASON 3, EPISODE 9

Cheryl Hines told *TV Guide* that her favorite episode of the series was the 2002 Christmas one in which her family visits and Larry eats a cookie version of baby Jesus—a story line that came from Hines's own family. "When I was home in Florida, my family had made a manger scene out of cookies and everyone was walking around saying, 'Don't eat baby Jesus.' And I immediately called Larry and said, 'If you were at my house right now, you would eat baby Jesus and my family would go crazy.' And then we started talking back-and-forth and he [loved it]."

SUSIE ESSMAN IS CONSTANTLY TELLING *CURB YOUR ENTHUSIASM* FANS TO "GO FUCK THEMSELVES."

Essman's character, Susie Greene, has a foul mouth and makes a regular habit of unleashing streams of expletives on Larry and her on-screen husband,

Jeff (Jeff Garlin). Essman explained to the Paley Center audience how fans constantly come up to her and ask to be berated. "My life has become extremely bizarre that people just come up to [me] wherever I am . . . begging me to tell them to go fuck themselves. It's like, I'm buying produce, I'm shaking a melon. 'Call me a fat fuck.' I'm not always in the mood." During an interview with *Esquire*, Essman said, "People are visibly disappointed that when they meet me I'm not this screaming, yelling crazy person."

AT ONE POINT, DAVID PUT THE ODDS OF A NINTH SEASON OF *CURB YOUR ENTHUSIASM* AT SIX TO ONE.

At the end of 2014, David told *Grantland*, "I guess, right now, the odds would be against it, probably six to one," and stated that, following his experience with the *Seinfeld* finale, he had no desire to do another episode "to wrap things up." In 2015, HBO's then-president of programming Michael Lombardo saw David and told *The Hollywood Reporter* that David had pointed to a notebook and said he was working on a new season of *Curb*. "I don't think it's out of [Larry's] system," said Lombardo. "I think he wants to have something to say."

In 2016, a ninth season of the series was officially greenlit and it premiered on October 1, 2017. Just two months later, a tenth season was confirmed; it premiered on January 19, 2020. On June 30, 2020, it was announced that *Curb* had gotten the green light for yet another season—season 11. "Believe me, I'm as upset about this as you are," David said of the decision. "One day I can only hope that HBO will come to their senses and grant me the cancellation I so richly deserve."

5 TV SHOWS THAT WERE IMPROVISED

Curb Your Enthusiasm isn't the only show that helps the environment by reducing the number of script pages. Here are a few other shows that have let their performers wing it.

RENO 911!
(2003–2009; 2020)

This absurd comedy about a troupe of inept Nevada cops was based largely on outlines, some consisting of just a few words ("Someone pooped in the book donation box" among them). Series co-creators and stars Thomas Lennon, Robert Ben Garant, and Kerri Kenney-Silver and others improvised dialogue, with Garant estimating it took about forty minutes of riffing for every ninety seconds of usable footage.

WHOSE LINE IS IT ANYWAY?
(1998–2013)

Through its various iterations, including the British original, *Whose Line Is It Anyway?* put a group of improv specialists at the mercy of various scenarios and made a star out of Wayne Brady. (Host Drew Carey was already well known, and later went on to do the similarly-themed *Drew Carey's Green Screen Show* in 2004.)

WILD 'N OUT
(2005–PRESENT)

This novel MTV series hosted by Nick Cannon blends sketch with stand-up with roast battles. Notable cast members include Katt Williams, Pete Davidson, and Taran Killam.

INSTANT COMEDY WITH THE GROUNDLINGS
(1998–2000)

The legendary Los Angeles-based improv group that honed the skills of everyone from Phil Hartman to Pee-wee Herman got a single season on FX in which then-current cast members took suggestions for sketches from the audience and let fly.

EASY
(2016–2019)

This Netflix anthology series from director Joe Swanberg took a cue from his low-budget "mumblecore" independent film roots and left the dialogue to the actors.

DEADWOOD (2004—2006)

CREATED BY: David Milch

SEASONS: 3

EPISODES: 36

OTHER SHOWS BY DAVID MILCH:
NYPD Blue (1993–2005)
John from Cincinnati (2007)
Luck (2011–2012)

Like many of the prestige dramas that HBO aired in the wake of the success of *The Sopranos*, David Milch's *Deadwood* managed to attract a small but rabid fan base that has only grown with time, as new generations get the chance to discover the series via streaming services like Amazon Prime Video.

Set in the late 1800s not long after Custer's Last Stand, the show mixes fact with fiction as historical characters including Wild Bill Hickok (Keith Carradine), Calamity Jane (Robin Weigert), and Wyatt Earp (Gale Harold) make their way in and out of Deadwood, South Dakota. Its main characters—Seth Bullock (Timothy Olyphant), Sol Star (John Hawkes), and Al Swearengen (Ian McShane)—were also real people. And while *Deadwood* includes all of the tropes we've come to expect of a great western, including gunfights, gold rushes, and fun-filled brothels, the series, which ran for just three seasons, is really about the evolution of civilization and how we build communities out of chaos—with a lot of F-bombs dropped (mostly by McShane). While admirers of the dark western crime drama have long lamented its too-short run on television, they got a second dose of the series with 2019's *Deadwood: The Movie*.

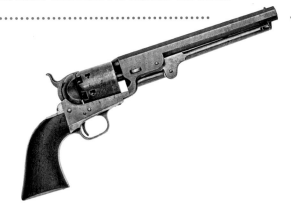

WHAT EVENTUALLY BECAME *DEADWOOD* WAS ORIGINALLY SUPPOSED TO BE A SHOW ABOUT NERO'S ROME.

Unbeknownst to David Milch, however, HBO had already greenlit *Rome*, a historical drama from John Milius, William J. MacDonald, and Bruno Heller. But the creator was undaunted: Milch believed his fascination with how society can form from chaos could be explored in another historical setting, so he set his sights on the Black Hills of the Old West and rewrote the story.

THE SERIES WAS BASED ON THE REAL DEADWOOD, SOUTH DAKOTA.

In the 1870s, Deadwood, South Dakota, was a place full of criminals and entrepreneurs. Milch rigorously researched the real Deadwood by reading its newspapers, the diaries of its residents, and formal historical accounts like Black Hills expert Watson Parker's book *Deadwood: The Golden Years*.

THE REAL SETH BULLOCK WAS CALLED "A BAD MAN WITH A GUN."

As in the show, Seth Bullock came to Deadwood with his friend Sol Star to open a hardware store. He invested in the community, headed health care boards, and became the town's first sheriff. That last vocation earned him the aforementioned reputation, which endeared him to Theodore Roosevelt, whom Bullock later successfully helped campaign for the vice presidency of the United States. The *Chicago Tribune* ran a delightful description of Bullock: "Bullock attracted general attention around the White House today. He has a fierce looking melodrama mustache and wears a sombrero."

THE REAL AL SWEARENGEN WAS NO ROMANTIC ANTIHERO.

In *Deadwood*, Ian McShane's Al Swearengen is a pimp, crook, and murderer, but he is also the protector of the "crippled" Jewel and he is grimly civic-minded. And, let's face it, he's somehow sort of likable. The real Swearengen was much less admirable: He was a sex trafficker, tricking women into coming to Deadwood to work in his various business ventures—like a theater—but then forcing them into prostitution. His wife publicly accused him of domestic abuse. Eventually, he was run out of Deadwood and was later found dead near some railroad tracks, either from an accident or a willful act of murder.

MILCH DIDN'T EVEN WANT IAN McSHANE TO AUDITION FOR THE ROLE OF AL SWEARENGEN.

Milch was convinced that McShane would be miscast as Swearengen. "Physically, Ian was absolutely wrong for the part. I didn't even want to read him," Milch wrote in *Deadwood: Stories of the Black Hills*. "I had imagined Swearengen as a physically imposing specimen. But when Ian came in, he neutralized all of that, because he had Swearengen's essence, which was fierce matter-of-factness. He was who he was, unadulterated."

MILCH WAS DETERMINED TO GET GARRET DILLAHUNT ON *DEADWOOD*.

If you noticed that Wild Bill's killer Jack McCall and the kinky and sadistic geologist Francis Wolcott looked similar, that's because they were played by the same actor: Garret Dillahunt. Milch was intent on casting Dillahunt in the show, but his road to *Deadwood* was paved with false starts. He initially auditioned for the role of Seth Bullock, then for the part of Doc Cochran, before being cast as McCall. After the rogue fled *Deadwood* for good in season 1, Milch decided to bring Dillahunt back in season 2. First, Milch considered him for the role of Hearst, but ultimately chose him to play Wolcott, minus the prosthetics that marred his appearance in season 1.

CALAMITY JANE AND WILD BILL HICKOK WERE NOT AS CLOSE AS THE SHOW MADE THEM OUT TO BE.

It's suspected that Jane and Wild Bill's connection has been conflated over the years as a part of the blossoming tall tales of the Old West. The pair *did* come to Deadwood together, but they hadn't known each other long before that. However, in her memoir, Jane described Bill as a friend. And the two, who died nearly thirty years apart, were buried beside each other in Deadwood's Mount Moriah Cemetery.

PAULA MALCOMSON MAY HAVE SAVED TRIXIE'S LIFE.

Over the seasons, Trixie the prostitute became an indelible part of *Deadwood* and the makeup of the town. But early on, the actress who played her feared her stint on the series would be short-lived. According to Malcomson, this all changed with "Reconnoitering the Rim," in which Trixie shaves the calluses off Al's feet with a straight razor.

The scene originally didn't have any direction, but Malcomson suggested the foot shaving business—something her father used to do for her grandmother—would give the pair's relationship a greater sense of depth and intimacy. She improvised the line, "Shall I do the other foot?" McShane replied, "Please." She recalls, "The minute he said, 'Please,' I knew it was a new place for us." And Trixie was preserved.

FREEZE FRAME ▶

**"DEADWOOD" //
SEASON I, EPISODE I**
When Timothy Olyphant
was first cast as
Deadwood's reluctant
sheriff Seth Bullock, his
mom was thrilled her son
would be in a western. But
she was taken aback by
all the violence and
four-letter words when
Olyphant showed her the
first episode—and made
sure to let him know it.
"I told all the ladies at
church you were finally
gonna be in something
they could watch," she
told Olyphant, "and
now I've got to call
them all back."

**THOUGH MANY OF
DEADWOOD'S CURSE
WORDS MAY BE
ANACHRONISTIC,
CURSING
ITSELF WAS NOT.**
Milch was dedicated to getting the tone of the Black
Hills right. It was a dangerous and gruff place where
men toiled, fought, and cursed. But the curse words
of the 1870s would seem downright laughable today,
even with the glowering Ian McShane delivering
them. So *tarnation* and *goldarn* were swapped out for
contemporary cursing's heavy hitters, even though *fuck*
didn't come into popularity until the 1920s.

**YES, THERE ARE LOTS OF F-BOMBS, BUT MARTIN
SCORSESE USED MORE.**
Along with being praised for being an impeccably
written show with outstanding performances, *Deadwood*
earned attention for its aggressive use of *fuck*.
According to one dedicated viewer, the entire series
clocked in with 2,980 uses of the word. While that beats
out the estimated 569 times the word was used in *The
Wolf of Wall Street*, Martin Scorsese's curse-laden white-
collar crime drama wins when you break it down by
uses per minute, boasting 3.16 to *Deadwood's* 1.56.

MILCH REJECTED HBO'S OFFER FOR A FOURTH SEASON.

Deadwood fans reeled when news of the show's cancellation came just ahead of its season 3 premiere in the spring of 2006. Common speculation has laid the blame at the feet of Milch's then-greenlit new show, *John from Cincinnati*; however, Milch himself admitted HBO offered a six-episode order for season 4. He turned it down, saying, "For my part, I did not want to accept a short order. We couldn't have done the work the way we wanted. I didn't want to limp home. My old man used to say, 'Never go anyplace where you're only tolerated.'"

DEADWOOD ROSE AGAIN IN 2019.

Not long after *Deadwood*'s finale aired, rumors popped up of movie specials that would tie up the loose threads left behind by season 3. But hope for a long-awaited and craved finale dwindled to dust as time passed, especially in 2009, when McShane told *The Daily Show with Jon Stewart*, "No hope. That's dead." Milch confirmed this sad news himself in 2012, admitting, "We got really close about a year ago," but adding: "Never say never."

In early 2017, reports began to surface that Milch was working on a script for a *Deadwood* movie. In April of that year, a number of outlets began reporting that Milch had finished the script and turned it in to HBO. In 2018, HBO officially confirmed that the movie was a go. And on May 31, 2019, *Deadwood: The Movie* premiered.

6 OTHER TIMES TIMOTHY OLYPHANT PLAYED A LACONIC LAWMAN

Timothy Olyphant made a name for himself as *Deadwood*'s moral-minded Seth Bullock, but it wasn't his first experience playing a man of the law—nor was it his last. Here are six other times we've seen the actor as a drawling harbinger of justice whose long, slow glances seem to say, "Less talk, more action." (He's not *always* wearing a flat-brimmed hat. Sometimes, he's just holding one.)

High Incident // (1996–1997)
Gone in 60 Seconds // (2000)
The Crazies // (2010)
Justified // (2010–2015)
Fargo // (2020)
The Mandalorian // (2020)

5 TV CHARACTERS WHO WERE INSPIRED BY REAL PEOPLE

From Hollywood superstars to political fixers, the small screen is filled with fictional characters who are at least partly inspired by real people, as *Deadwood* certainly proves. Here are a few more.

1 OLIVIA POPE // *Scandal*
Shonda Rhimes based *Scandal*'s Olivia Pope (Kerry Washington) on crisis manager Judy Smith, who served as special assistant and deputy press secretary to George H. W. Bush and has represented a diverse slate of clients including Monica Lewinsky, Michael Vick, and Paula Deen. Smith also served as a co-executive producer and technical advisor on the hit drama.

2 VINCENT CHASE // *Entourage*
The character of Vincent Chase (Adrian Grenier) on *Entourage* is partly based on the series' executive producer, Mark Wahlberg, who had a very similar group of friends and rise to stardom in Hollywood. "My assistant wanted to film my friends around me, because he just thought it was hilarious," Wahlberg told *The New York Times* in 2004. "Initially we wanted to kind of go for someone who was more like myself…but we didn't think that, like, the entourage fighting amongst themselves, like hitting each other with bottles…was going to work. So we wanted it a little bit lighter."

3 LUCIOUS LYON // *Empire*
Empire co-creator (and former *Buffy the Vampire Slayer* star) Danny Strong based the character of Lucious Lyon (Terrence Howard) on rapper and media mogul Jay-Z because of his past criminal life and rise to stardom through hip-hop. "The Jay-Z story, which very much inspired…certain elements of Lucious Lyon, was that story," Strong said. "For me, the story of people who have some sort of criminal past, or gangster past, are not limited to Black culture.…Our goal is to tell a great story, and to do the best show we can."

4 ABED NADIR // *Community*
Community creator Dan Harmon based the character of Abed Nadir (Danny Pudi) on his friend and colleague, Abed Gheith. The pair worked together on Channel 101, a monthly film festival that showcased mini-shows in Los Angeles and New York. According to Gheith, "I think I'm a bit more aware socially. I can tell when people are uncomfortable…It seems like the one on the show has no idea that he's around other people. Like he's watching them on TV. So he's kind of a kidlike version of me."

5 BASIL FAWLTY // *Fawlty Towers*
John Cleese based his *Fawlty Towers* character Basil Fawlty on a real-life hotel owner and manager named Donald Sinclair. In the early seventies, the Monty Python guys were guests at the Gleneagles Hotel in the seaside town of Torquay, England, where they came across the strict hotel proprietor. According to Cleese, Sinclair wouldn't bring in Eric Idle's suitcase because he thought there was a bomb in it. Cleese, who co-created *Fawlty Towers* with his then-wife Connie Booth, described Sinclair as "the most wonderfully rude man I have ever met."

DEXTER

(2006–2013)

CREATED BY: James Manos, Jr. (based on *Darkly Dreaming Dexter* by Jeff Lindsay)

SEASONS: 8

EPISODES: 96

"Homicidal" has not traditionally been a character trait jotted down by television writers in the hope of landing on a sympathetic lead. With *Dexter*, Showtime's dark—and darkly comic—drama, they got away with murder. Built on the considerable talent and charm of *Six Feet Under* star Michael C. Hall, and based on Jeff Lindsay's book series that began with *Darkly Dreaming Dexter*, the show asks viewers to sympathize with Dexter Morgan (Hall), a blood-spatter lab technician at the fictional Miami Metro Police Department by day and a serial killer by night.

Dexter's murderous impulses, which he can't seem to ignore, are directed at villains the world would seemingly be better off without. His detective sister, Deb (Jennifer Carpenter), grounds him in a loose family unit, while a succession of love interests attempt to pull genuine emotion from Dexter's shackled heart. The series is a police procedural crossed with the Grand Guignol gore shows of French theater, all of it anchored by Hall's struggle between being human and indulging in his inner monster (or, as he calls it, his Dark Passenger). Vigilante ritual killings are wrong, of course, but in Hall's knife-wielding hands, we sometimes have to remind ourselves of that.

MICHAEL C. HALL WASN'T INTERESTED IN MAKING ANOTHER TV SHOW WHEN HE WAS APPROACHED ABOUT *DEXTER*.

Hall's first starring turn, the funeral home drama *Six Feet Under*, went off the air in 2005, so he wasn't looking to jump back into TV again in 2006. And while he liked the pitch for *Dexter*, it meant going back into some dark and depressing places. So, as Hall told *Entertainment Weekly* in 2013, he had to ask himself: "Do I want to be surrounded by dead bodies for another indeterminate number of years?" He read the book and the script and decided he liked that Dexter "operates in a morally gray area."

"The tragedy of Dexter is that it's not his homicidal behavior that's gotten the people in his life in trouble but it's his appetite to play at becoming a human being—his desire to have real relationships," Hall said. "I guess a lesson that's emerged is that you can't have your cake and kill it, too."

ACTOR DAVID ZAYAS WAS A NEW YORK CITY POLICE OFFICER.

Zayas, who portrayed Sergeant (later Lieutenant) Angel Batista on *Dexter,* had been a cop in real life, too, and studied acting while working for the New York Police Department. "The moment I was involved in that world, it electrified me, and I realized that it was something that I wanted to do," Zayas told NPR in 2015. He didn't tell many of his co-workers he was trying to become an actor, but his partner knew. "I remember riding in the cars with [my partner] during the midnight shifts, and he would run lines with me for my audition the next day," Zayas said.

JOHN LITHGOW THINKS DEXTER AND TONY SOPRANO HAVE A LOT IN COMMON.

During an interview with the *Los Angeles Times*, Lithgow—who played the Trinity Killer, the main antagonist in *Dexter*'s fourth season—revealed who some of his favorite villains were. "The great evil creation of the last 10 years has been Tony Soprano, and I see a lot of similarities between Dexter and Tony," Lithgow said. "Obviously, there are a lot of huge differences, but he's a captivating character. You can't get enough of Tony Soprano: Even when he was slapping a Russian prostitute on the butt or killing people in the most gruesome manner, you're still with him all the way. I think Michael C. Hall and James Gandolfini are both great, smart actors who really understood that duality, that's what made it so hypnotic.

SPOILERS! JULIE BENZ MADE A JOKE OUT OF HER CHARACTER'S DEATH.

Benz played Dexter's girlfriend-turned-wife, Rita, until the end of season 4. She was shocked when she learned that her demise was coming: "I found out an hour before they put out the script," Benz told MTV. "Then I only found out an hour before we shot the scene how I was going to die—they wouldn't tell me or anybody." But Benz made the most of her memorable passing—and because she had a few days to process the news, she was able to have a little fun with it. "I brought in a Styrofoam tombstone and I floated [it] in the bathtub…[it] said R.I.P. Just to make a joke," Benz said. "I needed some kind of levity! Saying goodbye to my character, my job and people I love, was just too heavy."

LITHGOW DIDN'T THINK THE TRINITY KILLER WAS PURE EVIL.

During an interview with the *Los Angeles Times*, Lithgow—who won an Emmy for playing the Trinity Killer—said his character was "far more than one-dimensional. Even in the first episode, you see him commit this horrific murder, and it looks like pure evil, but the next time you see him, he's in that scalding shower, torturing himself with remorse…There's a lot more going on here than just sadism and evil."

When he's not killing people, Lithgow's character, Arthur Mitchell, tries to be a family man and fit in with society, which humanized his character. "To me, the most fascinating thing is that he's an evil man who does not want to be evil," Lithgow said. "In that sense, he's sort of a mirror image of Dexter, just a much, much more extreme case."

YVONNE STRAHOVSKI DIDN'T THINK HER CHARACTER WOULD SURVIVE SEASON 8.

Strahovski played Hannah, Dexter's serial-killer girlfriend, in seasons 7 and 8, and was one of the few people who had enough emotional attachment to Dexter to survive. "I was surprised when I got to the end of season 7, and I read that scene where she leaves the black orchid at his doorstep, I thought, 'Wow, this is a pretty open ending. This might mean that they want me back,'" she told Collider. "And sure enough, season 8 happened and I thought, 'Well, I probably will end up dying in this season, seeing as I didn't die in season 7, and traditionally, most of the guest stars on that show usually die.'"

SPOILERS! JENNIFER CARPENTER WANTED DEB TO DIE.

Carpenter told *The Hollywood Reporter* she wanted her character to die, but didn't want Dexter to do the deed. "In a strange way, I wanted her [death] to be a suicide," she said. "I wanted Deb to take the one thing that was totally alive in his life away. But how it played out was much better. Deb deserved to die an organic death."

Carpenter also said if Deb had lived, she probably wouldn't have had a happy ending. "She always would have been making sure she was piling enough dirt on the secrets that existed with Dexter. I'm not sure a happy ending was possible for her. This was her happy ending."

SPOILERS! DEXTER WASN'T ALLOWED TO DIE.

The big question of the series finale was: Would Dexter live or die? He almost died in a hurricane, but Showtime was adamant he needed to live. "They [wouldn't] let us kill him," producer John Goldwyn said. "Showtime was very clear about that. When we told them the arc for the last season, they just said, 'Just to be clear, he's going to live.' There were a lot of endings discussed because it was a very interesting problem to solve, to bring it to a close. People have a relationship with Dexter, even if it doesn't have the size and the ferocity of the fan base for *Breaking Bad*. But it has a very core loyal following."

SPOILERS! **HALL THOUGHT THAT DEXTER GOT AN APPROPRIATE ENDING.**

"Sometimes I wish he'd offed himself, wish he'd died, wish Deb had shot him in that train compartment," Hall said of the show's finale. "Of course, that would have made an eighth season difficult to do.…But the idea that he imprisons himself in a prison of his own making I think is fitting [for the character]."

As it turns out, the series finale isn't the last we'll see of Dexter Morgan. In October 2020, Showtime announced that it will be producing a 10-episode revival of *Dexter*, with Hall on board to reprise his role.

DEATH BECOMES HIM: MICHAEL C. HALL TALKS *SIX FEET UNDER*

Michael C. Hall is well aware that he has in many ways become television's poster boy for death. Five years before he channeled his inner Dark Passenger to play Dexter Morgan, Hall's breakthrough role came in HBO's *Six Feet Under*. The five-season series, created by Oscar-winning screenwriter Alan Ball (*American Beauty*), is a quirky-yet-poignant meditation on life, death, and what happens at the place where those two things intersect.

A longtime stage actor, Hall had never been in front of a television camera when he was cast as *Six Feet Under*'s David Fisher, the closeted heir to his family's funeral business. "Luckily, I was playing a character who was very tense," Hall told Mental Floss in 2016.

The critical and commercial success of *Six Feet Under*, which ran from 2001 to 2005, was due in large measure to Hall's depiction of David as a man who often seems to be choking on his own repressed tendencies. While all of the Fishers had neuroses, David's sexual identity kept him on an emotional ledge.

David had a few "coming out" scenes. Was there one that stood out for you, or helped you understand the character in a more complete way?

Because of how well-drawn the character was, who he was, I often had a sense of where he was coming from. But the first scene and first person where he came out was to his mother. Playing that with Frannie [Conroy], what I remember is her hand, her fingers, touching mine on the couch in a way that was affectionate but also skittish. It was surprising and perfect.

David's relationship with Keith (Mathew St. Patrick) was often referred to as a new standard for depicting a complex gay relationship on television. Did you get a sense the character could be a catalyst for changing minds about same-sex couples?

It's a gratifying thing, as gratifying as anything I've done. People saying that spending time with the character, seeing that relationship, helped them change their idea of a gay couple, or to have people say the existence of David and his story gave them strength at a formative time, is amazing.

A lot of people discover shows on streaming services now. How do you think *Six Feet Under* holds up to that kind of marathon viewing?

Whatever people can stomach, I say go for it. If you want to watch five seasons in a week and a half, more power to you. But it was definitely one of those shows where, when it originally aired, people got together with friends or loved ones and made it kind of a Sunday night party. It was exciting to be part of something that brought people together. That was true of *Dexter*, too. But… by its nature, [*Six Feet Under*] might be harder to take in big, heaping shovelfuls.

(1963–1989; 2005–PRESENT)

DOCTOR WHO

CREATED BY: Sydney Newman

SEASONS: 38

EPISODES: 862

OTHER SHOWS BY SYDNEY NEWMAN:
The Avengers (1961–1969)

*D*octor *Who* is the kind of sci-fi juggernaut that can seem a bit daunting to anyone but hardcore fans of the genre. While the original incarnation has a definite sense of humor, the reimagined version of the series—which made its triumphant return to televisions worldwide in 2005—offers loads of kitschy fun. The series follows an alien called the Doctor (no, it's *not* Doctor Who) who travels through space and time in a vehicle known as the TARDIS, which is disguised as a British police call box, to help save the world with the help of his trusty (and ever-changing) companions.

Though the reboot kicked off with Christopher Eccleston playing the Ninth Doctor, part of the fun of the series is that regeneration is canon. So while the Doctor is technically always the same character, he (or she) can regenerate into a new face and body every time an actor leaves the show. David Tennant, Matt Smith, and Peter Capaldi followed Eccleston, and in 2017, viewers got their first glimpse of *Broadchurch* star Jodie Whittaker—the first woman to take on the role of the Doctor—in the Christmas special "Twice Upon a Time." While the series isn't afraid to take a deep dive into classic sci-fi tropes, it's also not lacking a social conscience; one 2018 episode had the Doctor interacting with Rosa Parks. With its quirky mix of history and sci-fi, and a talented cast of actors, it's hard to resist the Doctor's charms.

DOCTOR WHO WAS CREATED AS A CHILDREN'S SERIES.

Though it certainly maintains plenty of pint-size fans to this day, the original concept for *Doctor Who* was specifically an educational program aimed at teaching kids about science and history. In an interview with the BBC, Waris Hussein—who, at the age of twenty-four, directed the very first episode of *Doctor Who*—said that the series "was meant to be educational for kids. We were trying to educate kids about certain things about the human condition."

THE REGENERATION CONCEPT CAME ABOUT BECAUSE OF THE FIRST DOCTOR'S HEALTH PROBLEMS.

William Hartnell, who played the First Doctor from 1963 to 1966, was having health problems toward the end of his run on the series. To ensure that the show could go on without its original star, and to avoid enraging viewers who had come to love Hartnell, the showrunners decided that, instead, they would make the ability to regenerate part of the Doctor's mythology.

THE DOCTOR'S REGENERATION IS SUPPOSED TO FEEL LIKE A BAD ACID TRIP.

Years after it was written, an internal BBC memo was uncovered that outlined the "metaphysical change" that would take place as the First Doctor became the Second Doctor. "It is as if he had had the LSD drug, and instead of experiencing the kicks, he has the hell and dank horror which can be its effect," the memo explained.

THE DOCTOR DIDN'T BECOME A "TIME LORD" UNTIL 1969.

The Doctor is a member of the Time Lords, a group of ancient aliens with the power to travel through time, but he wasn't actually identified as such until the series' sixth season The Doctor's (presumed) home planet of Gallifrey wasn't mentioned by name until 1973.

THE TARDIS ISN'T ALWAYS SUPPOSED TO LOOK LIKE A POLICE CALL BOX.

The TARDIS has always looked like a police box, but it turns out that's only because of a technical malfunction. In 1963's "An Unearthly Child," we learn that the TARDIS is supposed to blend into whatever time and place it has traveled to. But its cloaking device, known as a chameleon circuit, is broken. Oops!

IT TOOK THE BBC A FULL SIX YEARS TO TRADEMARK THE TARDIS.

In 1996, after years of selling TARDIS-branded merchandise, the BBC attempted to officially trademark the Doctor's preferred mode of transportation—but they were met with resistance from the Metropolitan Police, as the time-travel machine is essentially a police call box. Six years later, in 2002, the BBC finally won the case, while the Metropolitan Police were ordered to pay £850 (just shy of $2,000 in today's dollars), plus legal costs.

MORE THAN 2,500 VIEWERS ONCE ATTEMPTED TO CALL THE DOCTOR.

In the season 4 episode "The Stolen Earth," the Doctor's phone number was made clearly visible on the screen as Rose attempted to call him. Needless to say, this sent fans into a bit of a phone frenzy. More than 2,500 people reportedly tried to give the Doctor a ring when the episode aired. Sadly, it was a non-working number. (Also: The Doctor isn't real.)

RIDLEY SCOTT WAS SUPPOSED TO DESIGN THE DALEKS.

Considering what he did with *Alien* and *Blade Runner*, seeing what Oscar-nominated director Ridley Scott would have dreamed up for the Daleks would have been pretty fascinating. Unfortunately, we'll never have the chance. Though Scott, who worked for the BBC at the time of *Doctor Who*'s creation, was assigned the enviable task of designing the show's devilish Daleks, he ended up leaving the network to concentrate on becoming a director. Instead, we have Terry Nation and Raymond Cusick to thank for the Daleks' iconic design.

DOCTOR WHO'S LONG AWAITED RETURN WAS INTERRUPTED BY AN INFAMOUS AUDIO GAFFE.

Whovians were understandably eager to witness the long-awaited return of *Doctor Who* to TV screens when Russell T. Davies's reboot premiered in 2005. What they weren't expecting was…celebrity talk show host Graham Norton. But due to a technical oopsie, some audio of Norton excitedly hosting an episode of *Strictly Dance Fever* found its way into the *Doctor Who* soundtrack during the first few minutes—infuriating viewers.

In 2020, Davies hosted a live rewatch of "Rose" in honor of the reboot's fifteenth anniversary. At the exact moment where Norton's rogue audio had come into play so many years before, he retweeted a Eurovision promo featuring Norton, noting: "This is where Graham Norton interrupted. We laugh now but that night, we DIED. WE DIED. And I spent the whole episode waiting for it to happen again."

THE DALEKS ALMOST DIDN'T MAKE IT INTO *DOCTOR WHO*'S REVIVAL.

When *Doctor Who* made its triumphant return to television in 2005, it almost happened without the Daleks. The estate of Terry Nation, who created the mutants, had initially attempted to block their return to the new series, claiming that the BBC was trying to "ruin the brand of the Daleks." At one point, when negotiations between the BBC and Nation's estate seemed to have broken down, the show's producers even created a new villain. Fortunately, they were able to work it out, and the Daleks have continued to "Exterminate!"

TOM BAKER HAD THE LONGEST ONSCREEN TENURE AS THE DOCTOR ON *DOCTOR WHO*.

Baker, the fourth Doctor. played a role for seven years and 172 episodes—longer than any other actor (though arguably that title could go to Sylvester McCoy, who first appeared as the Doctor in 1987 and, despite the series' cancellation in 1989, appeared in a 1996 TV movie to regenerate into Paul McGann, making him Doctor for nine years. As McGann wasn't seen regenerating until years after the reboot began, his status is less clear). As far as the rebooted series goes, David Tennant holds the record with six years and forty-seven episodes.

WHEN DOUGLAS ADAMS'S ABANDONED *DOCTOR WHO* EPISODE FINALLY SAW THE LIGHT OF DAY—NEARLY FORTY YEARS LATER.

In 1979, *The Hitchhiker's Guide to the Galaxy* author Douglas Adams was enlisted to pen a script for the finale of *Doctor Who*'s seventeenth season. Titled "Shada," the serial saw the Fourth Doctor (Tom Baker) and his companion Romana (Lalla Ward) land the TARDIS in Cambridge, England, to help a retired Time Lord stop an evil alien from hacking into the secrets of a lost planet turned prison for evildoers.

The script was written, and filming for the episode commenced…but then there was a BBC staffer strike, and filming was abandoned. But in 2017, nearly forty years after its intended air date, Whovians finally got to see the episode—just as Adams wrote it—when the original footage was mixed with animated re-creations and newly recorded voice-overs from both Baker and Ward to complete the episode.

It wasn't the first time the broadcaster had recreated one of the series' old episodes. In November 2016, "The Power of the Daleks" found new life in animated form fifty years after it first aired, and more than forty years after the original recording was destroyed.

"THE DOCTOR'S DAUGHTER" //
SEASON 4, EPISODE 6
This 2008 episode introduced viewers to the Tenth Doctor's (artificially created) daughter, Jenny, who was played by Georgia Moffett. It was some inspired casting, as Moffett is the real-life daughter of actor Peter Davison, who played the Fifth Doctor from 1981 to 1984. Moffett's appearance in the episode also led to another enviable real-life title: Mrs. Tennant. She and David Tennant, who met while filming the episode, married three years later.

DAVID TENNANT BECAME AN ACTOR WITH THE GOAL OF PLAYING THE DOCTOR.

When the Tenth Doctor was just a kid, he knew exactly what he wanted to be when he grew up: the star of *Doctor Who*. It was Baker's version of the Doctor in particular that inspired Tennant to become an actor. He carried around a Doctor Who doll and wrote *Who*-inspired essays at school. "*Doctor Who* was a massive influence," Tennant told *Rolling Stone* in 2014. "I think it was for everyone in my generation; growing up, it was just part of the cultural furniture in Britain in the seventies and eighties."

PETER CAPALDI WAS A MAJOR WHOVIAN—AND A THORN IN THE *DOCTOR WHO* FAN CLUB'S SIDE.

Capaldi, the Twelfth Doctor, was obsessed with the series as a kid, too. As a teenager, he created *Doctor Who* fan art and even managed to get some of it published. More than forty years before he became the Doctor, some BBC staffers already knew his name because he used to inundate them with letters requesting production photos and begging to be named president of the show's fan club.

"He haunted my time running the fan club, as he was quite indignant he wasn't considered for the post," recalled Sarah Newman, an assistant to the show's producer at the time, who was forced to tell the teenage future Doctor that they had already named a president.

CATHERINE ZETA-JONES WAS RUSSELL DAVIES'S FIRST CHOICE TO TAKE OVER FOR TENNANT.

Though Jodie Whittaker is the series' first official female Doctor, she's not the first actress to be considered for the role. Back in the 1980s, Sydney Newman had an idea for how to revitalize the show: Regenerate the Time Lord into a Time Lady. The show's producers toyed with the idea of making the Doctor a woman for years. In 2008, showrunner Russell Davies broached the idea yet again, citing Catherine Zeta-Jones as his top pick to replace Tennant. (No official statement was ever made on whether she was actually offered the role.)

BENEDICT CUMBERBATCH AND HUGH GRANT WERE BOTH CONSIDERED TO PLAY THE DOCTOR.

Catherine Zeta-Jones isn't the only famous could've-been Doctor. Hugh Grant was offered the role of the Doctor when the show was being revitalized, but reportedly turned it down because he worried it wouldn't be a hit. *Sherlock* star Benedict Cumberbatch was also reportedly considered, but that didn't work out. "David [Tennant] and I talked about it but I thought it would have to be radically different," Cumberbatch said.

JODIE WHITTAKER'S FIRST EPISODE WAS THE MOST WATCHED *DOCTOR WHO* INTRODUCTION IN MORE THAN TEN YEARS.

When Whittaker made her official debut as the Doctor in the fall of 2018, approximately 9 million people tuned in to watch, making it the highest rated *Doctor Who* launch episode in more than a decade. Only Christopher Eccleston's first episode, which was the debut of the series' reboot, beat Whittaker's numbers (9.9 million tuned in to that).

THE ELEVENTH DOCTOR'S LOOK CREATED A DEMAND FOR BOW TIES.

While Matt Smith, as the Eleventh Doctor, was finding his look in his first episode, he declared that "bow ties are cool"—and he was clearly on to something. In 2010, British-based retailer Topman said that "Since the new *Doctor Who* aired, we have seen a dramatic rise in bow tie sales; in [one month, sales] increased by 94 percent."

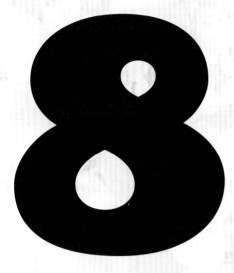

OF THE MOST BINGEABLE SCI-FI SERIES

While any television show has the potential to transport you to another world, the best science fiction can take you to worlds beyond. Here are a few of the sci-fi shows we recommend as being binge-worthy.

1 *12 Monkeys* // **(2015–2018)**
For four seasons, fans of Syfy's *12 Monkeys* watched as James Cole (Aaron Stanford), Cassandra Railly (Amanda Schull), Jennifer Goines (Emily Hampshire), and the rest of Team Splinter traveled through the past, present, and future in an attempt to thwart the Army of the 12 Monkeys, a nefarious cult that wants to destroy time and create the Red Forest—a place where neither time, nor death, exist—by spreading a deadly virus that could threaten all of mankind.

2 *The Twilight Zone* // **(1959–1964)**
Rod Serling's classic anthology series blended sci-fi and fantasy with modern social parables. Come for the morality lessons, stay for the wicked twist endings. (The show also led to three revivals: in 1985, 2002, and 2019.)

3 *Quantum Leap* // **(1989–1993)**
Scott Bakula stars as Dr. Sam Beckett, a physicist who can "leap" into the bodies of others at various points in time to prevent historical mishaps from occurring. Dean Stockwell is along for the ride as Al, who manifests as a hologram.

4 *Orphan Black* // **(2013–2017)**
Tatiana Maslany reinvents herself multiple times over in this clever thriller about a woman who steals the identity of one of her many clones.

5 *The 100* // **(2014–2020)**
A group of one hundred juvenile prisoners are the first humans returning to Earth after a nuclear apocalypse wipes out humanity. Upon arrival, Earth isn't quite as desolate as they expect it to be.

6 *Sense8* // **(2015–2018)**
Lana and Lilly Wachowski (*The Matrix*) and J. Michael Straczynski (*Babylon 5*) elevated streaming sci-fi with this Netflix series about eight people from around the globe who discover they're all emotionally connected with one another and race to discover their origins before the malevolent Biologic Preservation Organization does.

7 *The Expanse* // **(2015–PRESENT)**
A colonized solar system is the setting for this Syfy-turned-Amazon Prime Video drama about a spaceship crew navigating a political conspiracy.

8 *Snowpiercer* // **(2020–PRESENT)**
This adaptation of the 1982 graphic novel (which led to a 2013 film by Bong Joon-ho, the Oscar-winning director responsible for *Parasite*) sees a class system playing out on a train encircling a world that's frozen over. *Hamilton*'s Daveed Diggs co-stars.

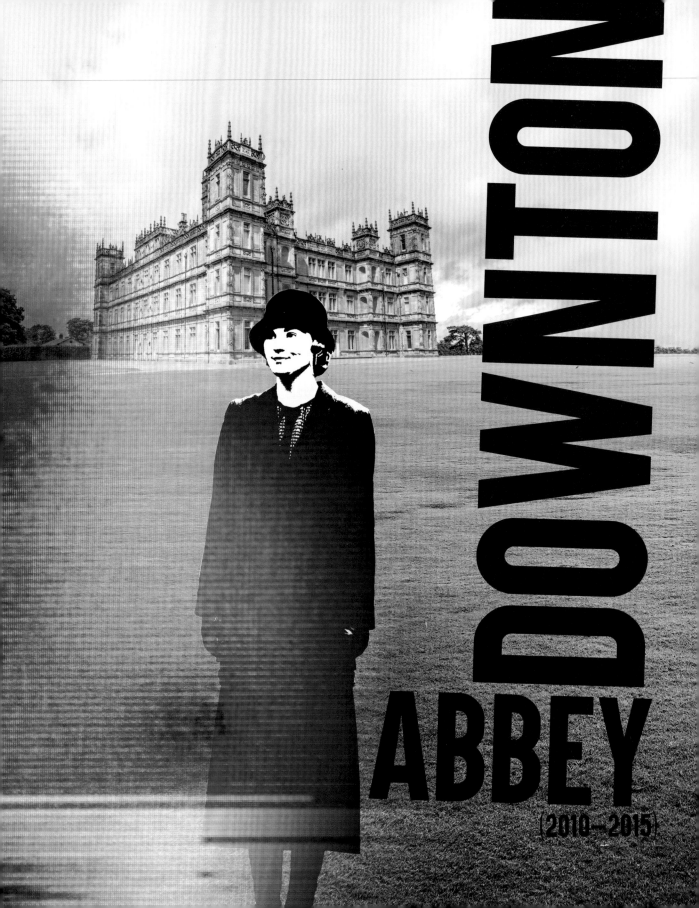

DOWNTON ABBEY (2010—2015)

CREATED BY: Julian Fellowes

SEASONS: 6

EPISODES: 52

OTHER WORKS BY JULIAN FELLOWES:
Doctor Thorne (2016)
Belgravia (2020)
The English Game (2020)

In the picturesque English village of Downton, Robert (Hugh Bonneville) and Cora Crawley (Elizabeth McGovern), aka the Earl and Countess of Grantham, have a problem: They've just received word that the earl's cousin James—his heir presumptive—and James's only son, Patrick (the unofficial fiancé of Robert's eldest daughter, Mary), have died aboard the *Titanic*.

Unfortunately for Mary (Michelle Dockery), there's no such thing as a female heir in 1912 England. So in addition to getting her married off to some well-to-do gentleman who will keep her social status intact, her parents need to track down the stranger who will end up inheriting their beloved estate and the bulk of their fortune. Enter Matthew Crawley (Dan Stevens), an upper-middle-class lawyer from Manchester, along with his meddling mother, Isobel (Penelope Wilton), who must find a way to adapt to the Downton way of life, and whom the family must learn to accept as the future master of the estate they love.

Even when it's at its most ridiculous (like amnesiac heirs coming back from the dead), the show's impeccable attention to detail—thanks to Julian Fellowes and historical advisor Alastair Bruce—and its *Upstairs, Downstairs*–like balance between the dramas that face a nineteenth-century aristocrat and the troubles of the trusty servants downstairs make *Downton* a completely addictive watch.

DOWNTON ABBEY'S STRUCTURE WAS INSPIRED BY ER AND THE WEST WING.
In developing the structure for *Downton Abbey*, creator Julian Fellowes and executive producer Gareth Neame found inspiration in some unexpected places. "Constructing *Downton*, I was consciously thinking in terms of those American structures," Fellowes said in Rebecca Eaton's book, *Making Masterpiece: 25 Years Behind the Scenes at Sherlock, Downton Abbey, Prime Suspect, Cranford, Upstairs Downstairs, and Other Great Shows.* "I had liked *ER*. There was something called *Chicago Hope* that I liked very much, and *thirtysomething*, with all these stories going at once." Executive producer Gareth Neame told Deadline the pitch for the show was "a weekly series that had the production values of the *Merchant Ivory* films and the pace of storytelling of *The West Wing*—a very contemporary feeling show, albeit set 100 years ago with multiple narratives."

DOWNTON ABBEY IS REALLY HIGHCLERE CASTLE.
Much of the series is filmed at Highclere Castle, an estate in Hampshire, England, that is home to the Earl and Countess of Carnarvon. The home regularly opens to the public and can be rented for weddings and parties. In addition to its iconic exterior, the library, dining room, drawing room, and grand hallway seen in *Downton Abbey* belong to the real-life Highclere Castle. Because the servants' quarters at Highclere Castle have

Andrew Lloyd Webber Wanted To Purchase Highclere Castle... For His Art Collection.

In 2010, composer Andrew Lloyd Webber (who lives in a neighboring estate) made an offer to purchase Highclere Castle, apparently as a home for his art collection. The Carnarvons kindly let Lloyd Webber know that the property was not for sale. "I think it has more to do with Andrew Lloyd Webber's desire to hang his art collection somewhere," Lady Carnarvon told the *Los Angeles Times*. "Maybe it might help with his estate duties. He was not a friend and, therefore, might not be aware of our own art collection."

In a letter to *The Daily Telegraph*, Lloyd Webber explained that he was "concerned that the Earl had proposed to develop housing in swathes of the north Hampshire Area of Outstanding Natural Beauty (AONB), relying on special English Heritage planning guidelines to raise money to restore the castle. Under these guidelines, this sort of development is only permitted if every other avenue is exhausted or if the sale of the building to be restored to a sympathetic buyer cannot be achieved." Hence his interest in possibly purchasing the property. FYI: The estate is valued at approximately $200 million.

FREEZE FRAME ▶

"EPISODE SEVEN" //
SEASON 5, EPISODE 7
One of the show's most beloved stars was its faithful pooch, Isis, who died of cancer in 2014. Though many thought the Labrador got the boot because of her name, star Hugh Bonneville set the record straight on that matter: "Anyone who genuinely believes the series 5 story line (1924) involving [Isis] was a reaction to recent world news is a complete berk."

FYI: All of the Crawleys' dogs have Egyptian-themed names as a nod to George Herbert, the 5th Earl of Carnarvon, who was one of the individuals who uncovered King Tut's tomb.

been modernized, the series' downstairs kitchen and attic living quarters were built at London's Ealing Studios.

CORA CRAWLEY WAS *NOT* CREATED FOR AMERICAN AUDIENCES.

Some critics of the show have questioned Fellowes's motive in developing a British series around an American character, with some assuming it was a strategic creative move in order to attract American audiences. "We weren't thinking in those terms about foreign sales," Fellowes told *The Independent*. "The advantage for me of having the American wife was it gave me a central character who was not dyed in the wool of the upper middle class upbringing, so you could have one of the principal characters who didn't take all that stuff for granted, and questioned it, as Cora did. She was not consciously written for America. The fact that we would have a central character for American sales was much more clever than we were really."

HUGH BONNEVILLE AND ELIZABETH HAVE BEEN MARRIED BEFORE.
If Bonneville and McGovern seemed at ease with each other playing husband and wife in *Downton Abbey*, that's probably because they've had some practice—on screen, that is. The actors played husband and wife on the BBC series *Freezing*.

IT BROKE AN EMMY AWARD RECORD.
With a total of sixty-nine nominations and fifteen wins, *Downton Abbey* is the most nominated non-US series in Emmy history.

DOWNTON ABBEY IS THE MOST SUCCESSFUL SERIES IN MASTERPIECE'S FIFTY-PLUS-YEAR HISTORY.
"Nobody in their right mind could have predicted what happened, when it sort of went viral," Julian Fellowes told *The New York Times* in 2013 of *Downton Abbey*'s unprecedented popularity. It's estimated that more than 120 million people around the world have watched the series at some point. The show was broadcast in 250 territories worldwide, and became a major hit in Russia, South Korea, and the Middle East, too.

QUEEN ELIZABETH II REPORTEDLY WATCHED THE SHOW.
According to *At Home with the Queen* author Brian Hoey, Her Royal Highness loved "to pick out the mistakes. [The show does] tend to get it right. However, the Queen did notice on one episode that there was a young so-called British officer wearing medals which had not been awarded when he was supposed to be alive. He was fighting in the First World War and the medals on his chest did not come in until the Second World War."

10 GREAT MOVIES THAT SPRUNG FROM TV SHOWS

Just because a TV series ends doesn't mean the journey of its characters does, too. In 2019, four years after the small-screen version of *Downton Abbey* aired its finale, fans got the chance to check in with the Crawley family and their dutiful servants as they prepared the estate for a royal visit from King George V and Queen Mary. (Hijinks ensued.) And they'll do it gain when the second *Downton* movie arrives in theaters in December 2021. But *Downton Abbey* isn't the only TV show that had fans clamoring for more. Here are ten other movies that originated on the small screen.

Borat // (2006)

The Fugitive // (1993)

In the Loop // (2009) from *The Thick of It*

The Inbetweeners Movie // (2011)

The *Jackass* Franchise // (2002–PRESENT)

MacGruber // (2010) from *Saturday Night Live*

The *Mission: Impossible* Franchise // (1996–PRESENT)

Monty Python and the Holy Grail // (1975)

Serenity // (2005) from *Firefly*

Twin Peaks: Fire Walk with Me // (1992)

THE COSTUMES CREATED A BIT OF A STINK.

In keeping with the show's dedication to authenticity, the producers maintained a "no-wash" policy with some of the costumes in order to keep them within the period look—which meant the actors could get a little stinky. "They have these weird patches, which are sewn into the armpits and which they wash separately," Sophie McShera (who played kitchen maid turned assistant cook Daisy) told the *Daily Mail*.

HIGHCLERE CASTLE REALLY DID OPERATE AS A HOSPITAL DURING WORLD WAR I.

During season 2, Downton Abbey is turned into a convalescent home for military officers. In real life, during World War I, the 5th Countess of Carnarvon *did* turn Highclere Castle into a recovery hospital for soldiers.

5 TV HOMES YOU CAN VISIT

Though the interiors of most TV houses are built on a set, their façades are often actual homes, much like *Downton Abbey*'s Highclere Castle. Some are private residences, while others allow tours and even overnight stays. Here are some TV homes you can visit in real life.

Rosebud Motel
LOCATION: ORANGEVILLE, ONTARIO, CANADA

You don't need to lose your video store fortune to wind up at this spot. It may have been the Rose family's last resort, but fans of *Schitt's Creek* eagerly flock to this former motel. Each of the eight rooms boasts a small kitchen and fridge, as well as enough space to display your collection of wigs.

Doune Castle
LOCATION: DOUNE, SCOTLAND

Fantasy fans will recognize this medieval fortress: It served as *Game of Thrones*'s Winterfell and

Outlander's Castle Leoch. You can tour the stalwart fourteenth-century castle, but don't expect to see any Starks or MacKenzies milling about.

Blair House Inn
LOCATION: MENDOCINO, CALIFORNIA

When she wasn't sleuthing around the fictional town of Cabot Cove, Maine, *Murder, She Wrote*'s Jessica Fletcher (Angela Lansbury) retreated to this Victorian home. It's a working inn, so book a room with an ocean view and get to work writing your own mystery thrillers.

The Binford Building
LOCATION: LOS ANGELES, CALIFORNIA

You can actually have your own *New Girl*–style loft adventures in

this building—it's full of apartments to rent. Just find some zany roommates and let the rounds of True American begin.

Seaview Terrace
LOCATION: NEWPORT, RHODE ISLAND

If you tuned in to the gothic soap opera *Dark Shadows*, you'll know this lavish manor as Collinwood Mansion. Fittingly for a structure that represented the setting of a spooky supernatural show, the mansion itself is purportedly haunted. Visitors have reported hearing people speaking, unexplained banging noises, and even phantom footsteps.

FARGO

(2014–PRESENT)

CREATED BY: Noah Hawley (based on the movie by Joel and Ethan Coen)

SEASONS: 4

EPISODES: 41

OTHER WORKS BY NOAH HAWLEY:
Legion (2017–2019)

Making the leap from movie to television show has rarely turned out to be a great idea (see the small-screen versions of *Ferris Bueller*, *Dirty Dancing*, and *Casablanca*). But *Fargo* is an exception to this rule. Brilliantly crafted, the show is technically designed as an anthology series, though there are small connections between each of its seasons.

Even better: The series doesn't try to retell the Coen brothers' Oscar-winning 1996 film, but it does pay tribute to their work—not just with its title or setting, but with its unique tone, quirky characters, and perfectly honed black comedy. Each season so far has taken a good guys versus bad guys approach, typically pitting the police against a handful of criminals, with a bumbling one usually thrown in for good measure.

Serious Coen fans will recognize all sorts of Easter eggs that relate not just to the show's big-screen predecessor, but several other movies in the brothers' filmography. The anthology series has been a hit for the network and for Noah Hawley, with four seasons airing through 2020.

THERE'S A REASON THE *FARGO* SERIES DIDN'T USE MARGE.

Fargo creator Noah Hawley had no desire to revisit Frances McDormand's Marge Gunderson character, the pregnant sheriff of Brainerd, Minnesota. Instead, as he told IndieWire in 2014, he wanted to tell new stories each season, and imagined that "after a season or two of the show, people who see the movie might say, 'That was a really great episode of *Fargo*,' because each season is a separate true crime story from that region, the movie now fits into the series."

THE COEN BROTHERS DIDN'T HAVE TO BE INVOLVED IN THE TV VERSION OF *FARGO*, BUT THEY WANTED TO BE.

Because MGM owns the rights to *Fargo*, they didn't necessarily need Joel and Ethan Coen's blessing to move forward. But when executive producer Warren Littlefield presented them with Hawley's script for the pilot, they decided to become involved. "They just said, 'We're not big fans of imitation, but we feel like Noah channeled us and we would like to put our names on this,'" Littlefield told HitFix in 2014. "And they didn't have to do that."

FX FELT THEY NEEDED BILLY BOB THORNTON FOR *FARGO*.

Oscar-winner Thornton portrayed philosophical hitman Lorne Malvo in the first season, a casting move that FX CEO John Landgraf said was mandatory for the show in order to find its footing. "We needed Billy Bob Thornton," Landgraf told a television critics panel in 2014, "but now the show, the title, the tone, the writing…are the star of that show."

NOAH HAWLEY WAS RELUCTANT TO CAST THORNTON.

Though the casting of Thornton, who worked with the Coens on *The Man Who Wasn't There* (2001) and *Intolerable Cruelty* (2003), in season 1 as a sociopath not unlike *No Country for Old Men*'s Anton Chigurh, may seem like another Coen Easter egg, Hawley was initially reluctant to consider Thornton for that very reason. He wanted the series to feel like the Coens but avoid any direct connection with them. "But the more I wrote this character, it just became clear that there was no other actor who could do [Lorne] Malvo justice," Hawley told the *Los Angeles Times*. "Billy just has that charm and charisma, and he perfectly plays someone who pushes civilized people to the point they revert to an animal mentality."

THE *FARGO* SERIES IS ALL TAKEN FROM A (FAKE) TRUE CRIME BOOK.

Hawley has been quoted as saying he thinks of the *Fargo*-verse as being influenced by a big book of Midwestern crime tales, with each season based on a different chapter. He cemented that idea in the ninth episode of the second season, opening with a close-up of a book titled *The History of True Crime in the Midwest*.

. . . WHICH MIGHT EXPLAIN THAT UFO.

In season 2, Patrick Wilson's Lou Solverson character is saved during the "Massacre at Sioux Falls" (originally referenced in the first season) by the appearance of a UFO hovering over a motel parking lot. Even by *Fargo*'s standards, it was a strange occurrence. According to Hawley, who was pressed for some kind of explanation during a June 2016 event, the scene stemmed from the idea that the show is ostensibly a "true story" and so these odd elements have to be included because they're the "truth-is-stranger-than-fiction" events recorded in the story.

It's also worth noting that *The Man Who Wasn't There* featured a similarly out-of-nowhere UFO scene.

THERE WAS A VOICE COACH ON THE *FARGO* SET.

If you've ever met anyone who wasn't a big fan of the Coen brothers' 1996 film, they probably pointed to the syrupy Minnesota accents as being too obnoxious to put up with for long. Hawley was cognizant of that, too. Although he kept a voice coach on set, he had the actors minimize any attempt to lay it on thick. The accent "became a caricature after the movie," he said. Allison Tolman, who played police deputy Molly Solverson in season 1, said her accent was inspired by listening to a Midwestern character on the 1990s Howie Mandel cartoon *Bobby's World*.

YOU NEED TO WATCH *FARGO* REALLY CLOSELY IF YOU WANT TO CATCH ALL THE COEN BROTHERS EASTER EGGS.

Hawley's *Fargo* doesn't just pay homage to the feature that inspired it; if you watch closely, you'll see obscure references to the Coens' entire filmography. A second-season episode featured a diner placemat with a circle on it and the line "You know, for kids!" in a nod to 1994's *The Hudsucker Proxy*. The word "unguent" is featured in both the film and show as a treatment for a bite and gunshot wound, respectively; a chalkboard ad for a white Russian drink special. A favorite of The Dude in *The Big Lebowski*—can be seen behind Martin Freeman in season 1.

EWAN McGREGOR FOOLED VISITORS ON THE SET OF *FARGO*.

In the third season, McGregor plays both Emmit and Ray Stussy, two brothers with vastly different lifestyles. While Emmit is "the parking lot king of Minnesota" with a fortune to match, the scheming Ray has gone to seed, with straggly hair and a paunch. McGregor told *Entertainment Weekly* that when a car mechanic came on set to discuss Ray's Corvette, he had a long conversation with the actor while McGregor was in makeup as Ray. The next day, the mechanic was (re)introduced to McGregor and had no idea he had already spoken to him.

 BAD HAIR IS A *FARGO* TRADITION

Jean Smart was cast in the second season as Floyd Gerhardt, the matriarch crime boss of a bunch of hooligan sons. The season was set in 1979, and sixty-three-year-old Smart was asked to cut and dye her hair to appear more matronly. "The first day they cut and dyed and styled my hair, I burst into tears," Smart said. "But after ten minutes, I was fine and I loved it. That it's not a glamour role is incredibly liberating. This must be what it's like to be a [male actor], where you're just thinking about what you're supposed to be thinking about—your character and the scene—instead of thinking, 'Oh my God, why are they shooting me from that angle?' You don't have to care about looking skinny, or where's the camera."

While Thornton sported an equally unfortunate cut in the first season, he seemed more pleased with it. "The weird haircut was actually a mistake. I got a bad haircut," he told Collider in 2014. "We had planned on dyeing my hair and having a dark beard, but I didn't plan on having bangs. But then, instead of fixing it, I didn't fix it because I looked at myself in the mirror and I thought, 'Hang on a second here, this is like 1967 L.A. rock. I could be the bass player for Buffalo Springfield. This is good. Or, it's the dark side of Ken Burns.'"

McGREGOR HAD ONE GOAL IN PLAYING DUAL ROLES: TO MAKE SURE IT WASN'T GIMMICKY.

McGregor is no stranger to the dual role thing; he's done it a couple times before in movies, including Michael Bay's *The Island* (2005) and Rodrigo García's *Last Days in the Desert* (2015). But *Fargo* presented a unique challenge because it required him to play two totally different characters who just happened to be brothers. "[T]he challenge for me really as an actor was to try and play the two parts without it being a hindrance to the audience," McGregor told *The Hollywood Reporter*. "My goal was to make people not see me playing Ray and me playing Emmit, but just see Emmit and Ray and forget that it was being played by the same actor…Otherwise, it's a gimmick, and a gimmick doesn't really hold over 10 hours of television."

CHRIS ROCK AGREED TO STAR IN *FARGO* WITHOUT EVEN READING A SCRIPT.

According to Hawley, Rock made a commitment to star in season 4 of the show without seeing much of anything on paper. Hawley phoned FX, told them the basic idea, and expressed interest in casting Rock. "Chris came to the set [of Hawley's 2019 film, *Lucy in the Sky*] two weeks later and I pitched him the thing and luckily he was a *Fargo* enthusiast and he was in," Hawley told *Entertainment Weekly*. "There wasn't a script for six more months. I've never done it that way before. There's always been a script first."

FOR HAWLEY, *FARGO* IS A MICROCOSM OF AMERICA.

The series may be called *Fargo* and many of its characters' mannerisms (and accents) are specific to the Midwest, but Hawley doesn't take its setting literally. "For me, *Fargo* has always been the story of America," he told *GQ* in 2020. "One of the things that I think you can say about Joel and Ethan's movie is that it is a quintessentially American film and that the characters in it are so unique and the exploration of this idea of basic decency in the face of greed and violence—there's something very American to that struggle. And so, certainly every year for me has been about expanding that conversation about America, and [in season 4], the focus of it moved on some level to this idea of, 'Well, what is an American? And who gets to be an American? And who gets to decide?'"

THE 1997 *FARGO* SERIES THAT NEVER TOOK OFF

One year after Joel and Ethan Coen's *Fargo* made its debut in theaters, rights holder MGM attempted a small-screen adaptation of the movie starring a pre-*Sopranos* Edie Falco as Marge Gunderson, the role originally played by Frances McDormand.

In writing about the 1997 pilot for *Fargo*, which was directed by Kathy Bates, *The New York Times* said that "it's got a quirky, *Northern Exposure* flavor mingled with a morbid vibe that presages *Six Feet Under*—it's a blend that might have found its way, over time. (On the other hand, a pre-*Sopranos* Edie Falco plays the lead, so perhaps it's a blessing that the show never made the cut.)"

The Coens were not involved in the show, which might have doomed the project from the start; it never went to series and sat on the shelf for six years until cable network Trio unearthed the pilot in 2003 as part of their block of unseen-programming specials. Ironically, NBC executive Warren Littlefield passed on this project—which eventually landed over at CBS—fearing it could never live up to the movie. He ended up becoming an executive producer on Noah Hawley's *Fargo* series in 2014.

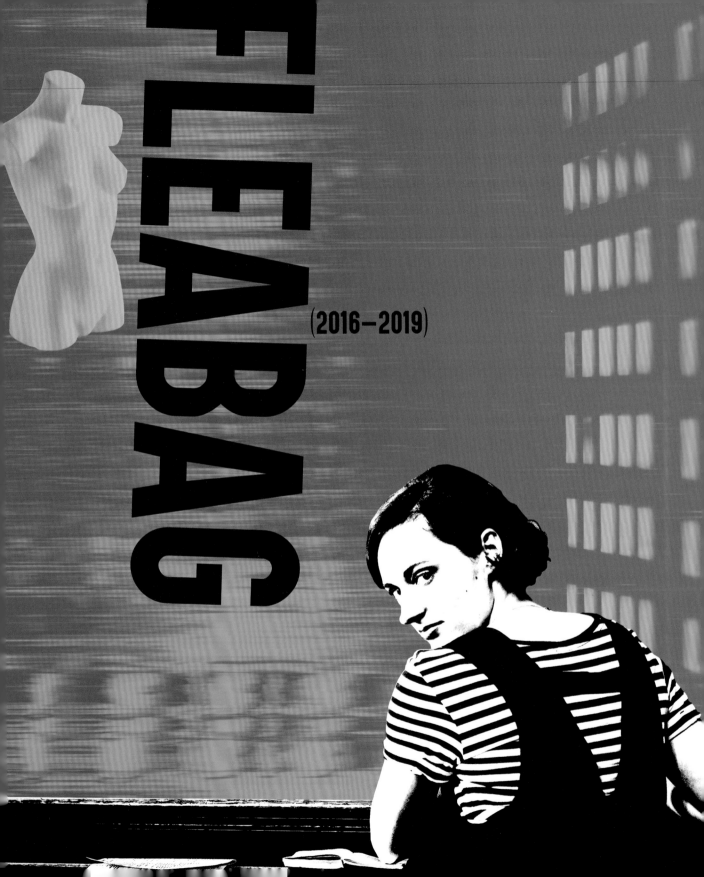

FLEABAG

(2016–2019)

CREATED BY: Phoebe Waller-Bridge

SEASONS: 2

EPISODES: 12

OTHER SHOWS BY PHOEBE WALLER-BRIDGE:
Crashing (2016)
Killing Eve (2018–PRESENT)

After the 71st Primetime Emmy Awards show in September 2019, Phoebe Waller-Bridge—clad in a gown—was photographed lounging at Los Angeles's famed Chateau Marmont with a cigarette in one hand and a cocktail in the other. The side tables were crowded with Emmy statuettes that saluted her as she, in a state of lazy ecstasy, exhaled smoke over the scene. *Fleabag* had nabbed a handful of Emmy Awards, and the photo—like so many other moments in *Fleabag*'s second and final season—went viral.

In just two short seasons, *Fleabag* made a lasting mark on television that won't soon be forgotten. Waller-Bridge's darkly hilarious series follows Fleabag, a thirty-something Londoner—played by the effortlessly funny Waller-Bridge—who is caught up living a life of late nights filled with booze and promiscuity in the wake of her mother's death. At first *Fleabag* appeared to be a simple half-hour comedy following the often naughty exploits of its quirky main character. But as the series progressed, it quickly proved itself to be a truly masterful piece of work with each episode adding more complicated layers and darker themes to which many viewers could relate.

Witty and frank about sensitive topics (for example, sex, death, and "losing the currency of youth"), the character quickly became the accident-prone alter ego of millennial viewers who saw aspects of their own messy, disillusioned lives depicted on screen. Season 2 introduced an additional reason to watch, in the form of Irish actor Andrew Scott as a sweary, irreverent (and nameless) cleric whom the internet zealously christened "Hot Priest." Though fans clamored for more, Waller-Bridge's post-Emmys glamour shot was *Fleabag*'s de facto finale. "This just feels like the most beautiful, beautiful way to say goodbye to it," she said after the awards ceremony. "It does feel nice to go out on a high. You can't get higher than this."

FLEABAG ORIGINATED AS A ONE-WOMAN STAGE PLAY.

It's hard to imagine what *Fleabag* might look like if it were stripped of all its chaotic characters and performed as a solo show, but that's exactly how it started. Before there was a TV show, Waller-Bridge staged *Fleabag* as a one-woman play at the Edinburgh Festival Fringe back in 2013. The title character addressed the audience in an hour-long, sexcapade-filled monologue, which was generally met with praise by theater critics. The TV show was created soon after and originally premiered on BBC Three in July 2016.

THE TITLE OF THE SHOW REFERS TO MORE THAN JUST THE MAIN CHARACTER.

The title *Fleabag* comes from a nickname given to Waller-Bridge by her family. Speaking to *This Morning* in April 2020, Waller-Bridge also revealed a deeper meaning for the name choice (which is never actually spoken in the show).

"A fleabag motel is something that's a bit rough around the edges," she explained. "I wanted to call her that because I wanted her persona and her outside aesthetic to give the impression that she was completely in control of her life, when actually, underneath, she's not."

ISOBEL WALLER-BRIDGE, PHOEBE'S SISTER, COMPOSED THE *FLEABAG* SOUNDTRACK.

The badass guitar chords played after every episode of *Fleabag* were composed by Isobel Waller-Bridge, Phoebe's very talented sister. Isobel studied music at Edinburgh University followed by a master's degree at King's College London, then pursued additional study at the Royal Academy of Music.

Isobel has firmly established herself in the music world. Like her sister, Isobel has received several awards, including Best Composer at the Underwire Film Festival. She also composed the chorused background music for *Fleabag*'s second season, which perfectly fit the religious theme.

SPOILERS! THE FOURTH-WALL BREAKS IN *FLEABAG* AREN'T JUST THERE FOR COMEDIC EFFECT.

Fleabag's hilarious fourth-wall breaks actually serve a deeper purpose for the character, which is realized by the end of season 1. Fleabag, who is deeply suppressing grief from the loss of her mother and best friend, uses these breaks to escape her troubled reality.

By season 2, the fourth-wall breaks become less of a crutch as the character becomes more engaged in her real life and even falls in love. By the end of the show, Fleabag retires from the audience altogether as she decides to face her reality going forward.

THE "HOT PRIEST" ROLE WAS WRITTEN SPECIFICALLY FOR ANDREW SCOTT.

Waller-Bridge worked with Scott years before she cast him to play the role of the Priest—aka "Hot Priest"—in *Fleabag*'s second season. Speaking to IndieWire in 2019, Waller-Bridge praised Scott's acting style, saying, "there's something really dangerous about how truthful he is as an actor…he just comes with so much complexity that your characters instantly become interesting." Waller-Bridge wrote the part once Scott agreed to it, and their perfectly tragicomic love story was born.

HAD SCOTT TURNED DOWN THE ROLE, A SECOND SEASON OF *FLEABAG* MIGHT HAVE LOOKED A LOT DIFFERENT.

Waller-Bridge was so set on getting Scott to sign on to play the Priest that she admitted a second season might never have even happened had he said no to the role. She knew that she wanted to somehow focus the season around religion, which is how the idea of featuring a priest as Fleabag's crush came to her—though she worried it could come off as a bit cliché. "But then the moment I imagined Andrew Scott in that role, and making this man complex and three-dimensional, and sort of a match for Fleabag, then I was like 'I've got the show now,'" Waller-Bridge told IndieWire, adding that if Scott hadn't been interested in the role, "I don't know if I would have actually been able to write that part."

6 BINGE-WORTHY AMAZON ORIGINAL SERIES TO ADD TO YOUR WATCHLIST

Amazon's transformation from online bookstore to "purveyor of everything" took a step forward in 2013 when it released its first original series, *Alpha House*. The political satire starring John Goodman was short-lived, running just two seasons, but over the years Amazon has proven itself a worthy competitor in the streaming wars, as *Fleabag*'s recent awards season domination proved. Here are a few more Amazon originals (and co-productions) well worth a watch.

BOSCH
(2014–PRESENT)

What could have been a rote police procedural is elevated into something richer by show creator (and *The Wire* veteran) Eric Overmyer and author Michael Connelly, who wrote the books the show is based on. *Bosch*'s charms are embodied in the finely drawn performance delivered by star Titus Welliver. Like the character himself, *Bosch* is just a bit smarter, funnier, and deeper than you might guess at first glance.

CATASTROPHE
(2015–2019)

The genius of this pitch-perfect "romantic comedy in reverse" is that it knows life is defined in many ways—not just by the grandiose scenes that would make up a film's third-act climax but by the quiet, messy moments that might otherwise end up on the cutting room floor. *Catastrophe*'s fictional Rob and Sharon (played with hilarious wit and surprising vulnerability by series co-creators Rob Delaney and Sharon Horgan) bring to life something crasser, funnier, and more beautiful than you'll see in a thousand mindless rom-coms: a real couple, trying their best to stay in love.

ONE MISSISSIPPI
(2015–2017)

Diablo Cody, the Oscar-winning screenwriter of *Juno*, and comedian Tig Notaro co-created this dark comedy. The partly autobiographical series sees Notaro return to her hometown in the wake of her mother's unexpected death and her own recovery from breast cancer. Even when the material isn't exactly ripe for laughs, Notaro's natural humor shines through.

THE BOYS
(2019–PRESENT)

In the real world, spandex-wearing superheroes have come to dominate cinema. In *The Boys*, superpowered characters are real and usually far less than heroic. Profane and often provocative, the show is both a repudiation of a worldview that equates might with right and an implicit acknowledgment that comic books can still provide fodder for morally complex and emotionally resonant storytelling.

THE MARVELOUS MRS. MAISEL
(2017–PRESENT)

By bringing to life Midge Maisel(Rachel Brosnahan), a plucky, would-be standup comedienne in late 1950s New York City, series creator Amy Sherman-Palladino achieves the apotheosis of the talky-but-breezy style she honed with shows like *Gilmore Girls*. The world of *Maisel* is an impeccably designed confection—the perfect visual realization of a world in which anyone is capable of dropping the perfect *bon mot*—but it's Midge and her manager/sidekick Susie (Alex Borstein) who make the rules.

UNDONE
(2019–PRESENT)

Star Rosa Salazar's Alma Winograd-Diaz is brought to life through an innovative production process combining live motion capture and rotoscope animation in this show from longtime *BoJack Horseman* writer Kate Purdy. The result is a dreamy, reality-bending meditation on life after near death, an evocative exploration of loss full of mysteries whose answers lie somewhere beyond the uncanny valley.

FREAKS
AND GEEKS

(1999–2000)

CREATED BY: Paul Feig

SEASONS: 1

EPISODES: 18

OTHER SHOWS BY PAUL FEIG:
Other Space (2015)

FREEZE FRAME ▶

"NOSHING AND MOSHING" // SEASON 1, EPISODE 15
Though the bulk of *Freaks and Geeks*'s budget was spent on licensing music, Neil Young's "Only Love Can Break Your Heart" is the tune that got away. According to Judd Apatow they got permission from Young to use it, but the series was canceled before the episode aired. The producers didn't think it made sense to spend a lot of money for a song to close out an episode that might never be seen, so they switched to Dean Martin's cheaper "You're Nobody 'til Somebody Loves You" –a decision Apatow still regrets.

Before Seth Rogen, Jason Segel, James Franco, and Linda Cardellini were starring in Hollywood blockbusters, they were coming of age on the set of *Freaks and Geeks*. In addition to its stellar cast, the show—which tells the story of siblings Lindsay (Cardellini) and Sam Weir (John Francis Daley) trying to navigate high school from two different social standings—may be best known for its early cancellation. It ran for a single, eighteen-episode season before it was pulled off the air in 2000.

It may not have received all the love it deserved during its run, but *Freaks and Geeks* has grown into a cult classic. It beat *Stranger Things* to the eighties nostalgia trend by seventeen years, and it remains one of the most painfully accurate portrayals of high school life ever shown on screen. The career trajectories of the actors and filmmakers behind the show have also helped its legacy. Series creator Paul Feig and executive producer Judd Apatow both went on to become comedy heavyweights in spite of *Freak and Geeks*'s untimely end—or, perhaps, because of it. Apatow said at a Q&A in 2008, "Everything I've done, in a way, is revenge for the people who cancelled *Freaks and Geeks*."

PAUL FEIG'S INSPIRATION FOR THE SHOW WAS HIS OWN LIFE—AND A 1920s-SET GERMAN MINISERIES.
Berlin Alexanderplatz, a fourteen-part West German TV miniseries that was directed by Rainer Werner Fassbinder and released in 1980, is also about an outcast—a man trying to make a new life for himself after accidentally killing his lover and serving four years in prison. It's based on the 1929 novel by Alfred Döblin.

JOHN FRANCIS DALEY WAS THE ONLY ONE OF THE MAIN HIGH SCHOOLERS PLAYING A CHARACTER HIS OR HER AGE.
Daley was fourteen in real life and as Sam Weir on TV. Linda Cardellini, then twenty-four, played his sixteen-year-old sister, Lindsay. Samm Levine (Neal Schweiber), Martin Starr (Bill Haverchuck), and Seth Rogen (Ken Miller) were all seventeen. Jason Segel (Nick Andopolis) was nineteen. Busy Philipps (Kim Kelly) and James Franco (Daniel Desario) were twenty and twenty-one, respectively.

MOST OF WHAT YOU SEE ON THE SHOW ACTUALLY HAPPENED TO FEIG OR ONE OF THE SHOW'S WRITERS.

To jump-start the writing process, Feig had writers fill out questionnaires about their own experiences in high school. Questions included: "What was the best thing that happened to you in high school? What's the most humiliating thing that happened to you in high school? What's the first sexual thing you ever did?" The answers were used to create the show. One exception to this autobiographical approach was made for episode seventeen, "The Little Things," in which Ken (Seth Rogen) is dating someone with ambiguous genitalia.

THE CAMERA CREW WAS UNDER STRICT ORDERS TO MAKE SCENES LOOK DRAB.

Freaks and Geeks takes place in the fictional town of Chippewa, Michigan, a suburb of Detroit. (There is a Chippewa County, Michigan, and the town is named for Chippewa Valley High School, Feig's very real alma mater.) The director of photography recalled Feig and Apatow saying, "This is Michigan in the fall and winter—pretend it's overcast all the time. Strip away all the turbocharged cinematography and get back to the basics of good storytelling."

TIMING—IN THIS CASE, BAD TIMING— WAS EVERYTHING.

Freaks and Geeks premiered on September 25, 1999, in one of NBC's deadliest time slots: Saturdays at 8:00 p.m. To make things worse, it wasn't aired continuously. The show was taken off the air during the World Series in October, and put against ABC's then red-hot *Who Wants to Be a Millionaire*. Reviews were great, but *Freaks and Geeks* couldn't keep an audience.

The producers created a website for the show, hoping that it would keep fans engaged and aware of upcoming episodes. But the head honchos at NBC refused to share the URL on ads, as they didn't want to promote internet use over watching TV.

FREAKS AND GEEKS WAS A CRITICAL DARLING, BUT WON ONLY ONE EMMY, FOR OUTSTANDING CASTING IN A COMEDY SERIES.

Casting is one of the Creative Arts Emmy categories awarded in a ceremony held separately from all the acting awards. Feig was also nominated for Outstanding Writing for a Comedy Series (in 2000 for the series pilot and in 2001 for the finale), but lost to *Malcolm in the Middle* both times.

NBC PRESSURED THE SHOW'S PRODUCERS TO STUNT-CAST CELEBRITIES IN SMALL ROLES TO BOOST VIEWERSHIP.

"[NBC] really wanted us to try and write Britney Spears into this," Feig said during the 2018 Tribeca Film Festival. "They were like, 'She's really popular now, maybe she could play a waitress or something.'" Though Feig didn't divulge why it never happened, word is that he and his fellow producers refused.

SAMM LEVINE'S WILLIAM SHATNER IMPERSONATION HELPED HIM LAND THE ROLE OF NEAL SCHWEIBER.

But not because it was good. Apatow thought it was extremely corny—exactly like something a geek would do.

FREAKS AND GEEKS'S FINALE WAS WRITTEN AND FILMED IN THE MIDDLE OF THE SEASON.

NBC originally ordered thirteen episodes of *Freaks and Geeks*. With the threat of cancellation looming, Feig wrote and directed the finale, "Discos and Dragons," so that the show could end on a strong note. Then NBC ordered five more episodes, which pushed the finale forward a few weeks. Three of the episodes never aired until Fox Family syndicated the show.

FEIG BRAINSTORMED SOME SEASON 2 STORY LINES.

What might we have seen if *Freaks and Geeks* hadn't been canceled? Feig imagined something bad happening to Lindsay while she was following the Grateful Dead, ultimately destroying her parents' trust in her. Sam was going to find his voice as a drama geek, while Neal joined the swing choir. Bill would become a late-blooming jock under the care of Coach Fredricks, who was dating his mother.

The freaks had more serious plot twists ahead. Daniel would end up in jail, Nick would probably join the army after graduation, and Ken's fate was never quite clear.

FEIG IS STILL HOLDING OUT HOPE THAT THE SHOW COULD COME BACK—AS A MUSICAL.

There's still some hope that *Freaks and Geeks* might come back someday, albeit with a new cast. As recently as 2020, Feig has said he'd still love to see a musical adaptation, which would include a dodgeball dance scene.

5 AMAZING ONE-SEASON SHOWS

As *Freaks and Geeks* proved, a show's time on the air is a poor indicator of its quality. Whether because of unlucky scheduling, an unsupportive network, or too niche an audience, many great series have been canceled prematurely. Though they didn't air for very long, these one-season shows managed to make a major impact.

FIREFLY
(2002)

Joss Whedon's space western *Firefly* didn't garner the same mainstream success as his show *Buffy the Vampire Slayer*. *Firefly*, which follows the crew of the spaceship *Serenity* in the year 2517, was canceled in 2002 due to poor ratings. The show was a surprise hit on DVD, however, and it spawned a movie in 2005.

UNDECLARED
(2002–2003)

After bringing high school to prime time, Judd Apatow matriculated to college for his next show, *Undeclared*. He hired many of the actors from *Freaks and Geeks*—including Seth Rogen, Jason Segel, Busy Philipps, Samm Levine, and David Krumholtz—in guest or recurring roles. Rogen also worked as one of the show's main writers. Like *Freaks and Geeks*, *Undeclared* was canceled after one season but later developed a cult following.

THE GET DOWN
(2016–2017)

Netflix premieres (and cancels) a lot of shows each year, so a series needs to be special to stand out. *The Get Down* was just that: The 2016 musical drama created by Baz Luhrmann and Stephen Adly Guirgis follows a group of South Bronx teens during the rise of disco and hip-hop in the 1970s. Despite its brief run, the show managed to win over a devoted fan base.

MY SO-CALLED LIFE
(1994–1995)

My So-Called Life was among the more memorable teen melodramas on TV in the 1990s, as it didn't sugarcoat the teen experience and introduced the world to up-and-coming stars including Claire Danes and Jared Leto. The series also broke new ground by casting Wilson Cruz as Rickie Vasquez, making Cruz the first openly gay actor to play an openly gay character in a major role on prime time.

POLICE SQUAD!
(1982)

If you enjoy the *Naked Gun* movies, check out *Police Squad!* The six-episode series from David Zucker, Jim Abrahams, and Jerry Zucker led to the police-spoof film franchise, in which Leslie Nielsen reprised his small-screen role as bumbling cop Frank Drebin.

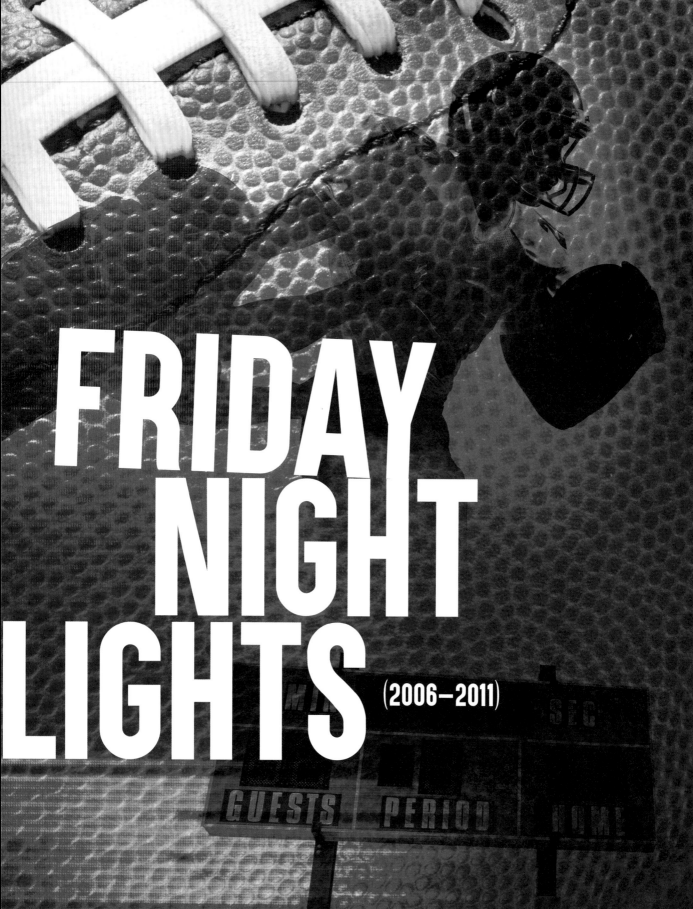

FRIDAY NIGHT LIGHTS

(2006–2011)

CREATED BY: Peter Berg (based on the book by
H. G. Bissinger and the movie by Peter Berg)

SEASONS: 5

EPISODES: 76

OTHER SHOWS BY PETER BERG:
Wonderland (2000)

I f you grew up in a small town where high school athletes were treated like celebrities and every Friday night football game was practically the Super Bowl, you might be sold on binge-watching *Friday Night Lights* based on that premise alone.

If you don't get or don't care about football, here are a few other reasons why you'll find yourself pressing "next episode" faster than you can say "Clear eyes, full hearts, can't lose": To watch the latest battle between Tim Riggins's (Taylor Kitsch) strong moral compass and alcohol-infused penchant for self-sabotage; to witness Tami Taylor (Connie Britton) juggle being an admirable mother, wife, and independent person with lots of compassion, patience, and sass; and, of course, to see Coach Eric Taylor (Kyle Chandler) slowly convince you that maybe you actually do care about football.

Like the high schoolers it follows, Peter Berg's small-screen adaptation of H. G. Bissinger's *Friday Night Lights: A Town, a Team, and a Dream*—which had already seen a big-screen adaptation (also directed by Berg) in 2004—initially struggled to find its footing. But thanks to the hard work of its creators and the perseverance of its fans, the series fought to survive a full five seasons.

PETER BERG WASN'T KEEN ON AUDITIONING KYLE CHANDLER FOR THE ROLE OF COACH TAYLOR.

Berg knew Chandler as the schoolboyish stockbroker from CBS's *Early Edition*, and his general vibe couldn't have been further from what Berg wanted for Coach Eric Taylor. After their first meeting, however, Berg completely changed his mind. Chandler—hot off a friend's fortieth birthday bash—had shown up on a motorcycle looking scruffy, sleep-deprived, and extremely hungover. "[Berg] goes, 'Whatever you did last night, I want you to keep doing it,'" Chandler recounted during a PaleyFest panel. "So I went home and said, 'Listen, honey, here's what I was told I have to do: I have to smoke a lot of cigars, drink a lot of wine, and watch a lot of football.'"

CONNIE BRITTON TURNED DOWN THE ROLE OF TAMI TAYLOR—REPEATEDLY.

Britton had played the coach's wife to Billy Bob Thornton's Coach Gary Gaines in Berg's 2004 film version of *Friday Night Lights*, and both actors had lamented how the movie failed to flesh out the female characters. Worried that the television series would be more of the same, Britton turned down the role of Tami Taylor several times. Finally, after Berg left her an impassioned voice mail vowing to make Tami a strong, multifaceted character, she accepted.

Writer and executive producer Jason Katims came up with the idea of having Tami become a guidance counselor at Dillon High School, which helped her connect with the teenage characters (and also set the scene for some captivating conflicts of interest with her husband turned colleague).

THE RIGGINSES' HOUSE WAS A HEALTH HAZARD. Instead of building sets, producers filmed *Friday Night Lights* at local sites around Austin, Texas. The Alamo Freeze, for example, is actually a functioning Dairy Queen. But not all locations were quite so well kept, especially Tim and Billy Riggins's ramshackle house. "It reeked. There was mold. The pool was filled with sludge," Kitsch told Grantland in 2011. "One of us got sick and we had a doctor come to set. He was like, 'You guys shouldn't be shooting in this house.'"

Adrianne Palicki, who played Tim Riggins's girlfriend, Tyra Collette, remembered sustaining insect bites, courtesy of the Rigginses' couch. Though certainly a health and safety nightmare, the one-story abode *did* fit the story. "Maybe it's just me, but I loved being in there," Kitsch said. "It was the Riggins brothers in a nutshell."

JESSE PLEMONS WAS THE UNDISPUTED CLASS CLOWN. At a 2013 cast reunion, Louanne Stephens (Lorraine Saracen) revealed that the funniest behind-the-scenes moments always involved Zach Gilford, who played her grandson, (Matt Saracen), and Jesse Plemons (Landry Clarke). Brad Leland (Buddy Garrity) agreed: "Jesse Plemons's face, any moment, ever." Gilford has admitted that certain shots were even edited so you couldn't see him laughing at Plemons in the frame. "I think he's the funniest person on the show," he said at PaleyFest. "I cannot keep a straight face around him."

TAYLOR KITSCH NICKNAMED JASON STREET "SIX" WHILE CAMERAS WERE ROLLING. Directors always kept the cameras rolling so scenes would feel as organic as possible, and they also encouraged the actors to improvise on set. One lasting ad-lib was Jason Street's nickname, "Six," which Kitsch made up when shooting Tim Riggins's initial visit to Jason in the hospital.

Another memorable line came from Connie Britton: After Coach Taylor finds his daughter and Matt Saracen (innocently) sharing a blanket on the couch, Matt hurriedly bows out and Coach presents the blanket to Tami as though he's uncovered some sort of smoking gun. Exasperated and amused, Tami says, "You're an idiot." It's Chandler's all-time favorite scene.

TV'S GREATEST COACHES

In any team sport, the head coach is the foundation of the whole organization. Head coaches devise strategies, maintain team chemistry, and make game-time decisions that can lead to glory or heartbreak. It's one of the most important jobs on any field, and that also extends to the actors playing the role of coach on TV. There might be no better coach than Kyle Chandler's Coach Taylor to lead a flock in Texas, but here are some other fantastic TV play-callers.

COACH (1989–1997)
As the man calling the plays for Minnesota State University's Screaming Eagles football team, coach Hayden Fox (Craig T. Nelson) has all the offbeat charisma of a sitcom star while also possessing a commanding presence perfect for leading a tackling drill. Fox's straight-man routine is backed up by his comic foils Luther Van Dam (Jerry Van Dyke) and Michael "Dauber" Dybinski (Bill Fagerbakke), whose witty chemistry helped *Coach* score a nine-season run.

GLEE (2010–2015)
Glee was far from a sports drama, but that didn't stop actress Dot-Marie Jones from imbuing her role as Coach Beiste (pronounced *Beast*) with a raw intensity that would make Dick Butkus blush. But Coach Beiste is far from a burly caricature; in *Glee*'s final season, the character is given real depth when he comes out as a transgender man, a rarity on network television.

TV SHOWS SAVED BY THEIR FANS

While ratings may be the end-all for television executives, a passionate fan base can encourage them to take a chance on a series that's underperforming. Such was the case with *Friday Night Lights,* whose dedicated viewers saved the show from cancellation by inundating NBC executives with packages full of light bulbs (a subtle way of suggesting they keep the lights on) and bottles of eyedrops (a nod to Coach Taylor's "Clear eyes, full hearts, can't lose" mantra). Here are six other shows that were spared the axe thanks to public support.

1 *Jericho* // (2006–2008)
This apocalyptic drama about a Kansas town coping with the aftermath of nuclear war got through two seasons before CBS lowered the boom. In response, fans took a cue from "Nuts!"—a line famously uttered by star Skeet Ulrich and inspired by World War II general Anthony McAuliffe's response when he was asked to surrender. More than 8 million peanuts were sent to CBS. The network gave in.

2 *La Femme Nikita* // (1997–2001)
The espionage thriller starring Peta Wilson aired on USA for several seasons before the end was announced. Fans wrote letters, but they also sent cold, hard cash—about $3,000 worth. Executives passed it along to charity, and a final order of seven episodes was produced.

3 *Roswell* // (1999–2002)
The Katherine Heigl series about aliens posing as prime-time teenagers hit a snag when the WB canceled it after one season. Fans deluged the network with six thousand bottles of Tabasco sauce—a popular beverage for the aliens. The WB didn't budge, but UPN did; the latter network picked the show up after fans shifted attention and sent twelve thousand bottles to *their* offices.

4 *Star Trek* // (1966–1969)
Gene Roddenberry's iconic sci-fi saga was nearly done in after two seasons. When NBC was deluged with letters in a campaign organized by fans John and Bjo Trimble, they reconsidered—for one more season.

5 *Twin Peaks* // (1990–1991)
David Lynch's eccentric series was in danger of being entombed after ratings fell and it entered into a hiatus in April of 1991. Fans formed COOP (Citizens Outraged at the Offing of *Peaks*) and sent logs, creamed corn, and stale donuts to ABC. *Twin Peaks* returned in June with a special double-episode finale.

TED LASSO
(2020-PRESENT)
After leading the Wichita State Shockers to a Division II college football championship, Ted Lasso (Jason Sudeikis) gets recruited to coach the *other* kind of football across the pond in this Golden Globe–winning Apple TV series. Though he's a fish out of water as a Premier League soccer club manager, Lasso proves his mettle as a top-notch sports mind and a genuine leader of men. That's not a bad résumé for a character that was originally created to be a one-note commercial mascot for NBC.

THE WHITE SHADOW (1978–1981)
The White Shadow was decades ahead of its time when it premiered in 1978. The hour-long drama focused on coach Ken Reeves (Ken Howard), a former NBA player and one of the only white members of the show's main cast, as he helped his inner-city high school basketball team navigate real-life issues like crime, drug use, and racial tension.

FRIENDS (1994–2004)

CREATED BY: David Crane and Marta Kauffman

SEASONS: 10

EPISODES: 236

OTHER SHOWS BY DAVID CRANE AND MARTA KAUFFMAN:
Dream On (1990–1996)
Veronica's Closet (1997–2000)

On September 22, 1994, *Friends* made its NBC debut and forever changed the face of American sitcoms. A group of friends—waitress Rachel Greene (Jennifer Aniston), chef Monica Geller (Courteney Cox), paleontologist and Monica's older brother Ross Geller (David Schwimmer), masseuse/musician Phoebe Buffay (Lisa Kudrow), struggling actor Joey Tribbiani (Matt LeBlanc), and corporate IT wonk Chandler Bing (Matthew Perry)—tries to make their way in New York City, but they mostly just hang out at their neighborhood café, Central Perk, or in Monica's enormous (and obviously rent-controlled) apartment to chat about their lives and make lots of nineties references that might go over younger viewers' heads entirely.

Though the premise of *Friends* was hardly groundbreaking, the show was popular enough to turn the six main actors into household names—and eventually some of the highest-paid actors in television history—and also helped a little magazine called *Mental Floss* (yep, that's us) find global recognition. Even today, *Friends* continues to find new fans thanks to the layer of nineties nostalgia that makes it oddly comforting to watch, even for first-time viewers.

THE ROLE OF ROSS GELLER WAS WRITTEN FOR DAVID SCHWIMMER.

This may come as a surprise, because Eric McCormack (best known as Will of *Will & Grace*) made news when he said that he auditioned "two or three times" for Ross. But executive producer Kevin Bright had worked with Schwimmer before, so the writers were already developing Ross's character in the actor's voice. And indeed, Schwimmer was the first person cast on the show.

THE CAST TOOK A TRIP TO LAS VEGAS TOGETHER BEFORE THE SHOW AIRED.

Pilot director James Burrows, who also went on to direct a handful of episodes for the show between 1994 and 1998, brought the six cast members to Vegas because he "had a feeling about the show." While they were at Caesar's Palace, he encouraged the group to enjoy themselves. "This is your last shot at anonymity," Burrows told them. "Once the show comes on the air, you guys will never be able to go anywhere without being hounded."

SPOILERS! CAESAR'S PALACE PLAYED AN IMPORTANT ROLE ON *FRIENDS* LATER ON.

Caesar's Palace played a key role in the fictional world of *Friends* as well. In "The One in Vegas," the season 5 finale, Joey is seen playing a gladiator at the Vegas hotel. This is, of course, the same episode in which Ross and Rachel get married in a drunken stupor and come stumbling out of a Vegas chapel while Monica and Chandler, who were about to get married, look on.

FRIENDS BY THE NUMBERS

5 ▷ 20

At the beginning of the series, Monica's door had the number 5 on it. The producers later realized that didn't make sense, as Monica lived on a higher floor. They changed her apartment number to 20. The number on Chandler's apartment changed as well—from 4 to 19.

4 ▷ 19

NONE OF THE SHOW'S STARS LOVED THE THEME SONG.

It's impossible to imagine *Friends* without also envisioning the opening credits, in which the cast members play in a fountain and dance along to the Rembrandts' "I'll Be There for You." But while appearing on *The One Show* in 2016, Aniston claimed that, "No one was really a big fan of that theme song." Then she appeared to backtrack: "I don't mean to say that. We felt it was a little, I don't know. Dancing in a . . . fountain felt sort of odd, but we did it."

SPOILERS! *FRIENDS* WAS FILMED IN FRONT OF A LIVE AUDIENCE, EXCEPT FOR CLIFF-HANGERS.

Shooting an episode of *Friends* was a lengthy process. Each typically lasted five hours, requiring multiple takes per scene and twenty minutes between shots to change sets. Still, the show was filmed in front of a live audience made up of three hundred fans—and that's the way the cast preferred it. "It's kind of like a test to see if the material works, if the jokes work, if the story tracks," LeBlanc said. Perry agreed: "Our energy just elevates every time there's an audience."

So what wasn't filmed in front of a live audience? One example is the cliff-hanger in the season 4 finale, "The One with Ross's Wedding." At the end of the episode, Ross is about to marry Emily, but accidentally says Rachel's name at the altar. "We couldn't have an audience for that," Aniston said. "We always remove the audience for the cliff-hangers because, obvious reasons, you don't want to spoil it."

FREEZE FRAME ▶

"THE ONE AFTER THE SUPERBOWL, PART 2" // SEASON 2, EPISODE 13

Ross's pet monkey, Marcel, was played by two monkeys: Monkey and Katie. Marcel was written out of the show in season 2 because it became too time-consuming to shoot scenes with a monkey. According to Katie's trainer, Nerissa Politzer, Monkey was once supposed to pick up a bra, but ended up throwing it at Aniston instead.

JAMES MICHAEL TYLER WAS WORKING AS A BARISTA WHEN HE WAS CAST AS GUNTHER.

In 2014, Tyler told BuzzFeed that he was working as a barista in real life at the Bourgeois Pig, a popular coffee shop in Hollywood, when he was cast on the show: "I was one of their first baristas—I think I started there in 1990 or so."

GUNTHER'S BLEACHED HAIR WAS ACCIDENTAL, BUT HE HAD TO KEEP IT FOR TEN YEARS.

In addition to being a real-life barista, Tyler's bleach-blonde hair was something he brought to the first day of shooting...which came back to haunt him. "I had a friend who wanted to be a hairdresser and wanted to practice bleaching someone's hair, so I offered what hair I had left at the time," Tyler told BuzzFeed. What he didn't expect was for his hair to turn white—the night before he was scheduled for his first day on set. As he was originally hired as a background actor, just to give the Central Perk set some authenticity, it didn't seem like a big deal...until his role became a recurring one. "I bleached my hair every week for ten years," Tyler said. "I did it myself after a while. It was just easier instead of coming in early to do it. I would just do it the night before."

THE ACTORS ON *FRIENDS* WERE THE FIRST TV CAST TO NEGOTIATE AS A GROUP.

During the first season, each cast member was receiving around $22,000 per episode. But allegedly, by the second season, each actor had a slightly different salary. In 1996, all six cast members refused to work until they each earned an equal salary of $100,000 per episode. This was big news. "Stars of hit shows often threaten to boycott their series in pursuit of higher salaries," *The New York Times* reported. "What is unusual is this cast's effort to use its solidarity as leverage."

This negotiation worked very well. By the final season, each cast member was earning $1 million per episode.

JOEY'S MAGNA DOODLE ART BECAME A JOB FOR THE CREW.

Over the years, a few crew members were responsible for drawing on the Magna Doodle on Joey's front door. But in the later seasons, it was primarily a job for Paul Swain, who was on the electrical crew.

The Magna Doodle became one of the show's stars. It sat right in the middle of Joey's door, so whenever a character walked through that door, the Magna Doodle was prominently displayed. Fans became obsessed with seeing what was written on the Magna Doodle in every scene shot in Joey's apartment. Unsurprisingly, LeBlanc had a soft spot for the Magna Doodle, too, and actually took it with him when the series ended. (He took the foosball table, too.) It even found a second life on his short-lived *Friends* spinoff, *Joey*.

THE IDENTITY OF "UGLY NAKED GUY" WASN'T DISCOVERED UNTIL 2016.

A dozen years after the series finale of *Friends* aired, intrepid HuffPost reporter Todd Van Luling finally uncovered the identity of the man who played "Ugly Naked Guy" on the show. The character—who lived in the apartment across from Monica and Rachel—was frequently referenced, but only ever appeared on the show twice, and in neither of those appearances was his face visible. But after a year of research, Van Luling finally had his answer: Ugly Naked Guy was likely an extra named Jon Haugen.

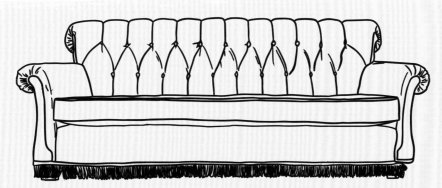

Watching Friends Could Help Ease Your Anxiety

They'll be there for you . . . especially when you're stressed out. In 2019, London-based clinical psychologist Marc Hekster told *Metro* that watching *Friends* could help to alleviate one's anxiety. "[A]mong other factors, it is the repetitive and relational nature of programs such as *Friends* and [*The*] *Big Bang Theory* that will be doing the trick," Hekster said of the healing properties of a show like *Friends*, which both sets up a problem and solves it in just thirty minutes or less.

According to Hekster, part of the reason for the psychological relief one can find in *Friends* is the predictability that, no matter the issues the characters are facing, they'll be back to their happy-go-lucky selves by the end of the episode. Watching *Friends*, Hekster says, "is about an experience of repair, of watching the characters in the show repeatedly having worries, which then get repaired and soothed, usually in the context of other relationships in their lives." Which means that while you might be feeling anxious about your relationship with your significant other or the dwindling dollars in your bank account, watching Monica keep it all together—and doing so with a sense of humor and dash of nineties style—can make you feel better. Kind of like magic!

"On the negative side," Hekster says of the downside of escaping into the world of Central Perk, "none of it is very real, and how can life ever be so . . . kind of perfect? It can't."

"THE ONE WITH THE SOAP OPERA PARTY" // **SEASON 9, EPISODE 20**

In this 2003 episode, Monica can be seen casually reading a new magazine called *Mental Floss* while hanging out at Central Perk. We really owe David Arquette a lifetime of gratitude, because he's the one who made it happen. "I thought it was so interesting," Arquette told *Entertainment Weekly* at the time, "[so] I gave it to [Courteney]."

ANISTON ALMOST DIDN'T RETURN FOR THE LAST SEASON.
By the time the show ended, Aniston was arguably the most famous cast member, thanks to films like *The Good Girl* and *Bruce Almighty*. Her then-husband Brad Pitt didn't hurt her celebrity status, either. With that fame came rumors that she had almost been responsible for the show ending prematurely. In a 2004 interview, Aniston admitted that she had hesitations. "I had a couple issues that I was dealing with," she said. "I wanted it to end when people still loved us and we were on a high. And then I was also feeling like, 'How much more of Rachel do I have in me?'" She eventually agreed to the final season.

Best Friends

In a 2016 survey by Comedy Central, *Friends* fans in the UK were asked to vote for their favorite cast member. Ross Geller came out on top with 25.6 percent of the vote, just edging out Chandler Bing, whom 25.4 percent named as their favorite Friend.

10

MOST-WATCHED TV SERIES FINALES EVER

Over the past several years, television audiences have said goodbye to some of the most acclaimed television series of all time, from *Game of Thrones* to *Breaking Bad*. And while their finales have made a lot of headlines, publicity doesn't always translate to eyeballs on the screen. These shows received both; here are the ten most-watched finales of all time, ranked by number of viewers.

1 M*A*S*H
105.9 million

In 1983, nearly 106 million viewers watched the Alan Alda–directed "Goodbye, Farewell and Amen" episode of *M*A*S*H*, which was not only the most-watched series finale ever, but the most-watched single-network television event ever—until 2010, when the Super Bowl topped it with 106 million viewers

2 Cheers
80.4 million

After eleven seasons, *Cheers* decided it was closing time. The final episode, "One for the Road" (which actually aired in two parts in 1993), featured the return of Shelley Long's Diane Chambers and drew a whopping number of viewers.

SPOILERS!

3 The Fugitive
78 million

Andrew Davis's 1993 film version of *The Fugitive* may have won an Oscar (for Tommy Lee Jones as Best Supporting Actor), but its original TV version has some major accolades as well. In 1967, an estimated 78 million people across the country tuned in to watch part two of the finale and see what would happen to Richard Kimble (David Janssen), the physician wrongly accused of murdering his wife. (He was exonerated.)

4 Seinfeld
76.3 million

One could safely estimate that at least half of the viewers who tuned in for *Seinfeld*'s finale in 1998 were sorely disappointed with what they saw. One critic deemed it a big "So long, suckers!" farewell to the audience who had made the show about nothing such a big hit.

5 Friends
52.5 million

Would Rachel and Ross live happily ever after? Could Chandler and Monica make it work in the suburbs? And where has Phoebe's "Smelly Cat" been? More than 50 million viewers tuned in to find out when *Friends* came to a conclusion in 2004.

6 Magnum, P.I.
50.7 million

Is Higgins really Robin Masters? What really happened to Lily? Will Rick get married? In 1988, more than 50 million other people wanted to know the answers to those questions, too.

SPOILERS!

7 The Cosby Show
44.4 million

In 1992, Theo graduated from NYU and Denise returned via phone to reveal her pregnancy. But the real shocker was when Cliff finally got the doorbell to work properly after he had been trying to fix it all season.

8 All in the Family
40.2 million

In 1979, more than 40 million viewers watched as Archie professed his love for an ailing Edith.

9 Family Ties
36.3 million

Some 36 million viewers tuned in to see if Alex would take his dream job in New York and leave the Keaton family in 1989.

10 Home Improvement
35.5 million

In 1999, *Home Improvement* edged out *Frasier* (#11), *Dallas* (#12), and *Everybody Loves Raymond* (#15) to crack the top ten.

10 Beloved Shows with Divisive Final Seasons

Pulling off a great series finale is no easy feat, as hundreds of showrunners and TV writers have learned the hard way. Just because a final episode manages to attract millions of eyeballs doesn't mean that viewers are loving what they're seeing. And while it's often that very final episode that bears the brunt of the love (or hate) that is talked about in postmortem TV discussions, the final season as a whole plays a major part in the lead-up to those final moments. Here are 10 shows that, according to their Rotten Tomatoes scores, amassed loyal followings . . . only to disappoint in their final seasons—sometimes to the point where fans actually felt betrayed by the creators (we're looking at you, *Game of Thrones*).

Arrested Development // (2003–2019)
FINAL SEASON RATING: **55%**

Game of Thrones // (2011–2019)
FINAL SEASON RATING: **54%**

Sherlock // (2010–2017)
FINAL SEASON RATING: **54%**

UnREAL // (2015–2018)
FINAL SEASON RATING: **50%**

Prison Break // (2005–2017)
FINAL SEASON RATING: **50%**

The Killing // (2011–2014)
FINAL SEASON RATING: **47%**

Entourage // (2004–2011)
FINAL SEASON RATING: **46%**

True Blood // (2008–2014)
FINAL SEASON RATING: **44%**

Weeds // (2005–2012)
FINAL SEASON RATING: **40%**

Dexter // (2006–2013)
FINAL SEASON RATING: **33%**

GAME OF THRONES

(2011—2019)

CREATED BY: David Benioff and D. B. Weiss
(based on George R. R. Martin's
A Song of Ice and Fire book series)

SEASONS: 8

EPISODES: 73

RIP on *GOT*

Injuries—specifically wounds to the head and neck region—were the most likely cause of death on the series until the end of season 7, while burning (a.k.a. the chief way to kill a wight, and a punishment Daenerys's dragons are very skilled at inflicting) was the second most common way to be knocked off.

Based on A Song of Ice and Fire, the fantasy book series by George R. R. Martin, *Game of Thrones* is a brilliantly realized epic detailing a power struggle that pits various factions against one another for the fate of the mysterious land of Westeros. Multiple plot threads are woven together to form a tapestry of violence, deception, and infighting, with a colorful army of characters that will either delight or disgust you (or maybe a bit of both).

The *Game of Thrones* cast is highlighted by breakout performances by Peter Dinklage, Emilia Clarke, Kit Harington, Maisie Williams, Sophie Turner, and Lena Headey, but though be cautious when getting attached to any of the show's characters. Author George R. R. Martin and showrunners David Benioff and D. B. Weiss had no problem killing off even the most beloved characters. Even if you're not a fan of high fantasy, the familial struggles and blockbuster action should be more than enough to keep you hooked.

THERE'S AN UNAIRED *GAME OF THRONES* PILOT.
The first pilot was so terrible it had to be shelved and reshot. "We got everything wrong on a very basic level with the writing of it," Benioff told *Variety*. One of the biggest problems? None of the friends he and Weiss invited to watch the pilot "realized that Jaime and Cersei were brother and sister, which is a major, major plot point that we had somehow failed to establish."

CATELYN STARK AND DAENERYS TARGARYEN WERE ORIGINALLY PLAYED BY OTHER ACTORS.
In the original pilot, Catelyn Stark and Daenerys Targaryen were played by Jennifer Ehle and Tamzin Merchant, respectively. By the time the show aired, they had been replaced by Michelle Fairley and Emilia Clarke.

ARYA STARK WAS THE HARDEST ROLE TO CAST.
While attending SXSW in 2017, Benioff recalled, "We probably looked at three hundred different young girls in England and could not find the right Arya."

They found Maisie Williams while going through audition videos in a Moroccan hotel lobby with bad Wi-Fi, and selected her video based on a small thumbnail that looked promising. "There was just something about that little tiny thumbnail face that seemed right," Benioff said. "We thought she was seven…So we clicked on the audition video and had to wait about forty minutes for it to download. And we finally saw her first audition for it and she was fucking awesome."

FREEZE FRAME

"A GOLDEN CROWN" // SEASON 1, EPISODE 6
The horse heart Daenerys had to eat was essentially a giant gummy candy—one that, per Emilia Clarke, tasted a little bit like bleach. (It also had pasta running through it to mimic arteries.) She ate twenty-eight hearts, and apparently did a lot of puking between takes. To make the proceedings even grosser, all the fake blood made Clarke so sticky that she got stuck to a toilet.

THE SHOW'S NUDITY WAS DIFFICULT FOR CLARKE.

Though Daenerys Targaryen turned out to be a career-changing role for Clarke, the actress admitted that her early days on set weren't easy. On her very first day of filming, she fell off a horse in front of the crew and, humiliated, cried. Plus, there was all the nudity required of her character—not to mention an infamous rape scene. "Once, I had to take a little time out," she told *Esquire* of filming the first season. "I said I needed a cup of tea, had a bit of a cry, and was ready for the next scene."

SOPHIE TURNER ADOPTED SANSA STARK'S DIREWOLF.

Turner, who played Sansa Stark, adopted Zunni, the Northern Inuit dog that played her pet direwolf on the series' first season. "Growing up I always wanted a dog, but my parents never wanted one," Turner told *Coventry Telegraph* in 2013. "We kind of fell in love with my character's direwolf, Lady, on set…My mum persuaded them to let us adopt her." Sadly, Zunni reportedly passed away in 2017.

SPOILERS! THE INTERNET SPOILED ROBB STARK'S FATE FOR RICHARD MADDEN.

While readers of the book series knew that Robb Stark's days were probably numbered on *Game of Thrones*, Madden—the actor who played him—decided to keep himself in the dark about the books as part of his preparation for the television role. But that didn't stop fans, or the internet, from telling the actor that his reign as King in the North would be short-lived.

"A thousand people spoiled it for me before I had a chance to pick up the third book," Madden told *Entertainment Weekly*. "I read [the books] season-by-season. I don't want to preempt where Robb is going and that's what I've done since the show started. I also made the fatal flaw of Googling. So that kind of reinforced what people were hinting—saying that something terrible was going to happen and giggling."

THE OFFICE'S DWIGHT SCHRUTE INFLUENCED DOTHRAKI.

In a 2012 episode of *The Office*, Dwight Schrute was teaching Dothraki and combined an accusative noun and a transitive verb to create the phrase *throat rip*. Linguist David Peterson, who worked with HBO to create the Dothraki language, hadn't considered doing that, but he liked it so much that he canonized it and called it a "Schrutean compound."

THE WHITE WALKERS HAD THEIR OWN LANGUAGE.

Peterson called that language Skroth. "It was actually going to be for the very first scene of the show where the White Walker comes and cuts that guy's head off. There are parts where you hear them kind of grumble and vocalize," Peterson said in 2015.

Ultimately, Skroth was scrapped because, according to Peterson, "I think ultimately they decided they didn't want them actually saying stuff and even subtitle it. That might have been a little corny, honestly, for the opening scene of the show." For season 2, a sound designer created an ice-cracking sound that finally brought Skroth to life, albeit without an actual language behind the sounds.

FREEZE FRAME

"BREAKER OF CHAINS" // SEASON 4, EPISODE 3
The unnamed Meereenese warrior who shouts a series of taunts at Daenerys is clearly a Monty Python fan. Among the insults that he hurls at her are lines taken directly from the iconic British comedy troupe, including: "Your mother was a hamster," "Go and boil your bottoms, sons of a silly person," and "I blow my nose at you"…in Low Valyrian, of course.

GAME OF THRONES BY THE NUMBERS

In the year 2014, per the Social Security Administration, Khaleesi was the United States's **755th** most popular baby name for girls, up from **1,021th** place in 2013. In England, Khaleesi, Arya, Tyrion, Brienne, Sansa, Bran, Sandor, and Theon also saw a rise in popularity after *Game of Thrones* began airing.

(What, no Dagmer Cleftjaw?)

JON SNOW'S CAPE FROM THE NIGHT'S WATCH WAS MADE FROM AN IKEA RUG.

Game of Thrones owes much of the credit for its characters' iconic looks to costume designer Michele Clapton, who oversaw a team of anywhere from seventy to one hundred costumers each season. In what might be the greatest testament to the costume team's creativity, Clapton revealed that several of the show's luxurious-looking capes are made from IKEA rugs. "We take anything we can; we cut and we shave them and then we added strong leather straps," she said. Following this admission, IKEA created a set of instructions for how to turn your SKOLD rug into a cape.

SPOILERS! JACKHAMMERS, BISON, AND SCREAMING FANS WERE AMONG THE NOISES USED TO CREATE THE DRAGONS' SOUND DESIGN.

Sound designer Paula Fairfield, who joined *Game of Thrones* in season 3, used many different techniques to create the sounds of the dragons. Among them were Tibetan chants and vocalizations from bison and her own dog. She used a jackhammer, screaming *Game of Thrones* fans, and dangling bones, among other things, to create the sound of Zombie Viserion.

THE TREES LINING THE KINGSROAD MIGHT NOT BE AROUND MUCH LONGER.

People have long flocked to Northern Ireland to explore the enchanting Dark Hedges, but the scenic location's appearance in season 2 of *Game of Thrones* really put the attraction on the map. Visitors who walk down the "Kingsroad" these days may notice something amiss, though. In 2019, powerful winds uprooted one of Ballymoney's famous beech trees, which have been a prominent feature of the town since the eighteenth century. There were once 150 beech trees at the site, but only sixty to ninety trees are still standing today, according to different estimates. Some fell victim to past storms, while others suffer from rot.

ONE ACTOR PLAYED FIVE CHARACTERS IN *GAME OF THRONES*.

Welsh actor and stunt performer Ian Whyte played a grand total of five roles. In seasons 1 and 2 he was a White Walker; also in season 2, he played Gregor Clegane (one of three actors to play that role). Whyte—who is more than seven feet tall—has played a giant many times. In seasons 3 and 4, he played Dongo the Doomed; in seasons 5 and 6, he was Wun Wun; and finally, in seasons 7 and 8, he played the unnamed wight giant taken down by Lyanna Mormont.

KIT HARINGTON NEEDED A SAFE WORD WHILE FILMING THE BATTLE OF THE BASTARDS.

In a behind-the-scenes featurette, longtime *Game of Thrones* camera operator Sean Savage shared that his very favorite scene to film over eight seasons was the moment during the Battle of the Bastards "when Jon Snow is forced to the ground and then trampled. And this seemingly immortal hero of ours looks like he's close to the end."

When Harington fell to the ground, Savage stood over him and filmed from above as tons of stuntmen piled on top of the actor. The scene wasn't entirely scripted, so in order to ensure that Harington wouldn't be injured, "we had a sort of safe word [so] that we could call it off at any point," Savage said.

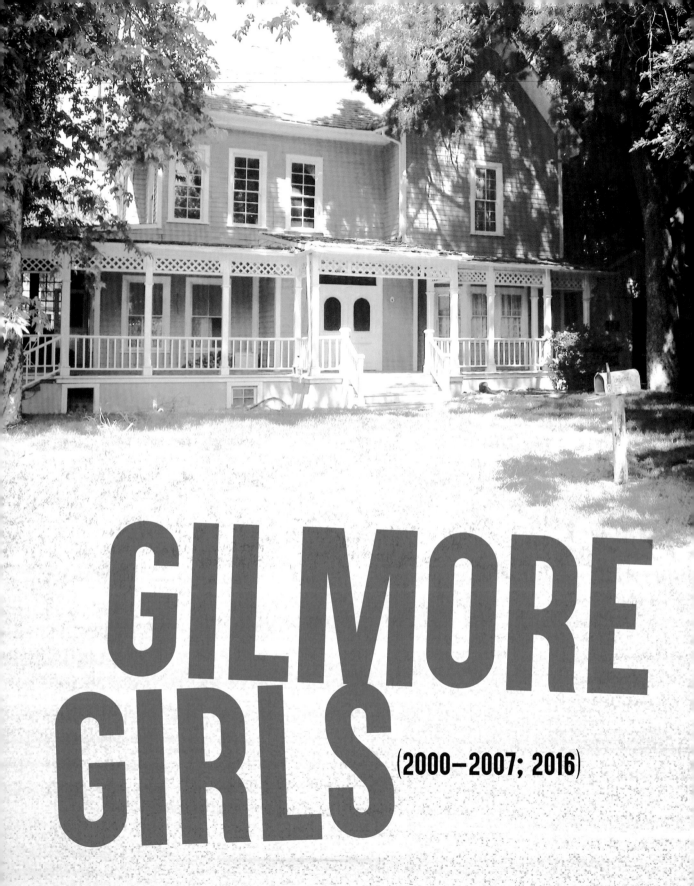

GILMORE GIRLS

(2000–2007; 2016)

CREATED BY: Amy Sherman-Palladino

SEASONS: 8

EPISODES: 157

OTHER SHOWS BY AMY SHERMAN-PALLADINO:
Bunheads (2012–2013)
The Marvelous Mrs. Maisel (2017–PRESENT)

For viewers with a high tolerance for caffeine and fast talking, *Gilmore Girls* presents an idyllic slice of small-town New England life. Lauren Graham plays Lorelai Gilmore, the unconventional single mom who defected from her upper-crust upbringing after getting pregnant at sixteen. Her daughter, Rory, played by Alexis Bledel, is much more studious and soft-spoken, but she shares her mother's love of coffee and pop culture.

Just as loveable as the main mother-daughter duo is the show's robust ensemble, which includes the quirky residents of the town of Stars Hollow, Lorelai's wealthy and out-of-touch parents, and Rory and Lorelai's numerous love interests (Team Jess forever). *Gilmore Girls* also introduced us to creator Amy Sherman-Palladino's rapid-fire brand of humor, which she has since recreated in *Bunheads* and *The Marvelous Mrs. Maisel*. But to fans of her first show, no characters have exemplified the art of gab quite like the Gilmores.

THE SHOW WAS INSPIRED BY A TRIP THAT CREATOR AMY SHERMAN-PALLADINO WAS ON.

The trip took her through the small town of Washington, Connecticut, where she stayed at an inn. "We're driving by, and people are slowing down saying, 'Excuse me, where is the pumpkin patch?'" she recalled. "And everything is green and people are out, and they're talking. And we went to a diner and everyone knew each other and someone got up and they walked behind the [counter] and they got their own coffee because the waitress was busy." Within twenty-four hours, she had worked out the show and written some of the pilot's dialogue.

ALEXIS BLEDEL HAD NEVER ACTED BEFORE SHE WAS CAST AS RORY GILMORE.

Bledel's only role at the time was as an uncredited extra in Wes Anderson's *Rushmore*. She was a student at NYU who was modeling part-time when she decided to try her luck and audition for the show. Other jobs she was applying for at the time: waitress and census taker.

ALEX BORSTEIN WAS ORIGINALLY CAST AS SOOKIE.

In 2019, Borstein took home the Emmy for Outstanding Supporting Actress in a Comedy Series for her work with Sherman-Palladino on *The Marvelous Mrs. Maisel*, but the two could have collaborated much more closely much earlier. Borstein was originally cast in the role of Sookie on *Gilmore Girls*, but had to turn down the part due to her work on *MadTV*. Melissa McCarthy ended up with the role. Borstein did end up making a few appearances as the harpist Drella, though.

FAST TALKING WAS ONE OF THE SHOW'S HALLMARKS.

In most series, one page of a screenplay accounts for about one minute of screen time. But for *Gilmore Girls* scripts, one page equaled about twenty to twenty-five seconds. There were also fewer close-ups than on shows with regular pacing, and they often reshot scenes to lose a mere few seconds of time.

THE CAST DIDN'T ALWAYS UNDERSTAND THE POP CULTURE REFERENCES, BUT THEY WENT WITH THEM.

"We'd have to look them up on our own typically," Bledel told *Entertainment Weekly*. "There were no explanations written in the script." Graham recalled Bledel asking her who the Waltons were and thinking, "I'm so old."

SPOILERS! SHERMAN-PALLADINO WROTE JESS ONTO THE SHOW SO THAT LORELAI AND LUKE HAD YET ANOTHER REASON NOT TO DATE EACH OTHER YET.

"We're dealing with two people who, if they just opened their eyes and stared across the table at each other, would go, 'Oh shit, it's you,'" Sherman-Palladino explained of Lorelai and Luke's will-they-or-won't-they chemistry. "So when you're playing that game, you have to find obstacles that are real to put in their way.'"

NORMAN MAILER MADE A CAMEO.

The Naked and the Dead author appeared in the season 5 episode "Norman Mailer, I'm Pregnant!" Originally, the script simply called for a well-known author. They asked Mailer, who initially said no—until the show asked his son to take a part as well. "I told them I couldn't memorize any lines; it had to be improvisation," Mailer told *New York* magazine in 2004. "The hard part was having to repeat things over and over."

SEBASTIAN BACH OF SKID ROW ALSO APPEARED ON THE SHOW.

Bach played Lane's bandmate Gil. "When I got the call, I was like, 'Do you guys have the

FREEZE FRAME

"HERE COMES THE SON" // SEASON 3, EPISODE 21

In 2003, one season after Jess (Milo Ventimiglia) first appeared on *Gilmore Girls*, there was talk of a spin-off for his character. This third season episode served as a kind of backdoor pilot (the term for using one or more episodes of a popular series to try to launch a brand-new spin-off series), which would have been called *Windward Circle*. Ultimately, the WB determined that it was too expensive to shoot in Venice Beach, where the show would have been set, and so progress stalled.

right phone number?'" he told *TV Guide*. "They wanted a 'rock star' to [play] the guitar player [in Lane's band] and [the casting director saw me on] VH1's *I Love the '70s*."

SHERMAN-PALLADINO LEFT THE SHOW BEFORE THE SEVENTH SEASON.

In 2006, Sherman-Palladino and her husband and creative partner Daniel Palladino released a statement that said, "Despite our best efforts to return and ensure the future of *Gilmore Girls* for years to come, we were unable to reach an agreement with the studio and are therefore leaving when our contracts expire at the end of this season." Later, she explained that she was particularly frustrated that the CW wouldn't allow the pair to hire more writers.

SPOILERS! IN 2016, LORELAI AND RORY CAME BACK TO TELEVISION SCREENS.

In 2016, Sherman-Palladino got the chance to write another chapter for the *Gilmore Girls* when she and her husband wrote and directed *Gilmore Girls: A Year in the Life*, a four-episode Netflix miniseries that caught up with Lorelai and Rory. It also allowed Sherman-Palladino to finally write that four-word ending she had long had in mind for the women: Rory telling her mom that she is pregnant. Though she said them nearly ten years later than Sherman-Palladino had initially intended, she thinks it worked out for the better.

"They both work on their own, because the purpose of leaving Rory in this position was always supposed to be that history repeats itself—daughter follows mother; where you lead I will follow. And that life throws you curveballs that you don't expect," Sherman-Palladino told *Vogue* in 2016. "So it works either way. One, is that she's just gotten out of college and she wants to start her life. And the other way is that she's older but she also thinks she's just figured out what her path is going to be, and she gets this curveball. I like it much better this way than that way, but who knew at the time?"

DEFUNCT SHOWS THAT WERE BROUGHT BACK FROM THE DEAD

Stars Hollow hadn't changed much when viewers revisited the dreamy Connecticut town in 2016 for *Gilmore Girls: A Year in the Life*. Thanks to Netflix, and a still-vibrant fan base looking to catch up with Lorelai and Rory, *Gilmore Girls* joined the ranks of other defunct TV classics that were (briefly) revived.

24: LEGACY
(2017)

From 2001 to 2010 (and again in 2014), Fox viewers got an intimate, action-packed look into the daily life of counter terrorist agent Jack Bauer (Kiefer Sutherland). The clock began ticking again—though this time for a new lead actor, Corey Hawkins—in 2017, when *24: Legacy* premiered.

ARRESTED DEVELOPMENT
(2013–2018)

The Bluth family's loss was comedy lovers' gain from 2003 to 2006, when fans followed the dysfunctional clan's attempts to navigate their downfall. The family returned to the screen in 2013 and again from 2018 to 2019 when Netflix rebooted *Arrested Development*.

FULLER HOUSE
(2016–2020)

Nineties kids basically grew up alongside the Tanner bunch. In 2016, D. J. Tanner (Candace Cameron Bure), a teen in the original, took the lead in the reboot as a widowed mom to three kids, helped of course by the members of her own full house.

TWIN PEAKS: THE RETURN
(2017)

The original *Twin Peaks* may have only lasted from 1990 to 1991, but that didn't stop the campy horror show from becoming a cult classic. Diehard fans were in for a treat when a third season appeared on Showtime in 2017.

VERONICA MARS
(2019)

Teenage sleuth Veronica Mars (Kristen Bell) began solving crimes in 2004. A grown Mars returned to the screen for a tragedy-packed, eight-episode revival in 2019.

WILL & GRACE
(2017–2020)

Will & Grace was a staple sitcom during the early 2000s. Dynamic duo Will Truman and Grace Adler (Eric McCormack and Debra Messing), along with sassy series favorites Jack McFarland (Sean Hayes) and Karen Walker (Megan Mullally) returned to TV for three seasons beginning in 2017.

GLEE

(2009–2015)

CREATED BY: Ryan Murphy, Brad Falchuk, and Ian Brennan

SEASONS: 6

EPISODES: 121

OTHER SHOWS BY RYAN MURPHY, BRAD FALCHUK, AND IAN BRENNAN:
Scream Queens (2015–2016)
The Politician (2019–PRESENT)

On May 19, 2009, a group of fictional high school misfits sang their way into the hearts of viewers across America when *Glee* previewed its pilot episode following the penultimate episode of *American Idol*'s eighth season (its first season officially kicked off about four months later). Co-created by Ryan Murphy, Ian Brennan, and Brad Falchuk, *Glee* was an instant smash.

After Will Schuester (Matthew Morrison) takes over McKinley High's show choir, New Directions, from a disgraced teacher, he recruits Rachel Berry (Lea Michele), Mercedes Jones (Amber Riley), Kurt Hummel (Chris Colfer), Artie Abrams (Kevin McHale), Tina Cohen-Chang (Jenna Ushkowitz), and Finn Hudson (Cory Monteith). Over the next six seasons, New Directions tries to achieve bigger and bigger goals—like beating rival glee clubs to compete at nationals—despite the interference of cheerleaders Quinn Fabray (Dianna Agron), Brittany S. Pierce (Heather Morris), and Santana Lopez (Naya Rivera) and their coach, Sue Sylvester (Jane Lynch).

Though sometimes derided for its over-the-top story lines, especially in later seasons, *Glee* also tackled serious issues like teen pregnancy, homophobia, domestic violence, cyberbullying, and eating disorders. The show became a bona fide phenomenon, winning numerous accolades, sending multiple songs to the *Billboard* charts, and turning its young actors into stars. Today, *Glee*'s legacy is decidedly complicated, but its standing as a cultural force of the early 2000s can't be denied.

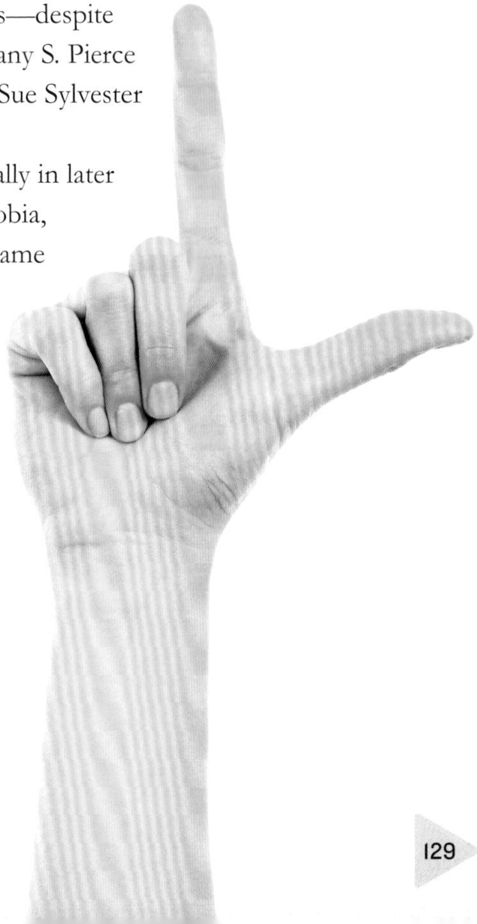

THE AUDITIONS FOR *GLEE* DIDN'T GO SMOOTHLY FOR MANY OF THE MAIN CAST MEMBERS.

Lea Michele totaled her car on the way to the *Glee* audition and walked in with glass in her hair; then the pianist flubbed her audition song ("On My Own" from *Les Misérables*). "The piano player skipped through the second verse," she later recalled. "So right in the middle of my song, I was like, 'Excuse me!' . . . Very Rachel Berry!" (Ryan Murphy had actually written the role specifically for Michele, who had been performing on Broadway for years.) Former boy-band member Kevin McHale auditioned by singing "Let It Be," but didn't know any more of the words when the casting director asked him to keep going. Jenna Ushkowitz sang a portion of "Waiting for Life" from the musical *Once on This Island*, to which she said the casting director responded, "Maybe you should think of a better cut next time." Dianna Agron, meanwhile, was the last actor to be cast—the night before filming began.

KURT HUMMEL WASN'T A CHARACTER UNTIL CHRIS COLFER CAME ALONG.

Chris Colfer originally auditioned for the role of Artie with "Mr. Cellophane" from *Chicago*. He didn't land the role—it went to McHale instead—but Murphy was inspired to create Kurt, a bullied, theater-loving gay teen, based on Colfer's background and experiences. The new character (who was named "Artie 2" in Colfer's contract) replaced an Indian character named Rajesh.

PRODUCERS WANTED A COLDPLAY SONG FOR THE PILOT, BUT COULDN'T GET IT.

According to music producer Adam Anders, the show didn't have much trouble clearing rights for music, not even at first. But there was an exception. Initially, producers wanted Coldplay's "Viva la Vida" to be the song that New Directions sings in the climactic performance of the show's pilot, but Coldplay wouldn't agree to it—so the show went with Journey's "Don't Stop Believin'" instead.

"I think it was meant to be," Anders told the *Los Angeles Times* of the Journey classic, which was featured on the series six times and became the show's first hit song (it reached number four on the charts in the US). "Don't Stop Believin'," according to Anders, "became the show. I don't think ['Viva la Vida'] would have been close to as good." When Coldplay eventually granted the show the rights to use its catalog in 2010, *Glee* covered "The Scientist" in its season 4 episode "The Break Up."

NO ONE EXPECTED *GLEE* TO BE A HIT.

In summer 2009, Murphy headed to Bali to shoot *Eat Pray Love* with Julia Roberts. Glee made its debut while he was there, and became an instant hit. When he came back, Murphy said it was like something out of

Beatlemania. "It was so crazy, like you could not go out with those kids," he said. It was so successful that the cast later went on tour and even shot a concert movie.

THOSE WERE REAL SLUSHIES BEING THROWN AT THE *GLEE* KIDS.

A running gag in *Glee* features the popular kids flinging slushies at the members of New Directions, and the show's production team opted to use the real thing when filming. "It literally takes the air out [of you]," Michele told Jimmy Fallon in 2010. "It's so cold I have to, like, recover for days." Beyond the initial shock, Michele said the drinks stained her body, and "the only way to get it off is to cover yourself with Gillette shaving cream."

BRITTANY AND SANTANA GOT SPOILERS! TOGETHER BECAUSE OF *GLEE*'S FANS.

Glee was known for its groundbreaking portrayal of gay relationships, including Kurt and Blaine (aka "Klaine") and Brittany and Santana (or "Brittana"). At first, producers meant for Brittany and Santana to simply be best friends, but the show's fans wanted them to get together, and they weren't quiet about it. "We sort of took it lightly at first," Rivera told *Vanity Fair* in 2011. "But then we thought it was something people really wanted us to do, that it was something we should tackle." Brittany and Santana dated—secretly, at first, as Santana struggled with being a lesbian and coming out to her family—broke up, got back together, and, eventually, got married.

Rivera's portrayal of Santana was lauded, and the character herself was a breakthrough. As Jarrett Barrios, then president of GLAAD, noted in 2011, her story was "one that hasn't been told on a prime-time network television show at that level, particularly by an LGBT teen of color." (Tragically, Rivera died in an accidental drowning in July 2020—almost seven years to the day that her Glee co-star, Cory Monteith, died from a lethal combination of heroin and alcohol on July 13, 2013.)

THE CAST DIDN'T HAVE MUCH TIME TO RECORD SONGS OR LEARN CHOREOGRAPHY.

When *Glee* first started, its stars, music producers, and choreographers were able to take their time recording songs and learning dances. That changed as the show got more and more popular. "We used to spend a whole day on one song. Now we have thirty minutes," Anders told *The Hollywood Reporter* in 2011, noting that he and his team were working on as many as ten songs at a time, literally around the clock (when he went to bed, his partner in Sweden would pick up where he had left off). "We finished a song in a day once, 'The Living Years,' but I don't ever want to do that again. That was awful." That same year, assistant choreographer Brooke Lipton told *Us Weekly* that "we're learning numbers in an hour, and they're performing, because time is so limited with the show rolling along."

THE SHOW ATTRACTED SOME A-LIST GUEST STARS.

The number of A-list stars who appeared on *Glee* is huge: *Wicked* star Kristin Chenoweth played a drunken classmate of Mr. Schuester's, while *Wicked*'s other star, Idina Menzel, played a rival glee club coach. (So did rapper Eve.) Gwyneth Paltrow appeared in several episodes as substitute teacher Holly Holliday. (Paltrow married *Glee* co-creator Brad Falchuk in 2018—four years after they met on the set of the show.) Gloria

Estefan played Santana's mom; Ken Jeong and Jennifer Coolidge were Brittany's parents; Jeff Goldblum and Brian Stokes Mitchell played Rachel's dads. Pop stars like Ricky Martin, Demi Lovato, and Adam Lambert also popped in. Britney Spears and Lindsay Lohan made cameos. Patti Lupone played herself.

SOME OF THE CAST DID MORE THAN JUST ACT IN THE SHOW.

Matthew Morrison made his directorial debut with *Glee*'s 2011 Christmas episode. Colfer wrote the season 5 episode "Old Dog, New Tricks." And Darren Criss, who played Blaine Anderson, wrote the series finale song, "This Time," for Michele to sing.

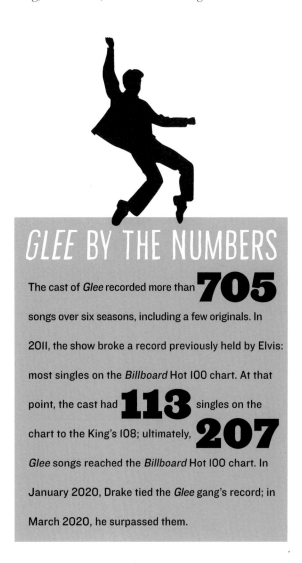

GLEE BY THE NUMBERS

The cast of *Glee* recorded more than **705** songs over six seasons, including a few originals. In 2011, the show broke a record previously held by Elvis: most singles on the *Billboard* Hot 100 chart. At that point, the cast had **113** singles on the chart to the King's 108; ultimately, **207** *Glee* songs reached the *Billboard* Hot 100 chart. In January 2020, Drake tied the *Glee* gang's record; in March 2020, he surpassed them.

7 GREAT TV SHOWS FOR MUSIC LOVERS

The popularity of *Glee* supports what musical fanatics have been trying to convince us of for decades: that it's actually very cool when people break into song in the middle of a program. If mash-ups of "Singin' in the Rain" and Rihanna's "Umbrella" still aren't quite your thing (or even if they are), here are seven other shows with ovation-worthy musical performances.

1 *Crazy Ex-Girlfriend* (2015–2019)

Creator and star Rachel Bloom turns all your inner thoughts about modern relationships into rousing musical numbers—e.g, "Research Me Obsessively" and "You're My Best Friend (And I Know I'm Not Yours)"—in this series about a New York lawyer who relocates to the California town where her high school boyfriend "just happens" to live.

2 *Empire* (2015–2020)

Family alliances are forged and betrayed against a backdrop of chart-worthy original R & B songs as Terrence Howard's Lucious Lyon decides which son should inherit his record label. His wife, Cookie's (Taraji P. Henson), recent release from prison complicates the process (but makes the series especially entertaining).

3 *Flight of the Conchords* (2007–2009)

Jemaine Clement and Bret McKenzie are Flight of the Conchords—a band that used to be "New Zealand's fourth most popular guitar-based digi-bongo acapella-rap-funk-comedy folk duo" but are now "the almost award-winning fourth-most-popular folk duo in New Zealand." They're also the stars of this delightfully absurd comedy where the slightest observation or most mundane conversation can turn into a surprisingly catchy tune like "Too Many Dicks (on the Dance Floor)."

4 *Mozart in the Jungle* (2014–2018)

Inspired by oboist Blair Tindall's eponymous memoir, *Mozart in the Jungle* is a clash between stuffy traditionalism and mercurial innovation in the fictional New York Symphony. Classical music may put some people to sleep, but the spirited musicians (led by Lola Kirke and Gael García Bernal) in this series most definitely will not.

5 *Nashville* (2012–2018)

Aging country music queen Rayna Jaymes (Connie Britton) fights tooth and perfectly lacquered nail to keep a sought-after new singer (Hayden Panettiere) from eclipsing her stardom. *Nashville* is both a fascinating look at the Nashville music scene and a CMT music video come to life.

6 *Smash* (2012–2013)

For the casual viewer, *Smash* is a drama about a bunch of triple threats jockeying for roles in new Broadway musicals. For musical theater buffs, it's more about recognizing the many familiar Broadway faces who appear in the show: Christian Borle, Annaleigh Ashford, and Leslie Odom, Jr., to name a few.

7 *Zoey's Extraordinary Playlist* (2020–PRESENT)

After an MRI goes awry, Zoey Clarke (Jane Levy) finds herself able to read minds—but people's thoughts are presented as full-fledged musical numbers. Hilarity ensues, as do a lot of unwitting emotional confessions that sound just like your favorite pop songs.

GOSSIP GIRL

(2007–2012)

CREATED BY: Josh Schwartz and Stephanie Savage (based on the book series by Cecily von Ziegesar)

SEASONS: 6

EPISODES: 121

OTHER SHOWS BY JOSH SCHWARTZ AND STEPHANIE SAVAGE:
The O.C. (2003–2007)
Runaways (2017–2019)
Dynasty (2017–PRESENT)
Nancy Drew (2019–PRESENT)

On September 19, 2007, just a few months after Josh Schwartz's *The O.C.* squeezed the last bit of life out of its nighttime teen soap domination, Schwartz teamed up with Stephanie Savage (a writer and producer on *The O.C.*) to swap the beachy vibes of California for the front steps of the Met and *Gossip Girl*. The series quickly became appointment television for America's teenagers—and a guilty pleasure for millions of non-teenagers.

Like a millennial version of *Beverly Hills, 90210*, the series—which was adapted from Cecily von Ziegesar's book series of the same name—followed the lives of a group of friends (and sometimes enemies) headed up by BFFs Serena van der Woodsen (Blake Lively) and Blair Waldorf (Leighton Meester) as they navigate the elite world of prep schools and just being plain fabulous on Manhattan's Upper East Side. They even learn to embrace the magical world of Brooklyn and its inhabitants—namely, the Humphrey family: Dan (Penn Badgley), Jenny (Taylor Momsen), and Rufus (Matthew Settle)—while the eponymous and ever-watchful blogger Gossip Girl tracks their every move and misstep.

IT WAS SUPPOSED TO BE A LINDSAY LOHAN MOVIE.
The original plan for adapting *Gossip Girl* didn't include a TV series at all. It was supposed to be a feature film, with *Gilmore Girls* creator Amy Sherman-Palladino writing the script and Lohan set to star as Blair Waldorf. When those plans fell through, the producers approached Schwartz—who was just wrapping up work on *The O.C.*—about taking his talent for creating enviable high school worlds to New York City's Upper East Side.

PENN BADGLEY INITIALLY TURNED DOWN THE ROLE OF DAN HUMPHREY.
Though he was hardly a household name when *Gossip Girl* premiered, Badgley had been acting for nearly a decade and had a lot of experience working on brand-new TV shows that never took off. So when he was offered the role of Brooklyn outsider Dan "Lonely Boy" Humphrey, his initial response was thanks, but no thanks.

In 2012, Badgley told Vulture that he originally turned the role down out of frustration. "I was frustrated and I was broke and I was depressed and I was like, 'I cannot do that again. I can't.'…Stephanie Savage, the [co-]creator, she said to me, 'I know you might not want to do this again, but just take a look at it.'" Badgley did, and he liked what he read. He was also genuinely grateful that they had thought of him for the project, but he just wasn't ready to invest so much of himself in another TV show that didn't go anywhere. When the producers couldn't find anyone else they liked for the role as much as Badgley, they came back to him. "Which is weird," the actor said, "because a million people could play Dan Humphrey—and she came back around, I was about to get a job as a waiter, and I was like, 'OK.'"

THE CREATORS GOT THE IDEA TO CAST BLAKE LIVELY FROM THE INTERNET.

According to *Vanity Fair*, when it came time to cast the show's main roles, they cruised some of the online message boards related to the *Gossip Girl* book series to see which actors fans of the books were suggesting. One name they kept seeing for the role of Serena van der Woodsen was Blake Lively, who had starred in *The Sisterhood of the Traveling Pants*. "We didn't see a lot of other girls for Serena," Schwartz said. "She has to be somebody that you believe would be sitting in the front row at Fashion Week eventually."

LEIGHTON MEESTER DYED HER HAIR TO LAND THE ROLE OF BLAIR WALDORF.

Because Blair and Serena were both best friends and occasional enemies, it was important to the show's creators that the characters did not look like the same person. That fact almost cost Leighton Meester the role of Blair.

"She came in and she was really funny, and really smart and played vulnerable," Schwartz recalled of Meester's audition. "But there was one problem: She was blonde. And Blake was blonde, obviously; Serena had to be blonde. So, [Leighton] went to the sink and dyed her hair. She wanted it." (Sounds like something Blair would do.)

THE NETWORK WAS WORRIED THAT ED WESTWICK LOOKED LIKE A "SERIAL KILLER."

Westwick, who originally auditioned for the role of Nate Archibald but ended up playing bad boy Chuck Bass, almost didn't land a role on the show at all. Though Schwartz and Savage loved the darker edge that

Westwick brought to the group of friends, *The Independent* reported that the CW worried "that he looked more like a serial killer than a romantic lead."

"He's menacing and scary, but there's a twinkle in his eye," casting director David Rapaport told BuzzFeed. "You want to hate him, but you would also probably sleep with him. He's one of those guys you hate for always getting away with things, but you also want to hang out with him and see what he's up to next." Fans clearly agreed.

WESTWICK CHANNELED HIS INNER CARLTON BANKS TO PLAY CHUCK BASS.

In order to perfect his posh American accent, West-wick—who was born in England—looked to another iconic American television character for help: *The Fresh Prince of Bel-Air*'s Carlton Banks (Alfonso Ribeiro). "There's a slight thing in Carlton Banks," Westwick told *Details* magazine in 2008, "that kind of über-preppy, that I did pick up on."

GRETA GERWIG AUDITIONED FOR THE SHOW . . . IN OVERALLS.

In 2015, Oscar-nominated actress and filmmaker Greta Gerwig talked to HuffPost Live about the mistakes she made early on in her career as an actress. "I have had moments when I was starting out when I was auditioning for things like *Gossip Girl*," she said. "And they would look at me like, 'Why are you wearing overalls to this audition?' And I'd be like, 'They said she was from a farm!' and they would be like, 'Well, this is *Gossip Girl*.'" (The role she was auditioning for, Eva Coupeau—a love interest for Chuck—eventually went to Clémence Poésy, who had played Fleur Delacour in the *Harry Potter* movies.)

GOSSIP GIRL WAS ONE OF TELEVISION'S FIRST INTERNET SUCCESS STORIES.

Years before *House of Cards* changed the way we watch, and even define, "television," *Gossip Girl* served as a sort of precursor to the streaming generation. While the show's Nielsen ratings were mediocre, *New York* magazine reported that, "New episodes routinely arrived at the No. 1 most-downloaded spot on iTunes, and then there were the hundreds of thousands who were downloading free week-old episodes on The CW's site. Even executives at Nielsen threw up their hands and admitted that *Gossip Girl* appeared to be speaking to an audience so young and tech-savvy they hadn't really figured it out just yet."

THE SHOW WAS BANNED BY SOME NEW YORK CITY SCHOOLS.

According to *Vanity Fair*, some of the elite New York City private schools that might have shared similarities with the show's fictional Constance Billard and St. Jude's banned their students from watching it (which, the outlet noted, "only served, in all likelihood, to make the students want to watch it more").

A WRITERS STRIKE HELPED THE SERIES GROW ITS VIEWERSHIP.

While the show struck a chord with certain audiences immediately upon its release, the 2007–08 Writers Guild of America strike proved to be a boon to the series. "The CW, because they couldn't just run repeats or game shows, [*Gossip Girl* was] all they had," Schwartz told *Vanity Fair*. "They kept re-running the show during the strike so more and more people were watching." Which led to even higher ratings when the show returned for a second season.

\\\\\\\ KRISTEN SPOILERS! BELL /////// PLAYED AN ESSENTIAL PART OF THE SERIES, BUT WAS NEVER CREDITED.

Though viewers had to watch all 121 episodes of *Gossip Girl* to learn the identity of the tattler in the title, Kristen Bell provided the voice for Gossip Girl for all six seasons, without credit. And while she sort of hoped that the finale would have revealed that she was indeed Gossip Girl all along, that ending was not meant to be. "I'm sure that it would've been really cool had I got to play some vicious part and actually come out as Gossip Girl, but I think it was appropriate for one of the main cast members to have surfaced as Gossip Girl," she told Perez Hilton.

Though she was a key part of the series, she didn't learn GG's true identity until the very end of the show—and she was surprised. "I don't know that I ever forethought it being Dan," she admitted. "That was a bit of a shocker!" (If it makes her feel any better, Badgley reportedly didn't learn Gossip Girl's identity until that scene was actually shot.)

FREEZE FRAME ▶

"*EASY J*" // SEASON 4, EPISODE 6
Over the course of the series, plenty of familiar faces popped up on *Gossip Girl*, but two in particular seem kind of funny in retrospect: Ivanka Trump and Jared Kushner played themselves in a club scene. (Ivanka was apparently a huge fan of the series.) "They did it for the money," Schwartz said, jokingly, to *Vanity Fair*.

20

TEEN DRAMAS TO BINGE

With lust, envy, and bespoke blazers in abundance, *Gossip Girl* could easily be called the quintessential high school drama of the twenty-first century. But not every teen series boasts a salacious blogger—some just have murderers, or vampires, or Superman. And even if your young adulthood was completely devoid of capital offenses and supernatural elements, there's something deeply relatable about watching any teenagers navigate locker-flanked halls and uncontrollable emotions. Here are twenty must-watch teen dramas that may or may not take you right back to chemistry class.

13 Reasons Why // **(2017–2020)**

All American // **(2018)**

Awkward // **(2011–2016)**

Beverly Hills, 90210 // **(1990–2000)**

Dawson's Creek // **(1998–2003)**

Degrassi: The Next Generation // **(2001–2010)**

Euphoria // **(2019–PRESENT)**

Love, Victor // **(2020–PRESENT)**

My So-Called Life // **(1994–1995)**

Never Have I Ever // **(2020–PRESENT)**

The O.C. // **(2003–2007)**

One Tree Hill // **(2003–2012)**

Pretty Little Liars // **(2010–2017)**

Riverdale // **(2017)**

Sex Education // **(2019–PRESENT)**

Skins // **(2007–2013)**

Smallville // **(2001–2011)**

Teen Wolf // **(2011–2017)**

The Vampire Diaries // **(2009–2017)**

Veronica Mars // **(2004–2007; 2019)**

GREY'S ANATOMY

(2005–PRESENT)

CREATED BY: Shonda Rhimes

SEASONS: 17

EPISODES: 369

OTHER SHOWS BY SHONDA RHIMES:
Private Practice (2007–2013)
Scandal (2012–2018)

I t's hard to remember a time when Shonda Rhimes wasn't a household name. But it's *Grey's Anatomy*—the longest-running prime-time medical drama in the United States—that originally put Rhimes on the map and paved the way to her throne as queen of Shondaland. As with any television show that's been on the air for nearly two decades, *Grey's Anatomy* has certainly had its fair share of ups and downs and seen some of its most popular stars come and go. It's also been at the center of more than one controversy.

Still, Ellen Pompeo—who stars as Dr. Meredith Grey, the Grey of the show's title—has remained at the center of it all. As viewers have watched her progress from newbie intern to chief of general surgery, they've gotten a glimpse into the personal and professional challenges doctors face at every stage of their careers, with plenty of love triangles thrown in. But Shondaland's first big hit still has a few secrets up its scrub sleeves.

SHONDA RHIMES GOT THE IDEA FOR *GREY'S ANATOMY* AFTER A CONVERSATION WITH A DOCTOR.

Rhimes told Oprah Winfrey that although she had always loved shows about surgery and emergency rooms, the unique angle for her show was sparked after a doctor mentioned how hard it was to shave her legs in the hospital shower. "At first that seemed like a silly detail," Rhimes said. "But then I thought about the fact that it was the only time and place this woman might have to shave her legs. That's how hard the work is."

THE WRITERS CONSULT REAL MEDICAL PROFESSIONALS.

To make sure they get it right, *Grey's* writers consult with a team of medical professionals on the proper jargon and phrasing. According to *Variety*, Rhimes said that during the writing process they just used the phrase "medical" as a dialogue placeholder, so Meredith would say "I need to medical the medical! Hand me the medical!" Rhimes did the same thing on shows like *Scandal*, where she instead used the word *political*.

THERE WAS ONE REAL DOCTOR ON STAFF THE FIRST SEASON.

The writers would come up with outrageous scenarios, often based on ripped-from-the-headlines stories, and then use emergency room doctor Zoanne Clack as their realist and fact-checker. "What was interesting was that the writers don't have those boundaries because they don't know the rules, so they would come up with all of these scenarios, and my immediate thought was like, 'No way!'" Clack said. "Then I'd have to think about it and go, 'But could it?'" Clack is now a producer and writer on *Grey's* and even once made a cameo as "Woman in Hall" during the fifteenth season in 2019.

THE "McDREAMY" NICKNAME WAS INSPIRED BY PATRICK DEMPSEY HIMSELF.

"When we were shooting the pilot, Patrick [Dempsey] was seriously the most adorable man we'd ever seen on camera," Rhimes told Oprah. "We'd watch the monitor and think, 'Look at his dreamy eyes!' So we started calling him Patrick McDreamy, and it stuck."

ROB LOWE COULD HAVE PLAYED McDREAMY.

Lowe was offered the role of Dr. Derek Shepherd before Dempsey was, but he turned the part down to make the short-lived drama *Dr. Vegas* instead. Lowe has no regrets over turning it down. "Me in that part isn't as interesting as Patrick in that part," Lowe told *Variety*. "If it'd been me [the fans] wouldn't have called me 'McDreamy,' they would have called me Rob Lowe."

THE WRITERS WERE CHASTISED FOR TALKING ABOUT FEMALE ANATOMY.

Rhimes and the writers received a note that they had used the word *vagina* too many times in one episode. "Now, we'd once used the word *penis* seventeen times in a single episode and no one blinked. But with *vagina*, the good folks at broadcast standards and practices blinked over and over and over," Rhimes said. "I think no one is comfortable experiencing the female anatomy out loud—which is a shame considering our anatomy is half the population."

THE SHOW WAS NOT EXPECTED TO LAST BEYOND THE FIRST SEASON.

After the first season wrapped, writers were asked to clean out their offices because showrunners didn't expect to get picked up for another one.

AFTER DEALING WITH SEVERAL SCANDALS WITH ACTORS ON *GREY'S*, RHIMES DEVELOPED A "NO ASSHOLES" POLICY.

She began implementing it on her next show, *Scandal*, which debuted in 2012. "There are no Heigls in this situation," she said in an interview with *The Hollywood Reporter*, referring to an infamous incident with actress Katherine Heigl, who withdrew her name from Emmy contention by saying the quality of scripts she received was not award material. "I don't put up with bullshit or nasty people," Rhimes said. "I don't have time for it."

> ## FREEZE FRAME ▶
>
> **"AS WE KNOW IT"** // **SEASON 2, EPISODE 17**
> The show's famous slang word for female genitalia was inspired by an off-camera exchange. "I heard one of our assistants using 'va-jay-jay' in place of 'vagina.' It was the greatest phrase I'd ever heard," Rhimes said. The phrase was first used by Miranda Bailey as she was giving birth. "Stop looking at my va-jay-jay," she told intern George O'Malley.

DEBBIE ALLEN CHANGED THE MAKEUP OF THE SHOW.

Allen rose to fame playing dance teacher Lydia Grant on Fame (1982–1987). She has been nominated for eighteen Emmy Awards and two Tonys, and she has won a Golden Globe Award. When Allen joined *Grey's* as director and executive producer, one of her goals was to hire 50 percent female directors and increase the number of Black male directors.

ONLY THREE OF THE ORIGINAL ACTORS REMAIN.

After the season 16 departure of Justin Chambers, who played Dr. Alex Karev, only three of the original actors are still on the show (not counting surprise returns in season 17): Chandra Wilson, who plays Dr. Miranda Bailey; James Pickens, who plays Dr. Richard Webber; and, of course, Ellen Pompeo, Dr. Meredith Grey herself.

THE BLOOD AND GUTS ON THE SHOW ARE REAL.

But they're not human blood and guts; they're cow organs. They also use cow blood, red Jell-O, and chicken fat to make all of those surgical scenes look extra realistic. The smell, according to some of the actors, is quite repulsive.

FREEZE FRAME ▶

"THE SOUND OF SILENCE" // SEASON 12, EPISODE 9

As part of Allen's goal of bringing more diversity behind the scenes of *Grey's Anatomy*, she brought on Denzel Washington to direct this season 12 episode. Though the choice may seem like an unconventional one for Washington, he didn't hesitate to agree, saying, "I'm going to say yes to Debbie Allen."

THE SHOW HAS SAVED AT LEAST ONE PERSON'S LIFE.

In 2011, when a Wisconsin woman collapsed during a severe asthma attack, her ten-year-old daughter and a friend administered CPR after seeing it done on the show. The woman made a full recovery.

RHIMES HAS SAID THAT WHEN POMPEO IS DONE, THE SHOW IS DONE.

In 2017, Rhimes told E! News, "Ellen and I have a pact that I'm going to do the show as long as she's going to do the show. So, the show will exist as long as both of us want to do it. If she wants to stop, we're stopping."

ELLEN POMPEO HAS ONE WISH FOR THE *GREY'S ANATOMY* FINALE.

Her request? That the original cast members come back. It could prove to be a challenge, as many of them have met their demise in the show. But in a series that has employed everything from ghosts to dreams to hallucinations, there's no telling what the showrunners have up their sleeves.

FREEZE FRAME ▶

"SONG BENEATH THE SONG" // SEASON 7, EPISODE 18

Just before joining the *Grey's Anatomy* clan in 2006 as Dr. Callie Torres, Sara Ramirez took home a Tony Award for Best Featured Actress in a Musical for their appearance as the Lady of the Lake in *Spamalot*. It inspired Rhimes to use Ramirez's chops in a musical episode she had long been thinking about. The episode is generally not considered one of *Grey's* best, but Ramirez always got rave reviews.

4 PEOPLE WHO REGRETTED LEAVING HIT TV SHOWS

Actors leave TV shows at the height of their popularity all the time, as Katherine Heigl proved when she departed *Grey's Anatomy* in 2010. But sometimes their exits come back to haunt them, as Heigl proved again in 2021, when she spoke about her departure from the show and admitted that she "could have handled it with more grace." These actors can relate.

CHRISTOPHER ECCLESTON // *Doctor Who*

In 2005, *Doctor Who* was rebooted for a new generation, and Christopher Eccleston was cast as the Ninth Doctor. Although the show was an immediate hit, Eccleston left after just one season due to creative differences with the show's producers. He was replaced by David Tennant.

"It was kind of tragic for me, that I didn't play him for longer," Eccleston said in 2016. "He's a beautiful character and I have a great deal of professional pride and had I done a second season, there would have been a marked improvement in my performance. I was learning new skills, in terms of playing light comedy."

JASON PRIESTLEY // *Beverly Hills, 90210*

In 1998, Jason Priestley left *Beverly Hills, 90210* during the show's ninth season. Although he earned two Golden Globe nominations for his role as Brandon Walsh and got the chance to direct a handful of episodes, Priestley believed he had explored every aspect of his character and could no longer play the role. However, he was disappointed with how the show ended and felt that if he had stayed on for one more season, it would have had a much more satisfying final year.

"Understanding what I do now about story and character, I believe that [Aaron Spelling] was pushing the story in a direction that would have had Brandon and Kelly end up together at the end of the show and I think I probably should have stuck around to its fruition," Priestley told CNN in 2014.

WIL WHEATON // *Star Trek: The Next Generation*

During the first four seasons of *Star Trek: The Next Generation*, Wil Wheaton played Wesley Crusher, the only son of Beverly Crusher, chief medical officer of the USS *Enterprise*. He left the show in 1990 to pursue more acting opportunities in movies and TV.

"I left *Star Trek: The Next Generation* when I was eighteen years old, and initially I thought it was a really smart business career move," Wheaton said during a *Star Trek* reunion at the Calgary Expo in 2012. "In some ways it was, and in more ways it wasn't. What I was unprepared for was how much I was going to miss the people that are on this stage. . . . After that ended, I just felt really ashamed of myself."

BRIAN DUNKLEMAN // *American Idol*

In 2002, during the first season of *American Idol*, there were actually two hosts: Ryan Seacrest and Brian Dunkleman, the latter of whom left the reality TV competition at the very beginning of its success. "[T]he undeniable truth is, I just didn't have the wisdom at the time to handle what was happening," Dunkleman wrote in *Variety* in 2016. "Do I regret not remaining on the show . . . Yes. Especially when I open my bank statements."

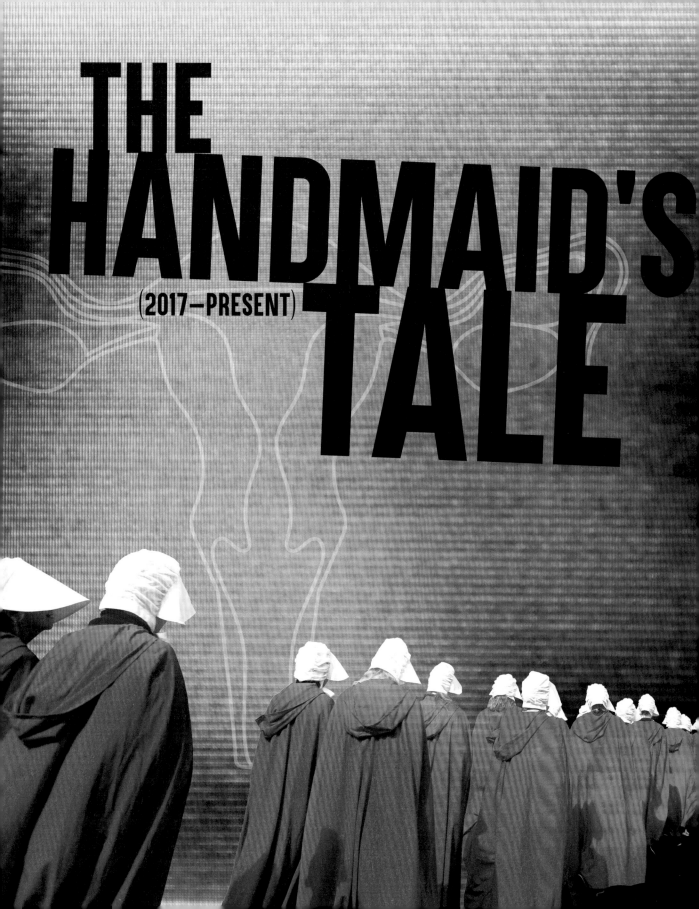

THE HANDMAID'S TALE

(2017—PRESENT)

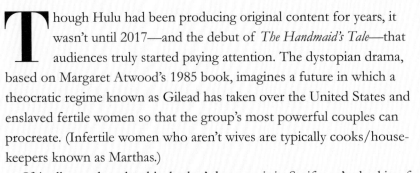

CREATED BY: Bruce Miller
(based on the novel
by Margaret Atwood)

SEASONS: 4

EPISODES: 46

FREEZE FRAME ▶

"OFFRED" // SEASON 1, EPISODE 1

Beyond just adapting the novel, Margaret Atwood has been a part of the production process on *The Handmaid's Tale* from the beginning, so she's had a hand in shaping the new version of the world. She also had a hand in slapping Offred on the back of the head. In the pilot, Atwood has a cameo playing an Aunt (one of the cruel taskmasters lording over the Handmaids) who hits Moss's character during her initiation into the fold. Playing an Aunt was Atwood's idea; the slap was Bruce Miller's.

Though Hulu had been producing original content for years, it wasn't until 2017—and the debut of *The Handmaid's Tale*—that audiences truly started paying attention. The dystopian drama, based on Margaret Atwood's 1985 book, imagines a future in which a theocratic regime known as Gilead has taken over the United States and enslaved fertile women so that the group's most powerful couples can procreate. (Infertile women who aren't wives are typically cooks/house-keepers known as Marthas.)

If it all sounds rather bleak, that's because it is. So if you're looking for a sunny pick-me-up, *The Handmaid's Tale* is not it. And while its story is an exaggeration of any male-dominated society that currently exists, there are many truths hidden within the series that speak to the realities of today. Elisabeth Moss stars as Offred, a fertile woman in an infertile land who is bound (practically literally) to a military officer (Joseph Fiennes) in Gilead's middle management. As a handmaid, it's Offred's job to bear children for this officer and his wife, but Offred (real name June Osborne) isn't big on being told what to do. Which is where the real story begins.

THE HANDMAID'S TALE IS THE FIRST STREAMING SHOW TO WIN THE EMMY FOR OUTSTANDING DRAMA.

The Emmy for Outstanding Drama Series has been bestowed on such hits as *The Sopranos, Homeland, Breaking Bad,* and *The West Wing.* But *The Handmaid's Tale* is unique in that it was the first streaming series to achieve this kind of acclaim, meaning it could only be accessed via a paid subscription to Hulu and viewed on your computer or other Internet-connected device versus a major network like NBC or a premium cable channel like HBO. Netflix tried for years to break into the gang with *House of Cards* and *Orange Is the New Black,* but Hulu sealed the deal in 2017 with this dystopian nightmare.

THE ACTORS HAVE TO RELY ON SOUND SINCE THE COSTUMES LIMIT THEIR VISION.

The "wings" the Handmaids wear are meant to hide their faces from others as well as obscure their own vision. Costume designer Ane Crabtree said they help "heighten the cages that [the Handmaids] were in mentally, physically, emotionally," but they also challenge the actors by removing sight from the equation. Moss and others spend a lot of time listening to their scene partners because, unless they're looking at them straight on, they can't see them. "What was actually a hindrance became quite a helpful vehicle for a new way of acting," Crabtree said.

THE ARTWORK IN COMMANDER FRED AND SERENA JOY'S HOUSE IS STOLEN.

A wry touch that nods toward how Nazi officers stole important, valuable pieces of art from Jewish houses is that the Waterford home is filled with stolen masterworks—but they aren't random. "All the paintings on the walls of the Commander's house are copies of pictures from the Boston Museum of Fine Arts, because the idea was that they looted them and put them in their houses, like the Nazis did," showrunner Bruce Miller explained.

A MARTHA WROTE A THESIS ON THE NOVEL.

Amanda Brugel plays Rita, a "Martha" who works in Commander Fred's household, but her connection to *The Handmaid's Tale* goes back much further. She first read the book in high school and wrote her college entrance essay on it—an essay that scored her a scholarship. The main focus of her piece? Rita.

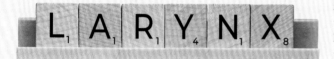

ONE CHARACTER HAS A SUBTLE *CASABLANCA* CONNECTION.

Nick (Max Minghella) doesn't have a last name in the book, but the creators made him Nick Blaine for the series. It's unclear whether the connection was intentional, but that makes his name incredibly close to *Casablanca* protagonist Rick Blaine, played by Humphrey Bogart. Both characters are initially seen as out for themselves before they reveal connections to the bad guys and ultimately aid the resistance.

COMPLACENCY IS A CENTRAL MESSAGE OF THE SHOW.

Reed Morano, who created the look of the show while directing its first three episodes, views the current political climate as a reason to feel more responsible in the art she's making. She was astonished by the number of people who don't vote (she voted absentee while shooting the show in Toronto). "That's the message, for me at least, in the first three episodes of *The Handmaid's Tale*. We're too complacent," Morano told *Esquire*. "We let things happen to us. And you don't have to let things happen to you. You can affect change."

4 INTRIGUING DYSTOPIAN TV SHOWS

For decades, makers of television have used imagined futures to make social commentaries on the present. *The Handmaid's Tale* is just one example of dystopian television. Here are more shows that work within the genre.

1 *12 Monkeys //* **(2013–2018)**
In the future world of this Syfy original series, which is inspired by Terry Gilliam's movie of the same name, an organization known as the Army of the 12 Monkeys has released a deadly virus that threatens humanity's survival. The show's protagonists must use time travel to try to stop the pandemic before it begins, taking viewers on a wild ride that never goes where (or when) they're expecting.

2 *Black Mirror //* **(2011–)**
There isn't just one dystopian setting in *Black Mirror*. The British sci-fi anthology series is as likely to explore futuristic societies as it is near futures that closely resemble our own time. The theme connecting each episode is the unwanted and sometimes horrifying effects of new technology. Prepare to want to cover the camera on your computer.

3 *The Man in the High Castle //* **(2015–2019)**
What if the Axis powers won the war? That is the question posed as the premise of Amazon's *The Man in the High Castle*. Adapted from Philip K. Dick's 1962 novel, it depicts a version of the US controlled by the Third Reich and Japanese Empire, where minorities are persecuted. Set in 1962, this dystopian show technically takes place in an alternate past.

4 *Watchmen //* **(2019)**
Based on the DC comic book series, *Watchmen* is set after an alternate version of the twentieth century. The HBO show follows outlawed vigilantes, but it isn't your typical superhero story. The unique blend of real historical events (like the Tulsa race massacre of 1921) with a dystopian future creates a fascinating social commentary on racism and police abuse.

HULU ORIGINAL SERIES YOU SHOULD ADD TO YOUR WATCHLIST

Hulu's slate of original programming doesn't just begin and end with its exemplary *The Handmaid's Tale* adaptation. The service is also the home of other world-class sci-fi series, dramas, and comedies that could become your next favorite binge-watches.

CASTLE ROCK
(2018–2019)

Stephen King's fictional town of Castle Rock, Maine, comes to life in this horror anthology series starring a rotating cast that includes Bill Skarsgård, Lizzy Caplan, André Holland, Melanie Lynskey, Jane Levy, Barkhad Abdi, and Sissy Spacek. Through its two-season run, *Castle Rock* expands upon King's universe, touching on everything from the Shawshank State Penitentiary to the family of *The Shining*'s Jack Torrance.

HARLOTS
(2017–2019)

In the male-dominated world of eighteenth-century London, running a brothel is one of the only ways for a woman to earn an independent living. But when Margaret Wells's (Samantha Morton) bordello comes under attack from both law enforcement and rival madams, she has to do everything within her power to preserve her way of life.

LETTERKENNY
(2016– PRESENT)

Not a whole lot happens in the town of Letterkenny—and that's exactly what makes for great comedy. This offbeat series revolves around the lives of farmers (Jared Keeso, Nathan Dales, and Michelle Mylett), hockey players, and other townsfolk who, more often than not, solve their problems with a well-placed insult or a right hook to the jaw.

NORMAL PEOPLE
(2020)

Based on author Sally Rooney's bestselling book, *Normal People* follows the complicated relationship between two mismatched Irish teens, Connell (Paul Mescal) and Marianne (Daisy Edgar-Jones), as they attend secondary school against the backdrop of the country's 2008 economic recession.

PEN15
(2019)

Somehow, *Pen15* takes the cringiest moments everyone suffered through as a teen and turns them into one of the most original comedies on any streaming service. This is all helped along by the sharp writing and by the performances of Maya Erskine and Anna Konkle, who play thirteen-year-old versions of themselves with impeccable authenticity.

RAMY
(2019–PRESENT)

Ramy Youssef stars in this dramedy about a young American Muslim who has to navigate his family's rigid faith, judgmental friends, and a modern culture that isn't always welcoming to people like him.

RUNAWAYS
(2017–2019)

Obviously, Disney-owned Hulu was going to wind up with a Marvel show at some point— and thankfully, the service landed *Runaways*, one of the comic publisher's most interesting properties. The series focuses on a group of super-powered teenagers (Rhenzy Feliz, Lyrica Okano, Virginia Gardner, et al.) who have to battle it out with their villainous parents and solve the mystery behind their origin.

THE GREAT
(2020–PRESENT)

The Great is basically Hulu's anti-historical answer to *The Crown*— and that's probably a description creator Tony McNamara would relish. It's a darkly satirical take on the rise of Catherine the Great (Elle Fanning) at the expense of her boorish, deranged husband, Emperor Peter III (Nicholas Hoult).

HANNIBAL

(2013—2015)

CREATED BY: Bryan Fuller (based on Thomas Harris's Hannibal novels)

SEASONS: 3

EPISODES: 39

OTHER SHOWS BY BRYAN FULLER:
Dead Like Me **(2003–2004)**
Wonderfalls **(2004)**
Pushing Daisies **(2007–2009)**
American Gods **(2017–2021)**
Star Trek: Discovery **(2017–PRESENT)**

I n 2013, Bryan Fuller set about crafting a new version of the Hannibal Lecter story. It was a daring proposition after the character and his world had been so clearly defined by Sir Anthony Hopkins's portrayal of the character and after Hannibal's presence in four novels and five feature films. But Fuller had an idea no one else had approached yet: He wanted to show what he described to Collider as "the bromance between Hannibal [Mads Mikkelsen] and Will Graham [Hugh Dancy]. Here are two crazy men, who are so unique in their insanity that they need each other to understand themselves." What audiences got was one of the most stylish, visually arresting, and psychologically complex shows ever to hit television.

Hannibal only lasted three seasons, but in its short time on the air it amassed loads of critical acclaim and a ravenous fan base known as "Fannibals," many of whom are still holding out hope for the show's return.

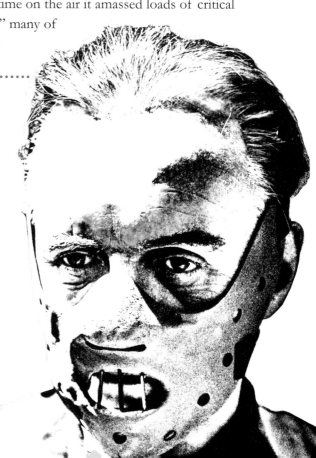

BRYAN FULLER GOT THE JOB BECAUSE OF A FATEFUL PLANE RIDE.

Fuller is a lifelong fan of horror, and a longtime fan of Thomas Harris's Hannibal Lecter novels. So it was fortuitous when he found himself seated near an old friend, producer Katie O'Connell, while on a flight to New York. O'Connell told Fuller she was developing a *Hannibal* series, and asked him what he thought. Fuller asked if she had the rights to Will Graham, the protagonist of Harris's novel *Red Dragon*, because he was fascinated by one line in that novel that signified a much deeper relationship between Graham and Lecter that audiences and readers had never quite seen.

"Because I had read the books, I knew how much more psychologically complex Will Graham is in the literature than he is in the film," Fuller said. "I thought, wow, there's a great opportunity to deliver on that line from *Red Dragon* that Hannibal Lecter says, which is,

'You caught me because you're as insane as I am.'"

Fuller's thoughts set in motion an idea for a kind of *Red Dragon* prequel that would also serve as a mash-up of all of Harris's writings on the character. That in turn led to a meeting with Martha De Laurentiis of the Dino De Laurentiis Company, which led to a meeting at NBC, which greenlit the show.

A REAL CHEF DESIGNED ALL THOSE CANNIBAL RECIPES.

Hannibal Lecter isn't just a cannibal—he is a cannibal gourmand, a lover of the finer things who doesn't just want to eat human flesh but to prepare it in exquisite ways. Fuller knew this, and he also knew he needed someone with tremendous food expertise to help him make the series. So he turned to celebrity chef and restaurateur José Andrés.

"I have a limited knowledge of the culinary," Fuller told the *The Hollywood Reporter*. "And Hannibal Lecter has to be smarter than I am in the kitchen. José gives insight into his expertise; he's omnipresent in every food scene." Andrés explained that every part of the human body is in some way edible, right down to the bones, which can be used as thickener. With this in mind, Fuller sought not just to write scenes in which Hannibal is cooking human body parts but to craft elaborate metaphors in each dinner scene.

SEVERAL ROLES WERE RACE- AND GENDER-SWAPPED.

In writing *Hannibal*, Fuller considered Harris's writing to be a kind of guiding bible, but that doesn't mean he didn't take liberties. For one thing, he aged up the title character, which removed Lecter's traumatic childhood experiences during World War II from consideration.

In an effort to increase the diversity of the cast, several key roles in the series were ultimately given to actors of different races and even genders than they were previously depicted. So *Hannibal* gave us Black actors in the roles of previously white characters Jack Crawford (Laurence Fishburne) and Reba McClane (Rutina Wesley), and the previously male characters Alan Bloom and Freddy Lounds became Alana Bloom (Caroline Dhavernas) and Freddie Lounds (Lara Jean Chorostecki).

CENSORS WERE ACTIVELY INVOLVED IN THE CREATIVE PROCESS.

For a show like *Hannibal*, elaborate crime scenes full of mutilated bodies were always going to be part of the process. Fuller took a very hands-on approach to crafting the various gruesome murders, with the help of NBC's standards and practices department. Rather than script or shoot something and then have to fight with network censors about what he couldn't show, Fuller reached out directly with his ideas first and then worked with them to create the most network-friendly version of the scene possible. As a result, he learned a few tricks to get around broadcast TV's violence limitations—like that the brighter the blood you feature in a scene, the less you can show.

THERE WAS ONE ELABORATE MURDER THE SHOW WASN'T ALLOWED TO FILM.

Despite working closely with the network's standards and practices department, *Hannibal* was still a series airing on network TV, not cable. That meant limitations were always inevitable, and at one point Fuller and the writers' imaginations reached further than NBC was willing to allow.

What's the one big murder scene NBC said no to? According to Fuller, it would have come in the season 1 episode "Rôti," in which Graham is pursuing escaped killer Dr. Abel Gideon (Eddie Izzard). The scene would have involved Lounds being lured into a room where one of Gideon's victims was waiting, still alive, with a slit in his stomach. Lounds would have then flipped a switch that triggered a ceiling fan, and it would have been revealed that the fan was actually attached to the man's intestines through the cut in his stomach. As the fan began to spin, it would disembowel him.

"That was the only one where NBC was like, 'I just don't know how you're going to do it,'" Fuller said. "We would have pushed back if we also hadn't been told that financially we didn't know how we could afford to produce such a gag, because you have intestines swinging around a ceiling fan."

THE SHOW'S BIGGEST CRIME SCENE USED REAL (LIVING) HUMAN BODIES.

The first case of *Hannibal*'s second season involved "The Muralist," a serial killer who abducted and killed people of different ethnic backgrounds, preserved their bodies with silicone and resin, then sewed them together in a massive and intricate pattern in the bottom of a silo to form the shape of a human eye. It was an intense and captivating visual even by *Hannibal*'s standards, and while the production used a computer program called form•Z to design the layout of the bodies beforehand, when it came time to actually film the scene there was no substitute for the real thing. Several dozen background artists were employed and asked to lie in an elaborate pattern on the floor of the set for two days of shooting, usually nearly nude.

ONE EPISODE NEVER AIRED ON NBC.

It was never any secret that *Hannibal* would be the kind of show that dealt with heinous crimes—its two main characters are a serial killer and a man who hunts serial killers, after all. Still, even Fuller has his limits, and after a particularly violent few months in America in late 2012 and early 2013, he asked NBC to pull the fourth episode of the show's first season.

"Oeuf," the episode in question, involved a woman (Molly Shannon) brainwashing children into killing their own families. Fuller felt that "given the cultural climate right now in the US, I think we shouldn't air the episode in its entirety," and cited in particular the Sandy Hook school shooting and the Boston Marathon bombing. "Oeuf" was still teased via a series of clips released to NBC's website, and the episode is now available on Blu-ray and through streaming services.

DAVID BOWIE WAS ALMOST A GUEST STAR.

In addition to a stellar main cast, *Hannibal* was always packed with interesting guest stars, from Zachary Quinto to Lance Henriksen. One particular guest star, though, was always *just* out of reach for the series. For the second season, Fuller offered the role of Hannibal's uncle Robert Lecter to legendary musician David Bowie, but Bowie was unavailable and the role was left uncast—though not without the hope that Bowie could eventually make time for the series.

"We were told by his people, when we got the pickup for the third season, to make sure to ask again about his availability," Fuller said in 2014. Sadly, Bowie never made it to *Hannibal*. He passed away on January 10, 2016.

10

MOVIES TURNED TV SHOWS

The remake trend that has overtaken Hollywood in the past few decades has been encroaching on small-screen originality, too, albeit with varying degrees of success. Here are some movies turned series that are worth seeking out.

Ash vs. Evil Dead // **(2015–2018)**

Bates Motel // **(2013–2017)**

The Dark Crystal: Age of Resistance // **(2019)**

Dear White People // **(2017–2021)**

Four Weddings and a Funeral // **(2019)**

Hanna // **(2019–PRESENT)**

She's Gotta Have It // **(2017–2019)**

Tremors // **(2003)**

Wet Hot American Summer // **(2015–2017)**

What We Do in the Shadows // **(2019–PRESENT)**

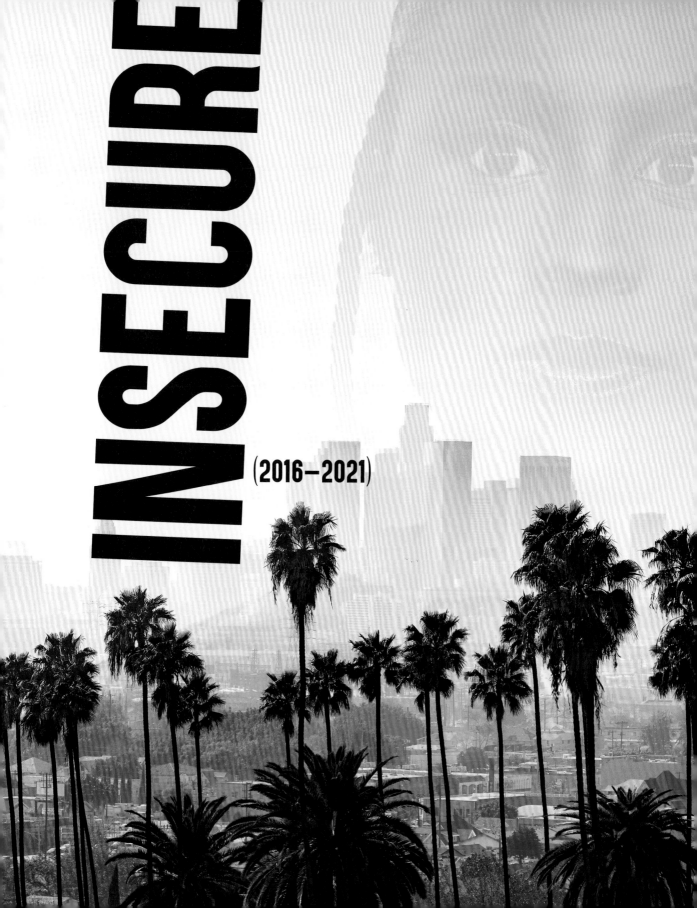

INSECURE

(2016–2021)

For more than a decade, Issa Rae has been busy carving out a unique space for Black female voices in Hollywood. It began with *Awkward Black Girl*, her witty YouTube web series, which grew up to become *Insecure*, the Emmy Award–winning HBO series Rae co-created with TV veteran Larry Wilmore.

Rae plays Issa Dee, a like-minded albeit fictional version of herself, who works at a nonprofit organization aimed at helping Black teens. With the help of her best friend, Molly (Yvonne Orji), a corporate lawyer whose professional success is in direct contrast to her romantic track record, Issa does her best to argue against there being "a universal way to be Black." The result is a painfully authentic portrait of the early days of adulthood, but through the eyes of two young Black women—a perspective not often seen on television.

WE ALMOST HAD A VERY DIFFERENT SHOW FROM ISSA RAE.

Most fans know that Issa Rae found initial fame from her award-winning web series *Awkward Black Girl*. Following the success of her web series, the actress-writer-producer was approached by Shonda Rhimes and her production partner, Betsy Beers. Rae pitched them a comedy about a woman trying to date image-obsessed Hollywood men titled *I Hate L.A. Dudes*. When the project eventually fell through, Rae told *The New York Times* that she felt she had "compromised my vision, and it didn't end up [being] the show that I wanted. It wasn't funny anymore." Time passed, new opportunities arrived, and now we have *Insecure*.

INSECURE IS A LOVE LETTER TO LOS ANGELES.

Much in the same way that its lead character has found her calling showcasing the best of her community, *Insecure* has always featured the city of Los Angeles as its own character. The block party episode, for example, featured different vendors from the area, which were chosen by soliciting suggestions from the show's staff, and also featured performances by local musicians.

INSECURE HAS ATTRACTED A LOT OF AMAZING DIRECTORS.

They include Debbie Allen, Melina Matsoukas, Stella Meghie, Tina Mabry, Kerry Washington, Oscar winner Regina King, and many more.

NATASHA ROTHWELL IS PULLING TRIPLE DUTY AS WRITER, PRODUCER, AND ACTRESS ON *INSECURE*.
The multihyphenate Rothwell was on the writing staff of *Insecure* when she was asked if she would like to play the newly created character (and future fan favorite) Kelli, and the rest is comedy gold.

***LOOKING FOR LATOYA*, *INSECURE*'S SHOW WITHIN THE SHOW, ALSO HAS A FICTIONAL PODCAST EPISODE.**
Each season of *Insecure* has included a show within the show that both the characters and the viewers enjoy, from the forbidden romance soap *Due North*, inspired by a writers' room joke, to *Kev'yn*, a spoof on nineties TV sitcoms and recent nostalgic reboots. Season 4 featured the mockumentary series *Looking for Latoya*, a satirical look at the ways that missing Black women are often ignored. It was such a hit, they created a fictional podcast episode.

SOLANGE IS A MUSICAL CONSULTANT FOR *INSECURE*.
She got involved with the show through Melina Matsoukas, who directed one of her videos. The show frequently showcases up-and-coming artists like Sonny747, St. Panther, Kirby, and many more.

***INSECURE*'S WARDROBE DEPARTMENT WORKS WITH SEVERAL UP-AND-COMING BLACK DESIGNERS.**
Insecure's costume designer, Shiona Turini, does a fantastic job capturing aspects of the American Black experience for all of the characters, with looks like Kelly's B.A.P.S. costume to Tiffany's baby wearing a Future AKA hat. This extends to the designers used on the show.

"Not only is it important to me to buy from and support the network of Black and, often, independent designers in the industry, but it's also equally important to our characters," Turini told *Teen Vogue*. "They're 'just like us'—diligent, mindful shoppers who are knowledgeable about the importance of supporting Black-owned businesses." Some of her favorite pieces have been the vintage T-shirts from BLK MKT Vintage and No Sesso.

THE CHARACTER OF ANDREW WAS ALMOST AUSTRALIAN (SORT OF).
Alexander Hodge, who plays Molly's boyfriend, Andrew, is Australian. Hodge recalls that during his chemistry read with Yvonne Orji, Orji learned he was Australian, which prompted her to stop the audition and launch into a conversation with Issa about whether Andrew should now be Australian while Prentice Penny, the co-showrunner, ate his lunch and waited for the two of them to finish. Ultimately, because the show is a love letter to L.A., it was decided that Andrew had to be American.

WHICH REALITY

Whether you broadcast your love for all *The Bachelor* franchises out loud or prefer to keep your obsession with *Vanderpump Rules* to yourself, there's no shame in loving reality television. It does, after all, comprise a major segment of programming for pretty much every network—streaming ones included. Whether you've just started

IF YOU LIKE:	YOU'LL LOVE:	THEN TRY:
THE BACHELOR (2002-PRESENT)	*TOO HOT TO HANDLE* (2020-PRESENT)	*BURNING LOVE* (2012-2013) ▶
TOP CHEF (2006-PRESENT)	*THE GREAT BRITISH BAKING SHOW* (2010-PRESENT)	*HELL'S KITCHEN* (2005-PRESENT)
RuPAUL'S DRAG RACE (2009-PRESENT)	*SKIN WARS: FRESH PAINT* (2014-2016)	*DANCING QUEEN* (2018-PRESENT)
THE REAL HOUSEWIVES (2006-PRESENT)	*BELOW DECK* (2013-PRESENT)	*LADIES OF LONDON* (2014-2017)
AMERICAN IDOL (2002-2016; 2018-present)	*THE VOICE* (2011-present)	*THE X FACTOR* (2011-2013)
KEEPING UP WITH THE KARDASHIANS (2007-2021)	*THE SIMPLE LIFE* (2003-2007)	*THE OSBOURNES* (2002-2005)
GHOST ADVENTURES (2008-PRESENT)	*GHOST HUNTERS* (2004-PRESENT)	*FINDING BIGFOOT* (2011-2018)
QUEER EYE (2003-2007; 2018-PRESENT)	*WHAT NOT TO WEAR* (2003-2013)	*MADE* (2002-2014)
VANDERPUMP RULES (2013-PRESENT)	*SOUTHERN CHARM* (2014-PRESENT)	*THE JERSEY SHORE* (2009-2012)
SHARK TANK (2009-PRESENT)	*THE PROFIT* (2013-PRESENT)	*BIG BRAIN* (2013-PRESENT)
THE REAL WORLD (1992-2009)	*THE CHALLENGE* (1998-PRESENT)	*SUMMER HOUSE* (2017-PRESENT)
SURVIVOR (2000-PRESENT)	*RUNNING WILD WITH BEAR GRYLLS* (2014-PRESENT)	*NAKED AND AFRAID* (2013-PRESENT)
90 DAY FIANCÉ (2014-PRESENT)	*MARRIED AT FIRST SIGHT* (2014-PRESENT)	*LOVE IS BLIND* (2020-PRESENT)
COPS (1989-2020)	*LIVE PD* (2016-PRESENT)	*UNDER ARREST* (1993-PRESENT)

▶ *BURNING LOVE* is not a reality series—it's a parody of *The Bachelor* that fans of the real thing will love, as it gets every detail just right (then goes slightly even more over the top).

SHOW IS RIGHT FOR ME?

digging into the genre or have vivid memories of watching the very first season of *The Real World* back in the day when **MTV** was still mostly music videos, let us help guide you on your reality **TV** journey.

PROJECT RUNWAY (2004-PRESENT)	*MAKING THE CUT* (2020-PRESENT)	*NEXT IN FASHION* (2020)
CHOPPED (2007-PRESENT)	*MASTERCHEF* (2010-PRESENT)	*IRON CHEF AMERICA* (2004-2018)
LOVE ISLAND (2015-PRESENT)	*BACHELOR IN PARADISE* (2014-PRESENT)	*TEMPTATION ISLAND* (2019-PRESENT)
DANCING WITH THE STARS (2005-PRESENT)	*THE MASKED SINGER* (2019-PRESENT)	*RHYTHM + FLOW* (2019-PRESENT)
THE AMAZING RACE (2001-PRESENT)	*AMERICAN NINJA WARRIOR* (2009-PRESENT)	*WIPEOUT* (2008-PRESENT)
HOUSE HUNTERS (1999-PRESENT)	*SELLING SUNSET* (2019-PRESENT)	*MILLION DOLLAR LISTING: LOS ANGELES* (2006-PRESENT); *NEW YORK* (2012-PRESENT)
AMERICA'S GOT TALENT (2006-PRESENT)	*SO YOU THINK YOU CAN DANCE* (2005)	*WORLD OF DANCE* (2017-2020)
TOP GEAR (2002-PRESENT)	*PIMP MY RIDE* (2004-2007)	*FASTEST CAR* (2018-PRESENT)
AMERICA'S NEXT TOP MODEL (2003-PRESENT)	*MAKE ME A SUPERMODEL* (2008-2009)	*8TH & OCEAN* (2006)
IMPRACTICAL JOKERS (2011-PRESENT)	*THE CARBONARO EFFECT* (2014-PRESENT)	*PUNK'D* (2003-2015)
LAGUNA BEACH: THE REAL O.C. (2004-2006)	*THE HILLS* (2006-2010)	*MY SUPER SWEET 16* (2005-2017)
UNDERCOVER BOSS (2010-PRESENT)	*THE SECRET MILLIONAIRE* (2008-2013)	*NATHAN FOR YOU* (2013-2017) ▶
PROPERTY BROTHERS (2011-PRESENT)	*FLIP OR FLOP* (2013-PRESENT)	*FIXER UPPER* (2013-2018)
THE GREAT POTTERY THROWDOWN (2015-PRESENT)	*BLOWN AWAY* (2019-PRESENT)	*THE BIG FLOWER FIGHT* (2020-PRESENT)

▶ While *NATHAN FOR YOU* is technically a reality series, it's also a Comedy Central series that sees a totally unqualified "expert" on everything try and help struggling businesses find their way (often with hilariously failed results).

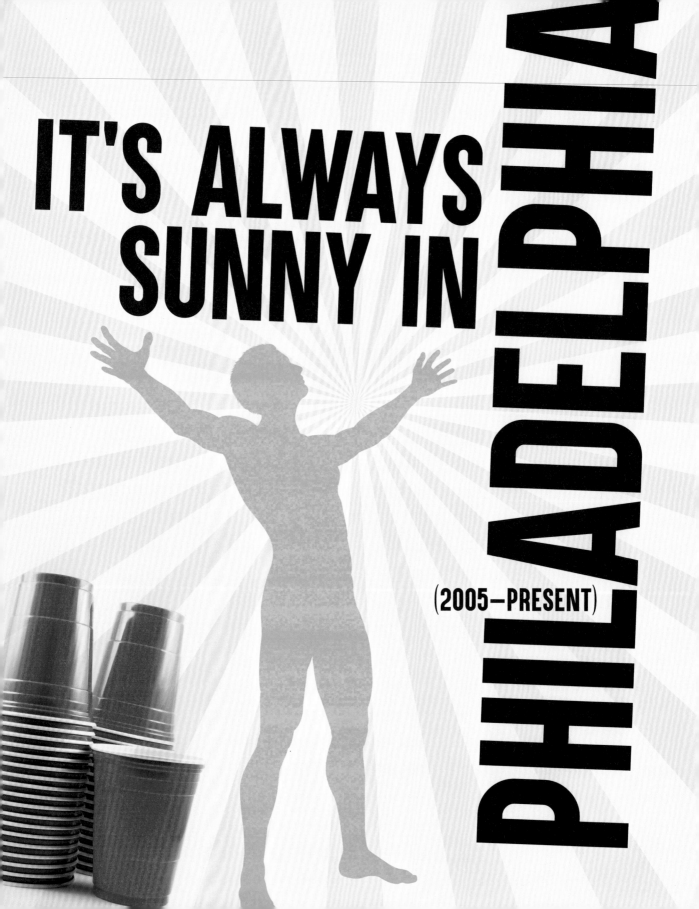

CREATED BY: Rob McElhenney

SEASONS: 14

EPISODES: 154

OTHER SHOWS BY ROB McELHENNEY:
Mythic Quest: Raven's Banquet
(2020–PRESENT)

The friends-just-hanging-out trope had been well established in sitcoms by the time *It's Always Sunny in Philadelphia* premiered in 2005. So had the notion that characters could be selfish narcissists (see *Seinfeld*). But *Sunny* had one advantage over Jerry and his crew of misfits: It was on basic cable, and network standards of decorum didn't apply. From its earliest seasons, with episode titles like "The Gang Finds a Dumpster Baby," the crew at Paddy's Pub has been able to mine humor from the most depraved of situations. Virtually none have any redeeming qualities. Ringleader Dennis Reynolds (Glenn Howerton) is a sociopath who may or may not have killed in the past; twin sister Dee Reynolds (Kaitlin Olson) suffers from self-delusion over her talents; guileless Charlie Kelly (Charlie Day) is prone to huffing gasoline; Mac (series creator Rob McElhenney, though he developed it with Howerton and Day) volleys from heavyset to super-fit in a pinball of self-image issues; Frank Reynolds (Danny DeVito), father(ish) figure to Dennis and Dee, has allowed his advancing years to remove any veneer of empathy from his actions.

These are all terrible people, prone to scheming, scamming, and exploiting others or themselves in the misplaced ambition to get ahead. If The Three Stooges used physical violence to abuse each other, the gang's aggression is almost purely psychological. Dennis preys on Mac's body dysmorphia and Dee's insecurity; Charlie's gullibility is exploited for personal gain; Frank gleefully betrays his own offspring. Their only redeeming quality? It's all darkly hilarious. Eventually—though not too soon, as *Sunny* will run at least through season 18—the gang will close its doors. Very few lessons will have been learned. Viewers wouldn't have it any other way.

THE PILOT COST $100 TO SHOOT.
Series leads McElhenney, Howerton, and Day were unknowns when they produced a pilot in 2004 titled "*It's Always Sunny on TV*", about struggling actors competing for the role of a cancer patient. The shot-on-video episode, which was intended to be more of a calling card than a polished production, cost less than one $100 to make. After shopping it to different networks, they found a supporter in FX president John Landgraf; he gave them $400,000 to shoot a proper pilot with an actual crew. The setting was changed to dive bar Paddy's Pub in Philadelphia.

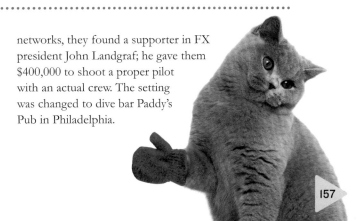

McELHENNEY CONTINUED WAITING TABLES DURING *SUNNY*'S FIRST SEASON.

Despite FX's endorsement, *Sunny* still had just a third of the budget of a typical network sitcom and was so strapped for cash that the actors shared a trailer. McElhenney made such a meager salary for the season that he continued waiting tables at a West Hollywood restaurant after he finished shooting for the day.

THE PILOT FEATURED A DIFFERENT DEE.

The original camcorder pilot was missing both the bar and actress Kaitlin Olson, who plays "Sweet" Dee Reynolds. The prototype Dee was played by Jordan Reid, then McElhenney's girlfriend, who was expected to continue on when the series was picked up by FX. But according to Reid, her breakup with McElhenney led to her role being recast on the show. *Saturday Night Live* actress Kristen Wiig was considered before the part went to Olson, who later married McElhenney.

DANNY DeVITO SAVED THE SHOW.

After a brief seven-episode first season, *Sunny* was neither a critical darling nor a commercial success. Low ratings prompted FX to mandate that the show cast a "name" actor in order to attract attention for a second season. DeVito knew Landgraf and agreed to meet with McElhenney; after talking about the show—and noting his kids were fans—DeVito accepted the role of absentee dad Frank Reynolds.

HULU ALSO SAVED THE SHOW.

While DeVito provided a stay of execution, the show's ratings were still mediocre. It wasn't until FX released episodes on DVD and on Hulu that people were able to sample the series, leading to the show becoming one of the service's most watched offerings. Demand for reruns eventually grew so popular that Comedy Central shelled out $33 million for the rights.

THE LIVE MUSICAL VERSION OF "THE NIGHTMAN COMETH" HAPPENED BY ACCIDENT.

For a loose stage adaptation of a season 4 episode titled "The Nightman Cometh," the cast toured six cities in 2009. A kind of *Always Sunny: The Musical*, Day performed several original numbers the trio had written for the episode, in which Charlie attempts to seduce the otherwise-unnamed Waitress (played by Day's real wife, Mary Elizabeth Ellis) with song. The

tour came about after a West Hollywood nightclub erroneously advertised that the cast of *Sunny* would be doing an entire live production of "The Nightman Cometh" as opposed to just a couple of numbers.

McELHENNEY'S PLAN WAS FOR EVERYONE TO GET FAT.

As regular *Sunny* viewers are aware, the normally fit Rob McElhenney decided to cultivate sixty pounds of mass for the show's seventh season as a response to his theory that everyone on television gets progressively better looking. He ate 5,000 calories a day—most of it from nutritionally viable sources like chicken and vegetables, some of it from ice cream—to achieve his smooth, seal-like appearance. McElhenney's original idea, however, was to have the entire cast add bulk while DeVito would lose fifty pounds. Ultimately, McElhenney underwent his transformation alone.

FRED SAVAGE DIRECTED SEVERAL EPISODES.

Betraying his wholesome *The Wonder Years* roots, actor and director Savage has directed several episodes of *Sunny*; he's also listed as a producer on a handful of episodes. Savage sought out work on the show, he told NPR, because he saw his own "worst qualities" in the characters. McElhenney hired him because he "needed to know if he really loved Becky Slater or if it was just Winnie all the way."

McELHENNEY AND OLSON OWN A REAL BAR IN PHILADELPHIA.

After a few of McElhenney's high school friends floated the idea of buying a bar, he and Olson agreed to fund Mac's Tavern, a sports bar in Philadelphia that opened in 2010. In 2017, bar management—in true *Sunny* style—Facebook-shamed a couple who left without paying for their meal.

THEY ALMOST KILLED DeVITO.

DeVito has made it clear he rarely says no to anything the show asks of him, from being stuck in a playground coil to emerging naked from a sofa. Being so agreeable has sometimes led to problems, as in the case of a scene for season 11 when the cast was depicted holding hands under water. DeVito (who Day described as "buoyant") had to be weighed down so he would sink. After the scene was complete, the cast was able to rise to the surface, but DeVito remained stuck halfway down and needed to be assisted up by safety divers. He was apparently so upset he left for the rest of the day.

THERE'S A RUSSIAN VERSION OF *SUNNY*.

It's Always Sunny in Moscow is a Russian remake of the show that Americans learned about thanks to Reddit and *Philadelphia City Paper* in 2014. The latter ran the landing page of the show through Google Translate and provided a summary: "Four young heroes… They went to school together. They have their own business— a pub 'Philadelphia.' But revenue it almost does not work. All their hopes and plans—love and money—are crumbling, when confronted with reality. The reason for this—their selfishness, laziness, and stupidity." The faithful adaptation aired for sixteen episodes.

FREEZE FRAME

"THE GANG GETS INVINCIBLE" // SEASON 3, EPISODE 2

There's a real Green Man. Or men. In 2010, Charlie Day told *Vice* that his character's habit of dressing in a green Lycra body suit for sporting events was inspired by a friend of McElhenney's who did the same thing for Philadelphia Eagles games. The show went on to inspire at least two Vancouver sports fans to show up at hockey games in the same outfit.

5 OF THE LONGEST-RUNNING TV SERIES

It's Always Sunny in Philadelphia is the undisputed champion when it comes to live-action sitcom longevity. Other shows (like *Supernatural* and *Grey's Anatomy*) have also demonstrated surprising endurance. Setting aside the tenured soap operas, game shows, and news programs, take a look at some of the series that have made broadcast history (in order of longevity).

1 *The Simpsons* // **(1989–PRESENT)**
Fox's first animated family aired its first episode the same year Milli Vanilli was on the music charts. In 2018, it set a record for being the longest-running prime-time scripted series in TV history (by episode count).

2 *Gunsmoke* // **(1955–1975)**
Before *The Simpsons* ended their face-off, *Gunsmoke* and its 635 episodes was the undisputed champ.

3 *Lassie* // **(1954–1974)**
For twenty years and 591 episodes (first on CBS, then in syndication), *Lassie* provided wholesome family entertainment. (Just don't do the math on an average collie's lifespan.)

4 *Law & Order: Special Victims Unit* // **(1999–PRESENT)**
Renewed in 2020 for a historic twenty-fourth season that should take it through at least 2023, the Mariska Hargitay–led procedural is the longest-running live-action prime-time series in history. It's even squeezed past parent series *Law & Order*, which ran for a mere twenty seasons.

5 *Saturday Night Live* // **(1975-PRESENT)**
Satire never grows old, which is why *SNL* will likely cross the half-century mark.

AND ONE SHOW THAT DIDN'T RUN FOR VERY LONG:

Turn-On // **(8:30 p.m.–9:00 p.m., February 5, 1969)**
Some shows last thirty years. Others don't last thirty minutes. According to guest-host Tim Conway, affiliate station WEWS in Cleveland, Ohio, had an executive who despised the show so much he petitioned other ABC channels not to broadcast it and pulled it from the air after just 15 minutes. It was never seen again.

LAW & ORDER

(1990–2010)

POLICE LINE DO NOT CROSS

CREATED BY: Dick Wolf

SEASONS: 20

EPISODES: 456

OTHER SHOWS BY DICK WOLF:
New York Undercover (1994–1998)
Law & Order: Special Victims Unit (1999–PRESENT)
Law & Order: Criminal Intent (2001–2011)
Chicago Fire (2012–PRESENT)
Chicago P.D. (2014–PRESENT)
Chicago Med (2015–PRESENT)

FREEZE FRAME ▶

**"SECURITATE" //
SEASON 3, EPISODE 20**
The role of Finkle is
played by Jerry Orbach's
son, Chris Orbach,
who became a "repeat
offender" and appeared
as different characters
in two more episodes:
"Matrimony" in 1997
and "Ambitious" in 1999.
Also in 1999, he began
a short stint as Detective
Ken Briscoe, Lennie's
nephew, on *Law &
Order: SVU*.

At more than thirty years old, the *Law & Order* universe seems to have always been with us. Revolutionary when the mothership show (also known as "original recipe") premiered in 1990, *Law & Order* began in an era when the web browser was only just invented, and only 5 million Americans had a cell phone subscription.

NBC called it quits on the mothership in 2010, but the series—which cycled through dozens of stars playing cops (law) and lawyers (order), plus many soon-to-be stars as both victims and perpetrators (check out any Broadway playbill and see if you can find any actors who *don't* list a *Law & Order* series on their résumé)—is still with us in endless reruns. Ranked as the thirty-sixth greatest TV show of all time by *Rolling Stone*, *Law & Order* may be everywhere—but how much do you really know?

NBC WASN'T THE FIRST—OR EVEN THE SECOND—NETWORK *LAW & ORDER*'S CREATORS PITCHED.

The show's first episode was originally shot in 1988, with CBS as the intended airing network. (Fox had been considered at one point, then discarded when the then network head Barry Diller declared it wasn't "a Fox show," according to *Law & Order: The Unofficial Companion*.)

That pilot, written by Dick Wolf and titled "Everybody's Favorite Bagman," was meant to look documentary-style gritty, and so was shot on sixteen-millimeter film. But in the end, CBS didn't pick the pilot up. Wolf was liked at NBC thanks to his work with the network on *Miami Vice* and *Hill Street Blues*, and network president Brandon Tartikoff agreed to pick up *Law & Order*, ordering thirteen episodes for their fall 1990 schedule—two years after the pilot was shot.

LAW & ORDER'S ORIGINAL DISTRICT ATTORNEY ONLY APPEARED IN ONE EPISODE.

Roy Thinnes was originally cast as Alfred Wentworth, the show's district attorney, and appeared in the show's pilot, which ultimately was aired as episode number six. There was such a lag between when the pilot was shot and when the show was ultimately picked up that Thinnes had already been contracted to another series and could not reprise his role.

With Thinnes out, original *Mission: Impossible* cast member Steven Hill was hired as DA Adam Schiff and remained with the show for 228 episodes, departing in 2000. Hill, who died in 2016 at age ninety-four, was an Orthodox Jew who would not film on the Sabbath, so his scenes had to be worked around that schedule.

CHRIS NOTH WAS NOT A SHOO-IN FOR THE PART OF DETECTIVE MIKE LOGAN.

Though the actors who ultimately got hired in the key original roles will forever live in our memories as the only true possibilities, it turns out that future *ER* star Eriq La Salle was originally up for the role of ADA Paul Robinette (which went to Richard Brooks), and future *Reservoir Dogs* star Michael Madsen was being seriously considered for the role of Detective Mike Logan (which ultimately went to Chris Noth).

According to *Inside Television Producing*, which features a detailed look at the early production process for the show, Madsen was thought to have "great sex appeal," but didn't make a great match with George Dzundza, who played Sergeant Max Greevey for *Law & Order*'s first two seasons. Noth, by contrast, was a more "compatible choice."

WOLF'S DEAL WITH THE UNIONS BROUGHT PRODUCTION IN NEW YORK CITY BACK TO LIFE.

To Wolf, there was no question that *Law & Order* would shoot in New York City, on location. But in 1988 (and, to some extent, in 1990, when production truly began), the Big Apple had almost no production going on. Unions had long-standing rules in place that made sense for feature films but weren't practical for television series. Wolf went to the union heads and had what he described as a "major meeting. I think the phrase I used was, 'Hey guys, 90 percent of the wealth is better than no bread at all.'"

The unions agreed to some work rule concessions (the show wasn't charged a location fee for the first four seasons, for example), which made the city affordable enough for the show's budget. By 1997, Wolf estimated the show had spent around $200 million in the city. These concessions led to a renaissance in television production in and around the city that continues even today.

LAW & ORDER SET A RECORD FOR A BLACK ACTOR ON A TV SERIES.

S. Epatha Merkerson first appeared on *Law & Order* as a guest star in season 1, then was hired full-time in 1993 to play Lieutenant Anita Van Buren, who oversaw the homicide department of 27th precinct until the show concluded in 2010. She appeared for seventeen consecutive seasons and nearly 400 episodes—and today holds the record as TV's longest-running prime-time Black female character.

EVERYTHING REALLY TOOK OFF IN RERUNS.

Some of the unsung heroes of NBC's *Law & Order* success story are other networks. *Law & Order* came into being on the tail end of continuing dramatic stories through series like *St. Elsewhere* and *Hill Street Blues*. Those shows were critically acclaimed and beloved, but didn't rerun well because they relied on continuing story arcs. Wolf purposely wanted to create a procedural show that could rerun endlessly, so he made sure that very little of the characters' personal lives made it into scripts, and very few episodes linked to one another.

Enter A&E, hungry for something to fill holes in its programming schedules. The cable network began rerunning *Law & Order* multiple times a day beginning in 1995, which boosted their ratings—plus the ratings of new episodes on NBC—and made the show ubiquitous. Since then, reruns have aired on Ion Television, WEtv, TNT, and Bounce TV, and the full series is now streaming on Peacock.

THE *LAW & ORDER* UNIVERSE, EXPLORED

The *Law & Order* concept proved so popular that spin-offs were inevitable—and haven't finished yet. Here's the whole of the global *Law & Order* universe.

Law & Order (1990–2010)
Law & Order: Special Victims Unit (1999–PRESENT)
Law & Order: Criminal Intent (2001–2011)
Law & Order: Trial by Jury (2005–2006)
Conviction (2006)
Law & Order: UK (2009–2014)
Law & Order: LA (2010–2011)
Law & Order: True Crime (2017)
Law & Order: Organized Crime (2021–PRESENT)

GUEST ROLES SOMETIMES TURNED INTO PERMANENT WORK.

Going from guesting on the show to returning as a regular new character happened more than once: Merkerson guested in "Mushrooms" in 1990, then returned in 1993 as Lieutenant Van Buren; Jerry Orbach first appeared as an attorney in 1991's "The Wages of Love," then signed on as Detective Lennie Briscoe in 1992; and Jeremy Sisto appeared in 2007's "The Family Hour" and came back the following year as Detective Cyrus Lupo.

GUEST STARS RETURNED SO FREQUENTLY THEY WERE CALLED "REPEAT OFFENDERS."

Since *Law & Order* drew on the New York casting pool, it was inevitable that some actors would show up on multiple episodes as entirely different characters. Fans created a "Repeat Offenders" website, which attempted to list all the names and appearances. Among the best known repeat offenders were renowned character actor Philip Bosco (with five appearances, three of them as attorney Gordon Schell), *Six Feet Under*'s Lauren Ambrose (three appearances), and Christine Baranski (three appearances).

THE ICONIC VOICE THAT INTRODUCES EACH EPISODE HAS BEEN THERE FROM BEFORE THE BEGINNING.

Alongside its iconic 'dun-dun' sound effect *Law & Order* might be most famous for its opening narration that explains how the criminal justice system works. That voice belongs to Steve Zirnkilton, a former Maine-based real estate broker who met Wolf when the showrunner was buying a house in Maine. Zirnkilton told *Backstage Magazine*, "When the transaction was complete [Wolf] said, 'What do I owe you?' I immediately passed him a cassette tape which was my [voice-over] demo."

Eventually Zirnkilton was cast in *Law & Order*, but not for voice-over work. He played a detective in the pilot. When NBC decided to pick up the series, Wolf returned to Zirnkilton to read some lines and a decades-long narration over many, many different series was born.

EVEN BELOVED REGULARS DIED IN THE SHOW . . . WHETHER THEY KNEW IT OR NOT.

Over the course of the twenty seasons, three major characters died in the line of duty: Sergeant Max Greevey (George Dzundza) was shot; ADA Alexandra Borgia (Annie Parisse) was kidnapped, beaten, and choked on her own vomit; and ADA Claire Kincaid (Jill Hennessy) was killed by a drunk driver.

Hennessy exited in 1993, but Kincaid wasn't confirmed as dead on the show until 1999; "I found out they killed me off from a friend who watched the show and told me, 'Jill, they said you were dead!'" Hennessy told *TV Guide* in 2009. "I was surprised, because I always thought I would return." *Law & Order: Specter Unit,* anyone?

THE SHOW WAS A WAITING ROOM FOR DOZENS OF STARS-TO-BE.

The list of young actors who got some of their earliest starts on *Law & Order* is a rap sheet longer than your arm, but a few faces you might want to look out for in those reruns are: Sarah Paulson, Laverne Cox, Sarah Hyland, Idris Elba, Philip Seymour Hoffman, Jennifer Garner, Julianna Margulies, Claire Danes, Allison Janney, Laura Linney, Emmy Rossum, Amanda Peet, Courtney B. Vance, Ellen Pompeo, Peter Facinelli, Edie Falco, and Felicity Huffman.

The "Dun-Dun" Effect

What's the sound of 500 Japanese men stamping their feet? Call it *dun-dun, chung-chung, thunk-thunk,* or whatever else you think it sounds like. The iconic sound effect that underscores key moments in each episode of *Law & Order* was created by show composer Mike Post, who told *Entertainment Weekly* that he intended for the sound to mimic a jail cell slamming shut. It's a synthesized effect that combines about seven different sounds, including the sound of hundreds of Japanese men stamping their feet on a wooden floor.

By the way, Post, who also wrote the show's theme, gets a separate royalty credit every time the sound is used. Dun-dun!

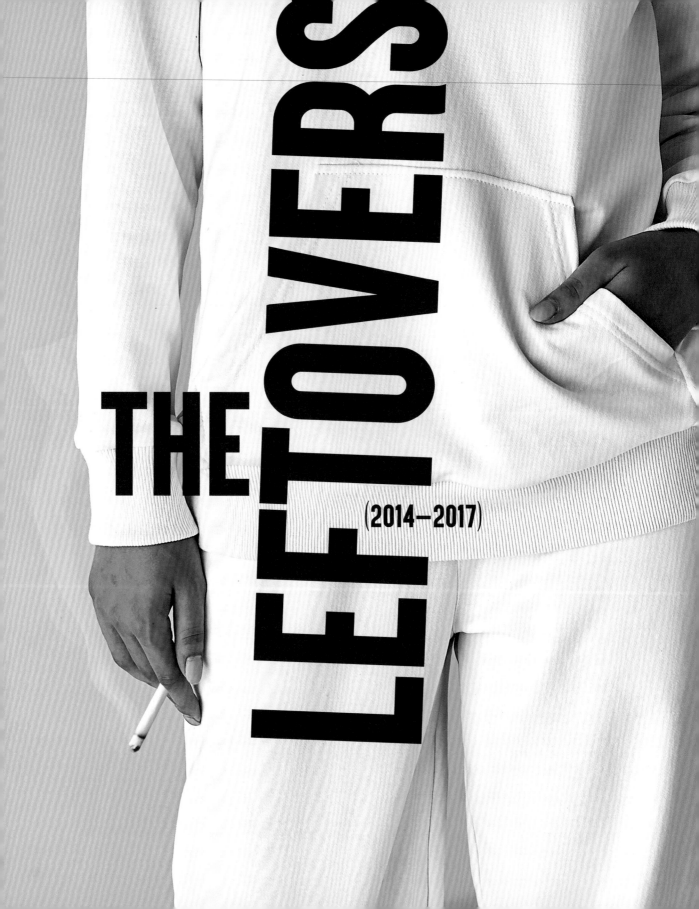

THE LEFTOVERS

(2014—2017)

CREATED BY: Damon Lindelof and Tom Perrotta (based on Tom Perrotta's novel)

SEASONS: 3

EPISODES: 28

OTHER SHOWS BY DAMON LINDELOF:
Lost (2004–2010)
Watchmen (2019)

A one-sentence summary of HBO's *The Leftovers* might sound something like this: "Three years after 2 percent of the world's population has vanished without a trace, suburban sheriff Kevin Garvey (played by Justin Theroux) and other survivors cope with the loss in different ways." In terms of comprehensiveness, that's a little like describing the Bible's New Testament as "a story about how God's son was born on Earth, made some friends and enemies, was killed, and came back to life."

The Leftovers was based on Tom Perrotta's novel of the same name, which imagines the world after an ostensibly non-religious rapture known as the "Sudden Departure." But creator Damon Lindelof had covered all of Perrotta's published territory by the end of season 1, which allowed him (with Perrotta's help) to expand the scope of the series in virtually every direction, first to a town untouched by the catastrophe, then to Australia, with increasingly frequent side quests into the subconscious and spiritual realms. Though not as commercially successful as Lindelof's previous series, *Lost, The Leftovers* is regarded by many as one of the most innovative shows of all time—and one that assumes its viewers are smart enough to draw their own conclusions.

SPOILERS! NOT EVEN TOM PERROTTA KNOWS WHERE THE MISSING POPULATION WENT.

Though the Sudden Departure hangs like a pall over everything else in the series, *The Leftovers* creators maintained from the get-go that they were never going to reveal why it happened or where the victims went. But they weren't exactly withholding much-coveted details from the audience; they simply never made up a backstory. When Lindelof first met with Perrotta about partnering on a TV adaptation, he asked the author if he at least knew what had happened to everyone. As Lindelof told *Variety*, "[Perrotta] said in the most kind and generous and authentically honest way: 'I got to be honest with you, man, I've never even thought about it.'"

In the end, the series does offer an explanation—if you believe it. In the series finale, Nora (Carrie Coon) tells

Kevin that she was able to travel to the other side in order to find her children, who were among the 2 percent of the population who disappeared as part of the Sudden Departure. But this parallel world was really just a mirror image of Nora and Kevin's reality, except that it was inhabited by the 2 percent who believed that 98 percent of the population disappeared. Ultimately, it's up to the viewer to decide whether they believe Nora's story.

THE CREATORS OF *THE LEFTOVERS* HAVE SHAKESPEARE (AND ALAN CUMMING) TO THANK FOR INADVERTENTLY FINDING THEM A COMPOSER.

While watching Alan Cumming's one-man performance of *Macbeth* on Broadway, Peter Berg, who directed the pilot of *The Leftovers*, was struck by the atmospheric instrumentals that punctuated each scene. He told Lindelof to track down the musician—a Berlin-born British composer named Max Richter who had some experience writing music for film, but never television shows. Richter signed on to score *The Leftovers*; he has since composed pieces for *Black Mirror* and *Taboo*, the latter of which earned him an Emmy nomination.

LINDELOF'S INFLUENCES INCLUDED *TWIN PEAKS*, *THE SOPRANOS*, AND *THE WIRE*.

Lindelof grew up watching David Lynch's *Twin Peaks*, and that show's blend of absurdism, mystery, and spirituality inspired similar motifs in *The Leftovers*. "There is no *Leftovers* without *Twin Peaks*, full stop," Lindelof told *Entertainment Weekly*. It's not the only show that influenced the series: Kevin Garvey's jaunt into the dream world in the season 2 episode "International Assassin" was a nod to Tony Soprano's time in limbo during *The Sopranos*. *The Wire*, which focused on a fresh cast of characters in season 2, inspired Lindelof to set the second season of *The Leftovers* in a different town and to introduce the Murphy family.

A RELIGIOUS SCHOLAR SERVED AS A CONSULTING PRODUCER FOR *THE LEFTOVERS*.

Upon discovering that religious scholar Reza Aslan was a fan of *The Leftovers*, then-HBO executive Michael Ellenberg suggested that Lindelof meet with him. Lindelof, who had read Aslan's book *Zealot: The Life and Times of Jesus of Nazareth*, agreed, and he and Aslan discussed the show's religious aspects over lunch. One idea that particularly appealed to Lindelof was Aslan's belief that Kevin Garvey was a shaman—someone who deciphered enigmatic messages from the spiritual world. Aslan ended up serving as a consulting producer for the show's second and third seasons.

THERE'S A REASON KEVIN GARVEY IS NAKED SO OFTEN.

The dogged protagonist seems to spend less time fully clothed than any other character, especially in later episodes. According to Lindelof, nudity generally symbolizes vulnerability, which Kevin has in spades. "The more vulnerable he feels, the more naked he should be," Lindelof explained to Vulture before the final season aired. "And he's feeling awfully vulnerable this year."

Theroux has also pointed out that his character often has reasonable explanations for being underdressed: Clothes might not make sense if you're "rebirthed into a different astral plane" or in bed with your spouse.

FREEZE FRAME

"PILOT" // SEASON 1, EPISODE 1
Christopher Eccleston, who plays the Reverend Matt Jamison, credits his role in *The Leftovers*, in part, for forcing him to rethink his longtime atheism. "I have huge rage at organized religion," he told NPR in 2016. "But I do feel, at the moment, a little more spiritually open to what may be religious beliefs."

"It's not *The Dick Van Dyke Show*," Theroux told *The New York Times*. "I'm not going to be wearing baby blue pajamas."

TWO NAMES FROM A WU-TANG CLAN NAME GENERATOR MAKE A CAMEO IN THE CREDITS.

At the end of the opening credits for "Don't Be Ridiculous" (season 3, episode 2), the slide flips quickly from "Created by Damon Lindelof and Tom Perrotta" to "Written by Tha Lonely Donkey Kong & Specialist Contagious." This, unlike the show's more mind-boggling metaphysical moments, has a clear explanation: The two writers typed their names into an online Wu-Tang Clan name generator (the same one, in fact, that *Community* star and *Atlanta* creator Donald Glover used to come up with his stage name, Childish Gambino). It's the first of a few Wu-Tang Clan references in the episode. Nora (Carrie Coon) later shows Erika (Regina King) the Wu-Tang Clan *W* tattooed on her forearm, and the two of them then spend some time bouncing on Erika's trampoline as Wu-Tang Clan's "Protect Ya Neck (The Jump Off)" blasts in the background. It reportedly cost HBO $30,000 to use the song.

THERE'S A *LEFTOVERS* EASTER EGG IN THE PILOT OF *THE GOOD PLACE*.

Michael Schur, a longtime Lindelof fan and avid viewer of *The Leftovers*, asked Lindelof to breakfast in order to bounce an idea off him. That idea became NBC's *The Good Place*, and Schur thanked his friend for the guidance via an Easter egg. In the first episode of *The Good Place*, a portrait honors Doug Forcett, the man who was 92 percent accurate in determining what the afterlife would look like. Beneath the portrait is a plaque bearing the date of that occasion: October 14, the same day of *The Leftovers*' Sudden Departure. (Later in the season, Kristen Bell's Eleanor finds out her soulmate is from Teaneck, New Jersey—Lindelof's hometown.)

SEVERAL CAST MEMBERS TOOK SOUVENIRS FROM THE SET.

Lindelof gifted Scott Glenn (who plays Kevin Garvey, Sr.) a didgeridoo, and Theroux claimed he was mailed the portrait of Kevin Garvey as a white-suited president from "The Most Powerful Man in the World (and His Identical Twin Brother)" (season 3, episode 7). Amy Brenneman made off with the lighter that Laurie Garvey's daughter gave her, and Coon absconded with something a little larger: Nora's bike.

FREEZE FRAME

"AXIS MUNDI" // SEASON 2, EPISODE 1
Mark Linn-Baker was unaware that there was a running joke about *Perfect Strangers*, the eighties sitcom that was his breakout hit, in *The Leftovers* when he auditioned to play Nora's boss at the Department of Sudden Departures in the first season. Lindelof said he gave a great audition, but he couldn't "cast him, because Mark Linn-Baker as himself is no longer there." Though Linn-Baker didn't get that role, he did appear in two episodes—this one and season 3's "Don't Be Ridiculous"—as himself.

LOST

(2004–2010)

CREATED BY: Jeffrey Lieber, J. J. Abrams, and Damon Lindelof

SEASONS: 6

EPISODES: 121

OTHER SHOWS BY J. J. ABRAMS:
Felicity (1998–2002)
Alias (2001–2006)
Fringe (2008–2013)

OTHER SHOWS BY DAMON LINDELOF:
The Leftovers (2014–2017)
Watchmen (2019)

On the surface, *Lost* might seem to be a typical adventure show featuring survivors of a plane crash who are stranded on a tropical island and must learn how to work together in order to survive. But the show doesn't take long to reveal its strange side, and the less you know about that going in, the better. Let's just say the island has many secrets…but not nearly as many as the survivors, whose pre-crash backstories are doled out in flashbacks.

Lost's many mysteries compelled audiences to try to figure out what was happening themselves, searching for clues, analyzing the science, and theorizing on social media and around the watercooler as few fan bases had ever done before. Its divisive ending has led to many debates about the show's legacy, but as *Entertainment Weekly*'s Jeff Jenson, a *Lost* superfan, wrote on the series' tenth anniversary, "What is certain is that *Lost* helped change the way we watch and talk about television."

JEFFREY LIEBER SPENT A YEAR WRITING THE ORIGINAL PILOT.

In 2003, ABC Entertainment chairman Lloyd Braun was vacationing in Hawaii when he saw the Tom Hanks film *Cast Away* and felt a show with a similar premise might work. Then he came up with the idea to pair the castaway aspect with *Survivor*. When Braun pitched his idea to other ABC execs, they weren't interested, but he pursued it anyway, with the help of Thom Sherman, head of drama development. They hired Jeffrey Lieber to write the pilot script, which the writer worked on over the course of a year. When Braun received Lieber's

script, it wasn't at all what he had hoped for. Not only had Lieber changed the name to *Nowhere*, the script "fell prey to many of the concerns that many people had when they first heard the idea," Braun told *Grantland*. "I was very disappointed."

Lieber's version of the show was "darker, emotionally," he told *Empire*. "At one point in the pilot, a kid runs up and says, 'Look! There are people swimming in the water!' And it's all these bodies of people who have drowned."

J. J. ABRAMS AND DAMON LINDELOF WERE HIRED TO REWRITE THE ORIGINAL PILOT.

Valuable time had passed, and Sherman wanted to shelve the idea until the following year. But ABC was struggling, and Braun knew that he might not be around for the next development season. So he made a phone call to J. J. Abrams, who was then working on *Alias*, and explained his idea. "I thought I could see that as a movie, but I didn't understand what that would be beyond the immediate aftermath," Abrams told *Nightline* in 2006. After thinking about it for a bit, he called Braun back. "I pitched a version where the island wasn't just an island," he said. "And I thought it was a little weirder than what they would want, but he said, 'No, I love that. Do that show.'"

Abrams was juggling a few other projects at the time, so ABC brought on Damon Lindelof to help with *Lost*. He quickly recognized that viewers would want everyone to get off the island, so to "defuse" that, he suggested giving the characters pasts that would make them want to stay, and showing flashbacks to their old lives, while Abrams came to the table with the ideas for the hatch and the Others. The duo wrote a twenty-two-page outline in five days; Braun called the following Saturday with a greenlight.

Lieber, meanwhile, was ultimately given a co-creator credit on the show thanks to his work on the original script, elements of which are in the aired pilot.

SPOILERS! *LOST*'S CREATORS HAD A DIFFERENT FATE IN MIND FOR JACK.

Many shows go through changes between the initial pilot script and filming, and *Lost* was no exception. Kate (Evangeline Lilly), for example, was not initially going to be a convict. And if Lindelof and Abrams had had their way, Jack Shephard would have died halfway through the pilot, which they thought would drive home the fact that no one was safe on the island. They even had Michael Keaton lined up to play the role.

But certain parties who read the script were against the idea; they thought it would destroy the audience's trust in the show. As they discussed it among themselves, the producers could see the logic of that. But Abrams wasn't convinced until he showed the script to his oldest friend, actor Greg Grunberg, who loved everything about it *except* the fact that Jack died—an element that he said made him furious. So Jack lived, causing Keaton to bow out and Matthew Fox to step in. Abrams then cast Grunberg as the pilot of Oceanic Flight 815…and had the island's mysterious monster kill him in the pilot instead.

THE TITLE CARD IS AN HOMAGE TO ANOTHER FAMOUS SHOW.

Abrams came up with the show's title card, which features the word *LOST* ever so slightly out of focus on a black background, a hat tip to the opening sequence of one of his favorite shows, *The Twilight Zone*.

THE LYRICS TO DRIVESHAFT'S HIT SONG CAME FROM *THE PHIL DONAHUE SHOW*.

On board Oceanic 815 when it crashes is Charlie Pace (Dominic Monaghan), bassist for the band Driveshaft. Producers knew they wanted the band to be a one-hit wonder, and they knew they wanted to put that song on the show—but they weren't sure what, exactly, the ditty would be. Monaghan even wrote a song with a friend for possible use, but *Lost*'s producers opted to go for an inside joke instead.

4 8 LOST BY THE NUMBERS 15

As they gathered around the video monitors watching the show's dailies, producers would often repeat a nonsensical quote from an audience member on *The Phil Donahue Show*, who had said, "You all everybody is acting like it's the stupid people wearing the expensive clothes." As producer Bryan Burk recalled in a DVD featurette, "At one point, in a delirious stupor, we realized that we had said it so many times, that that had to be the song."

Abrams came up with the melody for the chorus the day they shot the scene in the pilot where Kate is trying to figure out where she knows Charlie from and Charlie sings a bit of the song. The full quote and lyrics of the song, which they called "You All Everybody," appeared in the season 1 episode "The Moth."

CREATING "SMOKEY" WAS NO EASY FEAT.
Regular simulations didn't give the producers the effect they were looking for in conjuring "Smokey," their smoke monster; the smoke had to roil, move in different directions, and interact with the characters. Put simply, VFX artists accomplished what they needed to do by building a digital model in the computer that created smoke and controlled the monster's movement, then layered stock footage of real smoke over the effect. "You add layers of real smoke on top of it so when it's all meshed together, it has as analog a feeling as possible, even though a lot of the process is digital," Eden FX's John Teska told *Popular Mechanics*. In early seasons, making Smokey required so much computing power that rendering a single frame of the animation took hours; visual effects supervisor Mitch Suskin called their ability to get the effect done on schedule "miraculous."

SPOILERS! THE CREATORS DIDN'T KNOW HOW THE SHOW WAS GOING TO END.
Speaking with *Grantland*, co-showrunner Carlton Cuse compared the first season of *Lost* to "putting out an apartment fire with a garden hose. We had some general ideas of what we were going to do,

FREEZE FRAME ▶

"WALKABOUT" // **SEASON I, EPISODE 4**
Viewers didn't get a glimpse of what would come to be known as the Smoke Monster, aka Smokey, until the end of season I. Initially, its presence was announced by thrashing trees and its own unique sound, which was created using the noise of a taxi cab receipt printer (recorded by producer Bryan Burk) and the clicking of cicadas.

16   42

ONE OF THE NUMBERS WAS PICKED FOR A SPECIFIC REASON.

Lost fans can recite the Numbers (4 8 15 16 23 42) by heart. The digits worked their way into many facets of the show and, as Lindelof told *Entertainment Weekly*, "We had no idea, no grand design behind the Numbers. . . . This isn't to say that the Numbers don't mean anything.

We just had no idea it had this potential to get totally out of control." But at least one of the Numbers was chosen for a specific reason: "My father was into the Illuminati and the number 23," Lindelof said, and he was "a big reader of Robert Anton Wilson,"

a popularizer of the 23 enigma, which states that there is special significance to the number.

Meanwhile, fans of the show began playing the Numbers in the lottery, and some of them actually won a little bit of cash.

but we were making the show episode to episode," he said. It wasn't until after the first season that they were able to get the writers together and outline the larger mythology of the show. They initially wanted to wrap up after three seasons, but ABC wouldn't hear of it, saying, "You don't end shows people are watching."

That changed with season 3, which ABC split in half. After the first run of episodes, Lindelof told Collider that the network finally acknowledged "that we were working so hard to keep the characters on the island, and it was starting to be immensely frustrating. The flashbacks weren't good anymore."

ABC agreed to end the show. The network wanted ten seasons; Lindelof and Cuse wanted four. Ultimately, they compromised on three more seasons, with fewer episodes, which allowed the writers to switch from flashbacks to flash-forwards and map out an ending.

THE SHOWRUNNERS REGRETTED SOME STORY LINES.

Cuse told *Esquire* that among the story lines he most regretted was the season 3 introduction of Nikki (Kiele Sanchez) and Paulo (Rodrigo Santoro), characters who had apparently been present on the beach, but in the background, since day one. They wrapped up the characters' story line in a single episode, "Exposé," which quickly became the series' most hated. They also regretted exploring the origins of Jack's tattoos (also in season 3), which Cuse called "cringeworthy."

SPOILERS! SOME PLOT POINTS WERE KEPT SECRET FROM THE ACTORS.

Secrets were the name of the game on *Lost*, a rule that sometimes extended to the actors themselves. Terry O'Quinn, for example, didn't know until he got the script for season 1's standout episode "Walkabout" that his character used a wheelchair, or that he was playing a totally different character in Locke's skin in season 5. Michael Emerson, who was originally a guest star and later came on as a series regular to play Ben Linus, told Syfy that even after he was brought on as a series regular, he didn't know anything about his character—until he discovered the truth by accident. "I was asking simple actor questions about why might I do this, or what's going on here…and [the director] was being real cagey," Emerson said. "I thought something was up, and I went to him and I said, 'You know, what would be really cool is if I was actually the leader of the Others.' He blinked at me a couple of times and said, 'I can't discuss that with you.'"

Meanwhile, Néstor Carbonell, who played Richard Alpert, was in the dark about his character's origin until the series was nearly over. At a Paley Center event, the actor said his favorite moment on the show was "finally finding out who the hell I am. Three years of performing in a vacuum and finally I got a call from Carlton: 'OK, we're doing a backstory.' He wouldn't tell me even on the phone what it was about! . . . I've never done a role where I've never known my origin, so this was a departure to say the least."

SPOILERS! THE SERIES FINALE CREDITS CAUSED AUDIENCES TO MISINTERPRET THE ENDING.

When it came time to end *Lost*, the producers made the conscious decision not to try to answer every single lingering question, which they felt would have made for a finale that wasn't very interesting. Instead, recognizing that nothing they did would fully satisfy every single fan, Lindelof told *The Independent* that "we wanted to try to answer a mystery the show hadn't even asked up until that point…let's answer the mystery of what happens when you die and the process that you go through in order to achieve some fundamental level of grace." Hence, the show's finale scenes in a church (filmed in what was actually an elementary school), with most of the characters waiting for Jack—who has just saved the island and died—to finally arrive so they can all move on.

To keep viewers from having to endure a jarring commercial after the series' emotional ending, it was decided that B-roll footage of the crash site would play alongside the credits, which led some viewers to believe that the characters had actually been dead the whole time. (For the record, they were not.)

FREEZE FRAME

PREVIOUSLY ON *LOST*

Lloyd Braun left his position at ABC shortly before *Lost* began airing. To make him a part of the show, Abrams asked him to be the voice saying, "Previously on *Lost* . . ." at the beginning of most episodes. Braun agreed, on the condition that no one outside the *Lost* inner circle would know. Eventually, the secret got out.

UNFORGETTABLE TV CLIFF-HANGERS

As fans of *Lost* can attest, nothing unites a nation of TV watchers quite like a pulse-pounding cliff-hanger. Especially when it involves the collective misery of having to wait up to a year to find out the answer to whatever burning questions a series' season finale leaves behind. Here are a few of television's most famous.

Dallas // "A House Divided"
In 1980, the TV-watching world's collective heart stopped momentarily when, J. R. Ewing (Larry Hagman) was shot in his office by an unknown assailant. In the months that followed, fan theories ran wild about who shot the hit show's favorite love-to-hate antagonist. (The actual killer was revealed in season 4's "Who Done It" episode on November 21, 1980, with 350 million people tuning in worldwide.)

Dynasty // "Royal Wedding"
Not to be outdone, *Dynasty* opted to increase the body count when it closed out its fifth season in 1985 with what became known as the "Moldavian Massacre." What was meant to be the happiest day of soon-to-be-princess Amanda Carrington's (Catherine Oxenberg) life turned into something out of *Kill Bill: Vol. 2* when a group of terrorists descended on her royal wedding to Prince Michael of Moldavia (Michael Praed) and shot the chapel full of bullets, leaving nearly all of the key cast members lying lifeless on the ground. Fans had to wait until the next season to discover who had actually survived.

SPOILERS! Friends // "The One With Ross's Wedding: Part One"
By the time the fourth season of *Friends* rolled around in 1998, viewers had seen Ross and Rachel hate and love each other in equal parts. But as the season came to a close, the sometimes-couple's "break" seemed destined for permanency as the gang (minus Rachel and Phoebe) headed to London for Ross's wedding to Emily. But happily ever after turned into a big "uh-oh" when Rachel's last-minute arrival at the church led Ross to utter her name—not Emily's—while reciting his wedding vows.

The West Wing // "What Kind of Day Has It Been"
The West Wing didn't waste much time in getting down to business when, in 2000, they closed out the series' first season with a bang—literally—as gunshots rang out and the audience watched as President Josiah Bartlet (Martin Sheen) and all of his key staffers were thrown to the ground, pulled away, and/or placed into some other circumstance that left audiences wondering, "Who's been hit?" And that's exactly what the audience heard on the audio track as the episode faded out. Fun Aaron Sorkin fact: "What Kind of Day Has It Been" was also used to title the season 1 finales of Sorkin's *Sports Night* and *Studio 60 on the Sunset Strip* as well as the series finale of *The Newsroom*.

SPOILERS! Breaking Bad // "Gliding All Over"
OK, so 2012's "Gliding All Over" is technically a midseason finale. But as its conclusion wouldn't come until nearly one year later, we're calling "marketing-driven semantics" on that distinction. After years of watching Walter White vacillate in every aspect of his life—Is he a family man or a drug kingpin? Is he cooking meth for the money or the power? Will he ever choose boxers over briefs?—the character we got to know and like in the show's early days seemed to have returned. Walter has gotten out of the drug biz and is happily ensconced back in his home life, complete with a family dinner with his in-laws, Hank and Marie. But when a touch of gastrointestinal unease sends Hank to the bathroom, he flips through a copy of Walt Whitman's *Leaves of Grass* and sees an inscription that tells him all he needs to know: Walter White is the meth king he has been chasing. It's a moment that will undoubtedly go down in history as television's most compelling scene ever shot on a toilet.

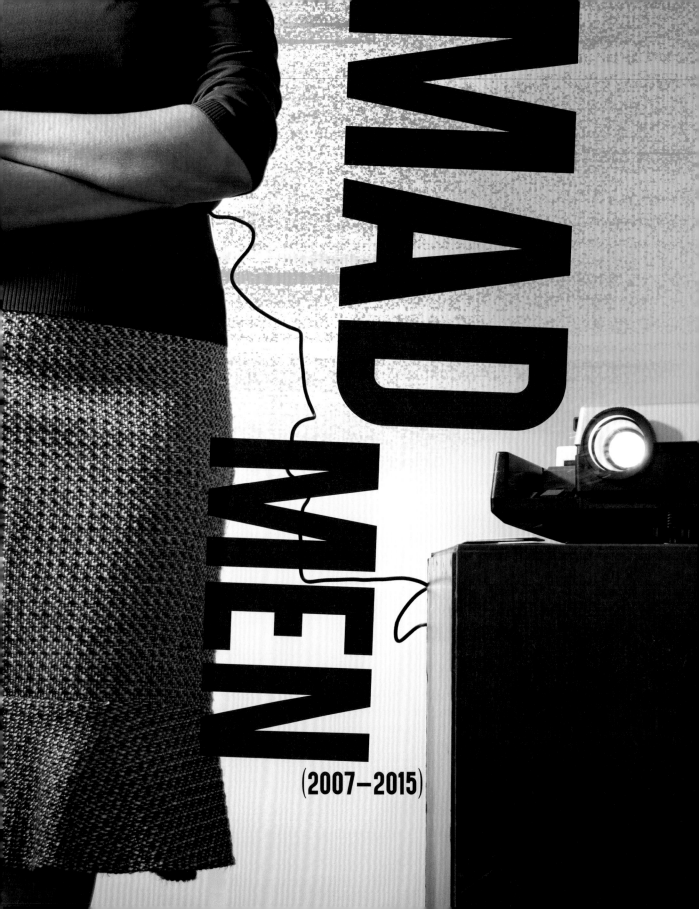

MAD MEN

(2007–2015)

CREATED BY: Matthew Weiner

SEASONS: 7

EPISODES: 92

OTHER SHOWS BY MATTHEW WEINER:
The Romanoffs (2018)

When *Mad Men* made its television debut in the summer of 2007, its story line seemed straight-forward enough: When he's not creating brilliant advertising campaigns for some of the country's biggest corporations, a handsome Madison Avenue executive named Don Draper (Jon Hamm) likes to smoke, drink, and cheat on his wife—and is often aided and abetted in these activities by his boss, the equally debonair Roger Sterling (John Slattery). But as the series continued, cracks began to show in Don's perfectly chiseled exterior, and it became clear that we were only beginning to scratch the surface of who, exactly, Don Draper was.

As such, *Mad Men* took on a slightly more mysterious tone as time went on—one that ultimately led devoted viewers to wonder whether the show had ever been straightforward at all, or if they had been hoodwinked, and *Mad Men* had been some sort of strange 1960s fever dream all along. There were bizarre fan theories (a popular one was that Draper was actually the notorious hijacker D. B. Cooper) and immediate suspicions if creator Matthew Weiner dared to let the camera linger on the image of an open elevator (what's he trying to tell us?). Was there anything to this heightened sense of paranoia? The best way to answer that question is to dive into the series and find out for yourself.

THE *MAD MEN* PILOT GOT MATTHEW WEINER HIS JOB AS A WRITER ON *THE SOPRANOS*.

In 2002, Weiner sent the *Mad Men* pilot to David Chase, creator of *The Sopranos*, as a writing sample. In 2012, *The New York Times* asked Chase how Weiner had come to his attention. "We were looking for writers, as we always were, and he was submitted," Chase recalled. "And what was submitted to me was the pilot for *Mad Men*. And it was quite good, and I met with him and he was hired. And then two or three years later, he took that pilot and apparently got somewhere with it."

HBO PASSED ON MAKING *MAD MEN*—AND IT'S ALL CHASE'S FAULT.

Before AMC signed on to broadcast *Mad Men*, Weiner spent some time shopping the script around. Considering its dark content, HBO seemed like the perfect fit. Chase thought so, too, and delivered the script for the *Mad Men* pilot to the network's executives himself. According to a 2009 story in *Vanity Fair*, both Chase and Weiner told the writer, "HBO indicated it would make *Mad Men* on the condition that Chase be an executive producer, and Chase said he had further discussion with Weiner about direct-ing the pilot, but despite being 'very tempted' by directing, he said no to both propositions, wanting to move away from weekly television."

DON DRAPER IS BASED ON A REAL PERSON.

At least parts of Don Draper are based on a real person: Draper Daniels, the legendary Chicago ad man who, while creative head at Leo Burnett, invented the Marlboro Man. In 2009, Daniels's wife even penned a piece for *Chicago* magazine about the real-life Draper, noting that Weiner "acknowledged that he based his protagonist Don Draper in part on Draper Daniels, whom he called 'one of the great copy guys.'"

THE PILOT WAS SHOT WHILE *THE SOPRANOS* WAS ON HIATUS.

Because the final season of *The Sopranos* was shot in two parts, Weiner took advantage of the hiatus to shoot the pilot of *Mad Men*. He was able to recruit several of his collaborators on *The Sopranos* to help. "Matt asked Alan Taylor to direct while all his buddies on *The Sopranos* were on hiatus," Rob Sorcher, AMC's former executive VP of programming and production, told *TV Insider*. "They shot the pilot in ten days in Queens."

THE FIRST AND SECOND EPISODES WERE SHOT ONE YEAR APART.

In *TV Insider*'s oral history of the series, Weiner said that nearly a year elapsed between shooting the pilot for *Mad Men* and its second episode. "There's seven years between when I first wrote the pilot, and then writing the second episode," Weiner explained. "A lot about my vision changed in terms of how the story-telling would be done. Ultimately it was done very much in the pilot the way we continued to do it. But I didn't know if it was just going to be a premise, or if we were going to be able to do something like that every week."

Mad Women

In 2009, *The Wall Street Journal* went behind the scenes of *Mad Men* and discovered something interesting: It was a female-dominated world. At the time, seven of the show's nine writers were female and five of the third season's thirteen episodes were directed by women.

WEINER WAS ALLOWED THREE "SHITS" PER SHOW.

In 2011, Weiner participated in a wide-ranging Q&A with *Curb Your Enthusiasm* star Jeff Garlin in Los Angeles. When asked about how *Mad Men* might have been different had it sold to HBO, Weiner replied, "*Mad Men* is TV-14, not even TV-MA. I'm allowed three 'shits' a show. I can say 'Jesus,' I can say 'Christ,' but I can't say 'Jesus Christ' unless he's actually there."

MAD MEN BOOSTED LUCKY STRIKE'S SALES.

The old-school cigarette brand, which played a recurring role on the show from its very beginning, likely benefited from its association with *Mad Men*: The company nearly doubled its sales during the show's run (selling an additional 10 billion cigarettes).

NO, THE ACTORS DIDN'T SMOKE REAL CIGARETTES.

"You don't want actors smoking real cigarettes," Weiner told *The New York Times*. "They get agitated and nervous. I've been on sets where people throw up, they've smoked so much." Instead, they smoked herbal cigarettes. "They're dis-gusting," Christina Hendricks, who played Joan, told *Esquire*.

JESSICA PARÉ SCORED A HIT WITH HER RENDITION OF "ZOU BISOU BISOU."

Paré, as the new Mrs. Draper, stole the season 5 premiere when she serenaded Don with her sexy take on "Zou Bisou." It didn't take long for her performance to transcend television and take over the music world, eventually becoming the number one song on *Billboard*'s World Digital chart.

FREEZE FRAME ▶

**"LADY LAZARUS" //
SEASON 5, EPISODE 8**
Weiner paid big bucks to close out season 5's "Lady Lazarus" episode, spending $250,000 to license the rights to The Beatles' "Tomorrow Never Knows."

PETE CAMPBELL AND STAN RIZZO WERE TEEN IDOLS IN THE 1990S.

Vincent Kartheiser and Jay Ferguson—who played Pete Campbell and Stan Rizzo, respectively—had a taste of what it feels like to be a teen idol back in the 1990s. Kartheiser's career kicked off in 1993 with a small role in the Christian Slater film *Untamed Heart*; bigger parts in *Little Big League*, *The Indian in the Cupboard*, and *Alaska* followed. Ferguson's fame came when he was cast as Ponyboy Curtis in the 1990 TV adaptation of *The Outsiders*.

THE DRAPERS' CREEPY NEIGHBOR GLEN IS WEINER'S SON.

The season 1 episode "Marriage of Figaro" marked the first appearance of Glen Bishop, the Drapers' creepy kid neighbor who obsesses over Betty before moving on to Sally. That creepy kid just so happens to be played by Weiner's son, Marten.

"He was cast because he was the best person available for the role," Weiner told NPR. "I would have never thought of him if he wasn't my son. It was actually someone else's idea, and I was counseled against it from all the complications that could happen from him failing at that job. But he really nailed it, and he's a really good actor."

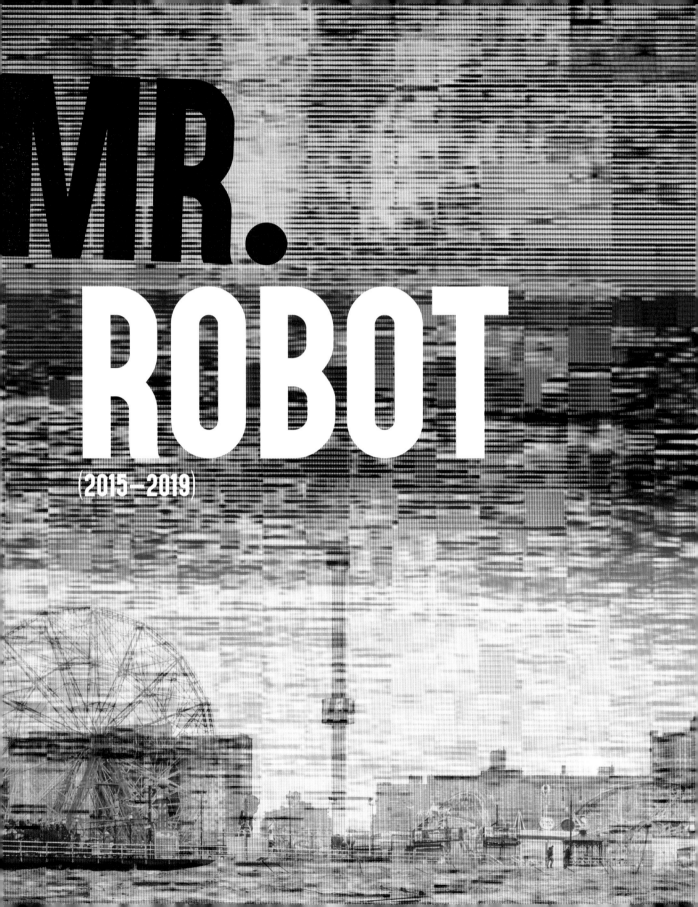

MR.
ROBOT

(2015—2019)

CREATED BY: Sam Esmail

SEASONS: 4

EPISODES: 45

On June 24, 2015, USA Network premiered *Mr. Robot*, a New York City–based—and shot—thriller-drama about Elliot Alderson (Rami Malek), an alienated and drug-addled vigilante hacker who uses his skills to hack into E Corp, one of the world's largest corporations, and erase all consumer debt. This financial shakeup is just one part of the mission of fsociety, a group of anarchist hackers who recruit Elliot to work with them, using their tech skills to change the world. Christian Slater played the eponymous Mr. Robot, the head of fsociety, who isn't what he seems to be.

For four seasons, the acclaimed series—created by and mostly written and directed by Sam Esmail—explored isolation, hacker culture, blurred reality, the deadly effects of capitalism, cybersecurity, mental illness, and family ties. Malek won an Emmy for his performance, and near the end of the show's run he also won an Oscar for the Freddie Mercury biopic *Bohemian Rhapsody*. On December 22, 2019, *Mr. Robot* logged off for good.

ELLIOT IS BASED ON SAM ESMAIL.
During a showrunner roundtable discussion with *The Hollywood Reporter*, Esmail revealed that *Mr. Robot* was partially autobiographical. "Elliot is a thinly veiled version of myself," he said. "I wrote what I knew because a lot of the details of his life and the loneliness were issues I've dealt with basically my whole life."

THE ARAB SPRING INSPIRED THE SERIES.
Esmail, who, like Rami Malek, is of Egyptian descent, followed the events of the 2010 to 2012 Arab Spring uprising closely, and told Gizmodo he went to Egypt after the movement ended. "My cousins are young and they were angry, but they were channeling that for positive change," he said. "The revolutionary spirit they had was so inspiring and moving—and they used Twitter and Facebook, and the controlling generation couldn't figure out a way to stop that. That to me was totally the final piece of the puzzle when I went into writing *Mr. Robot*."

FREEZE FRAME

"EPS1.9_ZERO-DAY.AVI" // SEASON 1, EPISODE 10
On August 26, 2015, a former Roanoke, Virginia, TV station employee killed two of his former co-workers, reporter Alison Parker and photojournalist Adam Ward, while they were on the air. *Mr. Robot's* season finale had been filmed before the tragedy and featured an eerily similar event in which an E Corp employee killed himself in front of cameras. The real-life incident spurred USA Network to postpone the finale by a week. The episode aired on September 2, 2015.

E CORP'S LOGO IS THE SAME AS ENRON'S.

Esmail hasn't said whether E Corp, aka Evil Corp, is based on a real corporation, but he did confirm to Gizmodo that the "E" is "totally the Enron logo. It's not like they're going to sue us for it."

ESMAIL WAS CONSIDERING ABANDONING THE PROJECT . . . THEN MALEK AUDITIONED.

The producers auditioned close to a hundred actors for the role of Elliot, but couldn't find the right person, because most of the actors just didn't feel right. "I thought we were in real trouble," Esmail told Recode. "I was contemplating not doing the show, because we were not finding the right guy. Then Rami came in and totally transformed the character. He added the warmth." Esmail went on to say a character who has a mental illness and rants about society might not be likeable. "It takes a really precise take . . . to add that warmth," he said. "This is all happening because he's in a lot of pain, and there's a forgiveness that you, as an audience member, can have when someone performs it like that."

FIGHT CLUB WAS A MAJOR INFLUENCE ON *MR. ROBOT*.

In an interview with Vulture, Esmail discussed films and TV shows that influenced the series, including *Fight Club*. "There is something audacious and exciting and entertaining about that film even though it is extremely political at the same time," he said. *Fight Club*'s "anti-establishment" spirit might be the most

obvious influence on the series, down to both the film and show using the Pixies song "Where Is My Mind" in pivotal scenes.

AMERICAN PSYCHO WAS ANOTHER INFLUENCE.

"We wanted to strike a balance between being straightforward and satirical," Esmail told Vulture of *Mr. Robot's* depiction of corporate America. As such, he looked to Mary Harron's adaptation of *American Psycho*, which is certainly a bit more extreme than *Mr. Robot*, but Esmail calls it "one of the best films about corporate politics even though it is not, I hope, a realistic representation."

REAL LIFE MIMICKED *MR. ROBOT'S* STORY LINES.

After Esmail filmed the pilot, USA decided to pick up the series on November 24, 2014—the same time the Sony hack occurred, some elements of which were later addressed by *Mr. Robot*. The pilot mentioned Ashley Madison, the infamous dating site for married people, and in 2015 real-life hackers breached the website and published private information belonging to its users, including Esmail (who had signed up for research purposes).

CHRISTIAN SLATER WORE HIS OWN HAT.

In 2019, Jimmy Kimmel asked Slater if he got to keep any mementos from the show, and Slater said he got to keep Mr. Robot's jacket and khaki-colored baseball hat. "[It] was originally mine anyway," Slater said. "They gave it back after four seasons." Slater said he wore the

famous hat to a wardrobe fitting. "It had my sweat in it. It was dirty. . . . It had a good, natural, raw quality to it."

MALEK USED AN EARPIECE TO RECEIVE HIS VOICE-OVER LINES.

Because the show features Elliot's running inner monologue, Malek had to wear a surveillance device in his ear called an earwig. "It's basically an earbud that fits into my ear and I turn it on whenever there's voice-over," he told *Vanity Fair*. A female production assistant read him his voice-over lines, and he reacted to them. "I tried out a bunch of people but for some reason there was something really soothing about this girl's voice, and so it just works for me." He said one time he had the PA yell the lines into his ear, which resulted in temporary damage. "I pulled the earbud out of my ear and it was covered in blood." He also said that to prepare for emotional scenes, he'd get music pumped into his earwig.

ESMAIL WANTED ALL THE TECHNOLOGY TO BE ACCURATE.

Esmail told NPR the hacker films and TV shows he grew up watching weren't always realistic, and he disliked the use of CGI; therefore, he wanted to make sure *Mr. Robot* was authentic. "One of the rules I have on my show is that we don't green screen…anything. So everything you see that we filmed is real," he said. "So the actors, I really wanted them to react to what is actually going on onscreen."

THE SHOW HIRED REAL-LIFE HACKERS AS CONSULTANTS.

To add to the show's authenticity, the producers hired Michael Bazzell as a technical assistant, who had done some hacking in his youth before working for law-enforcement agencies. "I felt this could be the first-ever show that cares about getting hacking right, even if it means altering a story line," Bazzell told Vulture. He helped test the show's hacks for accuracy and paid close attention to details. "We've had a couple of moments we altered that weren't devastating to the story line. The scripted technology didn't work. It wasn't plausible, and we didn't want to sell something not plausible to the audience." Overall, real-life hackers praised the show.

BD WONG'S TRANS CHARACTER TAPPED INTO "POWER DYNAMICS."

Wong—who played Whiterose, a transgender woman who heads up the China-based hacker group the Dark Army—received an Emmy nomination for his nuanced performance. The character was gender fluid: Sometimes they appeared as a man, other times as a woman.

"Here is a character that, for all intents and purposes—there is a poetry of Sam's utilization of this character as trans—is rather symbolic," Wong told *The Hollywood Reporter*. "What I mean is that he really wants to discuss in a big way on the show the power dynamics associated with gender. There's a great challenge in being a powerful woman in a powerful white man's world. I think that it's part of his choice to make her a person who needs to be gender fluid to get what she wants."

BIZARRE TV CROSSOVERS

Why have one TV show when you can have two? And why just have a TV crossover when you can have a really weird TV crossover? The TV crossover had something of a heyday in the nineties, when popular programs on the same network would routinely cross paths with one another as special events made to boost ratings. But sift through the run-of-the-mill must-see TV and you'll find some oddball crossovers that have taken place across the decades—like the time *ALF* and *Mr. Robot* met up.

ALF × MR. ROBOT

ALF really gets around. In 2016, decades after his show's cancellation, ALF came out of mothballs to make a cameo appearance in *Mr. Robot*. Paul and Linda Fusco, puppeteers for ALF in the original show (Paul, who co-created the series with Tom Patchett, also did the voice), returned for *Mr. Robot*'s season 2 episode "Eps2.4_m4ster-s1ave.aes," in which Elliot briefly finds himself inside a nineties-style sitcom. Writer Adam Penn, speaking to *The Wall Street Journal*, explained why ALF was the perfect choice for a cameo in the trippy techno-thriller about a man disconnected from reality: "While [ALF and Elliot] differ on a personality level, ALF was literally marooned on a planet away from home, isolated in a house, forced to try to fit in and connect with a family of strangers. There are certainly weird parallels between Elliot and ALF, which made the choice of our guest star seem like a no-brainer."

THE X-FILES × COPS

As a show, *The X-Files* was never too concerned with realism—unless one accepts that all varieties of monsters and little green men really do exist. So it was odd when the show's seventh season saw a crossover episode with *Cops*. "X-Cops" starts off like a normal *Cops* episode, only to see Mulder and Scully intrude on the police's hunt for what turns out to be an invisible monster that transforms based on the fears of its victims. Writer and producer Vince Gilligan had been trying to get a *Cops* episode made since season 4, but it took until season 7—when it looked like the show might be canceled—for *The X-Files* creator Chris Carter to give him the go-ahead.

DOCTOR WHO × EASTENDERS

British sci-fi institution *Doctor Who* has intersected a handful of times with British soap opera institution *EastEnders*. A two-part 1993 charity special called "Dimensions in Time"—which doubled as a thirtieth anniversary celebration for *Doctor Who*—sees the Third through Seventh incarnations of the Doctor attempt to stop the Rani (a renegade Time Lady) from capturing a human, which would allow her to complete her quasi-zoo of all sentient life forms. The Doctor and various companions find themselves bopping through different time periods around London's fictional Albert Square, where *EastEnders* takes place; in the process, they meet several characters from the show. *EastEnders* has been referred to several times within *Doctor Who* as the fictional show that it is, making its actual appearance in the *Who* canon a bit of a logical head-scratcher—nothing you wouldn't expect from a show about traveling through space and time in a police box.

ARCHER × BOB'S BURGERS

Archer and *Bob's Burgers* are wildly different shows with a few key similarities: They're both animated, they both exist under the Fox (now owned by Disney) television umbrella, and they both star, H. Jon Benjamin. So it made sense that there would be a crossover, even though *Bob's Burgers* is family-friendly and *Archer* is decidedly not. The crossover took place in *Archer*'s fourth season premiere and sees special agent Sterling Archer (Benjamin) suffering from amnesia. He's been living as *Bob's Burgers* patriarch Bob Belcher (also Benjamin) and running his restaurant with his family. Said family is drawn in the more realistic style of *Archer*, versus the more stylized look from *Bob's Burgers*.

CREATED BY: Christopher Lloyd and Steven Levitan

SEASONS: 11

EPISODES: 250

OTHER SHOWS BY CHRISTOPHER LLOYD AND STEVEN LEVITAN: *Back to You* (2007–2008)

I n the fall of 2009, ABC debuted a new sitcom called *Modern Family*. Except for TV veteran Ed O'Neill, *Married…with Children*'s Al Bundy, it featured no huge stars. (At least they weren't huge stars at the time.) And apart from its trendy mockumentary style, it promised no gimmicks. Yet this simple story of three different types of "modern families" became a ratings hit and unbeatable Emmy winner for ABC.

Jay Pritchett (O'Neill) is the family patriarch who is remarried to a much younger woman named Gloria (Sofia Vergara), who has a son, Manny Delgado (Rico Rodriguez), from her previous marriage. Jay's daughter, Claire (Julie Bowen), and her real estate agent husband, Phil Dunphy (Ty Burrell), have three children: Haley, Alex, and Luke (Sarah Hyland, Ariel Winter, and Nolan Gould); while Jay's son, Mitchell (Jesse Tyler Ferguson), and his husband, Cameron (Eric Stonestreet), raise their adopted daughter, Lily (Aubrey Anderson-Emmons for most of the show's run). With its whip-smart writing and talented cast of comedic actors, *Modern Family* became an award magnet, winning the Emmy for Best Comedy Series five years in a row.

FREEZE FRAME ▶

"PILOT" // SEASON 1, EPISODE 1
When Julie Bowen auditioned for the role of Claire Dunphy, she was heavily pregnant with her twin sons, Gus and John. Although she was convinced this would take her out of the running, she won the part anyway. But she still hadn't reached her due date when it came time to shoot the pilot, so she masked her belly with things like strategically placed cereal boxes.

THERE WAS AN EXPLANATION FOR THE SHOW'S MOCKUMENTARY STYLE.

Why are the Dunphys and Pritchetts always talking to the camera? There's no reason given, but originally the show had one. *Modern Family* was initially conceived as a documentary shot by Geert Floortje, a Dutch filmmaker who had lived with the Pritchetts years ago as a teenage exchange student and came back to the US as an adult to film them. But Geert got cut before *Modern Family* entered production because, according to Levitan, his documentarian openings, closings, and interview questions "risked becoming an appendage that you had to serve every week." The show was simply shot documentary-style, without the fictitious camera crew.

ROB HUEBEL "AGGRESSIVELY" TURNED DOWN THE PART OF PHIL DUNPHY.

Huebel was being considered for the part of Phil Dunphy. "When I read the script for it, I just hated it," he told Splitsider. "That's what an idiot I am. It's the most popular show in the country, and I love that show now…I'm just a fuckin' idiot because I read the script for it, and I didn't even go into the audition because I just hated it so much. I told my agent I didn't just wanna pass on it. I wanted him to call them and aggressively pass, which is not even a real thing." Clearly there were no hard feelings, as Huebel went on to play Glen Whipple, Phil's nemesis, in one episode—fittingly titled "The One That Got Away."

A SET OF TWINS PLAYED BABY LILY, AND THEY HATED IT.

Mitch and Cam's adopted daughter, Lily, was initially played by twin sisters Ella and Jaden Hiller. The baby girls appeared in the series for the first two seasons, but acting quickly wore them out. As their mom, Michelle, explained to *Woman's Day*, "Halfway through season 2 their personalities had started to develop, and it was really clear to us that they weren't enjoying their time on set. So we told the producers the girls wouldn't be coming back." Those producers apparently tried to sway the Hillers with more money, but they wouldn't budge. So Aubrey Anderson-Emmons was chosen as a replacement. She took over the role of Lily in 2011 and played it through the series finale in 2020.

ERIC STONESTREET WAS FIZBO THE CLOWN AS A KID.

Stonestreet began dressing up as Fizbo when he was nine years old; his dream was to be a clown in the circus. By the time he was eleven, he was performing at kids' birthday parties. "It was my way then as a young man to express my desire to entertain and perform," he told *The Kansas City Star*. "I didn't know what I was saying then was that I wanted to be an actor. I had parents, fortunately, who didn't think I was weird. They thought it was funny and cute and encouraged me

to do it. And I had a grandma who would make my costumes." Stonestreet has said his father came up with the name, but he doesn't know where it came from.

THE WRITERS WROTE JESSE TYLER FERGUSON'S ATTEMPT AT COMING OUT INTO THE SHOW.

In real life, Ferguson (whom producers initially wanted for the role of Cameron) had to come out to his father three times in order for him to accept it. The writers made that part of Mitchell's story on *Modern Family*.

SOFIA VERGARA THOUGHT ED O'NEILL SPOKE SPANISH.

Vergara watched *Married . . . with Children* when she was growing up in Colombia, where the voices were dubbed into Spanish. She didn't realize that it wasn't Ed O'Neill saying Al Bundy's lines in Spanish and was surprised to find when they first met that he couldn't speak her native language. "He had a very sexy Antonio Banderas voice, the guy who was dubbing him," according to Vergara.

O'NEILL'S CHARACTERS HAVE BEEN READING THE SAME NEWSPAPER FOR ALMOST THIRTY YEARS.

Eagle-eyed viewers noticed that O'Neill's Jay reads the same prop newspaper on *Modern Family* that O'Neill's Al Bundy read on *Married . . . with Children*. Many shows use the same prop newspaper because all of the photos and text have been cleared legally.

THE ACTOR WHO PLAYS LUKE DUNPHY IS ACTUALLY A GENIUS.

Nolan Gould's character may not be bright, but Gould has been a member of Mensa since he was four years old. He has an IQ of 150 and graduated from high school when he was thirteen years old.

MODERN FAMILY IS ESPECIALLY POPULAR WITH RICH PEOPLE.

Each year, Nielsen tracks data on TV viewership to find out who's watching which shows. After the company released its 2015 stats, Vulture discovered an interesting fact: Rich people love *Modern Family*. It was the second most popular show among viewers in the eighteen-to-forty-nine age bracket whose households earned an average annual income over $200,000. (*The Walking Dead* was number one.)

THERE'S AN INSIDE JOKE ABOUT O'NEILL'S JIU-JITSU SKILLS.

In the first season, Jay shows off his Brazilian jiu-jitsu chops when he puts Mitchell in a sleeper hold. "I learned this choke from the Gracie brothers," he tells Mitch. Jay is referencing the legendary Gracie martial arts family. The Brazilian clan has produced several generations of competitive fighters, who have passed on their techniques through the Gracie Jiu-Jitsu Academy in California. O'Neill is actually a student there. He's a black belt now, but it took him a while to earn that status.

THERE WAS A FACEBOOK PETITION FOR MITCHELL AND CAMERON TO KISS.

In 2010, the "Let Cam & Mitchell Kiss on *Modern Family*!" Facebook petition was launched. In September of that year, the characters kissed on camera for the first time in the background of a scene—though as Ferguson told *Entertainment Weekly*, " That was something that [the writers] had in the works very early on."

LIN-MANUEL MIRANDA HAD A PRE-HAMILTON CAMEO.

A full four years before *Hamilton* became the hottest Broadway ticket in town, the *Modern Family* casting team decided to tap Miranda for an episode. Miranda won casting director Jeff Greenberg over with his impressive knowledge of the show. "He came in and quoted episode after episode, line after line, joke after joke, and we loved him," Greenberg told *The Observer*. He gave Miranda a part as someone Gloria brings in to ask Jay for business advice. "Thank God we did [cast him] because now he gets me *Hamilton* tickets," Greenberg said.

7 MOCKUMENTARY-STYLE SITCOMS TO BINGE

Though it has seen a decline in recent years, the mockumentary format used in *Modern Family* was all the rage for sitcoms in the early to late 2000s. Here are some other great shows where people talk to the camera . . . for reasons rarely talked about.

Parks and Recreation **(2009–2015)**
The Comeback **(2005; 2014)**
The Office **(UK) (2001–2003)**
The Office **(US) (2005–2013)**
Twenty Twelve **(2011–2012)**
W1A **(2014–2017)**
What We Do in the Shadows
(2019–PRESENT)

THE OFFICE
UK
(2001–2003)

CREATED BY: Ricky Gervais and Stephen Merchant

SEASONS: 2

EPISODES: 14

OTHER SHOWS BY RICKY GERVAIS AND STEPHEN MERCHANT:
Extras (2005–2007)
The Ricky Gervais Show (2010–2012)
Life's Too Short (2011–2013)

I f your only experience with *The Office* is via NBC's long-running American adaptation of the BBC series, you're missing out. While the original series falls firmly into the "comedy" genre, it's that very specific—and unnerving—brand of cringe comedy (think *The Larry Sanders Show*, *Curb Your Enthusiasm*, or *The Comeback*) that separates the series from its more straightforward comedy competitors. And when it comes to the fine art of awkward comedy, there's no more talented practitioner than Ricky Gervais.

Whereas Dunder Mifflin's Michael Scott (Steve Carell) is a rather sweet social misfit who just wants to be liked, Wernham Hogg's David Brent (Gervais) is a self-centered jerk who regularly tries, and desperately fails, to command respect from those around him. And when things don't go Brent's way, he unleashes the childish beast inside, leading to the series' finest moments. His attempt to out-dance his immediate superior, who has everything David wants, is the kind of thing you'll have to rewind and rewatch—if only to prove that Martin Freeman (as paper sales rep Tim Canterbury) has *the* perfect facial response to every situation.

THE OFFICE RECEIVED SOME OF THE POOREST FOCUS GROUP SCORES IN BBC HISTORY.

Though the series became a massive hit around the world, the early reviews for *The Office* were not great. In fact, when the network put it in front of focus groups, it garnered one of the lowest scores in BBC history. "It was the joint lowest, [tied] with women's bowls," Gervais told the *Chicago Tribune*. "And that's not [American] bowling; bowling is exciting compared with women's bowls. This is women rolling a little white ball at a big black ball, somewhere in the north of England."

Over the years, Gervais has regularly reminded people that one critic even called it "a summer stinker."

The ratings were so poor that *The Office* was nearly canceled in its first season.

THE BBC LEFT GERVAIS AND STEPHAN MERCHANT TO THEIR OWN DEVICES.

Despite the poor audience reaction, the BBC trusted Gervais and Merchant enough to allow them to proceed with the show as is. "We didn't change a thing," Gervais told *The Sun*. "We knew how good it was, but that doesn't guarantee success. For us, 'success' just meant getting our own way and having it turn out exactly as we wanted."

SOME OF THE STORY LINES WERE SEMI-AUTOBIOGRAPHICAL.

In an interview with NPR, Gervais explained that the environment he created for Wernham Hogg was familiar to him. "I worked in an office for eight years," Gervais said. "That's where I got it all from. I was a middle manager. I went to management training seminars where the speakers talked rubbish for two days." That particular experience informed much of season 1's "Training" episode, in which Brent turns a training seminar into an NSFW role-playing game then into what feels like an episode of *MTV Unplugged* when he whips out his guitar.

GARETH IS BASED ON A REAL PERSON.

When asked about his inspiration for some of *The Office*'s more outlandish characters, Gervais told *The Sun*, "Gareth—played by Mackenzie Crook—is based on a bloke I went to school with. He once said, 'If you get captured by cannibals, they show you pornographic pictures so you get an erection and there's more meat.' I used his gems for Gareth."

DAVID BRENT SHOT SOME TRAINING VIDEOS FOR MICROSOFT.

In 2004, Microsoft UK convinced Gervais and Merchant to shoot a couple of training videos for the company, with Gervais in character as Brent. (Yes, he did break out his guitar at one point.) It didn't take long for the clips to be leaked online, which irked the tech giant, who said that they "were never intended to be viewed by the public."

THERE WASN'T A LOT OF IMPROVISATION.

Though the show has a very naturalistic style, similar to Larry David's *Curb Your Enthusiasm* (which is mostly improvised), Gervais and Merchant said *The Office* "was 95 percent scripted, with some improvisation here and there."

BRENT'S INFAMOUS DANCE WAS NOT REHEARSED.

In a series full of uncomfortable moments, one of the most cringeworthy might very well be when Brent shows off his dance moves. If you think that routine was choreographed, think again. "It wasn't rehearsed,"

FREEZE FRAME ▶

"JUDGEMENT" // SEASON I, EPISODE 6
One of *The Office's* most unique characters is Gordon, the janitor who pops up in a few episodes and silently stares into the camera for an uncomfortable amount of time. In real life, Gordon is Ron Merchant— Stephen's dad. "Yes, he is my dad and we put him in because we thought he had a funny face," Merchant explained.

Gervais said. "I just went berserk for thirty seconds, then had to have a sit-down for twenty minutes."

IT WAS THE FIRST BRITISH SITCOM TO WIN A GOLDEN GLOBE.

In 2003, *The Office* was nominated for a Golden Globe for Best Television Series—Comedy or Musical. When it won the award, it became the first British series ever to do so. (Gervais also took home a statue for Best Actor.)

MERCHANT DOESN'T THINK *THE OFFICE* COULD HAVE BEEN MADE TODAY.

In a 2015 interview, Merchant admitted that he doesn't know that the series would have been made had they pitched it today. "I feel like we're living in an age now where everyone is constantly apologizing for everything they say," Merchant told *The Telegraph*. "This idea that we have to police ourselves, that we might say the wrong thing and upset someone or something. It's not fun…I don't think *The Office* would have got off the ground if we'd made it now."

THE AMERICAN VERSION OF *THE OFFICE* IS NOT ITS ONLY ADAPTATION.

In addition to the UK and America, *The Office* has made its way onto television screens around the world. More than eighty countries have broadcast the original series, from Canada to Australia. The series has also been adapted for audiences around the world. Among the international updates are versions in France (*Le Bureau*), Germany (*Stromberg*), Canada (*La Job*), Chile (*La Ofis*), Israel (*HaMisrad*), and Sweden (*Kontoret*).

FREEZE FRAME

"APPRAISALS" // SEASON 2, EPISODE 2
According to Gervais and Merchant, the scene in which David gives Tim a performance appraisal required seventy-four takes. "We kept laughing and couldn't get through the dialogue," they said.

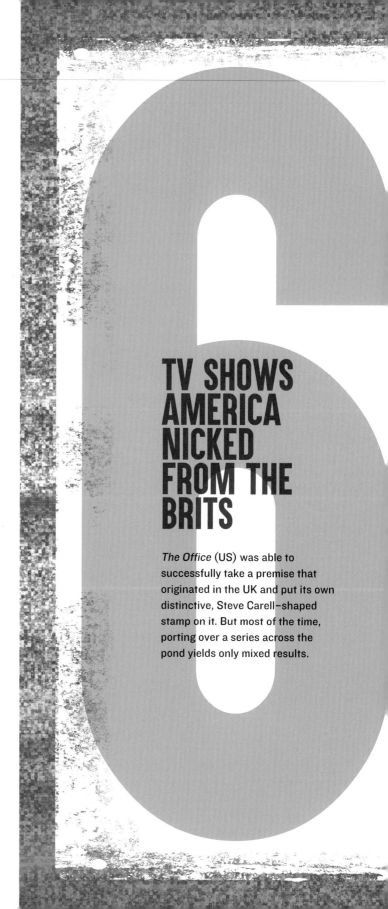

6 TV SHOWS AMERICA NICKED FROM THE BRITS

The Office (US) was able to successfully take a premise that originated in the UK and put its own distinctive, Steve Carell–shaped stamp on it. But most of the time, porting over a series across the pond yields only mixed results.

BROADCHURCH
(2013–2017)

This crime drama about a small coastal town besieged by murder was remade by Fox as *Gracepoint* in 2014 and gave itself every possible chance of success. It even recast original series star David Tennant (*Doctor Who*), doing an American accent. Viewers failed to see the point, as the original was already a hit on BBC America, and *Gracepoint* bowed out gracefully after one season.

TILL DEATH DO US PART
(1965–1975)

Actor Warren Mitchell starred as bigoted blue-collar worker Alf Garnett in this long-running series. When American television producer Norman Lear heard the premise, he immediately sought out the rights and brought it to the States as *All in the Family* with Carroll O'Connor as Archie Bunker. That ran from 1971 to 1979, with O'Connor continuing the role in *Archie Bunker's Place* from 1979 to 1983.

THE IT CROWD
(2006–2013)

This workplace comedy about tech support employees starring Chris O'Dowd and Richard Ayoade was so irresistible to US producers that it was remade twice, first in 2007 with Ayoade and Joel McHale and again in 2014. In 2017, a third attempt was announced, this one involving original series creator Graham Linehan. None of these have seen the light of day.

FAWLTY TOWERS
(1975–1979)

Who would dare touch this priceless John Cleese and Connie Booth classic about irascible innkeeper Basil Fawlty and his misfit band of employees? Two golden girls. Betty White appeared in *Snavely*, a 1978 remake with Harvey Korman. Then there was *Amanda's*, a 1983 effort with Bea Arthur portraying a gender-swapped iteration of Fawlty. Finally, John Larroquette (*Night Court*) took a swing in 1999 with *Payne*. It lasted just over a month.

THE INBETWEENERS
(2008–2010)

This sharp, raunchy sitcom about teenagers was critically-acclaimed in the UK Over in the US, it left less of an impression. A 2012 remake with episodes directed by Taika Waititi (*Thor: Ragnarok*) failed to graduate to a sophomore season.

COUPLING
(2000–2004)

This racy series written by Steven Moffat (*Doctor Who*) was snapped up by NBC in 2003 because it bore a slight resemblance to the network's massive hit *Friends* and its three-men, three-women dynamic. It was dropped after four episodes, which led to a spat between Moffat and NBC. After network executive Jeff Zucker said some of that season's programming "sucked," Moffat retorted, "It's not *Coupling* that sucks, it's NBC." Maybe the making of *Coupling* would have made for a better show.

THE OFFICE

US

(2005–2013)

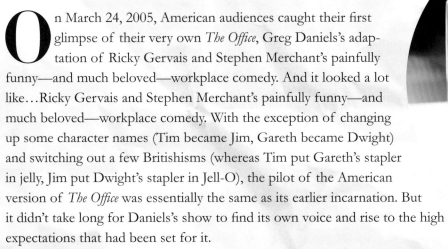

DEVELOPED BY: Greg Daniels

SEASONS: 9

EPISODES: 201

OTHER SHOWS BY GREG DANIELS:
King of the Hill (1997–2010)
Parks and Recreation (2009–2015)
Upload (2020–PRESENT)
Space Force (2020–PRESENT)

On March 24, 2005, American audiences caught their first glimpse of their very own *The Office*, Greg Daniels's adaptation of Ricky Gervais and Stephen Merchant's painfully funny—and much beloved—workplace comedy. And it looked a lot like…Ricky Gervais and Stephen Merchant's painfully funny—and much beloved—workplace comedy. With the exception of changing up some character names (Tim became Jim, Gareth became Dwight) and switching out a few Britishisms (whereas Tim put Gareth's stapler in jelly, Jim put Dwight's stapler in Jell-O), the pilot of the American version of *The Office* was essentially the same as its earlier incarnation. But it didn't take long for Daniels's show to find its own voice and rise to the high expectations that had been set for it.

Over the next eight years, *The Office* carved out its own comedic path that has put its pop culture impact on par with earlier mega-hits like *Seinfeld* and *Friends*. Michael Scott may not have been the world's best boss, but he sure made for a lovable—though cringeworthy—character. With a slew of "that's what she said" jokes and a string of human resources violations, Scott (Steve Carell) helped introduce audiences to the wacky inner workings of the Dunder Mifflin Paper Company in Scranton, Pennsylvania. The characters—Dwight Schrute (Rainn Wilson), Jim Halpert (John Krasinski), and Pam Beesly (Jenna Fischer), to name a few—practically perfected the deadpan as they regaled the fake mockumentary crew with their own takes on the office's daily shenanigans. The American reboot aired from 2005 to 2013, and it only got sillier as it went along, which is probably why some fans have theorized that the staff is suffering from the effects of radon poisoning, or that the office is actually hell on Earth. Whatever the case, even today, years after the show left the airwaves, new viewers are still regularly discovering the magical world of *The Office*. In 2020 alone, Americans spent more than 57 billion minutes streaming it, which is one accomplishment Michael Scott really would have reason to brag about.

DUNDER MIFFLIN'S OFFICE ADDRESS IS AN HOMAGE TO THE BRITISH SERIES.

The Scranton branch of Dunder Mifflin is located at 1725 Slough Avenue. That's not a real street in Scranton, Pennsylvania, though; it's a reference to the original version of the show, which takes place in Slough, England.

BOB ODENKIRK WAS THE ORIGINAL MICHAEL SCOTT.

Every series has a few could-have-beens when it comes to casting, and *The Office* is no exception. Adam Scott auditioned for the part of Jim, while Seth Rogen was in the running to play Dwight. Eric Stonestreet auditioned for Kevin before going on to star in *Modern Family*. Before being cast as Angela, Angela Kinsey auditioned for the part of Pam. Most notably, *Better Call Saul* star Bob Odenkirk was originally cast as Michael Scott, but was replaced by Steve Carell when *Come to Papa*, the show Carell had been working on, was canceled. Toward the end of *The Office*'s final season, Odenkirk played a Michael Scott-ish manager looking to hire Pam.

PHYLLIS SMITH WAS CAST WHILE SHE WAS CASTING THE SHOW.

Smith was working as a casting agent and reading the script with some auditioning actors when director Ken Kwapis decided that she should be cast.

JOHN KRASINSKI IS LUCKY GREG DANIELS HAS A SENSE OF HUMOR.

Krasinski's audition for *The Office* went about as well as Jim Halpert trying to impress Charles Miner (Idris Elba). First of all, he was supposed to audition for Dwight, but he convinced the casting directors to let him read for Jim. Secondly, he got into some trouble in

FREEZE FRAME ▶

"BOOZE CRUISE" // SEASON 2, EPISODE 11
When it came time to choose the show's opening theme music, Daniels let the cast choose. He gave them four different songs and let them vote on the winner. The now-iconic song came from a demo by composer Jay Ferguson, which was then re-recorded by musician Bob Thiele, Jr. and a group later dubbed the Scrantones—the same band performing on the booze cruise.

the waiting room. A man eating salad in the room asked him if he was nervous. Krasinski answered, "You know, not really. You either get these things or you don't. But what I'm really nervous about is this show. It's just I love the British show so much and Americans have a tendency to just really screw these opportunities up. I just don't know how I'll live with myself if they screw this show up and ruin it for me." The man responded, "My name's Greg Daniels, I'm the executive producer." Oops! Fortunately, Krasinski managed to nab the role.

NO ONE WAS OPTIMISTIC ABOUT THE SHOW.

Krasinski wasn't alone in his skepticism. It was hard for many members of the cast and crew to have faith early on. During the first season, NBC executives would bring a lot of pessimism to the set. According to Krasinski, they would say things like, "This episode is so good—unfortunately, it's the last one we're going to do."

THE SHOW OWES ITS SUCCESS, IN PART, TO APPLE.

One thing that helped save the show was iTunes. Around the second season, when NBC made the show available on the platform, it took up four of the top five slots for downloaded television shows. That's when the people behind the show learned that their audience skewed young, rather than the white-collar workers they thought would be watching.

THEY LITERALLY MADE THE SHOW BRIGHTER FOR SEASON 2.

In an attempt to boost ratings after the first season, the producers pivoted the show's style away from the British version to make Michael Scott more likable and make the episodes more optimistic. According to B. J. Novak's DVD commentary track for "The Dundies," the first episode of the second season, they also made the lights in the office brighter to help complete that tonal shift.

THE DOCUMENTARY CREW MAY HAVE HAD A TRAGIC REASON FOR COVERING DUNDER MIFFLIN.

In the season 2 episode "Performance Review," Michael reads papers from his suggestion box, including one from "Tom," who wrote, "We need better outreach for employees fighting depression." Then he's reminded that Tom died by suicide. During a 2007 *The Office* convention, a group of the show's writers proposed that this suicide was why the documentary crew showed up in Scranton. They wanted to investigate the suicide before turning to simpler story lines. They further postulated that the reason Ryan had been called in as a temp in the first place was to fill Tom's role.

JIM'S FAKE RAIN-FILLED PROPOSAL WAS EXPENSIVE.

The writers had a clear vision for how Jim's proposal to Pam would look. They wanted to shoot it at an actual rest stop on the Merritt Parkway, but it would have cost $100,000. Plus, they wouldn't be allowed to use fake rain, which was important to the scene. So the crew built a replica of the parkway and a rest stop. The shot ended up costing $250,000. Daniels described the scene as "the most expensive and elaborate shot we've ever done, but it's also sort of the highlight of five years of storytelling."

THE CPR EPISODE HELPED SAVE SOMEONE'S LIFE.

In the season 5 episode "Stress Relief," Michael arranges a CPR training session for his staff that quickly devolves into a very Scranton-y debacle. But even if no one at Dunder Mifflin learned anything, someone at home actually did. On the show, it's said that the chest compressions should be done to the beat of the popular Bee Gees song "Stayin' Alive," and this tip helped an *Office* fan from Arizona successfully perform CPR on a woman he found slumped over in the seat of her car. She regained consciousness after about a minute of CPR and was brought to the hospital, where she recovered and was later discharged.

MICHAEL HAS A DIFFERENT FISH IN EACH EPISODE OF THE "MICHAEL SCOTT PAPER COMPANY" ERA.

He starts with a goldfish and ends up with a black beta. Maybe he's not good at keeping fish alive? At least it's good practice for falling into a koi pond.

PAM AND MICHAEL HAD A GENUINE GOODBYE.

For their goodbye scene at the airport in Carell's last episode, Fischer was told by production, "Just say whatever you would want to say to Steve. Just say goodbye and we'll tape it and when you're finished, just give each other a hug and go your separate ways." Fischer revealed in 2018, "Those were real tears and a real goodbye."

CARELL HAD HIS NUMBER RETIRED.

When Carell left the show after seven seasons, he was still adored by the cast and crew. Up until that point, he had always been number one on the call sheet. So, when he left, they "retired" the number one, and it didn't appear on the call sheet again.

 SHOWRUNNERS KEPT CARELL'S FINALE APPEARANCE A SECRET FROM EVERYONE.

The showrunners didn't even tell network executives that Carell was going to appear in the finale. According to Daniels, "We shot the Steve stuff and we kept it out of the dailies and didn't tell them about it. At the table reading, we gave the Steve Carell lines to Creed."

FREEZE FRAME

"GAY WITCH HUNT" // SEASON 3, EPISODE 1
Carell improvised his kiss with Oscar. "We were just supposed to hug, and he kept hugging me," Oscar Nunez recalled. "And that particular take he came in really close, and I'm like, 'Where is he going with this?' Oh, dear, yes, here we go."

ORANGE IS THE NEW BLACK

(2013–2019)

CREATED BY: Jenji Kohan (based on the memoir by Piper Kerman)

SEASONS: 7

EPISODES: 91

OTHER SHOWS BY JENJI KOHAN:
Weeds (2005–2012)

FREEZE FRAME

THE OPENING CREDITS
Those are real former prisoners you see in the opening credits. Jenji Kohan hired non-actresses to pose for the opening credit sequence—all of them formerly incarcerated women. In order to get the right facial expressions, the women were asked to visualize three things: "a peaceful place," "a person who makes you laugh," and finally, "something that you want to forget."

Back when original content was still a relatively new concept for streaming platforms, Netflix unveiled *Orange Is the New Black* to viewers. Loosely based on the memoir of real-life ex-felon Piper Kerman, the dramedy follows Piper Chapman (Taylor Schilling) as she leaves her cushy life for prison after being convicted of drug-related charges. Though prison has been explored in media countless times, *Orange Is the New Black* was one of the first shows to spotlight female convicts exclusively. The setting also opened the door for the show's makers to tell the stories of women rarely represented on screen.

It may have started out as Piper's story, but *Orange Is the New Black* evolved into an impressive ensemble showcase over its seven seasons. To date, it remains the longest-running narrative series on Netflix—an impressive achievement in today's cutthroat streaming landscape. With so many shows to watch in the company's catalogue, many viewers still gravitate toward "Red" (Kate Mulgrew), Nicky (Natasha Lyonne), "Crazy Eyes" (Uzo Aduba), Poussey (Samira Wiley), and the rest of the inmates at Litchfield Penitentiary.

COMPETITION FOR THE RIGHTS TO PIPER KERMAN'S MEMOIR WAS STIFF.
Jenji Kohan, who was already well known for creating *Weeds*, read Kerman's memoir and thought it would be perfect for a TV show adaptation. As Kohan told NPR: "I'm always looking for those places where you can slam really disparate people up against one another, and they have to deal with each other. There are very few crossroads anymore. We talk about this country as this big melting pot, but it's a mosaic. There's all these pieces, they're next to each other, they're not necessarily mixing. And I'm looking for those spaces where people actually do mix—and prison just

happens to be a terrific one."

Kohan wasn't the only one who wanted to adapt Kerman's book; in fact, she had to call Kerman and "beg" her for the rights. Kerman was particularly impressed with Kohan's devotion to telling the story properly, as "she asked [her] question after question after question."

KOHAN ALWAYS HAD BIG PLANS FOR THE SHOW'S OTHER CHARACTERS.
Kohan knew that Taylor Schilling's Piper would appeal to network execs, but she wanted to go much deeper than that story. "In a lot of ways Piper was my Trojan

horse," Kohan said. "You're not going to go into a network and sell a show on really fascinating tales of Black women, and Latina women, and old women and criminals. But if you take this white girl, this sort of fish out of water, and you follow her in, you can then expand your world and tell all of those other stories. But it's a hard sell to just go in and try to sell those stories initially."

THE REAL-LIFE ALEX VAUSE HAS SPOKEN OUT ABOUT WHAT REALLY WENT DOWN.

Catherine Wolters, the inspiration for Alex (played by Laura Prepon), has claimed that the show gets a lot wrong when it comes to Alex and Piper's relationship. The two had already been involved in the trafficking business long before they began their relationship, according to Wolters. She also said that their relationship definitely didn't carry over to prison, where they only spent about five weeks in the same facility. But Wolters admitted that making the show about their real relationship would have been "so wretched and stinky, it would quite possibly result in a collapsed universe. So I guess it's a good thing Piper and Jenji stick with the fun little tidbits."

UZO ADUBA WAS OFFERED THE ROLE OF "CRAZY EYES" ON THE SAME DAY SHE DECIDED TO QUIT ACTING.

Aduba had auditioned for a different role before she was offered the part of Crazy Eyes. The former Boston University sprinter came in and read for Janae Watson, the track star. Frustrated that she hadn't heard back, she decided to quit acting and go to law school instead. Little did she know that Kohan thought she'd be perfect for a different part: The very same day she "quit" acting, Aduba was offered the part of Suzanne "Crazy Eyes" Warren.

ADUBA TAPPED INTO HER INNER CHILD TO PLAY CRAZY EYES.

In the first script, Aduba claimed that Crazy Eyes was described as "innocent like a child, except children aren't scary." She used that description to develop her character's distinctive persona and mannerisms. As Aduba put it, "That felt like the key to the door that might open this character because someone who is innocent like a child, to me, meant somebody who operates out of impulse…who acts and then thinks."

Children don't have agendas. They're not calculating."

TARYN MANNING RESEARCHED DIFFERENT RELIGIOUS GROUPS TO PLAY PENNSATUCKY.

Manning watched a number of documentaries about religious groups, including *Jesus Camp*. She also spent time studying YouTube videos of faith healing and other rituals used in some evangelist churches.

KERMAN CONTINUED TO GIVE NOTES FOR THE SHOW, EVEN WHEN IT DEVIATED FROM HER BOOK.

Though the series eventually deviated from the stories Kerman recounted in her memoir, Kohan continued to look to the author for advice. "She gives notes, mostly about accuracy," Kohan said. "You know, 'I don't think that would happen.' And she comes to set for visits, which must be strange for her. But she's really kind of trusted us with her baby and we really, completely took off from where she started."

THE WRITERS VISITED A REAL WOMEN'S PRISON.

Kohan and her writing staff visited a women's prison in California. Kohan also spoke with the prison's warden, who explained how social groups tend to form in both men's and women's prisons. He told her that, generally speaking, women are more communal and seek out groups, rather than spend time alone.

REGINA SPEKTOR WROTE THE THEME SONG SPECIFICALLY FOR THE SHOW.

Singer-songwriter Spektor and Kohan had already collaborated a couple of times. (Spektor did a cover of "Little Boxes" for the opening of an episode of *Weeds*.) Because of their solid working relationship, Kohan reached out to her and asked if she'd write the theme song for *Orange Is the New Black*. In order to write it, Spektor was sent a few unfinished episodes in the middle of filming season 1. She has said that seeing the characters come to life helped her put together a finished version of the song.

LAVERNE COX'S BROTHER PLAYS SOPHIA PRE-TRANSITION.

Cox's twin brother, musician M. Lamar, stepped in to play a pre-transition Sophia. The casting director auditioned a ton of actors before she discovered that Cox had a twin. "She insisted that he should audition for the role," Cox told HuffPost. "He auditioned, and he got the part."

JODIE FOSTER DIRECTED TWO EPISODES.

Foster pursued the gig: After reading the book, she asked her agent if she could somehow get involved. The Oscar winner ended up directing one episode in each of the show's first two seasons.

LORRAINE TOUSSAINT HAD NO IDEA VEE WAS GOING TO BE SO EVIL.

Toussaint didn't meet Kohan until her very first day on set, when she decided to pick the showrunner's brain about Vee, the inmate she was about to play. "I had some basic questions I needed answered so I could at least finish out that first day," Toussaint later recalled. "Somewhere in the conversation was an 'Oh, by the way, she's a sociopath.' I said, 'Huh? Really? Um…' and she said, 'Oh, yes, a bona-fide, complete and absolute sociopath.' I thought, Oh! I wish I had known that! I might have thought twice about this."

THE COSTUME DESIGNER HAD TO GET CREATIVE.

Costume designer Jennifer Rogien has described the job of dressing the inmates as "a creative challenge." She had to use real prison uniforms—either orange or beige—without altering anything too dramatically, unless the alterations were something a prisoner could have done herself. Rogien had to rely on subtle touches that served to set the characters apart, such as rolled sleeves or hems. Her time to really shine came during the flashback scenes, set in various decades and places. Rogien saw those as an opportunity not only to define the characters, but to "highlight the contrast between the world inside and the world outside."

THE CAST AND CREW LIKED WORKING ON A SHOW THEY KNEW PEOPLE WOULD BINGE-WATCH.

The people behind *Orange Is the New Black* were well aware that audiences were going to binge-watch their show, and they even adapted their production process accordingly. For instance, Kohan didn't worry as much about writing each character into every single episode because she knew that the audience didn't have to wait a full week for the next installment featuring their favorites.

5

FASCINATING FACTS ABOUT NETFLIX

Netflix has become the world's intravenous line for filmed entertainment. Like any media empire, it has a few stories of its own to tell.

1 NETFLIX WAS ORIGINALLY CALLED KIBBLE.

Choosing a name for the company was a drawn-out process. Directpix.com, Replay.com, and other names were considered; so was Luna.com, which was the name of co-founder Marc Randolph's dog. When the company was being incorporated, he named it Kibble until they could decide on something permanent.

2 EARLY NETFLIX SUBSCRIBERS GOT A LOT OF CHINESE PORNOGRAPHY.

In 1998, Netflix was still in the business of selling as well as renting DVDs. To try to offer consumers something new, Randolph decided to offer footage of President Bill Clinton's grand jury testimony about his involvement with Monica Lewinsky. But, according to the book *Netflixed*, the duplicating house had a mix-up: Of the more than 1,000 customers who ordered Clinton's interview, a few hundred received discs full of hardcore Chinese pornography.

3 NETFLIX EXECUTIVES USED TO MAKE HOUSE CALLS.

From the beginning, Netflix has been preoccupied with seeing how users interact with its software in order to select titles. In the late 1990s, subscribers near the company's location in Los Gatos, California, were contacted via telephone and asked a series of questions. Then staffers would ask if they could stop by to watch them use the site. Surprisingly, most

agreed. Netflix brought them a Starbucks—a small investment for gaining valuable information about their use of the software.

4 NETFLIX HAS MADE A SCIENCE OUT OF SPOILERS.

Because so much of Netflix's high-profile content can be binged in a single weekend, the company commissioned cultural anthropologist Grant McCracken to examine how spoilers affect a person's viewing habits. McCracken identified classifications of spoiler-prone people by whether they ruin a plot twist intentionally or hold it over others. (Some people are "Coded Spoilers," who according to Netflix "speak the language of spoilers so fluently, they can sneak them into conversations where only another fan can find them.") His verdict? Some people enjoy the power they get from having knowledge of spoilers. But if a show is good enough, knowing about key scenes won't dissuade viewers from watching.

5 NETFLIX STAFFERS THINK YOU MIGHT BE KIND OF A LIAR.

You can stop trying to impress Netflix with the streaming equivalent of keeping *Ulysses* on your coffee table. In a 2013 *Wired* interview, Carlos Gomez-Uribe—the company's vice president of product innovation from 2010 to 2016—noted that viewers often report viewing documentaries or esoteric foreign movies. "But in practice," he said, "that doesn't happen very much."

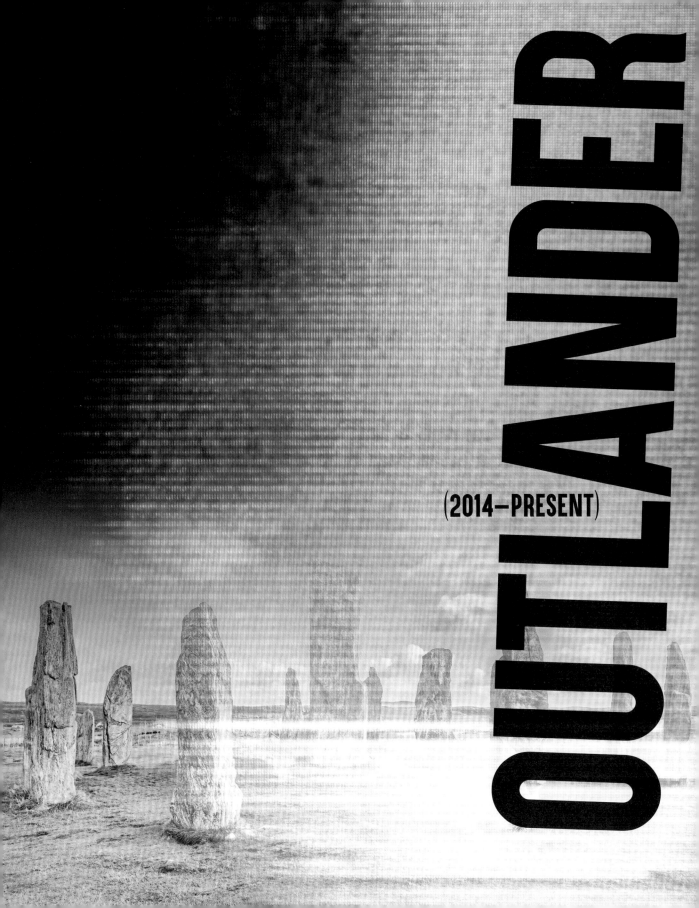

OUTLANDER

(2014–PRESENT)

DEVELOPED BY: Ronald D. Moore (based on Diana Gabaldon's Outlander book series)

SEASONS: 5

EPISODES: 67

OTHER SHOWS BY RONALD D. MOORE:
Battlestar Galactica (2004–2009)

In 2014, Starz debuted *Outlander*, a historical drama that defies easy categorization (unless historical time travel romantic drama is indeed already a genre). Based on Diana Gabaldon's beloved and bestselling book series—which itself was influenced by an episode of *Doctor Who*—the show is centered on Claire Randall (Caitriona Balfe), a married military nurse who takes a second honeymoon with her husband, Frank (Tobias Menzies), following the end of World War II…where she tumbles through some Scottish standing stones that transport her from 1945 to 1743.

It's in the past that she meets—and marries—Jamie Fraser (Sam Heughan), a Highlander with strong values and stronger muscles. If you've been chasing the high of a Disney princess movie for your entire adult life, you've just found it. This one, however, isn't rated G, and the heroine gets to do a lot more than *Sleeping Beauty* ever did.

IT COULD HAVE BEEN A KATHERINE HEIGL VEHICLE.
Before it was developed as a TV series, *Outlander* was being developed with Heigl as Claire. In 2010, *The New York Times* ran a profile of the former *Grey's Anatomy* star in which she hinted that she was leaning toward *Outlander* as her next project. "Scotland? 2012? What do you think?" Heigl asked.

CLAIRE WAS CAST NOT LONG BEFORE FILMING STARTED.
Though Claire is the central figure in the series, Caitriona Balfe was only offered the role of Claire a few weeks before filming began. "At the outset, I told everyone that we would find Claire first and then Jamie would be the last one cast, and of course it was exactly the opposite," Ronald Moore told E! News. "Sam came in really early in the process and he was literally the first one we cast. We saw the tape and we were like, 'Oh my god, there he is. Let's snatch him up now.' And then

Claire just took a long time. A lot of actresses, a lot of tape, looking for really ineffable qualities. She had to be smart, she had to have a strength of character, and really, she had to be someone that you could watch think on camera. But then suddenly Caitriona's tape came in and we had that same light-bulb moment."

IN TRUE SCOTTISH FASHION, THE ACTORS AREN'T WEARING ANYTHING BENEATH THOSE KILTS.
"I'm a true Scotsman, and…one of the joys of working on the show is wearing the kilt," Heughan said. "It can actually be very comfortable."

DAVID CAMERON ASKED THAT THE SERIES DELAY ITS UK PREMIERE.
Among the many Hollywood secrets that were made public in the wake of the 2014 Sony hack was the fact that then-prime minister David Cameron met with Sony to request that they delay the series' premiere in the UK.

His reason? The UK was just weeks away from a historic vote to determine whether Scotland should remain part of the UK or become its own independent country, and he thought it would be better if a series about Scottish rebels wasn't airing at the same time. Whether the result of Cameron's request or not, the series was delayed in the UK by several months.

THE COSTUMES ARE AGED WITH EVERYTHING FROM BLOWTORCHES TO CHEESE GRATERS.

In order to give the show's costumes the worn-in look they need for authenticity, the crew resorts to all sorts of tricks. Cheese graters, blowtorches, sandpaper, and pumice stones are just a few tools the costume department uses to give the show's clothing a lived-in appearance. Some of the clothes are tied up and baked, while others are burned with blowtorches.

HEUGHAN SPENDS THE MOST TIME IN THE MAKEUP CHAIR.

Heughan spends a lot of time in makeup—mainly to create the beaten and scarred look required for his character's back. "It's ridiculous," Heughan said. "I'll get into makeup at four a.m. and be there until eight or nine. And you have to be standing for most of it."

HALF OF *OUTLANDER*'S AMERICAN AUDIENCE IS MALE.

Heughan told *Elle* that "something like fifty percent of our audience in the US are men. And that's interesting. And the show wasn't made specifically for women, you know. It just happens to have a female lead character. I think there's something in there for every guy. There's a lot more graphic scenes, but not just intimate scenes. There's violence."

YOU CAN VISIT MANY OF THE SHOW'S KEY LOCATIONS IN REAL LIFE.

In order to capitalize on the show's success, the website VisitScotland has assembled a map to some of *Outlander*'s real-life locations, like Doune Castle, near Stirling, which portrays Castle Leoch. Blackness Castle in West Lothian plays the part of Fort William. Craigh na Dun, the prehistoric stone circle that sends Claire back in time, doesn't exist, but you can pay a visit to Kinloch Rannoch to see the area for yourself.

10

BINGEABLE BOOKS TURNED TV SHOWS

When it comes to creating TV hits, writers don't always have to start from scratch. Some of today's most acclaimed series are actually based on books. Here are ten shows that made the jump from page to screen.

1 **Good Omens // (2019)**
After three decades of waiting, fans of Terry Pratchett and Neil Gaiman's *Good Omens: The Nice and Accurate Prophecies of Agnes Nutter, Witch* finally got to lay their eyes upon an adaptation of the classic work of comic fantasy—and it was an all-star affair. Real-life pals Michael Sheen and David Tennant played the angel Aziraphale and his demon BFF Crowley, respectively.

2 **Bridgerton // (2020)**
On Christmas Day 2020, Netflix audiences were introduced to the deliciously lavish (and sometimes naughty) existence of the Bridgerton family, originally brought to life in Julia Quinn's series of historical romance novels.

3 **The Queen's Gambit // (2020)**
Walter Tevis's 1983 novel saw renewed interest in 2020 when Netflix turned the book—about the life of fictional chess prodigy Beth Harmon—into a seven-episode miniseries starring Anya Taylor-Joy.

4 **The Witcher // (2019–PRESENT)**
Polish author Andrzej Sapkowski's fantastical book series about a monster hunter was a monster of a hit for Netflix, becoming the most watched first season of an original series at the time of its release (until *Bridgerton* came along).

5 **Watchmen // (2019)**
Damon Lindelof, the co-creator of *Lost* and *The Leftovers* (an adaptation of Tom Perrotta's novel), took on a Herculean creative task by attempting to adapt Alan Moore and Dave Gibbons's *Watchmen*. Not only is the title regularly cited as one of the greatest graphic novels ever written, but it has a deeply devoted fan base who are well aware of Moore's distaste for adaptations. But along with critics, even longtime Moore devotees seemed to agree that this adaptation was more than worth of its source material.

6 **Killing Eve // (2018–PRESENT)**
In 2018, *Fleabag* creator Phoebe Waller-Bridge took on the enviable task of bringing Villanelle—the killer for hire at the center of Luke Jennings's novel series—to the small screen. But Villanelle is no by-the-books assassin. She's a manic psychopath with a hypnotic charm. She's vile, reprehensible, and oh so satisfying to watch as she leaves a trail of mayhem in her stylish wake.

7 **Patrick Melrose // (2018)**
Edward St Aubyn's semi-autobiographical novels about life in upper-class English society got the all-star treatment when Benedict Cumberbatch starred as the title character, who deals with his traumatic past by abusing drugs and alcohol, in Showtime's acclaimed miniseries.

8 **House of Cards // (1990; 2013–2018)**
Michael Dobbs's 1989 novel about a lethally manipulative politician has received the TV treatment twice: first in the 1990s via the BBC, then again in 2013, when Netflix put an American spin on the British tale.

9 **Call the Midwife // (2012–PRESENT)**
Jennifer Worth's *Call the Midwife* trilogy recalls Worth's own time spent bringing new life into London's East End. The BBC's take on the series goes beyond Worth's memoirs to introduce some new characters to Nonnatus House.

10 **Big Little Lies // (2017–2019)**
HBO cast some of Hollywood's biggest names—including Reese Witherspoon and Nicole Kidman—to bring Liane Moriarty's murder-filled bestselling novel to the screen.

(2017–PRESENT)

OZARK

Getting on the wrong side of the wrong people is a classic mistake, but Marty Byrde (Jason Bateman) went ahead and did it anyway—and dragged his family along for the ride. The Netflix series *Ozark* is a bit like *Breaking Bad*…if Walter White had come clean about making drugs early on, and Skyler (in this case, Laura Linney's more than complicit wife, Wendy Byrde) had been completely on board.

It's dark and twisty, and every success promises a failure. Byrde and his family flee Chicago because of his run-in with a drug cartel, only to run into a drug cartel in his new Missouri home. If that kind of thing happens, you've got to assume you're the problem.

One of the latest hit shows about a troubled middle-class white dude won Bateman an Emmy for Outstanding Directing for a Drama Series in 2019 and earned Julia Garner an Emmy for Outstanding Supporting Actress in a Drama Series in 2019 and 2020 for her role as Ruth Langmore.

OZARK'S CO-CREATOR CRAFTED THE SHOW WITH HIS OWN MEMORIES.
Missouri native and show co-creator Bill Dubuque chose to set *Ozark* at Lake of the Ozarks because he worked there as a teenager for the Alhonna Resort and Marina. He has a deep love for the place, even if his characters despair at moving to the "Redneck Riviera."

NEITHER BATEMAN NOR LAURA LINNEY WAS INTERESTED IN STARRING IN A TELEVISION SERIES WHEN OZARK CAME ALONG.
Linney wasn't interested in doing a series, but she was intrigued because of Bateman's involvement and the possibility of watching him stretch his acting range. But Bateman almost wasn't on board because he, too, was uninterested in doing another series when the project came to him. Reading the pilot and being offered the opportunity to sign on as a producer and direct several episodes of the show persuaded him to say yes.

OZARK'S CREATORS ATTEMPTED TO GET PETER MULLAN ON BOARD BEFORE THERE WAS EVEN A SCRIPT.

Mullan is a fierce character actor—not to mention a writer and director—known for *My Name Is Joe* and smaller, powerful roles like the fascist guard in *Children of Men* and the wealthy owner of Delos on *Westworld*. Bateman desperately wanted to cast Mullan in *Ozark* after seeing him in Jane Campion's *Top of the Lake*, so he and the show's creators "aggressively pursued" Mullan before they'd even finished the script.

LINNEY PUSHED TO MAKE HER *OZARK* CHARACTER MORE THAN "JUST A WIFE."

Linney was definitely drawn to the script when she read it, even though she saw her potential character as one that needed more dimension: As initially written, Wendy was "just a wife," defined entirely by her relationship to Marty. She took her concerns to Bateman, who agreed they needed to flesh the character out, and now Wendy is a monster all her own.

MARTY WEARS THE SAME SHOES EVERY BATEMAN CHARACTER DOES.

If you focus on shoes whenever you're watching a show or movie, you'll probably notice that Bateman wears a lot of New Balance. That's no different in *Ozark*, where his character is rocking the J. Crew x New Balance M1400DM, which is potentially bad product placement because you can't buy them anywhere.

SYMBOLS HIDDEN IN THE "O" OF THE *OZARK* TITLE CARD FORESHADOW THE EPISODE.

Emerging from the brooding title music, the show teases what you're about to see with icons embedded in the title's first letter. A spilled oil drum, a gun, a man on his knees. A rat, a swimming pool ladder, a child's playground. Designed by Fred Davis, the title cards are an ingenious tool in an era when fans are desperate to catch and solve narrative clues. *Ozark* primes that pump and offers fans something to search for.

BATEMAN FEELS BAD ABOUT KILLING OFF CHARACTERS ON *OZARK*.

Finally, a TV producer who admits to feeling what we all feel. The shocking deaths that keep us hooked to a show are also lamentable. It's safe to say we miss some characters when they're gone, and Bateman gets that. "Selfishly, you want everyone to stick around," he told *The Hollywood Reporter*. "We had a really great group of actors. It's terrible when these people have to go, but that's the trade-off of doing these kinds of shows. You have to be willing to make big moves because that's where everything is at nowadays."

LINNEY HAS TROUBLE KEEPING WENDY'S MORAL COMPASS STRAIGHT ON *OZARK*.

Linney's Wendy has evolved into one of the most complicated characters on the show because of her readiness and capability to take on immoral and illegal actions. It's part of the challenge of knowing where the character is during any given story line, especially when Linney doesn't know how her story will end. "It really is a partnership between the actor and the writers and the director as well," she told *Vanity Fair*. "To sort of let things unfold in a way that . . . feels right and is organic so that you don't get too far ahead of yourself or too far behind yourself."

OZARK'S PRODUCTION TEAM LEARNED HOW TO LAUNDER MONEY FROM THE FBI.

In order to make the show as realistic as possible, *Ozark*'s writers needed to develop a firm understanding of how money laundering works in real life. Naturally, they called the feds. "We had an FBI agent who investigates money laundering come and sit down with us for a day so we could pick her brain," producer Chris Mundy said.

OZARK FEATURES A FEW SUBTLE NODS TO ARRESTED DEVELOPMENT.

Since it covered so much ground and made so many references of its own, it's probably impossible for Bateman to be involved in anything without noticing some *Arrested Development* nods. For *Ozark*, that includes Marty stuffing pallets of cash into the walls of the resort (sans banana stand) and waxing intellectual about maritime law (all aboard the *Queen Mary*!).

BATEMAN SEES WENDY AS BETTER EQUIPPED TO HANDLE ALL THE BAD STUFF.

Maybe that's why Bateman sees his character's spouse as the more capable figure in their illegal schemes. While he called Wendy a "ninja" who has got what it takes to keep going, he also told Deadline that, at the end of season 2, Marty has "reached his limit [of] his ability to cope with things."

THE SUCCESS OF OZARK LED TO THE OPENING OF A REAL-LIFE BAR IN MISSOURI.

Just as *Atlanta* caused a fictional chicken wing order to become real, *Ozark* has bled into the tourist scene in Missouri. If you're visiting Lake Ozark, Missouri, you can hit up Marty Byrde's Bar and Grill for Del's Nachos, Ruth's Smoked Wings, or Wendy's Philly Steak Sandwich.

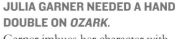

JULIA GARNER NEEDED A HAND DOUBLE ON OZARK.

Garner imbues her character with grit and tenacity—but she had to call for backup during a scene involving a mouse, because she hates rodents. She was supposed to pick up a mouse and drop it into some water, but she was on the verge of a panic attack, so they got a hand double to do it. "The whole crew was laughing at me," Garner told *W* magazine. "It was so embarrassing, and I couldn't even lift it."

OZARK IS FILMED IN ATLANTA.

Even though the show takes place in the Ozarks and was inspired by the Alhonna Resort, much of the show is filmed near and around Atlanta, Georgia, where a large production industry has bloomed over the last decade. Specifically, *Ozark* shoots in Eagle Rock Studios for its interior scenes, at Chateau Elan for Del's sprawling estate, and, when they need to hit the water, Lake Allatoona, which is about an hour outside of Atlanta.

THE OWNER OF THE REAL-LIFE RESORT HOPES PEOPLE REALIZE OZARK IS A PIECE OF FICTION.

Is a popular show set in your neck of the lake good for tourism? Shirley Gross-Russel hopes so. Her family owns the resort where *Ozark* is set (the same one where Dubuque worked at as a teen), and although it may not be everyone's cup of tea to be associated with a story about drug running, money laundering, and death, Gross-Russel is banking on people knowing that a TV show is just a TV show. She hopes guests won't go ripping the walls apart looking for hidden cash.

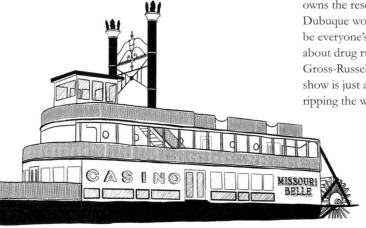

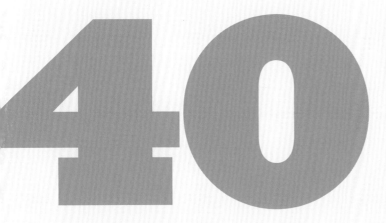

40 GREAT ORIGINAL NETFLIX SERIES

Ever since *House of Cards* became the first streaming series to win a slew of Emmy Awards in 2013, Netflix has been the streaming network to beat when it comes to high-quality programming. Here are some of the streamer's most bingeable series to add to your watchlist (or re-watchlist).

1. *Call the Midwife* // **(2017–2018)**
2. *Big Mouth* // **(2017–PRESENT)**
3. *Bloodline* // **(2017–2018)**
4. *BoJack Horseman* // **(2014–2020)**
5. *Bridgerton* // **(2020–PRESENT)**
6. *Chilling Adventures of Sabrina* // **(2018–2020)**
7. *Cobra Kai* // **(2018–PRESENT)**
8. *The Crown* // **(2016–PRESENT)**
9. *Daredevil* // **(2015–2018)**
10. *Dead to Me* // **(2019–PRESENT)**
11. *Dear White People* // **(2017–2021)**
12. *The End of the F***ing World* // **(2017–2019)**
13. *Glow* // **(2017–2019)**
14. *I Think You Should Leave with Tim Robinson* // **(2019–PRESENT)**
15. *Jessica Jones* // **(2015–2019)**
16. *Lady Dynamite* // **(2016–2017)**
17. *Love* // **(2016–2018)**
18. *Master of None* // **(2015–PRESENT)**
19. *Mindhunter* // **(2017–2019)**
20. *Narcos* // **(2015–2017)**
21. *Never Have I Ever* // **(2020–PRESENT)**
22. *The OA* // **(2016–2019)**
23. *On My Block* // **(2018–PRESENT)**
24. *One Day at a Time* // **(2017–2019)**
25. *Orange Is the New Black* // **(2013–2019)**
26. *Ozark* // **(2017–PRESENT)**
27. *The Punisher* // **(2017–2019)**
28. *The Queen's Gambit* // **(2020)**
29. *Queer Eye* // **(2018–PRESENT)**
30. *Russian Doll* // **(2019–PRESENT)**
31. *Santa Clarita Diet* // **(2017–2019)**
32. *Sense8* // **(2015–2018)**
33. *Sex Education* // **(2019–PRESENT)**
34. *She's Gotta Have It* // **(2017–2019)**
35. *Stranger Things* // **(2016–PRESENT)**
36. *The Umbrella Academy* // **(2019–PRESENT)**
37. *Unbelievable* // **(2019)**
38. *Unbreakable Kimmy Schmidt* // **(2015–2020)**
39. *The Witcher* // **(2019–PRESENT)**
40. *You* // **(2018–PRESENT)**

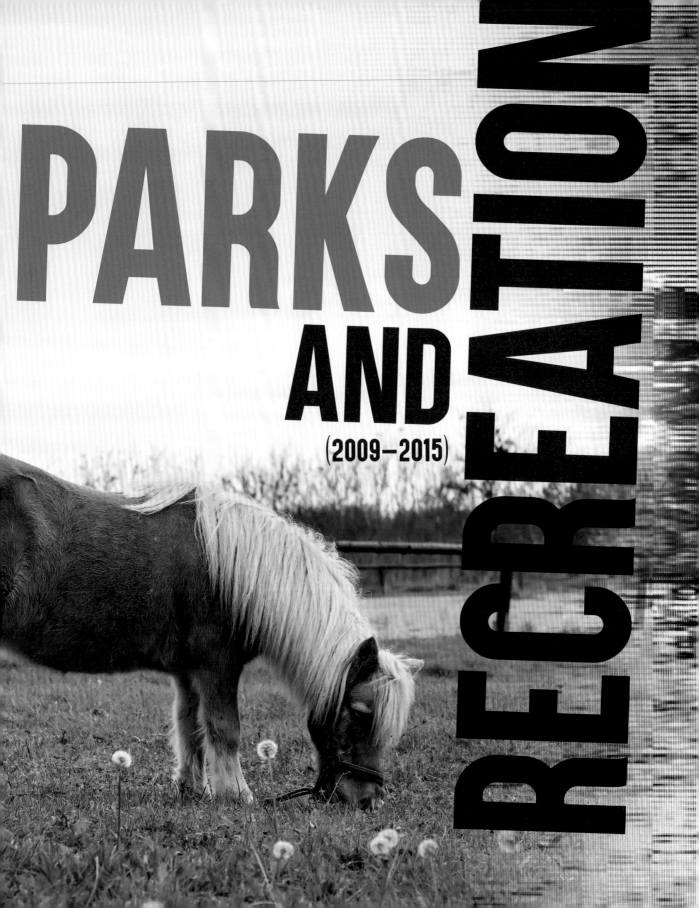

PARKS AND (2009–2015) RECREATION

CREATED BY: Greg Daniels and Michael Schur

SEASONS: 7

EPISODES: 126

OTHER SHOWS BY GREG DANIELS:
King of the Hill (1997–2010)
Upload (2020–PRESENT)
Space Force (2020–PRESENT)

OTHER SHOWS BY MICHAEL SCHUR:
Brooklyn Nine-Nine (2013–PRESENT)
The Good Place (2016–2020)

P*arks and Recreation* proved that the bureaucracy of small-town government is a gold mine for serious comedy. Amy Poehler stars as Leslie Knope, the optimistic and easily excitable deputy director of Pawnee, Indiana's parks and recreation department. Her boss, the mustachioed Ron Swanson (Nick Offerman), is the polar opposite of Leslie, which makes life easier for him—Leslie's overachieving ways allow him to get by with doing as little work as possible. They're surrounded by an all-star cast of comedic actors, including local nurse and Leslie's BFF, Ann Perkins (Rashida Jones); the entrepreneurial-minded Tom Haverford (Aziz Ansari); office manager and Tom's favorite sidekick, Donna Meagle (Retta); cynical intern April Ludgate (Aubrey Plaza); disgraced wunderkind and Leslie's eventual love interest, Ben Wyatt (Adam Scott); eternally optimistic government official Chris Traeger (Rob Lowe); and dim-witted but lovable musician Andy Dwyer (Chris Pratt).

It was an enviable cast with an undeniable chemistry, even when they were losing political battles or planning a memorial service for a tiny horse (RIP Li'l Sebastian). More than a decade since it originally premiered, *Parks and Recreation* is remembered for ushering in a new era of offbeat albeit feel-good sitcoms.

· ·

PARKS AND RECREATION WAS ALMOST A SPIN-OFF OF *THE OFFICE*.

In light of the popularity of *The Office*, NBC was eager to recreate its success. The network tapped *The Office* developer Greg Daniels to make a spin-off of the show, and he asked writer Michael Schur to help him develop it. This is how the idea for *Parks and Recreation* was born. Briefly there was an idea to have an episode of *The Office* end with the faulty copy machine from Dunder Mifflin's Scranton office ending up in Pawnee. Daniels and Schur ultimately abandoned *The Office* connection and made *Parks and Rec* a standalone show, though some similarities—like the mockumentary format and workplace setting—remained.

THE CREATORS WERE INSPIRED BY REAL GOVERNMENT EMPLOYEES.

To make *Parks and Recreation* feel as authentic as possible, co-creators Daniels and Schur visited real local government offices in California to do some research. There they learned that some of the comedic concepts they had planned for the show were even closer to reality than they had hoped. In one government office, they found the real-life version of Ron Swanson. When they described this character to a Burbank public servant, she told them, "Well, I'm a libertarian, so I don't really believe in the mission of my job." She said she was aware of the irony.

POSITIVITY WAS IN *PARKS AND REC'S* DNA.

Parks and Recreation premiered in 2009, a time when cynicism was all the rage in sitcoms. That type of humor would have been easy to replicate in a show about small-town bureaucracy, but Schur decided to take it in a different direction. Instead of relying on unhealthy dynamics for conflict, he wanted to create characters who liked and appreciated each other. "I've never liked mean-spirited comedy," Schur told The Take. "The characters on our show make fun of each other, but not in a biting, angry way. And there's no shortage of conflict in the world of government."

THE EARLY REVIEWS WERE NOT KIND.

Parks and Recreation wasn't an immediate hit. In fact, even today, the show's first season feels a bit different than the rest of the series. Focus groups and critics felt that it was essentially the same show as *The Office*, just in a slightly different setting. *The Washington Post*'s Tom Shales called *Parks and Rec* "a too-obvious imitation of the network's imported hit *The Office*," while others complained that Amy Poehler was being underutilized. The *Contra Costa Times*'s Chuck Barney wrote that the show "betrays Poehler by failing to provide her with material worthy of her talents. Whose idea was it anyway to take a woman gifted with a sharp comedic wit and turn her into a trite dumb blonde? She deserves so much more than that."

THE CAST AND CREW DIDN'T KNOW IF THE SHOW WOULD GET A SECOND SEASON.

With the negative reviews, *Parks and Recreation*'s creators and cast weren't sure they'd actually get to see a second season. In an interview with Vulture, Chris Pratt talked about how the cast had been "working our asses off to stay on the air. Up until now, we've always been sitting on a giant bubble. Right from the beginning it was like, 'Oh, fuck, there's a good chance this could be our last week.' At the end of season 1 [of] *Parks and Rec*, you hug the people really, really fucking tight because you just don't know."

SEVERAL PROMINENT POLITICIANS MADE CAMEOS.

Parks and Recreation is about a small local government, but some big-name politicians showed up over the course of the show's seven-season run. There were notable cameos from Cory Booker, John McCain, Newt Gingrich, and Michelle Obama. Future president/ Leslie's crush Joe Biden made not one but two guest appearances on the show—much to Knope's delight.

SURPRISINGLY, *THE WIRE* WAS ONE INFLUENCE ON THE SHOW.

The acclaimed HBO drama *The Wire* seems like an unlikely source of inspiration for *Parks and Recreation*, but the two shows share some surprising commonalities. They both look at how government works on a local level, and Schur once said he would love to make *Parks and Rec* the comedic answer to *The Wire*. The former show, however, ends on a much more optimistic note than the latter.

"*The Wire* was about calcified systems that were impenetrable from any angle," Schur told HuffPost. "This is the comedy-show equivalent of that, which is to say, those systems are screwed up and calcified and they beat you down, but the comedy version of that is, if you just keep plugging away and you work hard and you are tireless and you sleep three hours a night, [a difference can be made]."

A CONTEST HELPED CHOOSE THE THEME SONG.

To find a theme song for the show, the producers of *Parks and Rec* had a mass email sent out to potential composers. Candidates had five days to compose their music and submit it, and the best theme would receive $7,500 in exchange for the song rights. Vincent Jones and Gaby Moreno's cheery and fast-paced composition was chosen for best representing life in small-town America.

(2013—PRESENT)

BLINDERS

PEAKY

CREATED BY: Steven Knight

SEASONS: 5

EPISODES: 30

OTHER SHOWS BY STEVEN KNIGHT:
Who Wants to Be a Millionaire? (1998–2013)
All About Me (2002–2004)
Taboo (2017–PRESENT)
See (2019–PRESENT)

This BBC series was inspired by the real-life Peaky Blinders gang that operated out of Birmingham, England, during the nineteenth and early twentieth centuries. (They reportedly got their name from the razor blades they sewed into the brims of their caps, though there's no evidence they actually did this.)

Cillian Murphy stars as Tommy Shelby, the gang's reluctant but fiery leader, who must take over the family business out of a sense of criminal duty. Scored with a modern soundtrack (it boasts the greatest use of Nick Cave and the Bad Seeds' "Red Right Hand" ever) and shot with a classically staged intensity, *Peaky Blinders* gets its bingeability from constantly confronting the viewer with how people doing such wrong could seem so right. The series also features a talented lineup of recurring actors, including Sam Neill, Anya Taylor-Joy, Paddy Considine, Adrien Brody, Charlotte Riley, Aidan Gillen, Sam Claflin, and frequent Steve Knight collaborator Tom Hardy as the marble-mouthed Jewish gangster Alfie Solomons, the ruthless leader of a rival gang.

PEAKY BLINDERS IS MEANT TO BE MORE LIKE A WESTERN THAN A GANGSTER DRAMA.

Since its debut in 2013, *Peaky Blinders* has been compared to everything from *The Wire* to *Boardwalk Empire*. But in Knight's mind, the show is more of a western, which is why viewers first meet Tommy Shelby, leader of the Peaky Blinders, racing a horse through Birmingham. "I wanted [the show] to do what Americans did with westerns and take a real period of history, a real geographical location, and turn it into a dream," Knight told *The Observer*. "That's what Americans created with westerns around the nineteenth century."

THE SERIES IS PARTLY BASED ON KNIGHT'S OWN FAMILY.

Growing up, Knight's dad, George, a blacksmith, would tell him stories about his own youth in Birmingham. One day, when George was eight or nine years old, he was given a handwritten message on a piece of paper and told to go deliver it to his great uncles. "He ran through the streets barefoot, knocked on the door, the door opened and there was a table with about eight men sitting around it, immaculately dressed, wearing caps and with guns in their pockets," Knight told *BBC History* magazine. "The table was covered with money—at a time when no one had a penny—and they were all drinking beer out of jam jars because these men wouldn't spend money on glasses or cups. Just that image—smoke, booze, and these immaculately dressed men in this slum in Birmingham—I thought, that's the mythology, that's the story, and that's the first image I started to work with." Those family members were the Sheldons, whom Knight turned into the Shelbys for the series (for legal reasons).

THE SHOW COULD HAVE STARRED JASON STATHAM.

When it came time to cast the lead role of Tommy Shelby, Knight had it narrowed down to two people: Cillian Murphy and Jason Statham. "I met them both in Los Angeles to talk about the role and opted for Jason," Knight said. "One of the reasons was because physically in the room Jason is Jason. Cillian, when you meet him, isn't Tommy, obviously, but I was stupid enough not to understand that." Fortunately, Murphy was smart enough to follow up with a text that said, "Remember, I'm an actor," which he sent to Knight. "Which is absolutely the thing because he can transform himself," Knight said. "If you meet him in the street he is a totally different human being."

KNIGHT WANTS THE SHOW TO FEEL LIKE A PERSONAL MEMORY.

Just as Knight feels a personal connection to the characters and stories of *Peaky Blinders*, he wants the audience to feel the same way watching it. "From the beginning, *Peaky* is almost the recollections of someone who experienced something as a child," Knight said. "A kid remembering something that happened when they were young. Everything's bigger and better."

COMPARE *PEAKY BLINDERS* TO ANY OTHER PRESTIGE DRAMA YOU WANT—KNIGHT PROBABLY HASN'T SEEN IT.

If you see any sort of similarities between *Peaky Blinders* and other so-called prestige TV shows like *The Wire* or *Boardwalk Empire*, it's likely just a coincidence, as Knight has probably (and purposely) avoided watching those others. "I do try to avoid watching other TV shows and films that may be similar," he told *Variety* in early 2021. "I think even subconsciously, if you immerse yourself in lots of other stuff, it starts to rub off on you."

LIVERPOOL PLAYS THE ROLE OF BIRMINGHAM.

Though the world of *Peaky Blinders* is centered in Birmingham, most of the series is shot in Liverpool. Fans of the show can even sign up for a guided tour of the many locations that have been used for the show via a *Peaky* locations tour.

KNIGHT HAS A RULE ABOUT SHOOTING VIOLENCE.

It would be nearly impossible to create a compelling gangster epic without a little bloodshed, but the amount and level of violence in *Peaky Blinders* has proven divisive. The late Helen McCrory, who starred as Tommy's Aunt Polly, once called the show "disgustingly violent." But she said it had a right to be, and Knight seems to agree.

PEAKY BLINDERS BY THE NUMBERS

CILLIAN MURPHY ISN'T A SMOKER, BUT HE SMOKES A LOT.
The actor, who smokes herbal cigarettes for filming and doesn't inhale, asked the prop department to count how many cigarettes the show used in a single season. They counted

3,000

"With *Peaky*, always if there is an act of violence, there is a consequence," he told *The Independent*. "So if somebody gets injured, they're injured for a long time, they stay injured. It's not like what's more pernicious is when you watch over the shoulders of your kids as they're playing a computer game and they're battering the hell out of each other and there's no consequence."

MURPHY DIDN'T THINK THE MODERN SOUNDTRACK WOULD WORK.

As *Peaky Blinders* is a period drama, one of its most surprising elements is its modern soundtrack. "Red Right Hand" by Nick Cave and the Bad Seeds is the show's theme song, and the series has featured songs by the likes of Radiohead, Jarvis Cocker, Arctic Monkeys, David Bowie, PJ Harvey, Tom Waits, and The White Stripes over the years. It was a bold choice by Knight, and Murphy was one person who wasn't sure it would work.

"I thought it was a terrible idea when someone told me first that it would be contemporary music against a period story," the actor admitted. "I didn't think it would work but then something happened where it just clicked and we always— you know the people that made the show—we always talked about whether a tune is '*Peaky*' or 'not *Peaky*.' You just seemed to know whether it is and it's really hard to define what that is but I think it seems to be an outlaw quality to the music."

DAVID BOWIE WAS A MAJOR FAN OF THE SHOW.

Shortly before Bowie's death, Knight learned that the legendary singer was a huge fan of *Peaky Blinders* and wanted to see his music featured on it. On December 30, 2015, reps from Bowie's label arranged to come to Knight's home and preview Bowie's *Blackstar* album, which had not been announced yet, in the hope that they could use something from it on the show. "And then we heard that he'd passed away," Knight said. "It seems that his people were keen to establish that we could use it before he passed on." The show featured one of Bowie's songs in its third season.

After Bowie's death, Murphy shared that he had sent him Tommy's hat from season 1. "We were friends and I sent him the cap from the first series as a Christmas present," Murphy told Birmingham Live. "He was a very sweet man and a genuine fan of *Peaky Blinders*, and I was a huge, huge David Bowie fan."

25

BINGEABLE PERIOD DRAMAS

Period dramas can be addictive. Even with its modern flourishes,
Peaky Blinders manages to transport viewers back to the early twentieth century.
From the carefully curated costumes and set designs to the colorful language
and turns of phrase, it's easy to get caught up in the old-timey details
of a great series that takes you back in time.

1. *A Suitable Boy* // **(2020)**
2. *Belgravia* // **(2020)**
3. *Bridgerton* // **(2020–PRESENT)**
4. *Cable Girls* // **(2017–2020)**
5. *Call the Midwife* // **(2012–PRESENT)**
6. *Downton Abbey* // **(2010–2015)**
7. *Gentleman Jack* // **(2019–PRESENT)**
8. *Harlots* // **(2017–2019)**
9. *North and South* // **(2004)**
10. *Outlander* // **(2014–PRESENT)**
11. *Poldark* // **(2015–2019)**
12. *Pride and Prejudice* // **(1995)**
13. *Sanditon* // **(2019–PRESENT)**
14. *The Borgias* // **(2011–2013)**
15. *The Crown* // **(2016–PRESENT)**
16. *The Forsyte Saga* // **(2002–2003)**
17. *The Great* // **(2020–PRESENT)**
18. *The Knick* // **(2014–2015)**
19. *The Spanish Princess* // **(2019–2020)**
20. *The Tudors* // **(2007–2010)**
21. *Upstairs, Downstairs* // **(1971–1975)**
22. *Upstairs Downstairs* // **(2010–2012)**
23. *Versailles* // **(2015–2018)**
24. *Victoria* // **(2016–PRESENT)**
25. *Wolf Hall* // **(2015)**

POSE (2018—2021)

CREATED BY: Ryan Murphy, Brad Falchuk, and Steven Canals

SEASONS: 3

EPISODES: 25

OTHER SHOWS BY RYAN MURPHY AND BRAD FALCHUK:
Glee (2009–2015)
Scream Queens (2015–2016)
American Horror Story (2011–PRESENT)

FREEZE FRAME

"LOVE IS THE MESSAGE" // SEASON I, EPISODE 6

This season I episode was extremely personal to Murphy, who co-wrote the episode with director Janet Mock—specifically, the speech that Pray Tell gives about remembering what it's like to not live in fear of AIDS. "That was me," Murphy told *The Hollywood Reporter.* "I would drive myself to the emergency room in college every IO days, even when I was celibate, and get a blood test and I would wait for two weeks and lose I5 pounds and throw up in the middle of the night in fear because I thought I was going to die. I thought that loving someone meant death, and I think a large group of young people don't have that experience. That was my experience, so I was able to, with the HIV/AIDS story, really lean into my pain."

Not long after its 2018 premiere, *Pose* began making history. The series, which dramatizes New York City's underground drag ball scene of the late 1980s and early 1990s, was co-created by Steven Canals and über-showrunners Ryan Murphy and Brad Falchuk. Like so many of their other series, *Pose* puts representation at the forefront of the show. Without ignoring the hardships facing its characters—many of whom would be relegated to the margins of other shows—*Pose* brings to life a unique culture full of joy and perseverance, and has been heartily embraced by viewers and critics.

POSE WAS INSPIRED, IN PART, BY A DOCUMENTARY.
Jennie Livingston's *Paris Is Burning* (1990) exposed a relatively mainstream audience to the world of ballrooms, including future *Pose* co-creators Steven Canals and Ryan Murphy, as well as writer, director, and producer Janet Mock. At times, the show seems to mine plot points directly from the film. In *Paris Is Burning,* real-life performer Venus Xtravaganza muses about how any relationship can become transactional, creating a hypothetical scenario in which a "regular" woman must sleep with her husband in order to get the washer and dryer she wants. In the show, tension arise when that "regular" woman, Patty (Kate Mara), insists that her husband provide her with a dishwasher, raising similar thematic questions.

THE CREATORS WERE FLEXIBLE IN THE CASTING PROCESS.
Series regular Dyllón Burnside plays Ricky, a character who didn't exist until the creative team wrote the role for him after he auditioned for another part. Angelica Ross's Candy Ferocity was created under similar circumstances, despite Ross believing that she had blown her audition for one of the series' leads. And while Indya Moore auditioned for multiple roles and said they related most to the motherly Blanca, their casting as the beautiful but conflicted Angel certainly rings true for fans of the show.

THE IMPROBABLE OPENING HEIST REALLY HAPPENED.
The series begins with members of the House of Abundance hiding out in a museum at closing time so that they can raid an exhibition of royal clothing for use in their performances. As unlikely as it seems, Murphy said that the scene only came to be on *Pose* because of

New York City ballroom icon Hector Xtravaganza, who served as one of the show's consultants. "Hector was a huge influence on the development of the script; in many ways he was the Grandfather of the house scene (and that is how he identified)," Murphy wrote following Xtravaganza's death in 2018. "So many scenes in the script—including the opening Royalty museum heist—were actually inspired from stories he told me, always with a glimmer in his eye."

THE SHOW IS A HIGH-WATER MARK FOR TRANS REPRESENTATION.

While the gender identity of real-life ballroom performers ranged widely and defied easy categorization, contestants in the "femme queen" competition category were primarily transgender women. With well over one hundred trans actors and crew members, from star Indya Moore to writer and producer Janet Mock, *Pose* sets a new standard for telling compelling stories about trans people. It doesn't ignore their gender identity but recognizes that no person can be reduced to a single label.

MURPHY CONSIDERS HIMSELF AN ADVOCATE ON *POSE*, NOT A SHOWRUNNER.

Pose is a very different sort of project for Ryan Murphy (co-creator of *Glee*, *American Horror Story*, *Scream Queens*, and *The Politician*), and one that he wanted to use in order to give back to the LGBTQ community. As such, Murphy told *The Hollywood Reporter,* "I'm not showrunner here, I'm an advocate for this community, and my job is to take care of them and provide for them and to give them access into a mainstream world that they have been denied for so long." As part of this dedication to giving back, Murphy donates the profits from *Pose* to LGBTQ and trans charities. In addition, he has plans to continue raising more funds for these organizations via charity screenings and benefits, and he would like to set up scholarships for LGBTQ and trans kids in need. It's no wonder he has said that *Pose* is "without question the highlight of my career."

19 IMPORTANT MOMENTS IN LGBTQ HISTORY ON TV

1971: *All in the Family* became the first sitcom to feature a gay character—a macho type named Steve, who shocked Archie Bunker (Carroll O'Connor) by coming out—in the season 1 episode "Judging Books by Covers." Unfortunately, it was Steve's only appearance in the series.

1972: The made-for-TV movie *That Certain Summer* starred Hal Holbrook (before his turn as Deep Throat in the film *All the President's Men*) and Martin Sheen as a couple in love. It was lauded for its sympathetic portrayal of gay men, though Sheen recalled some people worried it would damage his career. It won the Golden Globe for Best Television Movie.

1973: The PBS series *An American Family,* often credited with being the first reality show, followed the Loud family of Santa Barbara, California. Openly gay son Lance became a breakout star of the series and an icon for paving the way for gay representation in mainstream television.

1977: *The Jeffersons*, a spin-off of *All in the Family*, is often credited with featuring the first transgender character on a sitcom. In the episode "Once a Friend," George Jefferson's old Navy buddy Eddie revealed that she's a woman named Edie.

1977: Billy Crystal portrayed Jodie Dallas, a gay dad, in the campy comedy *Soap*. The character displeased both religious moralists and gay rights activists, but his character became important in the TV landscape. *Soap* also had one of the first lesbian characters on a sitcom, Jodie's friend Alice, played by Randee Heller.

1992: Ryan Philippe played TV's first openly gay teenager on the soap opera *One Life to Live*, in which his character came out to his parents in a dramatic scene involving practically the whole town of Llanview.

1994: Though it aired for only one season, the influential show *My So-Called Life* tackled homophobia in a story line that featured Wilson Cruz playing Rickie Vasquez, the first openly gay teen in prime time.

1994: ABC fed the culture wars when it announced a forthcoming scene in its hit sitcom *Roseanne*, in which Roseanne Barr and Mariel Hemingway would share a kiss at a gay bar. More than 30 million people tuned in to the episode "Don't Ask, Don't Tell."

1994: As reality TV was becoming more and more dominant, MTV's *The Real World: San Francisco* introduced Pedro Zamora, a gay activist who was also HIV positive. Zamora proved to be a powerful voice on the series, creating the sort of teachable moments that resonated with young viewers. He died just hours after the final episode of *The Real World: San Francisco* aired.

1997: Ellen DeGeneres—playing a character based on herself in her sitcom *Ellen*—came out in "The Puppy Episode," a culture-shifting moment that went way beyond television (DeGeneres herself came out a few weeks before the episode aired). A 2015 *Variety* poll found that DeGeneres did more to sway Americans' attitudes about gay rights than any other celebrity.

1999 and 2000: *Queer as Folk* premiered in the UK, then on Showtime in the US as an American remake of the original Russell T. Davies series. It was the first hour-long drama to feature a cast of gay characters dealing with same-sex marriage, gay adoption, cruising, and other relevant topics. In April 2021, it was announced that the series was being rebooted for NBC's Peacock streaming network.

2003: *Queer Eye for the Straight Guy* (later shortened to *Queer Eye*) premiered on Bravo as one of the first reality shows featuring an all-gay cast. In each episode, its five lifestyle experts made over a less-than-chic guy or girl.

2009: *RuPaul's Drag Race* debuted on Logo TV and was an instant hit, thanks to its lovable host and the cutthroat competition to find America's "next drag superstar."

2014: Laverne Cox became the first openly trans person to be nominated for an Emmy Award for acting for her work on *Orange Is the New Black*, a show that addresses a number of LGBTQ issues.

2014: Amazon's *Transparent* broke new ground for trans actors with its cast, though some were critical that its star, Jeffrey Tambor, was a straight male actor playing a newly out trans woman. In 2018, multiple people accused Tambor of sexual harassment. Though the actor denied these allegations, these behind-the-scenes issues ultimately led to the show's conclusion.

2017: Asia Kate Dillon took on a major role as an intern named Taylor on Showtime's *Billions*, becoming one of the first non-binary characters on TV (and the first non-binary person to play one).

2018: The CW's *Black Lightning* included TV's first Black lesbian superhero, played by Nafessa Williams, in its universe.

2019: When Jenna Bans, creator of NBC's *Good Girls*, cast Isaiah Stannard in the role of Sadie Marks, she was unaware that the young actor was trans and used he/him pronouns. "We realized we had a really great opportunity to tell a story about a character who was gender non-conforming, but at the same time not necessarily have that be what leads the story," Bans told *Variety* in 2018. In the 2019 episode "Thelma and Louise," Sadie (now Ben) came out to his mother in a simple but moving scene. "We liked the idea that the character of Sadie was exploring her gender [expression] in the show," Bans said, "but I think what we responded to more was that the Mae Whitman character just couldn't care less."

SCHITT'S CREEK

(2015–2020)

MOTEL

Schitt's Creek

REFRIGERATED AIR

PUSH BUTTON PHONES

VACANCY

T-V IN ROOMS

CREATED BY: Dan Levy and Eugene Levy

SEASONS: 6

EPISODES: 80

If you've enjoyed Catherine O'Hara and Eugene Levy in any of their past film roles as an oddball couple, you won't be let down by *Schitt's Creek*. After they lose their entire video store fortune to the government because their business manager hasn't been paying their taxes, the Rose family—parents Johnny (Levy) and Moira (O'Hara) and their adult children, David (Daniel Levy, Eugene's son) and Alexis (Annie Murphy)—head to the only asset the government has allowed them to keep: the rural town of Schitt's Creek, which Johnny once purchased as a joke. The cosmopolitan Roses move into the local motel, where they share two adjoining rooms.

Schitt's Creek is a classic fish-out-of-water story, but at its heart it is a show about family. Though the Canadian show, which made its American debut on Pop TV, struggled to find its audience in the first few seasons (largely because most people had never heard of Pop TV), all that changed when *Schitt's Creek* dropped on Netflix and benefited from what is known as the "Netflix bump." Critics discovered the series, too; in 2020, *Schitt's Creek* swept all seven major comedy categories at the Emmys, and Daniel Levy became the first person in Emmy history to win all four major categories (producing, writing, directing, and acting) in a single year.

SCHITT'S CREEK WAS A FAMILY AFFAIR.

To flesh out his idea for *Schitt's Creek*, Daniel Levy turned to his dad, frequent Christopher Guest collaborator (and *American Pie* star) Eugene. The two had never worked together before; in fact, pre-*Schitt's*, Daniel had been adamant about doing his own thing. So why go to his father for *Schitt's*? As Daniel explained to NPR, he had seen the family-loses-it-all idea "played out on mainstream television and sitcoms, but I'd never really seen it explored through the lens of a certain style of realist comedy that my dad does so well. So I came to him and pitched the idea and asked him if he would be interested at all in just fleshing it out and seeing if there was anything there. And, fortunately, there was some interest and we started talking."

Eugene and Daniel weren't the only Levys on the show, either: Sarah Levy, daughter of Eugene and sister of Daniel, also appeared on *Schitt's Creek* as Twyla Sands, the lone waitress at the town's most happening diner, Cafe Tropical.

EUGENE CAME UP WITH THE SHOW'S TITLE.

"It was actually just out of coincidence really," Daniel told *Out* of the show's title. "He was having a dinner conversation a few weeks prior, about this theoretical town of Schitt's Creek: You would have Schitt Hardware and Schitt Grocers." When they were researching ways that people had lost their fortunes, they came across stories of people who had bought towns for various reasons and later ended up bankrupt. "We thought, well, what if this family, as a joke for the son's sixteenth birthday, found this town called Schitt's Creek, bought it as a joke because of the name and then ended up having to live there?" Daniel said.

The show's name made promotional tours interesting: Not all TV or radio outlets could say it, for fear of being fined for using profanity. On *The Late Show with Stephen Colbert*, for example, the name of the show had to appear on screen every time it was spoken aloud.

THE KARDASHIANS INFLUENCED SOME ELEMENTS OF *SCHITT'S CREEK*.

"It really just started with me being in Los Angeles, knowing that I wanted to write," Daniel told *Out* in 2015 of the show's beginnings. "I had been watching some reality TV at the time and was concentrating on what would happen if one of these wealthy families would lose everything. Would the Kardashians still be the Kardashians without their money?"

STEVIE BUDD WAS THE AUDIENCE'S STAND-IN.

Daniel has explained that Stevie (Emily Hampshire) was meant to be the character the audience could most connect with, which was something that resonated with Hampshire. "I think what I connected to in Stevie is that she really stands in for the audience in a way," Hampshire told *Mental Floss* in 2018, "and I felt like I just had to watch these people around me and take them in in an honest way and it would be funny."

In the character breakdown she received when she auditioned, Hampshire says that Stevie was described as "being from a small town, and she's very deadpan." But over the course of the show, Stevie evolved. In season 1, Hampshire said, "I don't think she had any attachment to the motel or to anyone—on purpose. To not be attached or kind of be emotionally invested in anything is a much safer place to be…she has opened up." Over the course of the show, Stevie "grows up a lot," Hampshire said, "and really learns to take responsibility for things that I don't think she ever wanted to take responsibility for."

O'HARA BROUGHT SOMETHING SPECIAL TO THE CHARACTER OF MOIRA ROSE.

It was Eugene who suggested O'Hara—his frequent collaborator in Guest's mockumentaries—for the part of Moira Rose. "I was not going to say, 'No, that's not a good idea,'" Daniel told *The New York Times*. "When he offers up Catherine O'Hara, you take it and run with it."

O'Hara told AwardsDaily that her character's voice is "kind of a mix of people I've met. There's one woman who's very feminine and lovely. She just has a unique way of putting sentences together." Inspiration can come from other sources, too. In the season 3 episode "New Car," O'Hara at one point had to use a British accent. "There's a woman on Sirius Radio who claims to be a dog whisperer or pet psychic. Have you heard this woman?" she asked AwardsDaily. "That's basically the accent I'm doing."

O'HARA USED ARCANE DICTIONARIES FOR MOIRA'S VOCABULARY.

Before shooting, O'Hara would look over Moira's dialogue and trade out conventional words with more unusual *bon mots*. "I have a couple of books that have arcane and archaic words that nobody's ever heard, and it's fun to play with my dialogue a bit and…*accessorize* with a few of those words," O'Hara told *Entertainment Weekly*. Those books included *Foyle's Philavery: A Treasury of Unusual Words* and *Mrs. Byrne's Dictionary of Unusual, Obscure, and Preposterous Words*.

THE LOCATION OF SCHITT'S CREEK WAS PURPOSELY AMBIGUOUS.

Schitt's Creek is a Canadian production, and the Rose family had a place in New York, but when people ask him where the town of Schitt's Creek is located, Eugene tells them it's wherever they think it should be. "We didn't set *Schitt's Creek* in any location or any country, it's just Schitt's Creek," he said at 92Y Talks in 2016. "We honestly wanted the focus of the show to be on this town, and if you put it in a country with real states or put it in a country with real provinces, then things become tangible…it kind of diffuses the focus to me."

THERE WASN'T A LOT OF IMPROV ON THE *SCHITT'S CREEK* SET.

That fact might surprise fans of Eugene and O'Hara's work on *SCTV* and in Guest films like *Waiting for Guffman* and *Best in Show*, where the cast works from an outline of the action with no dialogue rather than a traditional script. "[*Schitt's Creek*] is completely a scripted show, but we do an awful lot of playing around with the lines when we get to the set," Eugene told *The Hollywood Reporter*. "What looked good on paper doesn't always play when you hear the words out loud. So we do change things until they end up sounding right."

CHRIS ELLIOTT MADE EUGENE LEVY BREAK CONSTANTLY.

According to Annie Murphy, Eugene "giggles like a schoolboy" in scenes with Chris Elliott, who played Schitt's Creek Mayor Roland Schitt. "He's got my number," Levy said in an interview with YouTube's BUILD Series. "He's constantly making me laugh on set…He does it intentionally, of course, and he actually succeeds."

CAFE TROPICAL'S MENU WAS ANNIE MURPHY'S FAVORITE PROP.

Cafe Tropical's huge menu was often played for laughs on *Schitt's Creek*, and it was Murphy's favorite prop on the show. "I wish everyone could see the inside of the menu because it's very detailed and there's literally every dish you could possibly imagine," Murphy said at 92Y Talks in 2018. "There are literally 150 things you could order on this menu, and they're all described." The props department couldn't find a big enough real-life menu, so they ended up creating massive ones in a custom size.

AFTER PRODUCTION WRAPPED, EMILY HAMPSHIRE TOOK SOMETHING SPECIAL FROM THE SET.

Hampshire snagged the stag painting from behind the desk at the Rosebud Motel and took it home with her. These days, it lives in her home office. "It's in a *tiny* office," she says. "It's basically the entire office."

SCHITT'S CREEK SET AN EMMY RECORD.

The show swept the comedy category at the 2020 Emmys for its sixth and final season, and won nine awards in total—"the most ever for a comedy in a single year," according to *The New York Times*. O'Hara and Eugene Levy both won acting Emmys in the comedy category for playing Moira and Johnny Rose, while Daniel Levy and Annie Murphy won Outstanding Supporting Actor and Actress awards for their roles as David and Alexis Rose. The show also took home awards for directing, writing, casting, and contemporary costumes.

SPOILERS! *SCHITT'S CREEK* HAS BEEN LAUDED FOR ITS LGBTQ REPRESENTATIONS.

In addition to being painfully funny, *Schitt's Creek* has won accolades for its representation of gay characters. One of the show's main story lines is the developing relationship between David Rose (Daniel Levy) and Patrick (Noah Reid), which culminates in a wedding in the series finale. Unlike other series that would put the focus on David and Patrick being a "gay couple," on *Schitt's Creek* they're just a couple you're rooting for.

"I think getting to write that story line was incredibly cathartic for me for many reasons," Daniel told Deadline. "One, I don't get to see those kinds of relationships depicted on TV so I felt that it was an incredible responsibility to be given the opportunity and to try to tell it as authentic as I possibly could…By projecting a sweeter, gentler world, I feel that it was a political statement. It seemed to have an incredible effect on people."

13 SHOWS THAT BENEFITED FROM THE "NETFLIX BUMP"

Schitt's Creek isn't the only series that benefited from having a binge-watch just a few clicks away. Plenty of other beloved series found a much larger audience once they arrived on Netflix.

1. *Avatar: The Last Airbender* // (2005–2008)
2. *Breaking Bad* // (2008–2013)
3. *Community* // (2009–2015)
4. *Criminal Minds* // (2005–2020)
5. *Good Girls* // (2018–PRESENT)
6. *Grey's Anatomy* // (2005–PRESENT)
7. *How to Get Away With Murder* // (2014–2020)
8. *Outlander* // (2014–PRESENT)
9. *Riverdale* // (2017–PRESENT)
10. *The Blacklist* // (2013–PRESENT)
11. *The Good Place* // (2016–2020)
12. *The Office* // (2005–2013)
13. *The Walking Dead* // (2010–PRESENT)

SEX AND THE CITY

(1998–2004)

CREATED BY: Darren Star

SEASONS: 6

EPISODES: 94

OTHER SHOWS BY DARREN STAR:
Beverly Hills, 90210 (1990–2000)
Melrose Place (1992–1999)
Younger (2015–PRESENT)
Emily in Paris (2020–PRESENT)

Most romantic comedies revolve around some central question, like "Will they or won't they?" or "Which person will the protagonist choose?" Over the course of its six seasons, *Sex and the City* tackles all of them—and, thanks to Carrie Bradshaw, many more.

As Carrie (Sarah Jessica Parker) chronicles the New York City dating scene for her newspaper column, she can't help but wonder about everything from "Does a string of bad dates really equal one good one?" to "How much does a 'father figure' figure?" These intermittent soliloquies are a nod to the show's source material—Candace Bushnell's column in *The New York Observer*—and they also help link the individual romantic affairs of Carrie, a couture-loving journo, and her three BFFs: Miranda (Cynthia Nixon), a career-driven lawyer; Charlotte (Kristin Davis), a coy art gallerist; and Samantha (Kim Cattrall), an unapologetically lusty PR agent. In the end, the central question of *Sex and the City* isn't one posed by Carrie, but by the viewer: "Am I a Carrie, a Miranda, a Charlotte, or a Samantha?"

IT WAS THE FIRST CABLE SHOW TO WIN THE EMMY FOR OUTSTANDING COMEDY SERIES.
Although HBO has had great success with their dramatic series, *Sex and the City* was the network's first comedy series to win Emmy gold in 2001. It maintained that record until 2015, when *Veep* won the coveted award (which it won again in 2016 and 2017).

THE FOURTH-WALL BREAKING LASTED FOR LONGER THAN YOU PROBABLY REMEMBER.
Early episodes of *Sex and the City* feature one majorly jarring element that was later jettisoned from the rest of its run: Characters breaking the fourth wall and talking directly to the camera (which worked much better in *Fleabag*). Although Miranda, Charlotte, and random supporting characters did it in the pilot (even Skipper did it!), eventually only Carrie turned to the camera to chat it up—and even that got the axe by the early part of the second season.

CARRIE'S ADDRESS ISN'T REAL.

For the entire run of the series, Carrie lives in a very chic apartment in a rent-controlled Upper East Side brownstone located on East 73rd Street, between Park and Madison Avenues. Swanky location, right? Too bad it was doubly fictional. Carrie's building number was 245 (a nonexistent number that, if it did exist, would be located farther east, between Second and Third Avenues) and the exterior shots were actually filmed on Perry Street in the West Village—though the building's owners have since blocked off the stoop so that people will stop using their home as a photo op.

SAMANTHA AND MIRANDA'S ADDRESSES AREN'T REAL, EITHER.

Although the other ladies moved around during the course of the series, each of them had her own signature abode, none of which actually exist. Samantha's Meatpacking District loft at 300 Gansevoort Street isn't real (that address doesn't exist), and Miranda's Upper West Side apartment is also fictional. Charlotte's chi-chi address at 700 Park Avenue is, however, a real one, and it's home to a twenty-one-floor co-op that specializes in large apartments.

KRISTIN DAVIS USED TO HIDE THE SHOW FROM HER FAMILY.

Davis was concerned that the show's risqué subject matter—and even its title—would shock her family, so she didn't tell her grandmother about it and asked her parents not to watch it. But her attitude changed over time, and she later confessed that her parents had started watching the show after her grandmother passed away. Davis's dad, a psychology professor, really got into it, even using the show as part of his college lectures on marriage and sexuality.

KIM CATTRALL WAS WORRIED SHE HAD BEEN CAST AS SOMEONE'S MOTHER.

As the oldest member of the cast, Cattrall was a little blown away by the fact that the series wanted her to play the role of Samantha Jones, a sexy singleton, and not someone's mom. "I never thought I'd be playing this character at this age in my life," she said in 2002. "I thought I'd be playing somebody's mom."

THE SHOW DIDN'T INVENT THE COSMO, BUT IT CERTAINLY POPULARIZED IT.

The ladies' cocktail of choice, the pink-hued vodka sipper, may have risen to frothy fame thanks to the series, but the drink is believed to have been invented way back in the 1930s. Although its exact provenance is up for debate (no one can agree on whether it was first made in Provincetown or Miami or somewhere else), no one questions that its nineties popularity was due to its many, many appearances on the show. Pair it with a Magnolia Bakery cupcake, and you've got yourself one heck of a *Sex and the City* snack.

THERE WAS A REAL MR. BIG.

Given the true-life (and true-love) events that inspired Candace Bushnell's original columns, it should come as little surprise that there was a real Mr. Big *and* he has actually been identified. Although the series' Big (Chris Noth) was a big-time financier and entrepreneur, his inspiration—Ron Galotti—was a publisher whom Bushnell met at a party in 1995. The pair dated for about a year, but his presence was felt in her columns—and in Carrie's own story—for years to come.

NATASHA ONLY APPEARED IN SEVEN EPISODES.

Sex and the City featured a ton of very memorable recurring characters, from Candice Bergen as Enid Frick, Carrie's *Vogue* editor, to Frances Sternhagen as Bunny MacDougal, Charlotte's onetime mother-in-law. But few guest stars had quite the same impact as Bridget Moynahan as Natasha Naginsky, Mr. Big's second wife. Considering how deeply the introduction of Natasha changed Carrie's life (and her relationship with Mr. Big), it's surprising that Moynahan only popped up in seven episodes, spread out over the second and third seasons. Her last appearance? The seventeenth episode of season 3, "What Goes Around Comes Around," in which Carrie desperately tries to make amends.

THE SHOW ADDRESSED 9/11 IN ITS OWN WAY.

The September eleventh attacks occurred between half seasons, as the fourth season was split in two and the first run ended on August 12, 2001. When the show returned on January 6, 2002, the opening credits had been altered so as not to show the Twin Towers, which originally appeared twice: once with the show's title, once with "Starring Sarah Jessica Parker."

Of the change, led by producer Michael Patrick King, Parker—who watched the towers collapse—told *New York* magazine: "Like the rest of us, I had had all sorts of mixed feelings about the Twin Towers…But once they were gone, they were beloved." They were replaced in the credits by the Empire State Building.

PARKER PUSHED FOR DIVERSITY.

When Blair Underwood joined the cast as a love interest for Miranda back in 2003, it marked the injection of a long-needed bit of diversity in the show's cast. Of the casting, Nixon said, "We all of us, and no one more than Sarah Jessica, had lobbied for this for a long, long time…I'm a huge fan of the show, but if we had an area in which we really could use improvement, it's certainly this one…I think it's about time."

THE SHOW'S FINALE REALLY WAS INTENDED AS AN ENDING.

Although *Sex and the City* has spawned two feature films, as well as a revival series, producer Michael Patrick King (who directed both of the feature films) originally believed that the show ended just as it was meant to. In 2004, mere months after the show aired its final episode, King said at a panel, "Nothing we did in the series was altered to save something for the movie…This is exactly the way we wanted to end the series. We're proud of what we did."

IT'S STILL THE INSPIRATION FOR A BUS TOUR.

It makes sense that *Sex and the City*, one of those "oh, it's like New York City is its own character!" series, spawned a bus tour of the show's various New York City–set locations back in 2001. But it's a little surprising that the tour is still going. Run by On Location Tours, the three-and-a-half-hour tour has now been operating for more than seventeen years—nearly three times as long as the series was on the air—and it shows no sign of slowing down. It operates seven days a week, complete with stops at Magnolia Bakery (for cupcakes) and Bleecker Street (for shopping). And, yes, it does drive by Carrie's stoop (the one on Perry Street, naturally).

SEX AND THE CITY BY THE NUMBERS

TO CELEBRATE THE TWENTY-FIRST BIRTHDAY OF *SEX AND THE CITY*, THE CONTENT EXPERTS AT CEROS INSPIRE ANALYZED EVERY ONE OF THE SERIES' SCRIPTS TO GLEAN SOME FASCINATING STATS ABOUT THE SHOW. HERE'S WHAT THEY FOUND.

Over the course of six seasons, the show featured a total of **92** sex scenes. As there were **94** episodes in total, that works out to an average of just under **1** sex scene per episode (**.979** to be exact).

Who was getting the most action? Samantha, of course! Of those **92** intimate moments, **40** of them featured Samantha. While Charlotte may have been painted as the prudish one of the bunch, it was Carrie who had the fewest number of R-rated romps (**13** in total).

The ladies dated a variety of men in all sorts of professions, but bankers came out on top as far as love interests: All four women dated at least one for a collective total of **15** banker boyfriends. Artists were the second most popular paramour profession, with **9** in total (**7** of them Carrie's—hey, she had a type).

The women did a lot of talking, but Carrie and Miranda shared the most one-on-one exchanges: **1,827** of them, to be exact. Carrie and Samantha came in second, with **1,407** chats.

Though Carrie's massive shoe collection was practically its own character, her penchant for Manolo Blahnik shoes specifically was only ever mentioned in **7** episodes, and the brand wasn't mentioned at all in seasons 2 or 5. Go figure.

7 HBO SERIES YOU SHOULD ADD TO YOUR WATCHLIST

Though a famous early promo promised "It's not TV," over the years Home Box Office (HBO) has become synonymous with the Golden Age of Television. Here are a few shows that earned their place in the pantheon of prestige TV.

BARRY (2018–PRESENT)

Bill Hader isn't the first person you'd think of as a hit man, but he makes it work as Barry—someone who kills for a living but finds his escape from his high-violence world in the high-drama world of acting class. The show is an incredible feat of tonal balance that's equally comfortable going for humor as for heartache. It's something truly fresh and original, even by prestige TV standards.

EASTBOUND & DOWN (2009–2013)

If you're familiar with Danny McBride's body of work, you'll understand why *Eastbound & Down* is not for the easily offended. McBride is at his best when he's acting like a raging asshole, and he does that to an astonishing degree as Kenny Powers, an obnoxious former pro baseball player. The series tracks Powers's epic highs and painful lows—almost all of which he brings upon himself—and isn't afraid to say, do, or show things that no other series would dare.

THE FLIGHT ATTENDANT (2020–PRESENT)

In 2021, two years after *The Big Bang Theory* said farewell, Kaley Cuoco earned her first-ever Golden Globe nomination for her darkly comedic turn in this HBO Max series, based on Chris Bohjalian's bestselling novel. Cuoco stars as Cassie Bowden, a flight attendant who wakes up in a Bangkok hotel room (not her own) with a dead man by her side and no memory of what she did to get there.

I MAY DESTROY YOU (2020)

Michaela Coel's kaleidoscopic limited series is an investigation into the aftermath of trauma, a celebration and indictment of the power of social media, and a radical meditation on empathy. Incisive and surprising, the series will leave you sure of nothing but Coel's prodigious talent.

OZ (1997–2003)

Arguably the birthplace of a new generation of television, *Oz*'s "Emerald City" is an experimental unit inside an often hellish maximum-security prison. Telling unmistakably adult stories in an unsparing way, the show hinted at the possibilities of serialized storytelling on the small screen.

SILICON VALLEY (2014–2019)

Mike Judge's obsessively detailed satire of life in the tech industry follows Richard Hendricks (Thomas Middleditch) as he attempts to build a start-up around a revolutionary algorithm he created in his spare time. Pied Piper's ragtag team of coding misfits have the technical skills to change the world, if only they could stop getting in each other's (and their own) way. Martin Starr, Kumail Nanjiani, T. J. Miller, and Zach Woods co-star.

SUCCESSION (2018–PRESENT)

Brian Cox won his first Golden Globe in 2020 for his role as Logan Roy, the Rupert Murdoch-like media mogul who's as cutthroat when it comes to family matters as he is when his company is under threat of a hostile takeover. That's just what happens when you mix business with family, and have taught your kids—each one of whom is jockeying for the biggest piece of the pie—that life is a nonstop competition. Creator Jesse Armstrong's (*Peep Show*) distinctly black sense of humor has made *Succession* one of the most binge-worthy series in recent years.

SHERLOCK

(2010—2017)

CREATED BY: Mark Gatiss and Steven Moffat (based on the series of Sherlock Holmes novels and short stories by Sir Arthur Conan Doyle)

SEASONS: 4

EPISODES: 13

OTHER SHOWS BY MARK GATISS AND STEVEN MOFFAT:
Dracula (2020)

FREEZE FRAME

**"THE EMPTY HEARSE" //
SEASON 3, EPISODE 1**
Sherlock Holmes's parents
are played by actors
Timothy Carlton and Wanda
Ventham, aka Benedict
Cumberbatch's parents.

In 2012, the character of Sherlock Holmes became a Guinness World Record holder when Sir Arthur Conan Doyle's famed detective nabbed the title for "the most portrayed literary human character in film and TV" with a total (at the time) of 254 onscreen depictions. But you don't have to have seen even a fraction of those interpretations to know that Benedict Cumberbatch as the consulting detective and Martin Freeman as his trusty sidekick, Dr. Watson, brought a totally new spin to Doyle's works with *Sherlock*.

Set in modern-day London, *Sherlock* imagines a world in which Holmes has the benefit of Google and social media to help him in his investigations, with Watson regularly blogging about their strangest cases (which turns Sherlock into a kind of influencer). Though it may sound like a breeze to get through just thirteen episodes, most of them run about ninety minutes, so it's a bit more of an investment. But approaching each episode like a standalone film allows the show to experiment, including one episode that sees series co-creators Steven Moffat and Mark Gatiss send Holmes and Watson back in time to the era for which they were created.

A SHERLOCK LANDMARK HELPED MAKE THE SHOW HAPPEN.

For years, Steven Moffat and Mark Gatiss took a train to and from Cardiff while working on *Doctor Who,* and they discussed various projects they were interested in doing; one that kept coming up repeatedly was a modern-day adaptation of Sherlock Holmes. This reportedly went on for some time, with neither man making any particular effort to get it off the ground, until Moffat's wife, producer Sue Vertue (*Mr. Bean*, *Coupling*), decided to invite both men to lunch at the Criterion, a watering hole and eatery in London's Piccadilly Circus. It's the same place where the fictional John Watson, Holmes's best friend, first hears of the famed detective. The two got the hint and began working on the series.

THE ORIGINAL PILOT NEVER AIRED.

When Moffat and Gatiss conceived of a modern-day take on Holmes for the BBC in 2008, the expectation was that their hour-long adaptation of Arthur Conan Doyle's *A Study in Scarlet* would lead to a series. When they finished filming, however, those chances seemed slim: The pilot was more of a stodgy production than the cinematic, inventive style Gatiss and Moffat were hoping for. The BBC agreed to reshoot it with new director Paul McGuigan adding touches like having text messages appear onscreen. The less polished prototype is available on the DVD release.

BENEDICT CUMBERBATCH WASN'T IMMEDIATELY SOLD ON THE SERIES.

Though Sherlock Holmes is the role that brought Cumberbatch global recognition, saying yes to the part wasn't exactly a no-brainer for the actor. While speaking at a BAFTA event in 2014, Cumberbatch admitted that he was actually a little hesitant to sign on for the project. "I heard about it and thought that sounds like an excuse to [re-franchise] something to make money," he said. "Then I found out who was involved. . . . My mum had done [a few episodes of] *Coupling* . . . and Mark Gatiss was a huge hero of mine as a student with *League of Gentlemen*, so I knew the stable was good. I knew their involvement in *Doctor Who* and I knew what they'd done with that, and I thought 'I've got to read it.' And I read it and I completely fell in love with it."

SOME FOLKS AT THE BBC DIDN'T THINK CUMBERBATCH WAS "SEXY" ENOUGH TO PLAY SHERLOCK.

While speaking at the Hay Festival in 2014, Moffat talked about the BBC's track record in determining which actors might connect with audiences— Cumberbatch being one of them. "They said of casting David Tennant as *Casanova*, 'Damn, you should have cast someone sexier,'" Moffat said. "With Benedict Cumberbatch, we were told the same thing. 'You promised us a sexy Sherlock, not him.'"

Sue Vertue, a fellow producer on *Sherlock*, relayed a similar tale to *Entertainment Weekly*, telling the magazine: "When we first cast [Cumberbatch], people were saying, 'You promised us a sexy one!' . . . People weren't thinking of Benedict in that light at all." His name, apparently, posed another problem: "When people said, 'Who's playing Sherlock Holmes?' and we'd say, 'Benedict Cumberbatch,' everyone looked very vague," Vertue said. "Then we'd always have to spell his name."

MATT SMITH AUDITIONED FOR WATSON.

While Cumberbatch was the first and only choice for Holmes, Smith was among a number of actors considered for his counterpart, John Watson. The role eventually went to Martin Freeman (*The Office, Fargo*) because Moffat believed his chemistry with Cumberbatch was the best. Smith wound up auditioning for *Doctor Who* just a week later, and became the Eleventh Doctor.

Relativity, Dear Watson

Cumberbatch and *Sherlock Holmes* creator Sir Arthur Conan Doyle are sixteenth cousins, twice removed. The ancestral link between the two is the fourteenth- century Duke of Lancaster John of Gaunt, who was Doyle's fifteenth great-grandfather and Cumberbatch's seventeenth great-grandfather.

SHERLOCK HAS SOME FAMOUS FANS.

The quality of the series has not been lost on audiences, critics, or Harrison Ford: When the Han Solo actor appeared on *The Graham Norton Show* alongside Cumberbatch in 2013, Ford said that *Sherlock* was "amazing." Ford's wife, Calista Flockhart, told the *Radio Times* that she and Ford "can't stop watching" *Sherlock*. Another legendary actor who was excited to meet Cumberbatch was *Cheers* star Ted Danson. When asked during a Reddit AMA to share the "weirdest encounter you've had with a fan," Cumberbatch answered: "Ted Danson at a pre-Oscar party screaming across a floor of people like Leonardo DiCaprio, Ray Liotta, Kristen Stewart, Kirsten Dunst, et al. while pushing past them and knocking their drinks. 'OH MY GOD! OH MY GOD! IT'S FUCKING SHERLOCK HOLMES!'"

THE SERIES LED TO A RISE IN BOOK SALES.

The 2010 debut of *Sherlock* on BBC One correlated with a sharp uptick in sales of Arthur Conan Doyle's printed works. According to Nielsen BookScan, which tracks media sales, copies of Doyle's titles moved roughly 57,000 copies in 2009. The year after, it was 88,000, with sales the week after the show premiered doubling from the week prior.

FAN EXCITEMENT LED TO FEWER OUTDOOR SHOTS.

When word got out that *Sherlock* was filming exterior shots in Cardiff, fans gathered using a Twitter hashtag (#Setlock) to watch—sometimes up to three hundred at a time, all positioned behind barricades. Freeman has described the experience as something "I don't love," since the crowd is effectively an uninvited audience. (They once broke into applause when he opened a bag of potato chips.) Because of the distraction, Gatiss has noted that the show had to arrange for fewer scenes set outside. "Large dialogue scenes outside are quite tough," he said in 2014, adding that the actors had trouble concentrating.

PBS CUT A BIG CHUNK OUT OF EPISODES.

If your only exposure to the second season of *Sherlock* was on PBS in America, you've missed nearly a half hour of the show. In 2012, executive producer Sue Vertue told *The Independent* that eight minutes from each of the three episodes had been snipped in order to make room for sponsor spots in the United States.

THE
SHIELD
(2002–2008)

CREATED BY: Shawn Ryan

SEASONS: 7

EPISODES: 88

OTHER SHOWS BY SHAWN RYAN:
The Chicago Code (2011)
Last Resort (2012–2013)
Timeless (2016–2018)

When it comes to antiheroes, none have been quite as arresting as Vic Mackey (Michael Chiklis), the "different kind of cop" who murders, plunders, and lies his way through the politics of Los Angeles law enforcement in *The Shield*.

Chiklis won an Emmy for his portrayal of Mackey, and it's easy to see why: As Mackey's lies and deceptions continue to pile up, the actor does a fantastic job of keeping his character (almost) sympathetic. It's not that Mackey wants to blur the line between good and bad or right and wrong—he wants to erase it altogether. With *The Shield*, FX broke into the prestige drama landscape that had never before been occupied by a basic cable channel.

TRAINING DAY HELPED GET *THE SHIELD* ON THE AIR.

A series about a corrupt vice squad with law-breaking cops front and center was unusual for television at the time *The Shield* premiered. Although antiheroes like Tony Soprano of *The Sopranos* and the inmates of *Oz* were around, having a cop behave like a criminal was a risk. FX grew especially wary following the events of September 11, 2001, when law enforcement personnel were being heralded for their bravery. Their hesitations disappeared after the release of *Training Day* (2001), Antoine Fuqua's hit—and Oscar-winning—film about corrupt cop Alonzo Harris (Denzel Washington) making his own rules. Suddenly, Vic Mackey seemed more relevant than ever.

DONNIE BRASCO INSPIRED A PLOT POINT.

The 1997 film *Donnie Brasco* relates the true story of Joseph Pistone (Johnny Depp), an undercover cop who befriends low-level mobster Benjamin "Lefty" Ruggiero (Al Pacino). *The Shield* creator Shawn Ryan had watched the film and began wondering how shocking it would be for Ruggiero to discover Pistone was a cop midway through the film and kill him. That led to the pivotal moment in the show's pilot when Mackey murders a member of his unit, known as the Strike Team, named Terry Crowley (Reed Diamond), who had been sent to spy on them.

ERIC STOLTZ WAS CONSIDERED FOR THE ROLE OF VIC MACKEY.

Initially, executives had trouble visualizing Chiklis as Mackey. The actor was known for shows like ABC's *The Commish* (1991–1996), which embraced his softer side. FX instead considered Eric Stoltz (1985's *Mask*) for the role. According to Shawn Ryan, they even made him an offer. But when Chiklis showed up at his audition buff and growling, he won the part.

WALTON GOGGINS WAS ALMOST FIRED.

Goggins, who has had an incredible run on television with *The Shield*, *Justified* (2010–2015), and *Vice Principals* (2016–2017), among others, was a standout on the series thanks to his portrayal of Shane Vendrell, Mackey's right-hand man. But FX executives were apparently unhappy with Goggins in the pilot, declaring him "annoying" even though he only had four lines. Ryan convinced them to hang in there for the second episode, at which point they were sold on Goggins (and Vendrell).

THE LOS ANGELES POLICE DEPARTMENT THREATENED THE SHOW WITH LEGAL ACTION.

While *The Shield* clearly takes place in Los Angeles, the characters never explicitly refer to the Los Angeles Police Department. That's because the LAPD threatened Fox with legal action if they were ever mentioned by name in the series. The department didn't want any more publicity after the Rampart police corruption scandal—part of the inspiration for the show—which had rocked the city in the late 1990's. Mackey and his cohorts instead say "police," "PD," or the fictional "Farmington District." Fox even mandated that actors wear unique badges worn on the opposite side of where LAPD officers wear their own.

THE SHIELD HAD TROUBLE ATTRACTING ADVERTISERS.

The Shield was not initially attractive to advertisers because of its unflinching look at police corruption. During one screening, an FX executive asked prospective ad buyers if they liked the show. All of them raised their hands. When he asked how many would buy commercial time, no one raised an arm. That reluctance largely disappeared after the first season once the show had received considerable critical and audience acclaim, though FX still provided advertisers with advance copies of individual episodes in case they wanted to reconsider.

THE SHIELD CROSSED OVER WITH OTHER SERIES.

Ryan went on to helm *S.W.A.T.* in 2017, a remake of the 1970s cop series of the same name. In a 2019 episode, Detective Steve Billings (David Marciano), a regular on *The Shield* as a lackadaisical cop, made an appearance on *S.W.A.T.* And on *Sons of Anarchy*, which was created by onetime *The Shield* writer Kurt Sutter, biker gangs present in *The Shield* show up (specifically, the Byz Lats and One-Niners).

VIC MACKEY NEARLY POPPED UP IN A FEATURE FILM.

After *The Shield* ended in 2008, Mackey's story appeared to have come to an end. But Ryan revealed in 2017 that he once pitched Fox a film concept wholly separate from the series in which Mackey would appear at the midway point to surprise audiences. The project didn't move forward, but Ryan said he still wonders what Mackey—who was sentenced to a life of office purgatory—might be up to now. Maybe someday viewers will find out.

ARRESTING COP DRAMAS TO WATCH NEXT

7

Thanks to their inherent dramatic potential, cop dramas have been a staple of television practically since its invention. We've rounded up the usual suspects of other police shows that will arrest your attention.

Babylon Berlin // (2017–PRESENT)

This German series grabbed an international audience on Netflix with its twisty and stylish story of police inspector Gereon Rath (Volker Bruch) and flapper Charlotte Ritter (Liv Lisa Fries) operating in 1929 Berlin, which has yet to see the full impact of a certain Führer.

Bosch // (2014–PRESENT)

Titus Welliver brings author Michael Connelly's jazz-loving Los Angeles detective to life in this measured procedural, which makes the mundane details of police work as riveting as the shootouts.

Life on Mars // (2006–2007)

In 2006—a year before he was cast as the Master, the Doctor's nemesis on *Doctor Who*—John Simm starred as Sam Tyler, a modern-day cop who somehow wakes up in 1973 and has to navigate his bizarre new reality while tending to his detective duties. (You can safely skip the US remake.)

Line of Duty // (2012)

A British cop (Martin Compston) with the special license to carry a firearm is transferred to an elite investigative agency looking into corrupt cops in this BBC standout.

Luther // (2010–PRESENT)

Idris Elba moved from *The Wire* to this moody British drama about DCI John Luther, a haunted detective with the rough approach necessary to catch killers, including the seductive Alice Morgan (Ruth Wilson).

Mindhunter // (2017–2019)

Director David Fincher (*Se7en*) produced this unsettling drama about two FBI agents (Holt McCallany and Jonathan Groff) breaking ground with the bureau's criminal profiling unit in the late 1970s, with a parade of serial killers offering insight and menace in equal measure.

Narcos // (2015–2017)

DEA agents and other law enforcement chase down real-life drug kingpin Pablo Escobar in this Netflix hit seen through the eyes of cops Steve Murphy (Boyd Holbrook) and Javier Peña (Pedro Pascal).

THE SIMPSONS

(1989–PRESENT)

TM & © 2002 FOX

CREATED BY: Matt Groening

SEASONS: 32

EPISODES: 705

OTHER SHOWS BY MATT GROENING:
Futurama (1999–2003; 2008–2013)
Disenchantment (2018–PRESENT)

The *Simpsons* has been a television institution for more than thirty years. Since its debut on Fox in 1989, the series has accumulated a mountain of awards, worldwide acclaim, and an empire of merchandise—not to mention so many episodes that it would take more than two full weeks to binge-watch all of it in one session. But if you're looking to make a long-term commitment to a show that's smart, funny, and surprisingly heartfelt, this is the perfect series to have in your queue.

Homer, Marge, Lisa, Bart, and Maggie Simpson may be the titled stars, but *The Simpsons* is just as much about its robust ensemble. The number of memorable recurring characters in Springfield is made even more impressive by the fact that they're all voiced by a handful of well-respected actors. As the longest-running scripted show on prime time, it's no surprise that the history of *The Simpsons* is littered with interesting anecdotes, loads of cultural references, bizarre guest stars, offbeat writers, wild fan theories, and even a bit of drama.

THE SIMPSONS IS IVY LEAGUE COMEDY AT ITS FINEST.

The folks behind *The Simpsons* are smart. *Incredibly* smart. One look through the writers and producers who have passed through the show reveals graduates, scholars, and professors from some of the best universities on the planet. And many of them didn't start out by studying writing.

Al Jean, who has been the showrunner since 2001, began studying mathematics at Harvard when he was just sixteen. Writer Jeff Westbrook was an algorithm researcher and attended both Harvard and Princeton before becoming an associate professor at Yale. Writer David X. Cohen graduated from Harvard with a physics degree and University of California, Berkeley with a computer science degree. And this is just a sample of the brain power it takes to bring *The Simpsons* to life.

IN SPRINGFIELD, ONLY GOD HAS FIVE FINGERS.

The residents of Springfield—like most other cartoon characters—are notable for only possessing eight fingers (or six fingers and two thumbs, depending on your level of pedantry) and eight toes. It's an animation tradition, but one character bucks that trend: God. In the episode "Homer the Heretic," Homer meets the big cheese, who sports a long beard, flowing robe, and the standard five fingers on each hand. Just one of the perks of being in charge.

There is one inconsistency, though: Jesus is actually depicted with five fingers in the episode "Thank God It's Doomsday," but in subsequent appearances, he's back to four. Whether this is some profound message or a simple animator slip-up is a matter for your own interpretation.

THE *SIMPSONS* GOT INTO A PUBLIC WAR WITH THE BUSH FAMILY.

The very unlikely war between *The Simpsons* and the Bushes began in a 1990 issue of *People* magazine when then First Lady Barbara Bush said of the show, "It was the dumbest thing I had ever seen." Not looking to let that jab go unanswered, *The Simpsons* writing staff penned a pointed response to Mrs. Bush, but they wrote the letter in character as Marge Simpson.

The letter takes some good-natured shots at Mrs. Bush and pleasantly scolds her for the critique, including the line, "Ma'am, if we're the dumbest thing you ever saw, Washington must be a good deal different than what they teach me at the current events group at the church." (Bush responded to Marge with an apology, writing that, "I'm glad you spoke your mind; I foolishly didn't know you had one.")

The war was over…for a few months. Speaking in 1992, President George H. W. Bush vowed to strengthen American families, to make them "a lot more like the Waltons and a lot less like the Simpsons."

A year later, Bush was out, Clinton was in, and it seemed like *The Simpsons*—which would eventually more than triple the length of *The Waltons*' nine-season run—could move on. But the show wasn't done with the former First Family yet.

In the episode "Two Bad Neighbors," the Bushes move across the street from the Simpsons, and the former president engages in a battle of wits with Homer and Bart (and ends up with a rainbow wig glued to his head). Though the ex-president didn't voice the character, it provided a definitive end to the feud, as the family eventually drove the Bushes out of Springfield through the same idiotic behavior Barbara Bush had derided years earlier.

MATT GROENING REMOVED HIS NAME FROM THE EPISODE "A STAR IS BURNS."

One of the show's most memorable feuds went straight to the press, and it concerned the 1995 episode "A Star Is Burns," which featured the character Jay Sherman (voiced by Jon Lovitz) from the animated series *The Critic* coming to Springfield.

Feeling that the episode was just a cheap crossover, Groening removed his name from the episode's opening credits, which was the first and only time his name wasn't associated with the series. This led to a very

brief—but surprisingly brutal—war of words between Groening and executive producer James L. Brooks.

"The two reasons I am opposed to this crossover is that I don't want any credit or blame for *The Critic* and I feel this [encroachment of another cartoon character] violates *The Simpsons'* universe," Groening told the *Los Angeles Times*. "*The Critic* has nothing to do with *The Simpsons'* world."

Without responding to Groening directly, Brooks did give his side of the story, telling the *Los Angeles Times* that he was "furious with Matt. . . . Certainly he's allowed his opinion, but airing this publicly in the press is going too far. . . . This has been my worst fear . . . that the Matt we know privately is going public. . . . He is a gifted, adorable, cuddly ingrate. But his behavior right now is rotten. And it's not pretty when a rich man acts like this."

THE SHOW HAS LANDED BOTH BANKSY AND THOMAS PYNCHON.

No one knows what Banksy's real name is, and the mystery surrounding reclusive author Thomas Pynchon has endured for decades. Yet somehow, they both contributed to *The Simpsons*—Banksy with a couch gag and Pynchon as a guest voice.

Pynchon appears (with a paper bag over his head to preserve his mystique) in two episodes, "Diatribe of a Mad Housewife," in which he endorses Marge's book, and "All's Fair in Oven War," when he eats some chicken wings she made. He even edited his own dialogue for the show, removing a line in which he was supposed to call Homer a fat ass. His reason? "Homer is my role model and I can't speak ill of him," he told the producers.

Banksy's couch gag was one of the show's most shocking, depicting Fox as a vile corporate cesspool that runs on employee misery. Jean said he was a little concerned with the nature of the couch gag at first, but he and Groening agreed to leave it in with minimal changes. And no, nobody on *The Simpsons* ever met Banksy. In both cases, the reclusive artists were tracked down by casting director Bonnie Pietila.

ELIZABETH TAYLOR VOICED MAGGIE FOR ONE WORD.

Maggie is famous for her pacifier and longtime vow of silence, but she did utter one word during the fourth season in the episode "Lisa's First Word." The voice behind Maggie was none other than Elizabeth Taylor, who was hired to say one thing: "Daddy."

The scene takes place at the end of the episode, once Homer leaves Maggie's room after tucking her in, so of course no one hears her. To get the line just right, Jean requested a number of takes from the Hollywood icon, culminating in Taylor jokingly telling Jean, "Fuck you," in her Maggie voice while the tape was still rolling.

Taylor reappeared on the show (as herself) in "Krusty Gets Kancelled," the final episode of the fourth season. She had a bit more to say here, but laying claim to Maggie's first word cemented her legacy in Springfield.

THE SIMPSONS BY THE NUMBERS

HOMER MAKES LESS THAN
$25,000
A YEAR AT THE NUCLEAR PLANT.

The Simpson family finances are . . . complex. In some episodes, they have to forego fancy quilted toilet paper to make ends meet, and in others Homer can pull wads of money out of his wallet if the plot calls for it. It's all part of the show's famous "rubber band reality," where continuity never lines up episode to episode (or scene to scene).

One of the only concrete pieces of evidence we have of the family's financial situation comes in the episode "Much Apu about Nothing," when we get a glimpse of Homer's weekly paycheck from the nuclear plant.

Apparently Homer takes home **$479.60** before taxes (**$362.19** after taxes) for a full work week, which averages out to just about **$11.99** an hour. That's **$24,395** per year, and **$37,416** when you adjust for inflation.

"Daddy."

JOHN SWARTZWELDER: SPRINGFIELD'S MAN OF MYSTERY

The Simpsons has churned out a number of great comedy writers who have gone on to mainstream success—Conan O'Brien and *The Office* developer Greg Daniels among them. But there's one whose legend eclipses nearly everyone else. Casual fans might not know him, but among *Simpsons* die-hards, the name John Swartzwelder is met with hushed awe. Multiple members of *The Simpsons* staff have declared him the best writer the show has ever seen, with former show writer Dan Greaney proclaiming him "the greatest writer in the English language in any form."

Google his name and you'll end up with more questions than answers. Most of the details of his life boil down to second- and third-hand accounts, as he never does interviews, refuses to lend his voice to DVD commentary tracks, and rarely pops up in photos (there are a handful on Google, and none look any more recent than the nineties).

The one time that show producers tried to call him during a commentary recording, the man on the other end of the line ended the awkward conversation by joking, "It's too bad this really isn't John Swartzwelder." Despite that, the man wrote fifty-nine episodes of the show during its first fifteen seasons, with many of them ranking among the series' most popular, like "Bart Gets an Elephant," "Radioactive Man," and "Homer's Enemy."

When other writers talk about him in DVD commentaries, he's described as a serious Libertarian who is a "self-declared anti-environmentalist" and would go on tangents about how there is more rain forest now than there was one hundred years ago. When describing a recycling center in one of his scripts, he called it "a couple of hippies surrounded by garbage." This led to Swartzwelder being called on to write some of the show's most environmentally conscious episodes, including "Whacking Day" and "The Old Man and the Lisa," to give them what other writers described as "a special zing" and "just the right level of sarcasm."

How deep does Swartzwelder's quirky legend go? During the commentary for "Grade School Confidential," Groening told a story about Swartzwelder usually writing his *Simpsons* scripts alone in a coffee shop while smoking cigarettes and guzzling coffee. When California outlawed smoking in restaurants, Swartzwelder simply bought a diner booth and had it installed in his home, and continued to work in the exact same manner. "Later, I added a second one, in a different part of the house," he told *The New Yorker* in 2021. "Diner booths are a great place to write. Try it." When he was able to renegotiate his contract after season 4, the producers allowed him to work from home, so he rarely showed his face in *The Simpsons*' writers' room again.

Though he's been out of television since 2003, he has since authored a series of novels, all of which retain his genius—and infinitely absurd—humor.

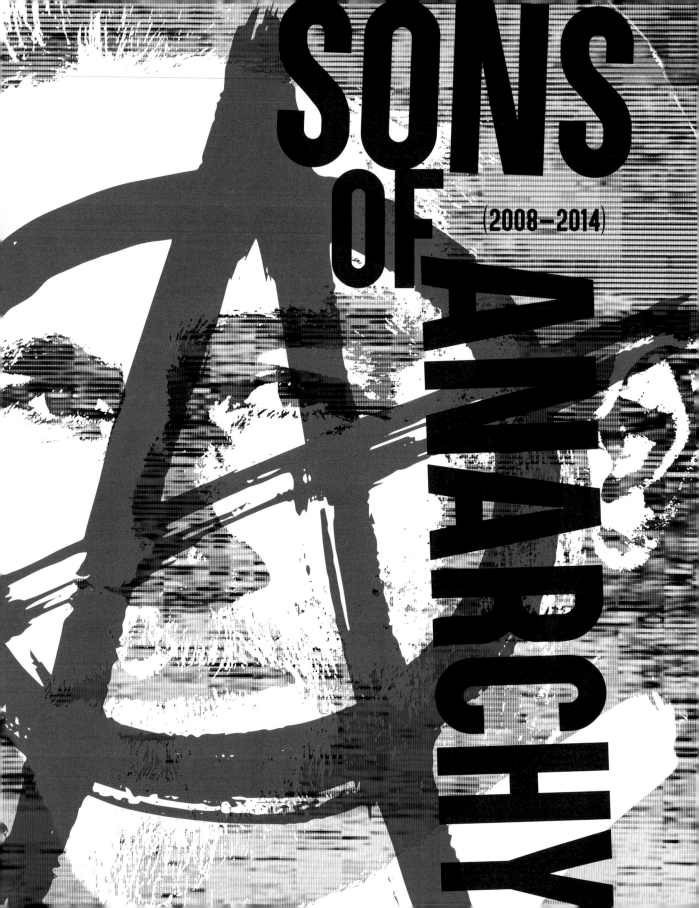

CREATED BY: Kurt Sutter

SEASONS: 7

EPISODES: 92

OTHER SHOWS BY KURT SUTTER:
The Bastard Executioner (2015)
Mayans M.C. (2018–PRESENT)

Influenced by *Hamlet*, *Sons of Anarchy* centered on a family (both related by blood and not) of grim reaper patch wearing outlaw bikers in a club known as SAMCRO (Sons of Anarchy Motorcycle Club Redwood Original), based in the fictional town of Charming, California. The show debuted on September 3, 2008, and, over the course of seven seasons, became FX's top-rated drama.

Katey Sagal plays the matriarch, Gemma, whose Harley-riding son, Jax (Charlie Hunnam), is the "Hamlet" character; he's caught between pleasing his mother and his stepfather, Clay (Ron Perlman), and honoring his dead father, John, a founding member of SAMCRO.

SOA courted controversy with its grisly scenes of violence, everything from a tattoo being burned off to a character being forked to death. But as the show's creator, Kurt Sutter, explained to *The Hollywood Reporter*, "For me, all that violence—because it's not who I am and it's not where I come from—it's all fantasy. I might as well be writing about wizards and fairies."

Before creating *SOA*, Sutter had been a producer and writer on *The Shield*. Shawn Ryan, creator of *The Shield*, recommended Sutter to producers Art and John Linson. They pitched Sutter a show about outlaw bikers and allowed him to build it from scratch. After ninety-two episodes of family drama (and multiple major character deaths), the show aired its final episode on December 9, 2014—though a spin-off, *Mayans M.C.*, is still going.

KURT SUTTER WROTE THE PART OF GEMMA WITH KATEY SAGAL IN MIND.

Sutter and *Married . . . with Children* star Sagal married in 2004 and have since collaborated on several projects. In an interview with NPR, Sagal said Sutter wrote the character of Gemma with her and their family dynamic in mind.

"If you asked him, what he would tell you probably is when he came into my life, I already had two children, and he's their stepparent, and I was very protective of my children," Sagal said. "He hadn't been around that kind of energy quite so much, so I think that's what

was the springboard for Gemma. It was not so much the heinous things she does; it was that at her core, her motivation is her children, is her child. At any cost, she will protect him and her club."

RON PERLMAN WASN'T THE FIRST CHOICE TO PLAY CLAY.

The original pilot featured Scott Glenn as Clay Morrow, president of SAMCRO. "The network decided that they weren't getting what they were hoping to get and… they loved the series enough [that] if they thought they found the right actor, they were willing to reshoot the pilot and restart the clock and greenlight the show for a whole first season, which is thirteen episodes," Perlman told NPR. The producers felt Glenn was too subtle and not dynamic enough. "So I understood going into it that, you know—that they were looking for a more operatic version of this guy," Perlman said. "I happened to be free that week."

Perlman auditioned for the show, unsure if he could play a character that lacked duality. "He has no feminine side whatsoever and I really didn't know whether I could, whether I had the chops to pull it off," Perlman told Collider.

TARA WAS "THE MORAL CENTER" OF THE SHOW.

While chatting with *Entertainment Weekly,* Maggie Siff—who played Jax's wife, Dr. Tara Knowles—agreed that her character was "the moral center of the show" for part of its run. "I think Kurt used her as a window, through which the audience could experience the club and the life of the club," she said. "You could see her loving these people in spite of herself, in spite of knowing better. I think she remained a moral center in that she continues to be one of the only [people] in [this] world who experiences real emotional conflict around the violence and the difficulty and the pain of the [criminal] life and wanting something better for her children."

PEOPLE LOVED TO GIVE CHARLIE HUNNAM KNIVES.

On the show, Hunnam's character, Jax, carries around a Ka-Bar knife. Hunnam said knives were part of biker culture, and California allows people to carry them. That signature accessory became a popular gift from Hunnam's fans: "I have dozens of Ka-Bars that military guys have given me and I've been told that a couple of them 'have been used,'" Hunnam told *GQ.* "Which is a little bit…grimy, you know? I'm not sure about the energy of that."

SUTTER RAN INTO ISSUES WITH STANDARDS AND PRACTICES.

Because FX forbade the use of the F-word, characters replaced it with "Jesus Christ." "There was one season where they were, like, counting my 'Jesus Christs' because somebody on the Fox food chain thought it was so blasphemous," Sutter told *Entertainment Weekly.*

John Landgraf, CEO of FX, took issue with some of Sutter's ideas, including the castration of a clown:

Sutter wanted the visual of the detached bit hitting the ground, FX did not. "I totally acknowledge the need for violence," Landgraf said. "It's a violent world and a violent show. He's portraying really tragic, dark consequences of violence. Kurt wants to show it in very graphic detail, and I want to leave more to the imagination."

Sutter told *GQ* that all of the violence had to be organic, not gratuitous. "When we're fucking burning a tattoo with a blowtorch off a guy's back, that is one of the most extreme decisions these guys may be making, but it's real to the world," he said. "I love being able to do things like that, and playing in worlds that allow me to do that."

SPOILERS! SAGAL WORRIED HER CHARACTER WOULD ALIENATE FANS.

During the season 6 finale, Gemma unexpectedly murders Jax's wife, Tara, using a carving fork. "When I first realized that Gemma was going to kill Tara, I had a moment like, oh shit, man, nobody's going to wanna see Gemma again. She's killing beloved Tara!" Sagal told *People.* Fortunately, the death didn't alienate fans as Sagal thought it would. "The very next day, I went to do an autograph session and people were showing up with forks for me to sign," Sagal said. "And I thought, 'Oh, OK.'"

SUTTER LIKED THE IRONY OF MOTORCYCLE CULTURE.

Sutter, who rides motorcycles in real life, told The Verge that motorcycle clubs "say they're all about 'ride free' and 'fuck the establishment.' But within the structure of these outlaw clubs, there are more rules and regulations than you or I have. They're like little military units. And I love the irony of that."

Sutter further explained that the club represents the ideal of how Americans "take care of our own," which is the theme of the show. "Yes, it's about family, but it's also about community and village and the organization you belong to…That's part of the positive stereotype we represent as a nation—that sense of no matter how fucked up or damaged these people are, and they are, there's something wholly familial about them."

WALTON GOGGINS CONVINCED SUTTER TO LET HIM PLAY A TRANSGENDER CHARACTER.

Sutter invited some former cast members from *The Shield* to cameo on *Sons of Anarchy,* but he was initially reluctant to have Goggins appear. "[Sutter said,] 'It would be very hard for our audience to accept them as anybody else,'" Goggins told *Entertainment Weekly*. "I called and said, 'That's bullshit! Come on!' And we went back and forth, like how would we do it? I wouldn't want to do it as anything that would be compared to *The Shield*." So Goggins came up with the idea of playing a transgender character. For six episodes between 2012 and 2014, Goggins played Venus Van Dam, a play on Goggins's *Shield* alias Cletus Van Damme.

HUNNAM HAD A DIFFICULT TIME LETTING GO OF JAX.

Hunnam played Jax for seven seasons. When it came time to end the show, he said it was emotional for him to separate himself from the character. "I found myself going back to set a lot," he told *Glamour*. "I knew the security guards and for a couple of days said, 'Oh, I forgot something,' so they'd let me onto the set, and I'd just walk around at night because I wanted to be in that environment and go through a personal process of saying goodbye. After a couple of nights I didn't really need the alibi to get in, and then after a while I just said, 'OK, enough, this is done.'"

WHEN STEPHEN KING SHOWED UP ON *SONS OF ANARCHY*

During "Caregiver," the third episode of *Sons of Anarchy*'s third season, Gemma and Tara (sort of) accidentally wind up with a dead body in the basement. So Tig (Kim Coates), SAMCRO's sergeant-at-Arms—in classic I-know-a-guy fashion—summons a self-employed "cleaner" named Bachman to disappear all the evidence. After rolling in on a shiny red Harley-Davidson Road Glide, Bachman conducts a creepy examination of the victim, gruffly asks how well the drain works, and declares that he's "in the mood" for some eighties music. If you didn't know any better, you might think the scene was lifted straight from a Stephen King novel—Bachman even bears a striking resemblance to King himself.

OK, it's actually Stephen King.

The horror writer had praised *Sons of Anarchy*, and word got around to Sutter that King was a fan. So Sutter invited King to participate in the series in whatever capacity he wanted. "All he said was that he wanted to ride a Harley," Sutter said on Twitter. "So I put the

Cleaner on a big red bagger and he came to play."

According to King, Sutter had also promised to come up with a "suitably nasty part" for him. The character's name was suitable, too: Bachman is a reference to King's pen name, Richard Bachman. King filmed his memorable cameo while in Los Angeles for an awards ceremony, and he was delighted to meet all the cast members on set. But nothing—not even the *Hellboy* photos that Ron Perlman autographed for King's three grandsons—excited the author more than the "bitchin' Harley" he got to ride. King later wrote that he "would have been glad to take it home (sadly, no deal)."

THE SOPRANOS

(1997–2007)

CREATED BY: David Chase

SEASONS: 6

EPISODES: 86

OTHER SHOWS BY DAVID CHASE:
Almost Grown (1988–1989)

I n the mafia, there's the family—the gang of career criminals, capos, bosses, and assorted misfits that drive an underground network of thuggery. And then there's family—the spouses, kids, and in-laws who can prove equally stressful. It's enough to drive a mobster to therapy, and that's where we find Tony Soprano (James Gandolfini), the simmering New Jersey crime boss, at the start of *The Sopranos*.

The demands of his crime brood are often in conflict with his domestic life. Wife Carmela (Edie Falco) tries to look the other way. Kids A. J. (Robert Iler) and Meadow (Jamie-Lynn Sigler) are no better off as a result of their father's murky profession. Tony breaks omertà, the mafia's code of silence, only with therapist Dr. Jennifer Melfi (Lorraine Bracco), but he might as well be talking directly to the audience, who had spent decades witnessing mafia antics in *The Godfather* and *Goodfellas* while only rarely pausing to explore its psychological effects. *The Sopranos*—which was originally developed as a movie pitch—drew its power and accolades from examining the collateral damage of violence. Like Tony, the show could explode in a moment's notice. Like Tony, it could also be introspective and quiet, lapsing into whispered dinner conversations and dream sequences. Is it the best television series ever made? With decades of "peak TV" in the can, that becomes more and more subjective. Was it television at its best? Fuhgeddaboudit.

• •

STEVEN VAN ZANDT WAS CHASE'S FIRST PICK FOR TONY.

Before he auditioned James Gandolfini, Chase wanted Steven Van Zandt, guitar player of Bruce Springsteen's E Street Band, to play Tony. "I used to listen to music a lot on headphones and look at [Springsteen's] LP, and Steven Van Zandt's face always grabbed me," Chase told *Vanity Fair* in 2012. "He had this similarity to Al Pacino in *The Godfather*. Then we were casting the pilot, and my wife, Denise, and I were watching TV. Steven came on VH1, when they were inducting the Rascals into the Rock and Roll Hall of Fame, and Steven gave

the speech. He was very, very funny and magnetic. I said to my wife, 'That guy has got to be in the show!'"

The producers didn't want to gamble on a first-time actor for the show's lead, so Chase offered to write a part for Van Zandt.

LIVIA SOPRANO WAS SUPPOSED TO DIE IN THE FIRST SEASON.

While Chase abandoned his movie idea, the tension between Tony and his mother, Livia, provided the central conflict for the show's first season, and that's where it was supposed to end. Chase originally intended for

FREEZE FRAME

"FOR ALL DEBTS PUBLIC AND PRIVATE" // SEASON 4, EPISODE 1

In all episodes prior to this one, as Tony exits the Lincoln Tunnel on his drive from New York to his Jersey 'burb in the opening credits, the Twin Towers can be seen in his rearview mirror (which itself is a bit of Hollywood magic, since the World Trade Center wasn't actually visible from the Lincoln Tunnel's exit). This shot was removed beginning in season 4, following the terrorist attacks on September 11, 2001.

Tony to succeed in suffocating his mother with a pillow after she tries to have him killed in season 1. However, Nancy Marchand, who played Livia, was sick with cancer during her time on the show. She asked Chase, "David, just keep me working." He graciously obliged.

Marchand passed away from lung cancer and emphysema on June 18, 2000, one day before her seventy-second birthday. Livia's final moments on screen were cobbled together from old footage, recordings of her usual choruses, and special effects (Marchand's head was CGIed onto a body double). At the time, critics panned the scene, deeming it awkward and convoluted.

DR. MELFI WAS MODELED ON CHASE'S REAL-LIFE THERAPIST.

In a 2006 interview with *Rolling Stone*, Chase revealed that Lorraine Kaufman, his therapist during the time he conceptualized *The Sopranos*, provided the inspiration for Dr. Melfi. "She had the same way of cutting through your bullshit," he said. Not only did Chase tell Dr. Kaufman of her influence, Kaufman became involved in the characters' psychological development. "After three or four seasons, she wrote me a breakdown of the Soprano family," Chase said. "This is not a bible, but every once in a while we get it out. Strangely enough, these fictional characters have, in fact, behaved in the way she predicted they might, even though we might have forgotten she ever wrote it."

MICHAEL IMPERIOLI THOUGHT HE BLEW HIS AUDITION.

As Imperioli, who plays Christopher Moltisanti, tells it, he almost didn't land the gig. "They brought me in, and I met with David. I thought he hated my audition, because David's a poker-faced guy," Imperioli told *Vanity Fair* in 2012. "He kept giving me notes and giving me direction, and I walked out of there, and I was like, 'I blew that one.'"

THE SOPRANOS WAS SO REALISTIC, THE REAL MOB THOUGHT THERE WAS A CONNECTED GUY ON THE INSIDE.

An FBI agent told *The Sopranos*' creative team that on Monday mornings all anyone could talk about was *The Sopranos*. And on the wiretaps they'd collected from the weekend, that's all the real-life mobsters could talk about as well. Writer and producer Terence Winter told *Vanity Fair*, "We would hear back that real wiseguys used to think that we had somebody on the inside. They couldn't believe how accurate the show was."

SPOILERS! CHASE SHOT MULTIPLE VERSIONS OF MANY SCENES SO THAT NOT EVEN THE ACTORS WOULD KNOW HOW THINGS TURNED OUT.

Were you shocked to see Sil whack Adriana in season 5? So was Drea de Matteo. De Matteo told *Vanity Fair* that David Chase had had the cast and crew film two different versions of the dramatic episode: one in which Adriana suspects something fishy and drives away after her final phone call with Tony, and one where—well, you know what happens.

According to de Matteo, this practice of filming multiple versions of the same scene to keep the cast and crew guessing (along with interviewers and fans) was a common occurrence.

IT WAS THE FIRST CABLE TELEVISION SHOW TO WIN THE EMMY FOR OUTSTANDING DRAMA SERIES.

In 2004, after being nominated for the award five times, *The Sopranos* won the Emmy Award for Outstanding Drama Series. It would continue to be nominated every year it was eligible, winning again for its final season in 2007. Matthew Weiner, who shared the Emmy with David Chase and the other executive producers, would go on to win the award the next four years for *Mad Men*, until *Homeland* broke his winning streak in 2012.

SPOILERS! IMPERIOLI IS CONVINCED HE HAS THE FINALE FIGURED OUT.

The famous cut-to-black—and impeccably truncated version of Journey's "Don't Stop Believin'"—in *The Sopranos* finale is heralded as one of the most shocking (and controversial) cliff-hangers of all time. Does Tony get shot? Does he get arrested? Or does the whole family finish their sundaes and go home?

No one but Chase can say for sure. But Imperioli is firmly in the "Ohmigod, they killed Tony!" camp. "I think he's dead, is what I think," Imperioli told *Vanity Fair* in 2012. "David was trying to put us in the place of the last things you see before you die. You remember some little details and something catches your eye and that's it. You don't know the aftermath because you're gone." And with that, the show was gone, too.

THE SOPRANOS BY THE NUMBERS

$33,333

To settle disputes over actors' salaries, Gandolfini gave each actor of his own money. After season 4, production on *The Sopranos* was delayed due to a pay dispute with HBO. According to Edie Falco, the cast staged a sort of "Occupy Vesuvio" sit-in that shut down the set. To help quell tensions, Gandolfini split his bonus among all the regular cast members, giving them each $33,333.

WHEN *THE SOPRANOS* BLACKED OUT

SPOILERS! In 2012, *The Sopranos* star James Gandolfini told *Vanity Fair* that he had a simple reaction after viewing the show's finale: "What the fuck?"

That brief review would be echoed by critics and fans in the days and even years following the episode's broadcast on June 10, 2007. "Made in America," the finale of *The Sopranos*, featured one last family supper with Tony, Carmela, Meadow, and A. J. The family meets up at Holsten's Ice Cream Parlor, and appears to be at least temporarily free of the stress Tony's life of crime has brought into their world. Tony orders onion rings, selects Journey's "Don't Stop Believin'" from the jukebox, and seems relieved his domestic life is intact.

Moments later, the screen goes black. "Don't Stop Believin'" is cut off so abruptly that many viewers believed they were experiencing a cable outage. It remained that way for eleven seconds before the credits rolled, a curious void of content that quickly became one of the most infamous endings to a series in TV history.

What happened in those final few moments is left open to interpretation. Viewers, however, didn't want to choose their own climax. Some became so incensed that they bombarded HBO's official website with complaints. (HBO shut its website down that Sunday night.) According to Yahoo!, searches for "*Sopranos* ending sucked" spiked.

When Chase finally spoke about the finale a few days later, he refused to answer the question of whether Tony was dead. He insisted that all the information a viewer needed was in the scene. "Anybody who wants to watch it, it's all there," Chase said.

When Chase pops up in media to discuss current projects, talk usually still turns to the furor caused by the blackout. While he has always demurred on the question of whether Tony survived his plate of onion rings, he has stated that he didn't intend to frustrate viewers. "I thought the ending would be somewhat jarring, sure," Chase said. "But not to the extent it was . . . I never considered the black a shot. I just thought what we see is black. The ceiling I was going for at that point, the biggest feeling I was going for, honestly, was don't stop believing. It was very simple and much more on the nose than people think. That's what I wanted people to believe. That life ends and death comes, but don't stop believing."

It's hard to know, once the initial shock of the closing moments wore off, whether viewers ever softened their stance on the finale. (At the time, newspapers were filled with quotes by fans calling it "unbelievably cruel" and accusing Chase of some kind of conspiracy to annoy them.) For at least one viewer, it took just one night of introspection to come to an entirely different opinion.

"After I had a day to sleep," Gandolfini said in 2012, "I just sat there and said, 'That's perfect.'"

STRANGER THINGS

(2016–PRESENT)

CREATED BY: Matt and Ross Duffer

SEASONS: 3

EPISODES: 25

The kids and monsters of *Stranger Things* own our Steven Spielberg–loving hearts. Set in the tiny town of Hawkins, Indiana, in the 1980s, the Netflix series is packed with homages and meta-references to the pop culture of the era—from *Dungeons & Dragons* to Stephen King. The series follows a group of kids, including the mysterious and psychokinetic Eleven (Millie Bobby Brown), as they navigate adolescence in a dangerous world filled with face-splitting beasts from an alternate dimension known as the Upside Down and phones that do not work unless they're tethered to the wall. Terrifying!

The second season of *Stranger Things* expanded the mythology of the Upside Down, while season 3 went even further while also exploring the relationship between Eleven and Mike (Finn Wolfhard). Even if you've seen every piece of eighties media that inspired *Stranger Things*, the show still has plenty of surprises—with more to come.

....

THE SHOW IS BASED ON A REAL TIME-TRAVEL PROJECT.

There aren't any transdimensional horror-beasts rampaging through quiet suburban towns (that we know of), but *Stranger Things* is based on real conspiracy theories about the American government conducting reality-bending experiments on children, specifically, the Montauk Project, which has been referenced in other fiction such as Thomas Pynchon's novel *Bleeding Edge*. Much of what Eleven experiences in the laboratory corresponds to the alleged activities of the Montauk Project. The show was also initially called *Montauk* and set on the far end of the Long Island peninsula.

STEPHEN KING HAD A HAND IN CASTING MILLIE BOBBY BROWN.

When you're going up against that kind of competition for a role, it helps to have someone influential in your corner. Millie Bobby Brown had a heavyweight. The master of horror saw Brown in the BBC America show *Intruders* and publicly praised her work on Twitter, giving her a leg up in the race to become a stranger thing.

THE SHOW WAS ALMOST AN ANTHOLOGY SERIES WITH DIFFERENT CHARACTERS AND SETTINGS EVERY SEASON.

The *Stranger Things* that we know almost didn't come to be. The Duffer brothers meant for it to kick off with a monster-centric flash of 1980s nostalgia, but then they wanted it to tell new eerie tales and progress through the 1990s, 2000s, 2010s, and then 2020 in a final season that would air in 2020. The show would have said goodbye to Eleven, Dustin, Will, Mike, Lucas, and the rest of the cast after the first season. Luckily, they realized how special the team they'd assembled was and chose to keep focusing on their original story.

DACRE MONTGOMERY HAD AN UNUSUAL SHIRTLESS AUDITION TAPE.

Montgomery played the greasy-headed Billy Hargrove in season 2. The character is thought to be a nod to the classic Stephen King villain Randall Flagg, who has appeared in several of the author's novels. But in his audition, Montgomery channeled a lot of other demons. He read through the prepared scenes, but then added a Duran Duran song in the middle of reciting the scene where he tries to run down Max's (Sadie Sink) new friends, started dancing, and then ended the entire thing without a shirt.

Ross Duffer said they hired him without needing to fly him out to Los Angeles. "I've watched thousands of auditions now, and it's by far the most bonkers that I've witnessed," he said.

STRANGER THINGS BY THE NUMBERS

THEY AUDITIONED 906 BOYS AND 307 GIRLS FOR THE MAIN ROLES.

The Duffer brothers and casting director Carmen Cuba undertook the gargantuan task of hearing from 1,213 child actors to get the right people for what would be crucial roles. They had them read scenes from the pilot as well as scenes from *Stand by Me*.

NETFLIX KNOWS EXACTLY WHEN YOU GOT HOOKED ON *STRANGER THINGS*

If you're like most people, you didn't get truly invested in *Stranger Things* until the second episode. According to Netflix's data, that was the episode that turned most viewers from casual to addicted. About 70 percent of viewers who finished the second episode ended up watching the first full season.

Other series tend to be more of a slow burn. Most people watch three episodes of *Narcos* or *Prison Break* before committing to the first season, while *Making a Murderer* and *Fuller House* both take about four episodes to get people really hooked. *Gilmore Girls* and *Jane the Virgin*, meanwhile,

both take around seven episodes to get people invested.

Netflix has previously broken down the same data with some of its other popular shows, like *Breaking Bad* (two episodes), *Pretty Little Liars* (four episodes), and *Mad Men* (six episodes).

ELEVEN IS MODELED AFTER E.T.

In the first season, Eleven dons a pink dress and absurd blond wig in an homage to *E.T.*, but the Easter egg is also a clue to her entire otherworldly character. "[The Duffer brothers] told me that the performance that they wanted me to resemble was E.T. and sort of that relationship between E.T. and the kids," Brown said. "I thought that was very interesting, and Matt and Ross were like, 'Basically you're going to be an alien.'" Accordingly, Eleven (like Spielberg's extraterrestrial wonder) does more with body language than dialogue.

BROWN ONCE SHOWED UP TO THE SET COVERED IN GLITTER.

While discussing the unique challenges of working with a young cast, the Duffer brothers like to point to a story where production halted for a brief period of time because Brown showed up to set inexplicably covered in glitter. No, they never figured out where the glitter came from. No, they never have to worry about that type of thing happening to David Harbour.

THE DUFFER BROTHERS PULLED A MORBID PRANK ON NOAH SCHNAPP'S MOTHER.

Schnapp plays Will Byers, whose disappearance sets the entire show into motion and whose fake dead body covers up the government's secret project (for about five minutes). The show ordered a prop body from Fractured FX, and when it arrived, they used it to freak out Schnapp's mom.

"We immediately took Noah's mom aside, told her we had something to show her, and led her into a dark closet where we had propped up this frighteningly realistic corpse of her son," the Duffer brothers said. "After the initial shock, she loved it." Schnapp's mom posed for pictures with the fake corpse, which she then texted to her friends.

THE GANG WENT TRICK-OR-TREATING TOGETHER.

It's probably a lot easier to remain anonymous when you're behind a mask, even if you're on a wildly popular Netflix show. All the kids are famous for being friends in real life (they have a group chat called Stranger Texts), and they've even ventured out on Halloween together. "This one kid was like, 'Are you the cast from *Stranger Things*?'" Brown explained. "And I was all like, 'No, I'm Harley Quinn.'"

BOB NEWBY ALMOST HAD A VERY DIFFERENT FATE.

Sean Astin's lovable lunk Bob Newby gave the second season a puzzle master and a Boy Scout's moral compass, but the character evolved in a lot of ways. At first, the Duffer brothers weren't sure they wanted Astin for the role because, while he's a living nod to *The Goonies*, he might have stood out for being too famous as a geek icon. Then they planned to kill him off early on, but Astin and the character were too good. What's really surprising, though, is the way they intended to dispose of him.

Evil Will was supposed to show up far earlier in the season and murder Bob. Fortunately, the plan was scrapped, and Astin convinced the Duffer brothers to give him a *Jaws*-like, gruesome death. You died a hero, Bob!

6

MINOR CHARACTERS WHO GAINED CULT FOLLOWINGS

Ask any showrunner what the secret is to creating a character that captures the world's attention and most of them, if they're answering honestly, will probably admit that it has a lot to do with luck. Whether it's an adorable mini-horse or a background actor who just happened to catch the audience's eye, here are six minor characters who found their way into audiences' hearts.

1 BARBARA "BARB" HOLLAND // *Stranger Things* (2016-PRESENT)

Barbara "Barb" Holland (Shannon Purser) was a minor character on *Stranger Things* who developed a major following for her pitch-perfect role as geeky-but-loyal BFF to the much more glamorous Nancy Wheeler (Natalia Dyer). Barb is that friend who knows your most embarrassing secrets and isn't afraid to call you out when you're acting like a jerk. She's also just one in a proud line of minor players who managed to stand out.

2 THE LOG LADY // *Twin Peaks* (1990–1991; 2017)

Catherine Coulson played the mysterious, wood-loving character who would pop up sporadically in David Lynch's surreal series and talk to her log. When Coulson had worked on Lynch's first film, 1977's *Eraserhead*, Lynch told her, "Someday I'll do a series and you'll play a girl with a log." Bizarre, but he stuck to his word.

3 CIGARETTE SMOKING MAN // *The X-Files* (1993-2002; 2016-2018)

The mysterious lurker with a taste for tobacco was originally just a background character in the pilot of *The X-Files*. From there, actor William B. Davis became part of the show's paranoid mythology, and was even brought back from the dead for the 2016 series revival.

4 & 5 SKINNY PETE AND BADGER // *Breaking Bad* (2008–2013)

In a show bursting with memorable characters, unmotivated meth addicts Skinny Pete (Charles Baker) and Badger (Matt Jones) managed to get a lot of attention. Though they were rarely germane to the plot, Jesse Pinkman's best buddies won fans over with their slacker vibe— a much-needed break from the stress of watching everyone else on the show circling the drain.

6 LI'L SEBASTIAN // *Parks and Recreation* (2009–2015)

The pony pride of Pawnee, Indiana, made an appearance in the NBC sitcom during its third season, but an untimely (off screen) demise made him an equine sensation. Fans got Li'l Sebastian tattoos, and the show later featured him as a hologram.

TRANSPARENT

(2014–2019)

CREATED BY: Joey Soloway

SEASONS: 5

EPISODES: 41

OTHER SHOWS CREATED BY JOEY SOLOWAY:
I Love Dick (2016–2017)

All the major streaming networks seem to have that one breakout hit. For Amazon Studios, it was Joey Soloway's *Transparent*. On February 6, 2014, Amazon began streaming the series' pilot, and both viewers and critics were immediately smitten. By the time the show's first full season debuted on September 26, 2014, viewers had fallen madly in love with the Pfeffermans, a difficult family trying to make sense of their lives in the wake of their father (Jeffrey Tambor) coming out as a trans woman named Maura. A slew of awards—BAFTAs and Emmys included—followed, making *Transparent* Amazon's first series to win a major award and the first streaming series to win a Golden Globe for Best Television Series. But *Transparent* wasn't just a triumph for Amazon; it also broke new ground for trans representation.

Unfortunately, like the dysfunction surrounding the Pfeffermans, there was trouble brewing on the *Transparent* set. In late 2017, at the same time the show's fifth season was being written, word spread that star Tambor had been hit with two sexual harassment claims from people close to the series. On November 19, 2017, Tambor quit the show; on February 15, 2018, Tambor was officially fired. And on September 27, 2019, *Transparent*'s final episode—a musical finale that took the place of a fifth season—aired, thus closing a chapter on the series. Still, there's no denying that it made an enormous difference for Amazon, as well as for the many viewers it touched.

A STORY ABOUT COURTENEY COX'S BUTT HELPED JUMP-START JOEY SOLOWAY'S CAREER.
While working their first L.A. writing gigs at *The Steve Harvey Show* and *Nikki* (which they called "the worst sitcom in the world"), Soloway had some time on their hands to mess around on a show called *Sit 'n Spin* with their friends. The show involved people reading monologues or fiction, for which Soloway penned the hilarious "Courteney Cox's Asshole," a work of fiction told from the perspective of Cox's personal assistant.

Soloway later sent the piece to a handful of literary magazines, while their agent passed it on to Alan Ball, executive producer of HBO's *Six Feet Under*. Ball was impressed, telling *Time* that the story, albeit a few pages long, was able to "convey the very real pain of a soul yearning to be authentic in a completely inauthentic world." Also: He felt confident Soloway would be able to "write the hell out of [characters] Claire and Brenda." Soloway won a spot in the *Six Feet Under* writers' room.

SOLOWAY AND LENA DUNHAM COMPETED FOR THE SAME HBO SLOT. (DUNHAM WON.)
This huge victory was not without a series of painful rejections, too. In what *The New Yorker* called a "downward slide"—the period immediately following their *Six Feet Under* residency in 2005—Soloway was fired from both

HBO's *United States of Tara* and *Grey's Anatomy*. Then they were beat out of what seemed to be a promising HBO slot by Lena Dunham (who would go on to create *Girls*). To add insult to injury, Soloway recalls people would frequently ask if they were related to Dunham: "People were, like, it's you, but younger and better."

TAMBOR USED MORE OF HIMSELF FOR THE CHARACTER OF MAURA THAN ANY OTHER ROLE.

Tambor anticipated the biggest challenge of playing a trans character would be the physical transformation, though this was quickly proven incorrect. He told Terry Gross in a *Fresh Air* interview that that part turned out to be "very, very easy" for him. The hardest part? Coming to terms with his true self. "I get to use more of Jeffrey than I've ever used in any role. Probably even in playing Jeffrey," he said.

IT WAS THE MOST TRANS-INCLUSIVE PRODUCTION IN HOLLYWOOD HISTORY.

Producer Rhys Ernst told *Out* that he felt strongly about casting a trans actor to portray a young Maura in season 3's flashback sequences, ultimately bringing twelve-year-old Sophia Grace Gianna (who had recently transitioned) on for the part.

This trans-inclusiveness was part of *Transparent*'s DNA. Ernst said that the show employed more than fifty trans and gender-nonconforming people in the capacity of "crew members or as actors with speaking roles." That doesn't include what he estimates to be "hundreds of extras."

TAMBOR WENT "METHOD" TO WARM UP TO HIS ROLE AS MAURA.

Ahead of shooting the pilot of *Transparent*, Tambor was taken on a field trip by producers Rhys Ernst and Zackary Drucker. To get to the heart of his character, Tambor was encouraged to put on his full wardrobe and go out in public for the first time. The scariest part wouldn't be the club-hopping the producers had planned but, in fact, the inevitable walk through the hotel lobby.

"I can remember my legs were shaking, literally trembling—not so much because we were going to a club, but I was so nervous about the walk through the hotel lobby," Tambor told the *Los Angeles Times*. "And I remember telling myself: 'Remember this. Don't forget this. Let this instruct every single one of your shots and your days.' And it did. It has nothing to do with the entirety of what being a transgender person is, by any means, but it informed me."

SOLOWAY EMBRACED IMPROVISATION.

Season 2 of *Transparent* opens with a four-minute scene so perfect and categorically "Pfefferman," it likely did not occur to you that the whole thing was predicated on a mistake. The whole family is gathering for a wedding portrait, and we hear the photographer mis-gender Maura. Maura doesn't let the flub go unnoticed, snapping back, "Did he just call me 'sir'? This is over."

Gaby Hoffman, who plays the youngest member of the Pfefferman family, told *Vanity Fair* that this scene began as a "one-line moment in the script." That is, Soloway stepped back and let "everybody [say] whatever the hell he or she was saying." It was Tambor who made the snap decision to incorporate this mistake into the scene.

FAITH SOLOWAY, JOEY'S SISTER AND SHOW WRITER, WAS HARI NEF'S CAMP COUNSELOR.

One of *Transparent*'s breakout stars was trans actress, model, and writer Hari Nef, who played Gittel. Faith Soloway, who was a writer on the show (and also Joey's sister) evidently knew of Nef because she had been her camp counselor at the Charles River Creative Arts Program in Dover, Massachusetts. Nef recalled that she received an email seemingly out of the blue from Joey asking if she'd be interested in being their date to a New York gala. "So I showed up, we hit it off, and she wrote me a part," Nef said.

TRANSPARENT'S EMMY AWARD–WINNING MAIN TITLE THEME MUSIC WAS COMPOSED ON AN EIGHTY-YEAR-OLD PIANO.

Do not underestimate the power of an eighty-year-old piano. The nostalgia-inducing composition at the beginning of each episode is the work of Dustin O'Halloran, who is largely responsible for setting the understated tone of the rest of the series. Speaking with Song Exploder, O'Halloran described coming up in a "hippie Methodist church" community and learning to play music.

O'Halloran said that he used a Swiss piano from the 1930s for the theme song, the same piano he had recorded *Piano Solos Vol. 2* on. He also admitted that he'd composed an earlier version to be used for the show but felt that it wasn't right. "I was probably thinking too much about it being an opening title piece—more of a statement, like '*the show is beginning!*'" he said. O'Halloran's secret for the finished tune: A "fuller" but still understated sound. Also, some killer harmonium.

TRUE BLOOD

(2008–2014)

CREATED BY: Alan Ball (based on Charlaine Harris's Sookie Stackhouse book series)

SEASONS: 7

EPISODES: 80

OTHER SHOWS BY ALAN BALL:
Six Feet Under (2001–2005)
Here and Now (2018)

Set in fictional Bon Temps, Louisiana, Oscar winner Alan Ball's *True Blood* deals with vampires trying to acclimate to living among humans, often with violent results. The Japanese invent Tru Blood, a synthetic blood beverage meant to satiate vampires so they won't seek out real blood, but it doesn't work out so well.

Ball, creator of *Six Feet Under*, based the show on Charlaine Harris's Sookie Stackhouse books. Sookie (Anna Paquin), part fairy and part telepathic human, falls in love with a 173-year-old vampire, Bill (Stephen Moyer). (In 2010, Moyer and Paquin married in real life.) Sookie's also drawn to Eric (Emmy Award–winner Alexander Skarsgård) and shape-shifting werewolf Alcide (Joe Manganiello).

Also along for the ride to battle vampires and other fantastical creatures are Sookie's well-meaning but dimwitted brother, Jason (Ryan Kwanten); Sookie's boss, Sam Merlotte (Sam Trammell); and her friends Tara (Rutina Wesley) and Lafayette Reynolds (Nelsan Ellis, who died in 2017).

The show debuted on September 7, 2008, and became a sensation—so much so that in 2010, Paquin, Moyer, and Skarsgård posed naked, covered in blood, on the cover of *Rolling Stone*. *True Blood* blended sex, violence, and humor in a way no HBO show had done before, which led to it becoming the network's highest rated show since *The Sopranos* (until *Game of Thrones* surpassed both shows).

TRUE BLOOD WOULDN'T HAVE HAPPENED WITHOUT A TRIP TO THE DENTIST.

Alan Ball had to get a root canal and showed up thirty minutes early to his appointment. With time to kill, he visited a Barnes and Noble across the street and saw Charlaine Harris's book *Dead Until Dark*, the first in a series of thirteen novels. "The tagline is, 'Maybe having a vampire for a boyfriend isn't such a bright idea,' which made me laugh," Ball told Emmy TV Legends. "I'm from the South, Charlaine's from the South. It had a very authentic Southern feel to it. It was this great mix of drama and comedy and horror and sex and violence and social commentary. She walked this line that was so incredibly entertaining that I couldn't put the book down." He read three more of her books in the series and thought it'd make a good TV show. At the time the book was under option to be made into a film, but when the option expired, Ball jumped at the chance. He filmed a pilot and two more episodes, and HBO greenlit the series.

ANNA PAQUIN PURSUED THE ROLE OF SOOKIE.

Ball hadn't considered the naturally brunette Anna Paquin for the role of Sookie until the day the Oscar winner's reps called Ball's casting director and said she wanted to audition. "At the time Anna was dark-haired, and certainly her body of work didn't lead me anywhere near Sookie Stackhouse," Ball told *The New York Times*. "But she aggressively pursued it."

Paquin welcomed playing a part that she described to *The New York Times* as being "about as radically different from me and a lot of the work I've previously done as you could possibly come up with." In an interview with *Rolling Stone*, Paquin explained how people saw her as too serious. "But it only takes one person with a little bit of imagination to go, 'You know, pale-skin girls with brown hair can also be blond girls with a fake tan,' and presto change-o, makeover. It's not rocket science."

HARRIS AND BALL HAD DIFFERENT IDEAS ON VAMPIRE REPRESENTATION.

Harris published *Dead Until Dark*, the first book in the series, in 2001. "When I began framing how I was going to represent the vampires, it suddenly occurred to me that it would be interesting if they were a minority that was trying to get equal rights," Harris told the *New York Post*. "It just seemed to fit with what was happening in the world right then."

Ball, however, didn't agree with her. "I have a hard time seeing the vampires as a metaphor for gays and lesbians," he told *Rolling Stone*. "Just because the vampires on our show are, for the most part, vicious murderers and predators, and I'm gay myself, so I don't really want to say, 'Hey, gays and lesbians are basically viciously amoral murderers.'"

BALL THINKS THE SHOW IS ABOUT "THE TERRORS OF INTIMACY."

While developing the show for HBO, the network asked Ball for a one-sentence pitch for what the show was about. "I thought, 'Oh, dear God, what am I going to say?' I said, 'Well, ultimately at its heart, it's about the terrors of intimacy,'" he told *The New York Times*. "Which is an answer I just pulled totally out of [nowhere] at that moment. But I do think that actually, there is some truth to that. That is kind of what it's about." Later, he would tell NPR that the show was about "how we deal with our primal desires. How do those elements of our psyche manifest themselves in a world where monsters were real?"

RYAN KWANTEN DOESN'T THINK JASON IS DUMB.

In an interview with Vulture, Kwanten was asked, "What are the challenges of playing someone that dumb?" He responded with, "I see him more as simple than dumb…He can get away with some of the things he does because of that innocence. Whereas being dumb, you don't really get sympathy for that."

ALEXANDER SKARSGÅRD DIDN'T ALWAYS ABIDE BY THE PROPER NUDITY PROTOCOLS.

To keep partially covered up during sex scenes, the show's female actors wore thong-like "patches" while the male actors had to wear socks on their private parts. But Skarsgård bucked the trend during the season 6 finale. Eric is sunbathing on a snowy landscape in the mountains of Sweden, but the crew set up a green screen and filmed it atop a parking structure in Hollywood. "And it was a very hot day, so I didn't need the sock," he told Vulture. At the end of the scene, Skarsgård got up from his chair and revealed, well, everything, so to speak.

SPOILERS! RUTINA WESLEY EMBRACED TARA'S CHARACTER ARC.

During the fifth season, Sookie's best friend Tara (Rutina Wesley) becomes a vampire. HBO threw no punches when they killed her off in the premiere episode. Wesley didn't mind, though. "I think it's great," she told *Entertainment Weekly*. "I think somebody had to go. To have a main character right off the bat go, that's gonna bring everybody into the show. It's like, OK, and the show has started.' . . . This is the final season. We can't all make it to the end."

DENIS O'HARE USED HISTORY TO CREATE HIS CHARACTER'S BACKSTORY.

Russell Edgington, a.k.a. the King of Mississippi, is a 2,800-year-old vampire played by O'Hare, who wanted to make the character come from "somewhere interesting," so it was decided to make him a pagan Celt. "They are just wild people," O'Hare told Film School Rejects. "They have a very different relationship to everything in terms of nature and in terms of their own belief system. I just love that. That kind of helped make him just a different kind of character."

JOE MANGANIELLO GOT HIS JOB WITH HELP FROM A BLOG.

Fans of Harris's book had a blog in which they listed who should play certain characters, and some people suggested Joe Manganiello for Alcide. Manganiello stumbled upon the site, read the books, and told his agent he wanted to audition.

"It had been my dream, since I was a little kid, to play a movie monster and a werewolf," Manganiello told Collider. He posted the blog posts to his website, and someone who was friends with a *True Blood* casting director saw them. "I guess he was out at breakfast with one of the casting directors and the waiter came up to their table and the casting director said, 'Oh, wow, that waiter would make a great werewolf, if only he was an actor.' And, this guy said, 'No, you know who'd make a great werewolf? This guy,' and he pulled up my picture and showed it to him."

Joe auditioned for a different werewolf part, but "I wound up being brought in a second time for that other werewolf character, and then they wound up bringing me back in for Alcide."

11

OF TV'S FIERCEST VAMPIRES

From silly to sexy to scary, you'll want to check out these bloodsuckers.

ERIC NORTHMAN // *True Blood*

Technically he's not *True Blood*'s main vamp, but Eric Northman (Alexander Skarsgård), the owner of Fangtasia and a key part of the show's central love triangle, is a scene-stealer. Eric is a bit of a jerk, and he's capable of incredible violence, but he can also be caring and loyal, especially to his maker, Gordic, and his protégé, Pam. Also: He's sexy as hell. You won't be able to look away.

BARNABAS COLLINS // *Dark Shadows*

Less than one year into its run, ABC's gothic supernatural soap opera *Dark Shadows* was struggling—until it introduced vampire Barnabas Collins (Jonathan Frid), arguably TV's first sexy vampire. Barnabas wasn't intended to be a main character, but he was an immediate hit with audiences, becoming the show's most popular character right up until the series ended in 1971.

NANDOR, NADJA, LASZLO, AND COLIN ROBINSON // *What We Do in the Shadows*

It doesn't get any funnier than a group of vampires living in Staten Island, especially when they're trailed by a film crew covering their every hilarious move (and murder). Whether Nandor the Relentless (Kayvan Novak), Nadja (Natasia Demetriou), and Laszlo Cravensworth (Matt Berry) are attempting to take more territory in New York, making a mess of things at their neighbor Sean's "Superb Owl" party, or "[cutting] loose to Pennsylvania because it sounds like Transylvania," you'll be laughing until you cry—and watching each season more than once. Special shout-out to Colin Robinson (Mark Proksch), a day-walking energy vampire who will probably remind you of more than a few co-workers.

THE COUNTESS // *American Horror Story: Hotel*

As with many Ryan Murphy shows, there is a *lot* going on in *Hotel* (Vampires! Ghosts! Serial killers! The ghosts of serial killers!). Still, Lady Gaga's compelling turn as the Countess—a glamorous, century-old vampire turned hotel owner who slits throats with a chain mail glove—makes the watch well worth it.

JOHN MITCHELL // *Being Human*

Being Human follows brooding vampire John Mitchell (Aidan Turner) as he fights his urge to feed and works a hospital job in an attempt to be a normal person. He shares a flat with his friend George Sands (Russell Tovey), a werewolf who is also fighting his supernatural powers, and Annie Sawyer (Lenora Crichlow), a ghost who haunts their apartment. The characters' struggles with their true natures aren't just relatable; they make for an addictively bingeable show, which lasted five seasons. The series also spawned an American remake, with Sam Witwer playing a vampire named Aidan, which lasted for four seasons.

MR. QUINLAN // *The Strain*

It's impossible to forget the inhuman features and horrifying stingers of *The Strain*'s vampire Strigoi—and though he keeps his nose and his ability to walk around in daylight, Mr. Quinlan (Rupert Penry-Jones) is just as scary. Driven by rage and carrying a sword with a human femur hilt, the vampire-human hybrid is on a mission to kill the Master, who is also his father. You won't want to stop watching until you know how it ends.

ANGEL AND SPIKE // *Buffy The Vampire Slayer*

No list of best vampires would be complete without Buffy's blood-sucking boyfriends. When they're bad, David Boreanaz (Angel/Angelus) and James Marsters (Spike) imbue their characters with a menacing, darkly humorous swagger—and when they're good, they're angsty and a little tortured—and, of course, they support the Slayer to help literally save the world. Either way, they challenge Buffy and help show her just how strong she is, whether they're on her side or not.

THE WALKING DEAD

(2010—PRESENT)

DEVELOPED BY: Frank Darabont (based on Robert Kirkman, Tony Moore, and Charlie Adlard's graphic novel series)

SEASONS: 11

EPISODES: 177

OTHER SHOWS BY FRANK DARABONT:
Mob City (2013)

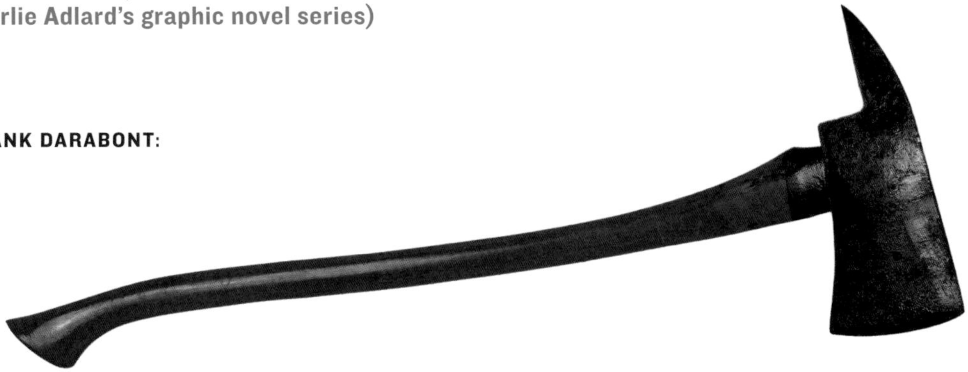

Zombies have always been a dependable crowd-pleaser, but *The Walking Dead* proves that tales of the living impaired can also spawn a multi-billion-dollar franchise complete with video games, toys, spin-offs, and all the other windfalls network executives dream of.

Based on the hit Image Comics series by writer Robert Kirkman and artists Tony Moore and Charlie Adlard, *The Walking Dead* already had an award-winning foundation when producer Frank Darabont brought the adaptation to AMC. The show itself mirrors its comic book roots by following Rick Grimes (Andrew Lincoln) and a group of other survivors (Jon Bernthal, Sarah Wayne Callies, Norman Reedus, and more) who have to eke out an existence in a post-apocalyptic world overrun by the undead. Human nature being what it is, they soon find themselves at odds with one another and other factions of survivors, proving that the flesh-eaters might not be their biggest threat after all.

THE SHOW DOESN'T USE THE WORD *ZOMBIE*.

The Walking Dead's low-key slogan is, "Don't say the zed word." That's a reference that no one in *The Walking Dead* universe would get because *Shaun of the Dead* (as well as other zombie-based entertainment) doesn't exist there. Robert Kirkman breaks his own rule in the comic book occasionally, but the show has stuck to calling them walkers, skin-eaters, deadheads, wasteds, deadies, rotters, and dozens of other names to avoid saying what we all know they are.

HBO WAS WILLING TO MAKE THE SHOW . . . IF THEY TONED DOWN THE VIOLENCE.

For a show like *The Walking Dead*, which contains a lot of R-rated elements, HBO is often a first choice when it comes to pitching a network.

And they were indeed interested in the possibility of making it an HBO series . . . but only if its creators agreed to soften the level of violence and gore.

Reminder: This is HBO we're talking about—home of *Oz*, *The Sopranos*, *True Blood*, and *Game of Thrones*.

THE ZOMBIES ARE EATING HAM.

Instead of chowing down on human flesh, the actors playing walkers wrap their lips around juicy bits of ham. They used to get barbecue sauce to help it go down, but the vinegar messed up their makeup, so now it's just ham with fake blood all over it. Actor Vincent Martella, who played Patrick in season 4, said it was a challenge to eat a person on the show, not because of the ham, but because of the mindlessness. "When you eat someone you have to look like an animal devouring prey," he told *Today*. "You can't look like you have any specific motive or where you're going to take a bite."

THE SHOW'S OPENING CREDITS ARE DETERIORATING.

Everything falls apart. That includes the lettering and logo for the show's opening credits, which have been yellowing and crumbling since the series began. The ninth season logo featured greenery, signaling a change in the story's direction, a sense of rebuilding, and the return of nature.

ZOMBIE ACTORS HAVE TO ATTEND ZOMBIE SCHOOL.

Before trying to eat Michonne or Daryl, aspiring "walkers" have to attend a seminar where they get tips on the specific style of the show's undead, followed by auditions where executive producer and horror effects legend Greg Nicotero chooses the best stumblers. Some keys to success include staying loose and avoiding sticking your arms straight out like Frankenstein's monster.

IT TAKES ABOUT 90 MINUTES TO TURN AN ACTOR INTO A WALKER.

Nicotero told CNN that the process of turning an extra into a zombie takes about 90 minutes. "The extras come into the trailers; we don't know who is coming in, and it's sort of like having a new canvas every single time," he said. "They all have contact lenses; they all have custom dentures; some people we like to make more rotted than others. It all depends on the character and what we want to do on that particular day."

THE SURVIVORS ARE SERIOUSLY OUTNUMBERED.

While it's obvious to anyone who has watched the show that the walkers outnumber the survivors, that's never explicitly stated on the show. The comic book is a different story. According to a blurb from Image Comics, the ratio of zombies to humans is 5,000 to one.

SPOILERS! THE SEASON 7 PREMIERE WAS A DIVISIVE EPISODE FOR VIEWERS.

The season 7 premiere—which saw Negan (Jeffrey Dean Morgan) brutally murder fan favorite character Glenn (Steven Yeun) with his beloved barbed baseball bat, Lucille—attracted a number of very

specific complaints. One Miami-based filmmaker and horror movie lover complained that, while they had no issue "seeing zombies hacked to pieces," the show had crossed the line with Glenn's death. "Watching human beings bashed over the head with a barbwire baseball bat over and over is just plain gore," the complaint read. "Here I am days later and still freaked out from what I saw and can't erase the image from my memory. It was that horrific…Viewers must be protected from extreme and excessive gore and violence. *TWD* crossed the line."

WHEN A CHARACTER DIES, THE CAST GETS TOGETHER FOR A LAST SUPPER.

As the rare show that kills its main characters with fierce regularity, *The Walking Dead* started its own tradition of holding Death Dinners for those about to bite the dust. "It gives everyone a chance to get properly sauced and say, 'We're going to miss the hell out of you,'" Sarah Wayne Callies (who played Rick's wife, Lori Grimes) told *Rolling Stone* in 2012. As the show grew in popularity, they began pretending that these get-togethers were cast birthday parties (so waitstaff or anyone who saw them out and about wouldn't get wise and spoil who's getting bitten next).

THEY USE CGI TO ERASE ZOMBIE BREATH.

The actors playing the zombies are amazing, but they can't hide their breath when it's cold outside. To add to the otherworldly nature of the monsters (and to be biologically accurate), the producers have to remove breath steam from the undead figures, who wouldn't be breathing.

A FAN BIT NORMAN REEDUS.

Five years into playing a character who could potentially outlast all 7 billion zombies, Reedus was unable to thwart an attack in real life when an overzealous fan bit him on the chest at New Jersey's

Walker Stalker Con. The actor took it in stride and didn't press charges, but the fan was banned from the convention for life. No matter how much you love a show, please don't bite people.

THE FCC GETS A LOT OF COMPLAINTS ABOUT THE SHOW.

In 2020, *Observer* filed a Freedom of Information Act request with the FCC in order to learn what sort of complaints the organization hears about *The Walking Dead*. Of the 28 pages of data they received, they learned that many of the issues people had with the show were somewhat repetitive: The show is too violent; there's a lot of bad language used; the commercials are much louder than the show (we're kind of with them on this one).

NON-FANS OF THE SHOW REGULARLY COMPLAIN ABOUT IT, TOO.

While fans of *The Walking Dead* took issue with particularly violent moments in the show, even non-viewers have a lot to say about the show—especially when its commercials interrupt their otherwise PG-rated programming. The bulk of complaints obtained were from non-fans of the show who were forced to endure watching just a few moments of it during commercial breaks on channels including Hallmark, Food Network, and CMT. One North Carolina resident wrote in to complain about a CMT ad that featured "a man cutting, sewing, and wearing the skin of another human as a mask. I'm watching *Princess Diaries 2* for goodness sakes, and now I have that vivid sickening image in my mind!" A Florida fan of Food Network's *Cake Wars* was watching the baking show with his 9-year-old daughter when an equally offensive ad ran.

FREEZE FRAME

"MERCY" // SEASON 8, EPISODE 1

The Walking Dead's first episode established the show's tone by having Rick shoot a teddy bear–holding little girl named Summer (Addy Miller). She was going to eat his face off, but the action still stole away a portion of Grimes's humanity. For its hundredth episode, the series brought Miller back to play a zombie very similar to the iconic one she played when she was ten years old.

WATCHING *THE WALKING DEAD* COULD FRIGHTEN YOUR NEIGHBORS.

If you're planning to binge-watch *The Walking Dead*, you might want to check the volume on your TV. In 2016, police in Great Falls, Montana, were called when a concerned citizen heard loud, strange noises and what he thought were gunshots coming from his neighbor's apartment. What the authorities discovered were some fans of the show watching the latest episode with the sound turned up and their windows open. Consider yourselves warned.

THE WEST WING

(1999–2006)

CREATED BY: Aaron Sorkin

SEASONS: 7

EPISODES: 155

OTHER SHOWS BY AARON SORKIN:
Sports Night (1998–2000)
Studio 60 on the Sunset Strip (2006–2007)
The Newsroom (2012–2014)

Aaron Sorkin's benchmark political drama was prestige TV before we even started using the term. *The West Wing* focuses on the presidential administration of the fictional Democrat Josiah Bartlet (Martin Sheen) and his trusty team of political wunderkinds, including best friend and chief of staff Leo McGarry (John Spencer), deputy chief of staff Josh Lyman (Bradley Whitford), communications director Toby Ziegler (Richard Schiff), deputy communications director Sam Seaborn (Rob Lowe), press secretary C. J. Cregg (Allison Janney), and personal aide Charlie Young (Dulé Hill).

The West Wing rose above early doubts to become one of most celebrated shows of its era, winning four consecutive Outstanding Drama Series Emmys and turning its ensemble cast into major stars. With its lightning-quick dialogue (a Sorkin signature), eye for authenticity, and plenty of walk-and-talks (another Sorkin technique), the series is as close as most of us are ever going to get to seeing how the White House operates during both moments of mundanity and complete chaos.

AARON SORKIN DIDN'T WANT TO MAKE A TV SHOW.
The seed for *The West Wing* was planted when Sorkin, fresh off the success of films including *A Few Good Men* and *The American President*, was asked to take a meeting with TV producer John Wells, who was still riding high from the success of *ER* at NBC. Sorkin agreed to the meeting, though he had "never thought of doing television." The night before meeting with Wells, he had a conversation with his friend, screenwriter Akiva Goldsman, who referenced Sorkin's *The American President* and suggested the idea of a TV series about a senior staffer at the White House. Sorkin still resisted the idea of a TV show, but he couldn't get the idea out of his head.

"The next day I walked into the restaurant and immediately saw this wasn't what I thought it was going to be," Sorkin told *Empire*. "This wasn't just a 'hello, how are you?' meeting, because John was sitting with a couple of agents and studio executives from Warner Brothers. Right after I sat down, he said, 'So what do you want to do?' And instead of saying, 'I think there's been a misunderstanding, I don't have an idea for a television series,' which would've been honest, I said 'I want to do a television series about senior staffers at the White House.' He said, 'OK, you got a deal.'" (Due to the pace at which productions happen in Hollywood, Sorkin's *Sports Night* ended up premiering in September 1998, one year before *The West Wing*.)

SORKIN DEMANDED THE DIALOGUE REMAIN EXACTLY AS HE WROTE IT.

Sorkin was famous for the rhythm and pacing of his dialogue, and by the time *The West Wing* came along, he'd taken great pains to make sure the language that was on his page was the same language spoken by his actors in the finished product. Martin Sheen later recalled that it was actually a part of Sorkin's contract that the dialogue he wrote had to be repeated exactly by the cast, and while the actors could make suggestions for rewrites, improvisation was never encouraged.

"I had been used to improvising, and even in the audition I was feeling free to rearrange Aaron's words a little bit, as lovely as they were. I didn't find out until after I got the part how furious Aaron was at me for doing that," Richard Schiff recalled. "They said, 'He was livid. He did everything in his power not to jump down your throat!' But I came to realize that Aaron was writing in meter and the rhythm of the language is very important."

THE PRESIDENT WAS ORIGINALLY SUPPOSED TO BE A RECURRING CHARACTER.

When Sheen accepted the role of President Josiah "Jed" Bartlet, he did it thinking he would be a recurring cast member only, appearing in just a handful of episodes each season. Sorkin originally intended to use the president sparingly on the show, keeping the focus on the staff out of fear that having the leader of the free world pop up all the time would "take up all the oxygen in a room." When Sheen showed up to work on the show, though, in the famous final scene of the pilot in which he berates a group of hypocritical ministers, everyone knew Sheen would be sticking around.

THE MS SUBPLOT CAME FROM RESEARCHERS.

In the season 1 episode "He Shall, from Time to Time," First Lady Abigail Bartlet (Stockard Channing) reveals to Leo McGarry that President Bartlet has multiple sclerosis. This secret, which wasn't really brought up as a plot device again until the season 2 premiere, became a driving narrative force in the show, as a Congressional investigation into whether or not Bartlet had defrauded the public by concealing his illness got underway. Bartlet's MS ultimately became one of the show's most potent dramatic elements, but during a 2016 panel at the ATX Television Festival, Sorkin admitted he initially gave the president the disease because Channing wanted to do more on the show. Sorkin thought she should be some kind of professional like a doctor, then combined that with an idea he had long had about the president having a sick day and watching daytime television. So he hit on the idea that Bartlet fell ill with something that looked like the flu but Abigail needs to rush back because she's the only one who knows it might be something else.

Sorkin picked multiple sclerosis and moved forward with the episode, only to find that the next time he faced questions from the Television Critics Association, everyone wanted to know when the MS story line would come up again. so Sorkin had to figure out what would happen next.

IT WAS THOMAS SCHLAMME WHO SUGGESTED THE NOW ICONIC "WALK-AND-TALK" SHOTS.

As *The West Wing* came together and Sorkin began delivering scripts, the design of the show's visuals fell to Thomas Schlamme, who quickly realized he had to find new ways of making a bunch of scenes that were essentially people having high-stakes meetings into something that would look dynamic and exciting on a TV screen. It was out of this need that the show's trademark "walk-and-talk" sequences of characters having long conversations while moving through corridors were born.

"I thought his language had motion, so why not get people up and have them say that language while they're also moving? It was driven by the idea that there is no wasted time," Schlamme said. "If you went from one place to another, that had to be a meeting!"

ONE PIECE OF THE ORIGINAL ENSEMBLE DIDN'T FIT.

Mandy Hampton (Moira Kelly) was a former Bartlet campaign staffer who was introduced in the show as a foil for Josh Lyman (Bradley Whitford) and ultimately became the Bartlet White House media director. But by the second season premiere the character had disappeared from the show entirely without explanation. Where did Mandy go? According to Sorkin, there's no great mystery to solve. It just didn't work out.

"Moira was a joy to work with, a total pro who understood as time went on that for whatever reasons—and those reasons had nothing to do with her considerable talent—it just wasn't working," he later said. "She was a model of graciousness."

SORKIN NEVER WATCHED THE SEASONS HE DIDN'T WRITE.

Though Sorkin's name was always on the show as a creator, the last episode he wrote was the season 4 finale, "Twenty Five," which left a cliff-hanger involving Bartlet's kidnapped daughter and a new interim president for John Wells and company to pick up in season 5.

As he left *The West Wing* behind, Sorkin got a call from another famous television writer who'd recently departed a hit series, who gave him a key piece of advice.

"Larry David had left *Seinfeld* a few seasons before the show ended and he called me and said, 'You can never watch *The West Wing* again. Either the show is going to be great without you and you're going to be miserable, or the show is going to be less than great without you and you're going to be miserable,'" Sorkin told *Empire*. Though he did attempt to watch the first episode shot without him, Sorkin said he didn't get more than fifteen seconds in before turning it off. "It felt like I was watching somebody make out with my girlfriend," he said. And he never looked back.

ALLISON JANNEY DIDN'T LIKE WHERE HER CHARACTER WENT.

With Sorkin gone, John Wells took over and set up creating some ambitious new plotlines that saw some of the show's key characters heading in new directions. Early in the sixth season, Leo McGarry suffered a near-fatal heart attack, and Bartlet named C. J. Cregg the new White House chief of staff. Though it added some new energy to the show, Janney wasn't exactly a fan.

"I liked the dynamics the way they were. Me having to be the boss of everyone wasn't as fun for me in the room and the comedy wasn't there," Janney recalled. "When C. J. became chief of staff it was a strange shift for me on the show and I wasn't comfortable in that shift."

SCHIFF WAS PISSED ABOUT WHAT HAPPENED TO HIS CHARACTER.
The change was even more radical for Toby Ziegler, who went from one of the president's most trusted advisors to a disgraced criminal when it was revealed in the season 7 episode "Mr. Frost" that he'd been responsible for leaking classified information about a military space shuttle to the press. Schiff hated the turn for his character and believed Toby would never have betrayed Bartlet.

"What was done to Toby [in the final season] was wrong. I was deeply, deeply hurt by that," Schiff said. "They gave me this scene where I reveal myself as the White House leak and I thought, 'Oh, maybe I'm taking the fall for somebody.' So I played that out kind of heroically, like maybe I'm falling on my sword. I did not know that they wanted to shorten the number of my episodes! I hope it was just a bad idea that they thought was great and that there was nothing beyond that— but it was a really bad idea and very insulting to me."

SORKIN CAME BACK FOR THE SERIES FINALE.
The seventh and final season of the show was full of reunions, including the returns of characters like Sam Seaborn and frequent guest Ainsley Hayes (Emily Procter) for an episode or two. Sorkin, too, wanted to at least be present for the farewell. He made a brief but prominent cameo appearance in the series finale, "Tomorrow," as a man seated on the stage during Matt Santos's inauguration.

MUST-WATCH POLITICAL SHOWS

The Good Fight // **(2017–PRESENT)**
The Good Wife // **(2009–2016)**
Homeland // **(2011–2020)**
House of Cards // **(2013–2018)**
The Politician // **(2019–PRESENT)**
Spin City // **(1996–2002)**
Tanner 88 // **(1988)**
The Thick of It // **(2005–2012)**
Veep // **(2012–2019)**

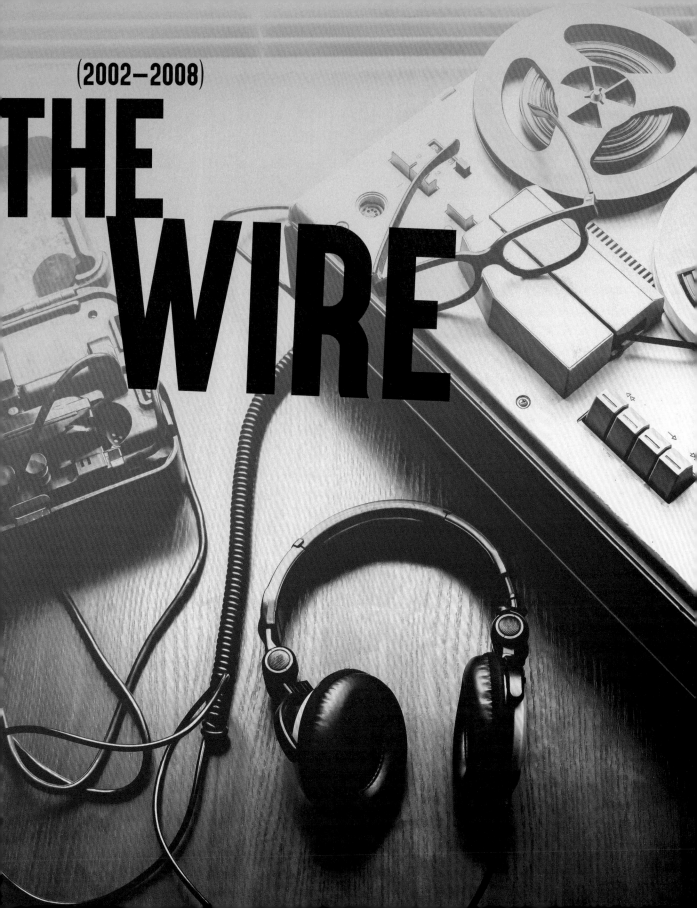

(2002–2008)
THE WIRE

CREATED BY: David Simon

SEASONS: 5

EPISODES: 60

OTHER SHOWS BY DAVID SIMON:
Treme (2010–2013)
Show Me a Hero (2015)
The Deuce (2017–2019)
The Plot Against America (2020)

In "The Wire," the sixth episode of *The Wire*'s first season, Detective Lester Freamon (Clarke Peters) tells perpetual screwup Roland "Prez" Pryzbylewski (Jim True-Frost), "All the pieces matter." Freamon says this while teaching the junior detective the basics of good police work and why it's essential to consider each bit of evidence both on its own and as part of the overall puzzle. While it could have easily been written off as a throwaway line, the idea that "all the pieces matter" came to embody the overall theme of *The Wire* itself, which is one of the most deeply layered shows ever to grace the small screen.

The series never garnered a ton of awards or even boasted solid viewer ratings during its time on the air, but *The Wire* undoubtedly ranks alongside *The Sopranos* and *Breaking Bad* as one of the greatest television shows of all time. On paper, it may sound like just another cops-versus-criminals series, but the truth—like the show itself—is far more complex. Over the course of its five seasons, the carefully plotted drama upends every cops-and-robbers trope television has ever seen. In doing so, it weaves an intricate portrait of the inner workings of the city of Baltimore and the role that not only its police and criminal element play in the shaping of Charm City, but its politicians, educators, and media, too. *The Wire* isn't an easy watch, though it is a rewarding one.

THE WIRE WAS ROOTED IN GREEK TRAGEDY.

Although *The Wire* has been compared to the works of William Shakespeare and Charles Dickens, David Simon told *Slate* that "the guys we were stealing from in *The Wire* are the Greeks. In our heads we're writing a Greek tragedy, but instead of the gods being petulant and jealous Olympians hurling lightning bolts down at our protagonists, it's the postmodern institutions that are the gods. And they are gods. And no one is bigger."

FREEZE FRAME

"OLD CASES" / SEASON 1, EPISODE 4

Baltimore homicide detective Terry McLarney once joked to David Simon that he and his fellow officers swore so much that "[one] day we're going to get to the point where we're all going to be able to just use the word *fuck* to communicate." Simon took it upon himself to do just that with *The Wire*'s famous "Fuck Scene," a nearly five-minute scene in which McNulty and Bunk communicate solely in F-bombs—or some variation of the word. It's uttered approximately forty times between the two. Pierce called the scene "one of the best displays of my acting in the whole series. I tell folks, 'Study that if you want to study what intent is,' because everyone understood exactly what we were doing at every moment, even though we were using just that one word or [a] variation thereof. That was one of the best-acted scenes that I did on the show."

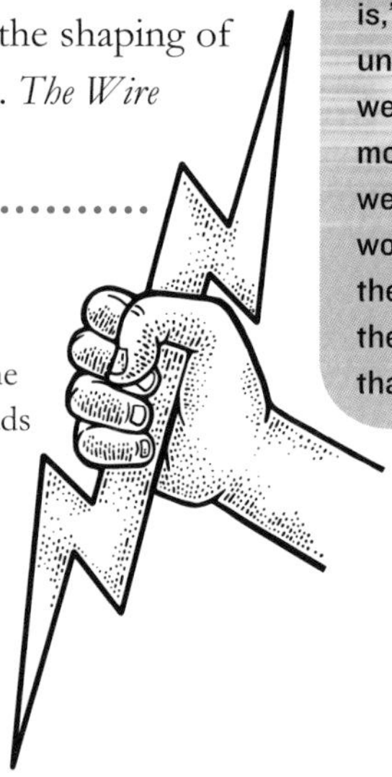

IT'S BARACK OBAMA'S FAVORITE TV SHOW.
The forty-fourth POTUS has never made a secret of his love for *The Wire*. In 2008, before he was president, Obama told the *Las Vegas Sun* that it was his favorite show, and even named Omar Little as his favorite character. "That's not an endorsement," Obama clarified. "[Omar's] not my favorite person, but he's a fascinating character…the toughest, baddest guy on the show."

FREEZE FRAME

"TOOK" // SEASON 5, EPISODE 7
Richard Belzer makes a brief cameo playing Detective John Munch, the longtime cop character he originated on *Homicide: Life on the Street,* the Emmy-winning NBC series based on David Simon's 1991 book *Homicide: A Year on the Killing Streets,* and later moved to the *Law & Order* franchise. Belzer appears in a bar scene with Jay Landsman, the real-life Baltimore detective on whom Munch's character is based. But *The Wire* also features a character based on Jay Landsman, named Jay Landsman and played by Delaney Williams. To make matters more confusing, Landsman himself appears on *The Wire,* playing Lieutenant Dennis Mello (who is in the scene with Belzer). Got that?

THE WIRE'S RATINGS WERE PRETTY ABYSMAL.
Though critics (and at least one president) have raved about *The Wire*, it was never a big hit with viewers while it was on the air. At the height of its "popularity," *The Wire* was attracting about 4 million viewers per week. By the time its final season aired, it was being watched by around 1 million people. Compare that to the nearly 20 million viewers who were tuning in to fellow HBO series *Game of Thrones* during its final season.

IT WAS NOT AN AWARDS SHOW DARLING.
Even today, more than a decade after it ended its run, *The Wire* is regularly cited as one of the best TV shows ever made. But a glance at the awards it won—or was even nominated for—would make that fact surprising. During its five seasons, *The Wire* received just two Emmy nominations, both for Outstanding Writing for a Drama Series, and lost both times (once to *House*, the other time to *Mad Men*). It was nominated for a BAFTA for Best International Show but was trumped yet again by Don Draper and company. At least the American Film Institute knew what was what; it named *The Wire* a TV Program of the Year at its 2003, 2006, and 2008 AFI Awards.

MUCH OF *THE WIRE* IS BASED ON THE EXPERIENCES OF WRITER AND PRODUCER ED BURNS.
Burns, Simon's longtime collaborator, logged twenty years with the Baltimore Police Department, where he worked in both the homicide and narcotics departments. In fact, it was while Burns was working as a detective that he first met Simon, who spent twelve years working as a crime reporter for *The Baltimore Sun*. Burns mined his own history as a detective for many of the characters and story lines in *The Wire*. "He did a lot of these protracted investigations, often of more than a year's time, into violent drug traffickers," Simon told Salon shortly after *The Wire*'s premiere in 2002. "It was largely based on his experiences and his frustrations in the department. And then it was also based on my experiences at my newspaper, which became a sort of hellish, futile bureaucracy."

MANY OF THE CRIMINALS WERE BASED ON REAL PEOPLE.
Simon has been quoted as saying that "all of our characters [are] a composite of attributes from a variety of people. No one is entirely fictional or entirely real." That being said, fans and journalists have teased out some of the potential inspirations for the show. Omar, Baltimore's most feared stickup artist, was based largely on Donnie Andrews. In 1986, in order to support his heroin habit, Donnie agreed to murder a drug dealer. But the guilt became too much for Andrews, so he surrendered himself to Burns. In 1987, Andrews was sentenced to life in prison. With the help of Burns and Simon, who lobbied for his release, Andrews left prison in 2005. He appeared in six episodes of *The Wire* playing Donnie, a friend of Omar's close friend and advisor Butchie. (Andrews died in 2012.)

A real-life version of confidential informant Reginald "Bubbles" Cousins (Andre Royo) has only been publicly identified as "Possum." Like Bubbles, Possum had a photographic memory and would help the police determine high-priority targets for investigations by having them try on different hats that he was trying to sell. Simon had been planning to write an article about Possum, but that turned into an obituary when Possum died in 1992 due to complications of HIV.

"Little" Melvin Williams, a notorious drug kingpin in Baltimore during the 1970s and eighties—who was arrested by Burns in 1985 following a wiretap investigation—informed much of Avon Barksdale's (Wood Harris) character. That same year, Simon wrote a five-article series on Williams for *The Sun* titled "Easy Money: Anatomy of a Drug Empire." Williams, too, later landed a role on *The Wire*, playing the Deacon in seasons 3 and 4.

BUNK MORELAND WAS THE FIRST CHARACTER CAST.

In Jonathan Abrams's excellent *All the Pieces Matter: The Inside Story of* The Wire, Simon recounts how each of the many roles in *The Wire* was cast and how Wendell Pierce in particular made a huge impression, not specifically because of his reading, but because he was so agitated when he came in to audition. "He was really pissed off," Simon recalled. "He had gotten in an argument with a cab driver. It was one of those sort of trying-to-hail-a-cab-while-Black moments in New York, and he came in and he was steaming. He was harried, like a bear who'd hit the hornet's nest. He had to focus on the scene, and he was apologizing for what he thought was a bad read, but it had that air of Baltimore—put-upon workaday Baltimore—homicide detective. As soon as he came in and read, it was like, 'That's our Bunk.'"

SEVERAL OF THE POLICE OFFICERS ARE PLAYED BY ACTUAL POLICE OFFICERS

Simon added authenticity to *The Wire* by casting several real police officers in key roles. Gary D'Addario, Leonard Hamm, Jimmy Rood, and Donald Worden were all Baltimore Police Department veterans who had bit parts on the show. As did Ed Norris, who happened to be Baltimore's very real police commissioner at the time he made his first appearance on *The Wire*. It was meant to be a cameo but turned into a recurring role, which ended when Norris was indicted on federal corruption charges for misuse of public funds. Eventually, he pled guilty and served six months.

DOMINIC WEST HAD A TOUGH TIME GETTING THE BALTIMORE ACCENT DOWN.

Though you might not guess it from the Baltimore accent he so ably pulls off on the show, West was born in Sheffield, England. He was cast in *The Wire* at a time when there weren't a lot of Brits playing American characters. Burns in particular remembers Simon attempting to teach West how to master Baltimore's distinct accent: "David and Dominic spent a lot of time: 'Now, say it like *po*-lice.' 'Police.' 'No, *po*-lice.'"

"Po-lice."

There is also the character of Sergeant Jay Landsman (Delaney Williams), right-hand man to William Rawls, who is based on real BPD homicide detective Jay Landsman. In season 2, the real Landsman joined *The Wire* as recurring character Dennis Mello.

SIMON WAS EYEING JOHN C. REILLY FOR THE ROLE OF JIMMY McNULTY.

While *The Wire* is an ensemble piece, one could make a strong argument that Jimmy McNulty was the main character in the show's early days. And while it was Dominic West who ended up playing the role, Simon initially saw John C. Reilly in the part. "I thought John C. Reilly could be a different McNulty, certainly not the same, but I thought he could carry all of the excesses and vices of McNulty in a different way," Simon said in *All the Pieces Matter*. "I've loved his work in a lot of stuff…Later on, Dom was working with [Reilly] on *Chicago* and they're looking at each other. They're so different, and Dom's like, 'What were they going for?'"

AN ENGLISH ACCENT COULD HAVE COST IDRIS ELBA THE ROLE OF STRINGER BELL.

West wasn't the only Brit cast in *The Wire*; the series marked the American breakthrough for Idris Elba, too, who played drug kingpin Stringer Bell, Avon Barksdale's second-in-command and longtime best friend. While Elba was initially considered for the role of Avon, Simon and company decided he would work better as Stringer, who serves as the brains of the Barksdale operation and would like to see the business go legit.

"Sheeeeeeeee-it!"

Fortunately for Elba, he made the wise decision to hide his British accent during his audition. "I was probably in a mode where if I was being asked to take on more Brits, or more anything, I would have been like, 'Come on, can't I get some tougher New Yorkers?'" Simon told *The Hollywood Reporter*. "I know I can't get a Baltimore accent, but can I at least get some Americans?" It wasn't until the first table read with the cast that Simon even learned Elba was British.

For Elba, the American accent was all a part of his prep for the role. "I didn't realize he was English initially, because he was talking the whole time in American and he was living in New York at the time," West said in *All the Pieces Matter*. "I was chatting to him, and eventually he said, 'Look, you've got to stop talking in that English accent because you're fucking me up.'"

SPOILERS! ELBA WASN'T HAPPY WHEN HE LEARNED ABOUT STRINGER'S FATE.

According to *The Hollywood Reporter*, Elba was "devastated" when Simon called to tell him that Stringer was being killed off. Given the character's popularity, Elba wasn't the only one who thought it was a bad idea. Author Laura Lippman, Simon's girlfriend at the time (now his wife), called him an "idiot" for killing the character. And while Elba didn't want to go, and feared whether he'd even work again, he became angry when he read his final scene. Originally, it was written so that after Omar shoots Stringer, "he then whips his dick out and pisses on him," Elba recalled. "I was pissed. I told [Simon] it was [an] absolute tragedy, that it was sensational, and that it wasn't going to happen." Simon agreed to remove that particular indignity from the scene.

IT WAS SPIKE LEE WHO FIRST INTRODUCED US TO ISIAH WHITLOCK, JR.'S "SHEEEEEEEEE-IT!"

In 2008, Isiah Whitlock, Jr. dove into the history of the comically exaggerated curse word with *Slate*, which he explained started with his uncle and was something he had been saying for years before he was cast in *The Wire*. In fact, the first time he ever uttered it onscreen wasn't even in *The Wire* at all; it was in Spike Lee's 2002 film *The 25th Hour* (which was adapted from a book by *Game of Thrones* co-creator David Benioff). Someone on *The Wire* writing staff knew all about Whitlock's love of the word, and wrote it into the script. For the record: The correct way to spell it is with *nine* Es and a hyphen: *sheeeeeeeee-it*.

SIMON PITCHED A POLITICAL SPIN-OFF OF *THE WIRE* CALLED *THE HALL*.

After *The Wire*'s third season introduced power-hungry councilman Tommy Carcetti (Aidan Gillen) into the mix, Simon saw the potential for a new series. "We actually went to [then HBO chairman] Chris Albrecht and said, 'Here's a pilot of a show called *The Hall* that follows the Carcetti character and his political career. And we want to run them in tandem,'" Simon told *Salon* in 2012. "So after season 3 of *The Wire* you would get season 1 of *The Hall*, then you'd get season 4 of *The Wire*, then season 2 of *The Hall*. This poor guy must have been listening to this and saying, 'Yeah that's what I need, I need two shows that nobody's watching in Baltimore'… He had to be laughing his ass off inside."

FANTASTIC PILOTS

Even great TV series don't always start out that way. Sometimes a show needs several episodes, or even a couple of seasons, to really find its feet. There's no shame in that, but it also means the shows that do nail their tonal and thematic intentions from the very first episode are rare creatures worthy of celebration. *The Wire* is just one of those shows.

1 *THE WIRE* // "**The Target**"
Forget the best pilots for a second and just think about the best opening scenes in the history of television, and *The Wire* might emerge right at the top of the list. One simple conversation between McNulty and a witness to a murder while cops process the crime scene in front of them managed to encapsulate much of what made the show great: Understated acting, brilliant dialogue, unpretentious realism, and thematic weight hanging from every word. The rest of the pilot somehow only managed to get better from there, and a TV legend was born.

2 *CHEERS* // "**Give Me a Ring Sometime**"
The mission statement of the titular bar in *Cheers* is right there in the theme song: It's a haven, a refuge, and a place of comfort. It's therefore quite brilliant, all these years later, that the show's very first episode is the chronicle of how a stranger—namely Diane (Shelley Long)—is initiated into this group of misfits who are always glad you came. Structurally, the pilot works because it allows an audience identification character to be introduced to the show's cast and home set. Emotionally, it works because it allows Diane, and by extension us, to find friends we want to see again and again.

3 *FUTURAMA* // "**Space Pilot 3000**"
Matt Groening created *The Simpsons*, the most successful animated series of all time. Even in 1999, when *Futurama* premiered, it was hard to imagine lightning like that would strike twice, but somehow Groening and co-developer David X. Cohen pulled it off. *Futurama*— the story of a delivery man named Fry (Billy West) who, after being cryogenically frozen by accident, emerges a thousand years into his own future—debuted as a sharp, audacious, and immediately inventive satire that managed to both call *The Simpsons* to mind and somehow avoid copying its own satirical instincts. "Space Pilot 3000" was an instant classic.

4 *HOW I MET YOUR MOTHER* // "**Pilot**"
How I Met Your Mother is a show with an ending that still divides fans, in part because it seemed to overshadow the entire mission statement of the show as laid out in the pilot. Taken on its own as an introduction to a series about friendship and what Ted Mosby's friends later term "emotional endurance," though, *How I Met Your Mother*'s pilot is a beautifully assembled piece of television, telling the story of Ted (Josh Radnor) and Robin's (Cobie Smulders) magical first hours together, and then totally subverting them by the end.

5 *TWIN PEAKS* // "**Pilot**" **aka "Northwest Passage"**
"She's dead; wrapped in plastic" remains one of the most iconic lines in television history, in part because it's one of the strangest ways to phrase a phone call in which you inform someone that you've just found a body. So began the central mystery of *Twin Peaks*, David Lynch and Mark Frost's strange, satirical TV mystery that merged mystery, soap opera, and pure Lynchian weirdness into something unlike anything else ever seen on television before or since.

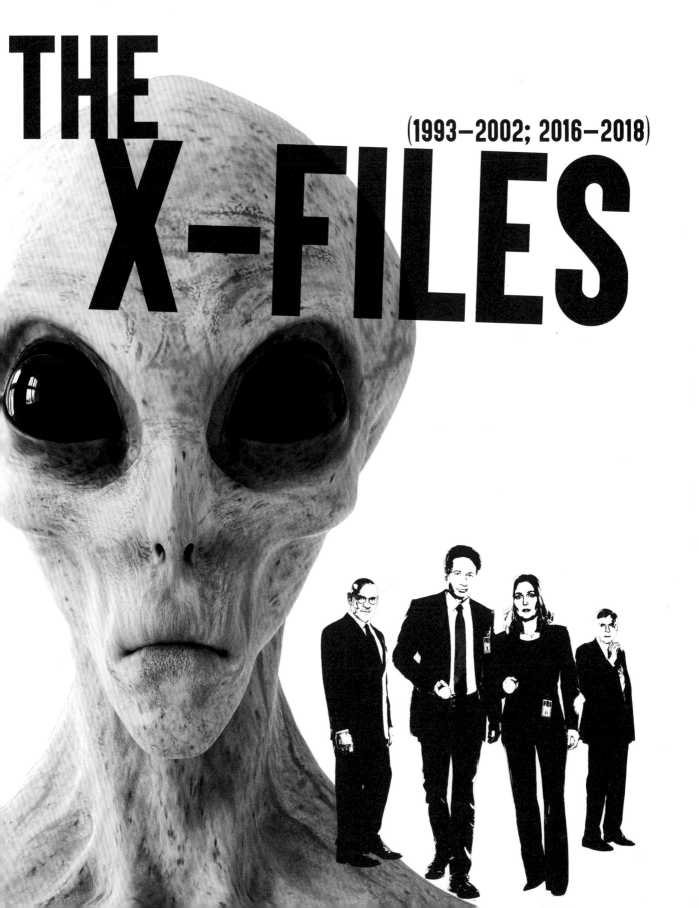

THE X-FILES

(1993–2002; 2016–2018)

CREATED BY: Chris Carter

SEASONS: 11

EPISODES: 218

OTHER SHOWS BY CHRIS CARTER:
Millennium (1996–1999)

*T*he X-Files drew its appeal from the pairing of the oddest of couples: FBI agents Dana Scully (Gillian Anderson) and Fox Mulder (David Duchovny). Scully is the skeptic, a doctor who believes in science; Mulder can't resist the idea that truth is simply an illusion, one perpetuated by grim-faced characters like boss Walter Skinner (Mitch Pileggi) and the mysterious Cigarette Smoking Man (William B. Davis).

The sci-fi series bounced between a grander mythology, which became increasingly difficult to unwind, and standalone episodes that featured the famous "monster of the week." *The X-Files* anticipated the internet's communal curiosity. All these years later, Mulder comes off as rather reasonable.

THE IDEA FOR *THE X-FILES* ORIGINATED WITH A PUBLIC OPINION SURVEY.

Chris Carter's interest in the paranormal was piqued when he read Pulitzer Prize–winning writer, psychiatrist, and Harvard Medical School professor John E. Mack's analysis of a 1992 Roper Poll survey, which estimated that 3.7 million Americans may have been abducted by aliens. "Abduction is tantamount to a religious experience," Carter told the *Los Angeles Times*.

DANA SCULLY WAS PARTLY MODELED ON CLARICE STARLING.

Carter has been vocal about his admiration for Jonathan Demme's Oscar-winning film *The Silence of the Lambs* and the influence it had on *The X-Files*. "It's not a mistake that Dana Scully has red hair like Clarice Starling in *The Silence of the Lambs*," Carter told *Smithsonian* magazine.

DAVID DUCHOVNY PUSHED FOR JENNIFER BEALS TO PLAY SCULLY.

Duchovny and the *Flashdance* star became acquainted when the two attended Yale. "I used to see David on the street—he tried to pick me up on several occasions," Beals recalled. "And I said, 'Um, I'm living with somebody.' And then I ended up taking this acting class in New York and who walks in the door but David Duchovny. And he's like, 'I swear I am not stalking you!' And we became really good friends…When he was doing *The X-Files* he had talked to me about doing that, but I think Gillian was much better suited for that part than me."

ENTERTAINMENT WEEKLY PRONOUNCED THE SERIES DOA.

In a preview of the 1993 fall television lineup, *Entertainment Weekly* declared, "This show's a goner," citing its genre and Friday night time slot as two indicators that the series wouldn't last. Today, it's one of the longest-running sci-fi series in television history.

FREEZE FRAME

"PILOT" // SEASON 1, EPISODE 1

William B. Davis, who played the Cigarette Smoking Man, wasn't a smoker—at least he wasn't when he was cast in the role. He had kicked the habit over a decade earlier, after smoking for twenty-five years. Though he was eventually given herbal cigarettes, the cigarettes were real for his first few appearances, and the job required him to inhale. "That was beginning to wake up some long buried desires," Davis said.

ANDERSON AND DUCHOVNY HAD A COMPLICATED RELATIONSHIP.

Though Anderson and Duchovny are tight nowadays, that friendship—while based on the work they did together—didn't really come about until after *The X-Files* ended. "The crucible of doing that show made monsters out of both of us," Duchovny told *Variety*, saying that it wasn't until filming the 2008 movie *The X-Files: I Want to Believe* that the two really clicked. "Once we got to step back, it was like, 'Oh, wow, we really like each other. I didn't know that was going to happen.' The way we work together has changed. Whatever rapport we have as actors, we earned."

"Our relationship has definitely become a proper friendship over the last few years," Anderson added. "I think we're more on each other's side. We're more aware of the other's needs, wants, concerns, and mindful to take those into consideration."

SCULLY'S CHARACTER HAD A BIG INFLUENCE ON THE TELEVISION LANDSCAPE.

Anderson told the *Chicago Tribune* that Carter had to fight extremely hard to cast her "rather than what used to be the version of women [on] television back then." And that in doing so, The X-Files actually changed the way women were perceived—both by the industry as well as by viewers. "This funny old series...had a huge influence on the history of television in many ways, from the lighting on television to the kinds of stories that were being told to the characters. The amount of things you see right now where they even just have a male and female as investigators. It's almost a joke. It's

like, somebody should come with something different now!"

THERE WAS A PAY GAP ISSUE.

In 2016, Anderson revealed that she had to fight to be paid the same amount as Duchovny—*twice*! The first time was when the show originally aired, then again when it came back for two new seasons beginning in 2016. According to The Daily Beast, Anderson was even initially mandated to always be a few steps behind Duchovny when they appeared onscreen together. It took Anderson a full three years to close the wage gap.

When the series was set to be revived in 2016, Anderson was shocked that she was offered just half of what Duchovny was paid to come back. "Even in interviews in the last few years, people have said to me, 'I can't believe that happened, how did you feel about it, that is insane,'" she told The Daily Beast. "And my response always was, 'That was then, this is now.' And then it happened again! I don't even know what to say about it."

THE CIGARETTE SMOKING MAN WAS ORIGINALLY CAST AS AN EXTRA.

When actor William B. Davis first appeared on *The X-Files*, it was as a background actor with no dialogue. At that time neither Davis nor the producers knew that he would end up becoming the show's main antagonist. "There was a time when I wasn't in any episodes, then all of a sudden I had a line or two and I thought, 'That was interesting,'" Davis told *The Palm Beach Post* in 1996. "And that just gradually increased. Then, finally I had a big scene where Mulder comes after me with a gun. That was the turning point where the producers decided this character is really interesting and I guess they felt I was OK to handle it."

THE SHOW EMPLOYED A NUMBER OF SCIENTISTS.

In an effort to make sure the series got its science right, the producers hired a number of scientists as consultants, including University of Maryland microbiologist Anne Simon, who was hired at the end of the first season and came back aboard for the tenth season reboot.

"You're not there to tell the writer, 'Chris, you can't have a Flukeman that's half-man, half-worm,'" she explained of her role in the production. "But you want to come up with something reasonable." (Simon is also the author of *The Real Science Behind the X-Files: Microbes, Meteorites, and Mutants*.)

THE X-FILES GAVE BIRTH TO *BREAKING BAD* AS WE KNOW IT.

Breaking Bad creator Vince Gilligan logged several years as a writer and producer on *The X-Files* (he also helped create *The X-Files* spin-off *The Lone Gunmen*). Among his many credits on the show is the season 6 episode "Drive," which stars Bryan Cranston as Patrick Crump, a "Monster-of-the-Week" who kidnaps Mulder. Cranston's performance stayed with Gilligan over the years, and is what led to his being cast as Walter White on *Breaking Bad*. "You don't have to like him," Gilligan said of the character. "But you need to sympathize and feel empathy and sorrow for him at the end of the hour."

Other future *Breaking Bad* stars Aaron Paul (Jesse), Dean Norris (Hank), Raymond Cruz (Tuco), Danny Trejo (Tortuga), and Michael Bowen (Uncle Jack) also appeared on *The X-Files*.

MITCH PILEGGI'S SHAVED HEAD ALMOST COST HIM THE ROLE OF WALTER SKINNER.

Pileggi auditioned three times before he landed the role of FBI Assistant Director Walter Skinner. "I thought, this guy [Chris Carter] either hates me or I must be a totally bad actor," Pileggi recalled. "But he told me later it was because my shaved head was too extreme for an FBI agent."

SCULLY MAY ALSO HAVE INSPIRED A NUMBER OF YOUNG WOMEN TO PURSUE STEM CAREERS.

In April 2018, a report from the Geena Davis Institute on Gender in Media claimed that Dana Scully served as a powerful role model for women who watched the show. The skeptical doctor helped inspire women to go into STEM (science, technology, engineering, and math) careers.

"In the world of entertainment media, where scientists are often portrayed as white men wearing white coats and working alone in labs, Scully stood out in the 1990s as the only female STEM character in a prominent, prime-time television role," the report explained. Previously, anecdotal evidence has pointed to the existence of a "Scully effect," in which the measured TV scientist—with her detailed note-taking, evidence-based approach, and desire to autopsy everything—inspired women to seek out their own science careers. This report provides the hard data.

FREEZE FRAME ▶

"NEVER AGAIN" //
SEASON 4, EPISODE 13
In the fourth season episode "Never Again," Jodie Foster (who won an Oscar in 1992 for her role as Clarice Starling) provided the voice of, a homicidal tattoo (yes, a homicidal tattoo).

MUST-WATCH SUPERNATURAL SHOWS

Sometimes, you just want to turn on the TV and escape into a world filled with magic and monsters. Here are a few shows where the supernatural reigns supreme.

Supernatural // (2005-2020)

When it comes to hunting monsters—or ghosts, or demons, or anything, well, *supernatural*—no one goes to greater lengths than the Winchester brothers. For a staggering fifteen seasons, fans watched as Dean (Jensen Ackles) and Sam (Jared Padalecki) literally went to Hell and back to save the world from a menagerie of evil forces.

Lucifer // (2016-PRESENT)

Hell's top demon has traded red skin and horns for a suave suit and a gig solving crimes in Los Angeles. Fed up with torturing souls, Lucifer (Tom Ellis) heads to the City of Angels to run a night-club and help the LAPD solve crimes.

Sabrina the Teenage Witch // (1996-2003)

If you thought your teenage years were tough, try navigating the traditional woes of adolescence while also learning you're a witch. Such is the life of Sabrina Spellman (Melissa Joan Hart), who, with the help of her centuries-old witchy aunts and a witty talking cat, must navigate a world that straddles both high school crushes and magical curses. In 2018, Netflix rebooted the series as *Chilling Adventures of Sabrina*, with *Mad Men*'s Kiernan Shipka taking over the title role.

True Blood // (2008-2014)

Vampires no longer have to hide from the human world in HBO's *True Blood*. The love story between a telepathic waitress and a 173-year-old vampire is filled with supernatural drama—and a lot of sex and violence.

Scooby-Doo // (1969-PRESENT)

Since 1969, various iterations of *Scooby-Doo* have dominated the world of supernatural cartoons. With his signature "Scooby-Dooby-Doo," the skittish Great Dane helps his crew of teenage sleuths solve all sorts of spooky mysteries.

6

TV SPIN-OFFS YOU DIDN'T KNOW EXISTED

The greatest testament to a television series' endearing popularity is the inability of viewers to let its characters say goodbye, which is why every time a popular show announces its finale date, rumors begin swirling about the people, places, and things that might provide strong fodder for an entirely new series.

Some of these spin-off ideas go the way of Dwight Schrute and *The Farm* (read: nowhere). Others buck the spin-off moniker altogether and end up being as successful as the original incarnation (see *Frasier*). And then there are those shows that make it to the small screen…only to find the sound of crickets chirping in place of a laugh track. These are some of those shows.

1 The Lone Gunmen // (2001)

Fox Mulder's favorite trio of conspiracy theorists, better known as the Lone Gunmen, went from recurring characters to leading men in 2001. While the show—which was co-created by Vince Gilligan (along with Chris Carter, John Shiban, and Frank Spotnitz)—was met with critical praise, audiences simply weren't tuning in. It was canceled after just thirteen episodes, but the producers had the unusual opportunity to address the show's (unintentional) finale's cliff-hanger in the ninth season of *The X-Files*.

2 AfterMASH // (1983–1985)

To be fair, attempting to replicate even a modicum of the success of *M*A*S*H*—one of the most beloved television shows of all time—would be akin to creating a show around the Drake following *Seinfeld*'s finale. It's not that it couldn't be entertaining; it's just too soon (and unnecessary). Which is exactly what audiences thought of *AfterMASH*, which chronicles the lives of Colonel Potter, Klinger, and Father Mulcahy after the Korean War. Though *AfterMASH* did make it to a second season and received an Emmy nomination for Outstanding Directing in a Comedy Series, it was canceled nine episodes in. *TV Guide* later called it one of the ten worst television shows of all time.

3 Deadline // (2000–2001)

Yes, even *Law & Order* has produced a clunker of a spin-off on occasion, including this one, in which Oliver Platt played a tabloid journalist for *The New York Ledger* (a fictional newspaper often used as a prop in the *Law & Order* series). Despite an impressive cast, including Bebe Neuwirth, Lili Taylor, and Hope Davis, the series was killed after thirteen episodes.

4 Models Inc. // (1994–1995)

Models Inc. was technically a spin-off squared, as it's a spin-off of *Melrose Place*, which is a spin-off of *Beverly Hills, 90210*. The show's only real purpose was to capitalize on the fact that supermodels like Cindy Crawford and Naomi Campbell were taking over the world in the mid-1990s. But *Models Inc.*'s only real contribution to the pop culture conversation was that it introduced the woman who would become Trinity—Carrie-Anne Moss—to the world.

5 The Golden Palace // (1992–1993)

Bea Arthur was the only main actress from *The Golden Girls* not to appear in this series, which sees Blanche, Rose, and Sophia becoming hoteliers after purchasing an Art Deco gem known as the Golden Palace Hotel. Despite Don Cheadle and Cheech Marin in supporting roles, *The Golden Palace* was booking at about 10 percent capacity.

6 Young Americans // (2000)

Trying to take yet another bite out of the young, beautiful people genre, *Young Americans* began its life on *Dawson's Creek*. Lead character Will Krudski was introduced as an old friend of the gang in *Dawson's* third season, when he visits during a break from Rawley Academy, a prep school where he hangs out with Kate Bosworth and Ian Somerhalder. It lasted for a fleeting eight episodes.

THE BEST TV SERIES FINALES OF ALL TIME

What makes a great TV series finale? It depends on the show, of course. But no matter what series you may be watching, you want a finale that ties up loose ends (or deliberately doesn't tie them up) without being annoyingly completist or seeming overly sentimental and an episode that makes you feel just as happy, sad, thrilled, or compelled as you did with each previous installment. It's a tricky needle to thread, and some series have undoubtedly done it better than others. Here are (some of) the other greatest series finales of all time.

SPOILERS!

BREAKING BAD
"Felina"

Few series finales have ever faced such high expectations and managed to rise to meet them so powerfully as *Breaking Bad* did with its final episode in 2013. "Felina" has everything you could ever want from a *Breaking Bad* send-off: Walt's final conversation with Skyler, an incredible revenge shoot-out, one main character's cry of freedom, and another's smile of victory. Some series finales deliver what you want; others deliver what you need. "Felina" somehow managed to do both.

HALT AND CATCH FIRE
"Ten of Swords"

Halt and Catch Fire never got the audience it deserved when it was airing, which means many people likely don't know just how brilliant and daring the show

became in its final seasons, which included a time jump, a shocking death, and the dawn of the internet age. "Ten of Swords" is all about closing old chapters and starting new ones, and sends the show's trinity of remaining major characters in promising new directions, even as they all come to terms with the fact that they can never again recapture what they once had.

SIX FEET UNDER
"Everyone's Waiting"

The final minutes of "Everyone's Waiting" are among the most famous in the history of television, and even if the rest of the episode had been a disappointment, they would still rank among the greatest farewells in the medium. As it is, *Six Feet Under*'s final episode with the Fisher family was a gripping, heartfelt, and bitterly funny gem, all building to that last montage which, as Sia's "Breathe Me" plays, reminded us that death takes many forms beyond mere tragedy.

THE AMERICANS
"Start"

The Americans quietly became one of the best shows on TV before finally winning a bunch of awards for its final season, and with good reason. The final adventures of Philip and Elizabeth Jennings as they contemplate a return to Russia and an end to their double lives in America were among the best the series ever delivered, all building to a final episode that stuck the landing in every possible way.

THE SOPRANOS
"Made in America"

"Made in America" is, infamously, the television episode that made millions of viewers briefly think that their cable had just gone out. In reality, *The Sopranos* creator David Chase had simply decided that the exact second where Tony Soprano's journey would end was one seemingly random moment. Fans still debate the meaning and merits of the final scene, but the sense of palpable unease Chase built up in those last moments—signifying Tony's perpetual state of watching his back—was a brilliant way to end a show that began as a meditation on existential dread in the first place.

THE WIRE
"–30–"

The Wire was never going to end anything in a clean, cut-and-dried way, but its series finale did manage to wield the various talents at play in the series to end everything on an ambitious and fairly comprehensive note. The finale reckoned with many of the same questions the entire series did, from the nature of justice to the fragility of power systems and how far people will go to keep them in place. One last montage reminded us that life goes on in Baltimore, whether the show's characters have reshaped it for the better or not.

TWIN PEAKS: THE RETURN
"Part 17 and Part 18"

Twin Peaks famously ended its early nineties run with a cliff-hanger, which then led to the joyous reception that accompanied *The Return*, an eighteen-hour monument to creative freedom that everyone hoped would finally provide some answers. In true David Lynch fashion, though, the answers we got were often difficult to parse. And by the time it was all over, we were left with even more questions. The final two hours of *The Return* are among the most mind-meltingly intense episodes of television ever devised, all building to a daring and stunning final scene that still has fans talking.

THE LEFTOVERS
"The Book of Nora"

Though it was never a ratings bonanza for HBO during the series' run, its flawless series finale—which has regularly been cited as one of television's best—led many viewers to discover the series later, via streaming. Though it had a tendency to enter surrealist territory (particularly in its penultimate episode), its series finale was simple, subtle, and quietly devastating. Perhaps most surprisingly, it answered the question that many people had forgotten they ever asked in the first place: What happened to the people who disappeared during the Sudden Departure.

MENTAL FLOSS
RECOMMENDS

Though it would be impossible to make mention of *all* the TV shows we love in a single volume, we'd be remiss not to recommend just a few more of our personal favorite binge-watches.

12 MONKEYS
(2015–2018)

RECOMMENDED BY: ERIN MCCARTHY, EDITOR-IN-CHIEF

This criminally underrated series, created by Terry Matalas and Travis Fickett, is no retread of Terry Gilliam's 1995 film: Though it borrows the basic premise and some character names (and places clever Easter Eggs as a nod to the movie), this *12 Monkeys* quickly goes its own way. In 2015, epidemiologist Cassandra Railly (Amanda Schull) is approached by a man named James Cole (Aaron Stanford) who claims to be from 2043, where a plague has devastated Earth. With the help of Jennifer Goines (Emily Hampshire, playing the part originated by Brad Pitt in Gilliam's film), Dr. Katarina Jones (Barbara Sukowa), and Theodore Deacon (Todd Stashwick), they must fight a nefarious organization known as The Army of the 12 Monkeys—and try to stop the plague from happening in the first place.

    12 Monkeys is heavy on the sci-fi and drama—after all, the world is at stake!—but it's also incredibly funny (Hampshire's performances, musical and otherwise, are not to be missed). Christopher Lloyd (*Back to the Future*), James Callis (*Battlestar Galactica*), and Hannah Waddingham (*Ted Lasso*) all show up in pivotal roles. And while there are so many twists and turns that you might expect plot holes, thanks to careful planning by Matalas and the show's writers, everything lines up—and, more than that, pays off in genuinely surprising, emotional, and satisfying ways. *12 Monkeys* sticks the landing, and at just four seasons, it's a show you'll want to binge more than once.

I MAY DESTROY YOU
(2020)

RECOMMENDED BY:
JENNIFER M. WOOD, MANAGING EDITOR

I May Destroy You is as much a warning to the viewer as it is the title of this 12-episode miniseries, created, written, produced by, and starring Michaela Coel (who won a BAFTA for her previous series, *Chewing Gum*, in 2016). While it feels reductive to try and summarize the series in just a few words, it's also one of those shows that is best entered into with as little information as possible, as it's the sum total of the entire experience that makes it so ground-breaking. What you do need to know is that it begins with Coel's Arabella—a social media star who ended up writing a bestselling book about the *Chronicles of a Fed-Up Millennial* and is currently struggling with her second book—

going out for a night with friends that ends in a blackout. But as flashes of the night come back to her, Arabella realizes she was the victim of a violent sexual assault that she can only remember in pieces. So rather than finish her new book, which her agents and publisher are waiting for, Arabella sets out on a journey to both piece together the evening and figure out who was responsible while also using her platform as the voice of a generation to rally others around her cause.

But *I May Destroy You* is about much more than the attack that kicks off the series. It's an exploration of the concept of consent (or, as is often the case, lack thereof); the murkiness surrounding rape culture; and what it takes to rebuild one's life in the aftermath of trauma. That the story is a semi-autobiographical one for Coel—who is mesmerizing to watch—makes it even more personal and effective. But her greatest achievement may very well be that, through all the pain, Coel still somehow manages to imbue to the script with her trademark humor. Making *I May Destroy You* one of the most surprising, stylish, frank, discomfiting, challenging, and, ultimately, most satisfying series to come along in a long time.

THE QUEEN'S GAMBIT
(2020)

RECOMMENDED BY:
MICHELE DEBCZAK, SENIOR STAFF WRITER

A show about chess has no right to be this entertaining. *The Queen's Gambit* owes much of its appeal to Anya Taylor-Joy's star-making performance as Beth Harmon—an orphan from Kentucky who shows an impressive knack for the game from a young age. As she rises through the competitive chess world, her struggles with addiction become the greatest threat to her success. Even if you don't know your knights from your pawns, the chess scenes in this Netflix miniseries are just as thrilling as any sports drama.

SUCCESSION
(2018–PRESENT)

RECOMMENDED BY: ELLEN GUTOSKEY, STAFF WRITER

HBO's *Succession*—which follows the corrupt, impudent, wealth-obsessed Roy family and its media empire—has a few things in common with *Game of Thrones*. For one, most of the major players are so morally bereft that there's really no viable option to root for a hero. There are also way too many disasters to leave any delusions about a happy ending. And then there are all the glorious memes, from Demi Adejuyigbe's remixed theme song ("Who will get a kiss from Daddy?") to unforgettable lines like "You can't make a Tomelette without breaking some Greggs." Sure, there could be people who don't think *Succession* is spit-take hilarious—but their last name is probably Murdoch.

BRIDGERTON
(2020–PRESENT)

RECOMMENDED BY:
ELAINE SELNA, COMMERCE WRITER

Bridgerton, a lavish Regency-era drama, is based on Julia Quinn's eight-book romance series about the Bridgerton children finding love. The breakout debut season follows the eldest Bridgerton daughter, Daphne (played by Phoebe Dynevor), finding a husband in 1813. She and Simon Basset, the Duke of Hastings (Regé-Jean Page), pretend to be courting so that Simon can keep the line of eager mothers trying to marry off their daughters to an "eligible" duke at bay and Daphne can attract more suitors by making them jealous. What could go wrong? A lot, it turns out.

PARTY DOWN
(2009–2010)

RECOMMENDED BY:
JUSTIN DODD, VIDEO PRODUCER

Party Down is the funniest show ever made about a catering company, and that's a fact. Comprised of just 20 episodes (though a reboot is on the horizon), the series is a staple of the prestigious pantheon of "cancelled cult classics." Each episode takes place at a different catered Hollywood event with the same hilarious, depressing cast of oddballs. Ken Marino's Ron Donald will forever be one of the greatest tragicomic characters on television. It'll only take a day or two to watch the whole series, but if you're going to watch just one episode, make it "Steve Guttenberg's Birthday."

MONEY HEIST
(2017–2021)

RECOMMENDED BY: JAKE ROSSEN, SENIOR STAFF WRITER

Dramatic series usually save their biggest twists and reveals for season finales. Álex Pina, the creator of the international Spanish language hit *Money Heist*, seemed to have a different quota in mind. In this tense thriller about a group of thieves who breach the Royal Mint of Spain, the plan (and plot) seems to get upended every 10 minutes. Recruited by the mysterious-but-brilliant Professor (Álvaro Morte), seven criminals with code names like Tokyo, Berlin, and Denver try to convince police a standard theft is underway while they focus on their real ambition: printing money 24 hours a day. Unspooling over five seasons, two jobs, and lots of criminal conflict, the series (a.k.a. *La Casa de Papel*) is a compulsive binge watch that succeeds in pulling off a third big heist: Stealing most of your free time.

WANDAVISION
(2021)

RECOMMENDED BY:
KERRY WOLFE, STAFF EDITOR

The Marvel Cinematic Universe came to the small screen with this Disney+ series starring Avengers Wanda Maximoff (Elizabeth Olsen) and Vision (Paul Bettany). Part sitcom, part action show, the series flashes through various eras of TV before pivoting to the epic battle sequences fans of the MCU have come to expect. *WandaVision* is more than a tribute to sitcoms of the past—it lets Wanda and Vision, two Avengers with noticeably less screen time in the feature films—showcase their humor, while also affording the characters a chance to grapple with and navigate undeniably human emotions and experiences.

STAR TREK: THE NEXT GENERATION (1987–1994)

RECOMMENDED BY: JASON SERAFINO, SPECIAL PROJECTS EDITOR

All the sci-fi shows you're streaming today owe their very existence to *Star Trek: The Next Generation*. Despite airing in syndication throughout its run, the series amassed a huge following, thanks to the strange new worlds and villains that appealed to longtime fans and sharp, witty character dynamics that transcended the genre. More than 30 years after its debut, *TNG* is still the standard-bearer for the franchise.

SEINFELD (1989–1998)

JON MAYER, SENIOR VIDEO PRODUCER

With its finely drawn characters and precise plotting, *Seinfeld* was never really a "show about nothing." It's often about unimportant things, but those trivialities are also entry points to comedically examine human weakness—from duplicity to vanity and jealousy to sloth. Its main characters are *just* self-aware enough to worry about how their immoral actions make them look to the world, allowing the audience, in turn, to recognize and laugh at our own worst qualities (not that there's anything wrong with that).

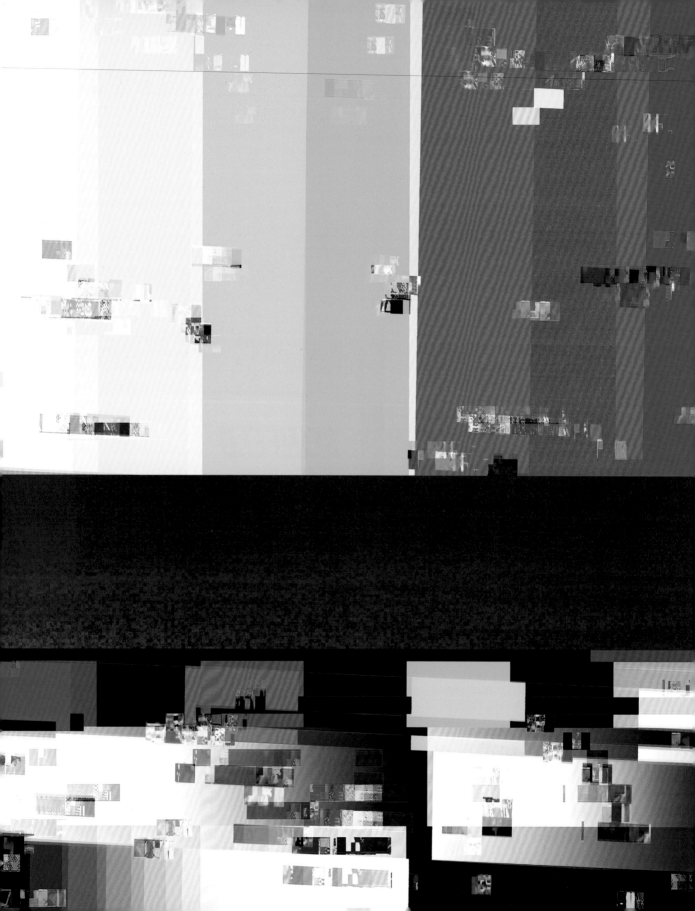

ACKNOWLEDGMENTS

"... and all the pieces matter."

—*Detective Lester Freamon*, The Wire

Just as no TV show is the work of a single person, no book is ever a solo effort—and *The Curious Viewer* is proof of that.

First, a huge thank you to our agent, Dinah Dunn at Indelible Editions, whose enthusiasm for this project has been a constant source of positivity (even when deadlines were tight . . . or being pushed). And to designer Carol Bobolts, whose artistry brought our words to life. Thanks to our publisher, Weldon Owen, Inc., especially Roger Shaw, Katie Killebrew, and Ian Cannon.

You wouldn't be holding this book if it weren't for the many talents of the entire Mental Floss team, especially editor-in-chief Erin McCarthy, who knows my bad habits and how to break me of them (most of the time) and whose advice, ideas, and counsel were invaluable. A very special thanks to Jake Rossen, who went above and beyond his duties as a staff writer to help plan and execute this book at every step; just like *Highlander*, there can be only one Jake (and he, too, looks great in a duster).

Deep gratitude is also owed to writers Michele Debczak and Ellen Gutoskey, who never balked when asked to write "just one more thing." And to editors Kat Long, Jay Serafino, and Kerry Wolfe; social media maestro Angela Trotti; and "V-boys" Jon Mayer and Justin Dodd for their enthusiasm and amazing contributions to this book. Special thanks to former Mental Floss staffers whose work also appears in this book: Colin Gorenstein and Abbey Stone.

The Curious Viewer would not have been possible without the tireless support of our Minute Media family, especially Matan Har, Ze'ev Rozov, Chad Payne, Kimberly Holland, and everyone else who was so enthusiastic about this project.

Thanks to fact checker extraordinaire Austin Thompson, whose meticulous notes are hilarious and worthy of their own book; copyeditor Becky Maines; and proofreader Ryan Smernoff.

Thank you to the amazing roster of freelance writers who contributed work to this book: Scott Beggs (*Atlanta, Better Call Saul, The Chi, The Handmaid's Tale, Ozark, Stranger Things, The Walking Dead*); Stacy Conradt (*Grey's Anatomy*); Meredith Danko (*30 Rock, Friends, Gilmore Girls, The Office, Orange Is the New Black*); Randee Dawn (*Law & Order*); Kate Erbland (*Sex and the City*); Faridah Gbadamosi (*Insecure*); Amanda Green (*Freaks and Geeks*); Matthew Jackson (*Battlestar Galactica, Hannibal, The West Wing,* The Best TV Spin-Offs, The Best TV Pilots, The Best Series Finales); Kristin Hunt (*Black-ish*); Rudie Obias (Actors Who Asked for Their Characters to Be Killed Off, Actors Who Regretted Leaving Hit TV Shows); Rebecca Pahle (*Game of Thrones*, Bizarre TV Crossovers); Garin Pirnia (*24, The Big Bang Theory, Broad City, Curb Your Enthusiasm, Dexter, Mr. Robot, Sons of Anarchy, True Blood*); Kristy Puchko (*Deadwood*); and Escher Walcott (*Fleabag*).

Last but certainly not least: love and thanks to James Menzies and the entire Wood-Menzies menagerie for being the best binge-watching partners anyone could ask for.

INDEX OF SHOWS, CHANNELS, AND NETWORKS

Note: Page numbers in **bold** refer to main discussions

PICTURE CREDITS

JENNIFER M. WOOD, Mental Floss managing editor and compulsive binge-watcher, oversees all of the entertainment content at the site.

MENTALFLOSS.COM, its social media accounts, and its YouTube channel have reached more than 1 billion people since 2001 with answers to life's big questions, fascinating facts, and stories so interesting that readers have to share them.